T0238262

IFIP Advances in Information and Communication Technology 322

IFIP – The International Federation for Information Processing

IFIP was founded in 1960 under the auspices of UNESCO, following the First World Computer Congress held in Paris the previous year. An umbrella organization for societies working in information processing, IFIP's aim is two-fold: to support information processing within its member countries and to encourage technology transfer to developing nations. As its mission statement clearly states,

> *IFIP's mission is to be the leading, truly international, apolitical organization which encourages and assists in the development, exploitation and application of information technology for the benefit of all people.*

IFIP is a non-profitmaking organization, run almost solely by 2500 volunteers. It operates through a number of technical committees, which organize events and publications. IFIP's events range from an international congress to local seminars, but the most important are:

- The IFIP World Computer Congress, held every second year;
- Open conferences;
- Working conferences.

The flagship event is the IFIP World Computer Congress, at which both invited and contributed papers are presented. Contributed papers are rigorously refereed and the rejection rate is high.

As with the Congress, participation in the open conferences is open to all and papers may be invited or submitted. Again, submitted papers are stringently refereed.

The working conferences are structured differently. They are usually run by a working group and attendance is small and by invitation only. Their purpose is to create an atmosphere conducive to innovation and development. Refereeing is less rigorous and papers are subjected to extensive group discussion.

Publications arising from IFIP events vary. The papers presented at the IFIP World Computer Congress and at open conferences are published as conference proceedings, while the results of the working conferences are often published as collections of selected and edited papers.

Any national society whose primary activity is in information may apply to become a full member of IFIP, although full membership is restricted to one society per country. Full members are entitled to vote at the annual General Assembly, National societies preferring a less committed involvement may apply for associate or corresponding membership. Associate members enjoy the same benefits as full members, but without voting rights. Corresponding members are not represented in IFIP bodies. Affiliated membership is open to non-national societies, and individual and honorary membership schemes are also offered.

Ángel Ortiz
Rubén Darío Franco
Pedro Gómez Gasquet (Eds.)

Balanced Automation Systems for Future Manufacturing Networks

9th IFIP WG 5.5 International Conference, BASYS 2010
Valencia, Spain, July 21-23, 2010
Proceedings

 Springer

Volume Editors

Ángel Ortiz
Rubén Darío Franco
Pedro Gómez Gasquet
Polytechnical University of Valencia
Research Centre on Production Management and Engineering
Edificio 8B, Acceso L, Planta 2, 46022 Valencia, Spain
E-mail: {aortiz, dfranco, pgomez}@cigip.upv.es

CR Subject Classification (1998): I.6, C.2.4, I.2.11, H.4, H.3, I.2

ISSN   1868-4238
ISBN-10   3-642-42254-3 Springer Berlin Heidelberg New York
ISBN-13   978-3-642-42254-6 Springer Berlin Heidelberg New York

springer.com

© IFIP International Federation for Information Processing 2010
Softcover re-print of the Hardcover 1st edition 2010
Typesetting: Camera-ready by author, data conversion by Scientific Publishing Services, Chennai, India
Printed on acid-free paper   06/3180

Preface

Manufacturing and operations management paradigms are evolving toward more open and resilient spaces where innovation is driven not only by ever-changing customer needs but also by agile and fast-reacting networked structures. Flexibility, adaptability and responsiveness are properties that the next generation of systems must have in order to successfully support such new emerging trends.

Customers are being attracted to be involved in Co-innovation Networks, as improved responsiveness and agility is expected from industry ecosystems. Renewed production systems needs to be modeled, engineered and deployed in order to achieve cost-effective solutions.

BASYS conferences have been developed and organized as a forum in which to share visions and research findings for innovative sustainable and knowledge-based products-services and manufacturing models.

Thus, the focus of BASYS is to discuss how human actors, emergent technologies and even organizations are integrated in order to redefine the way in which the value-creation process must be conceived and realized.

BASYS 2010, which was held in Valencia, Spain, proposed new approaches in automation where synergies between people, systems and organizations need to be fully exploited in order to create high added-value products and services.

This book contains the selection of the papers which were accepted for presentation at the BASYS 2010 conference, covering consolidated and emerging topics of the conference scope.

The contributions were organized in five sections:

- Co-innovation Networks in Industry
- Industry Ecosystems and Emergent Business Models
- Advanced Production Engineering
- New Trends in Digital Factories
- Agent-Based Simulation and Management of Complex Systems (Special Session)

The papers selected for this book cover the most relevant topics in the BASYS Conference scope and they may help readers gain a deeper understanding of next-generation systems for innovation and manufacturing.

We would like to express our gratitude to all the authors, presenters, reviewers and the entire Organizing Committee for their enthusiastic work and magnificent support during BASYS 2010.

Ángel Ortiz-Bas
Rubén Darío Franco
Pedro Gómez-Gasquet

Organization

Conference Chair

Ángel Ortiz Bas (Spain)

Program Committee Co-chairs

Luís M. Camarinha-Matos (Portugal)
Hamideh Afsarmanesh (The Netherlands)
Juan Carlos Beitialarrangoitia (Spain)
Rubén Darío Franco (Spain)
Erastos Filos (Belgium)

Program Committee

Afsarmanesh, Hamideh (The Netherlands)
Alfaro Saiz, J.J. (Spain)
Arauzo, José Alberto (Spain)
Andrés Romano, C. (Spain)
Azevedo, Américo (Portugal)
Barata, José (Portugal)
Burns, Neil (UK)
Camarinha-Matos, Luis M. (Portugal)
Carneiro, Luis (Portugal)
Carpanzano, Emanuele (Italy)
Cellary, Wojciech (Poland)
Copani, Giacomo (Italy)
Cunha, Pedro (Portugal)
Faria, José (Portugal)
Filos, Erastos (Belgium)
Fornasiero, Rosana (Italy)
Fuentes, Rubén (Spain)

Galán, José (Spain)
Gómez-Gasquet, Pedro (Spain)
Goranson, Ted (USA)
Hernandez, Cesareo (Spain)
Kopacek, Peter (Austria)
Kovács, Gyorgy (Hungary)
Kusiak, Andrew (USA)
Lario Esteban, Fco-Cruz (Spain)
López-Paredes, Adolfo (Spain)
Molfino, Rezia (Italy)
Onori, Mauro (Sweden)
Ortiz Bas, A. (Spain)
Paralic, Jan (Slovakia)
Pajares, Javier (Spain)
Pavón, Juan (Spain)
Pereira, Carlos (Brazil)
Pinho de Sousa, Jorge (Portugal)

Poler Escoto, R. (Spain)
Portugal, Paulo (Portugal)
Pranevichus, Henrikas (Lithuania)
Putnik, Goran (Portugal)
Rabelo, Ricardo (Brazil)
Rauber, Thomas (Brazil)
Rodriguez, Raul (Spain)
Shpitalni, Moshe (Israel)
Schreck, Gerhard (Germany)
Shen, W. (Canada)
Soares, A. Lucas (Portugal)
Smirnov, Alexander (Russia)
Tamura, Shinsuke (Japan)
Valckenaers, P. (Belgium)
Westkamper, Engelbert (Germany)
Zaremba, Marek (Canada)
Zelezny, Filip (Czech Republic)

Organizing Committee

Pedro Gómez Gasquet
Eduardo Vicens Salort
Maria del Mar Alemany Díaz
Faustino Alarcón Valero
Julio Lajara Asensio

Inmaculada Cano
Guillermo Prats
Llanos Cuenca
Andrés Boza

Technical Sponsors

IFIP WG 5.5 COVE
Co-Operation Infrastructure for Virtual Enterprises and
Electronic Business

SOCOLNET
Society of Collaborative Networks

Organizational Co-sponsors

Universidad Politécnica de Valencia
Valencia, Spain

Research Centre on Production Management and Engineering
Valencia, Spain

This work has been partially funded by The Ministerio de Ciencia e Innovación of the Spanish Government and the Polytechnic University of Valencia.

Table of Contents

Part III: Advanced Production Engineering

Part IV: New Trends in Digital Factories

Part V: Agent-Based Simulation and Management of Complex Systems

Part I
Co-innovation Networks in Industry

Cold Supply Chain Processes in a Fruit-and-Vegetable Collaborative Network

M. Victoria de-la-Fuente and Lorenzo Ros

Universidad Politécnica de Cartagena, ETSII,
Campus Muralla del Mar, 30202 Cartagena, Spain
{marivi.fuente,lorenzo.ros}@upct.es

Abstract. The work presented in this paper focuses on the construction of a prototype for strategic design of nodes in a logistics network (PROCONET project). It incorporates the necessary concepts, models and supporting tools related to the design of the process flow and the choice of technology. The operation of the prototype will be validated with global supply chain processes for perishable products. Global supply chain processes will consider both full loads and groupages. Special attention will be given to the impact of INCOTERM agreements. The prototype will support intermodal logistics processes as an added value.

Keywords: Cold chain, Collaborative network, Perishable goods.

1 Introduction

In the last thirty years the fruit-and-vegetable sector has become the first Spanish agriculture sector in terms of production and export value. Driven by strong competition, this dynamic area must continuously incorporate new methods and technologies.

As such, an ongoing effort has to be made by agricultural companies to implement innovative measures which add value to the sector and make it capable of appropriately responding to consumers' demands, of successfully facing competition and of maintaining leadership via new products and new forms of presenting them.

It is in this context of innovation and new technologies where the PROCONET Research Project is defined, initiated due to the need for improvements in logistics and transport of perishable goods (as discovered by the companies in this segment). A prototype of strategic storage nodes will be designed in a collaborative network framework, which facilitates the operation of the cold chain and transportation of products while ensuring traceability and food safety throughout the whole logistic process.

This paper is organized as follows: Section 2 presents a brief review of collaborative networks, their characteristics, their coordination of activities and the information mechanisms inside them. Section 3 deals with current issues in the Spanish fruit-and-vegetable sector. Section 4 discusses the objectives, the integration methodology and the framework for the fruit-and-vegetable collaborative network to

Á. Ortiz Bas, R.D. Franco, P. Gómez Gasquet (Eds.): BASYS 2010, IFIP AICT 322, pp. 3–10, 2010.

be developed in the project, and proposes the PROCONET architectural design and components of the fruit-and-vegetable collaborative network, information systems and network data exchange techniques. Section 5 presents the main conclusions and innovation aspects of the PROCONET project.

2 Collaborative Networked Organizations

Participation in networks has become very important for any organization that strives to achieve a differentiated competitive advantage. Among the wide variety of existing networks, collaborative networks are especially relevant. These have emerged over the last few years as a result of the challenges faced by both the business and scientific world, since collaboration has become the key issue to rapidly answer market demands in manufacturing companies through sharing competence and resources [5].

A collaborative network (CN) is constituted by a variety of entities (e.g. organizations and people) that are largely autonomous, geographically distributed, and heterogeneous in terms of their operating environment, culture, social capital and goals. Nevertheless, these entities collaborate to better achieve compatible goals, using ICT for supporting the development of collaborative business opportunities [3].

As dynamic inter-organizational models, CNs must display a distributed business process management system to support the means for obtaining, providing and managing production-related information from and about CNs, enabling enterprises to conduct their logistics more efficiently, and working better in an integrated and virtual environment [9]. In this context, communication mechanisms play a vital role, alongside coordination to support the exchange of information between interdependent activities / processes and among CN enterprises [2].

For this reason, the advantages in the ICT that support the concept of collaborative networks have allowed enterprises to move to more cooperative information-driven environments. Enterprise knowledge sharing (know-how), open source / web-based applications, and common best practices are ways to achieve both the concept of integrated enterprise and the implementation of collaborative networked enterprises for the manufacturing industry [5].

Finally, it must be noted that a growing number of collaborative networked organization forms are emerging as a result of the continuous advances in the field of ICT, which contributes to help SMEs face current social and market challenges. CNs are already recognized as an important survival instrument for organizations in a period of turbulent socio-economic changes [3,5].

3 The Fruit-and-Vegetable Spanish Sector: Problems and Necessities

In the last thirty years the fruit and vegetable sector has become the first sector of Spanish agriculture in terms of production value. Spain is the major producer of fruits and vegetables for consumption in fresh and the major exporter of these products.

The fruit-and-vegetable sector is extremely dynamic. It is continuously incorporating new methods and modern technologies, due to heavy domestic competition, and especially because of the development that is occurring in other regions and countries. An increasingly globalized market and competition from producers and distributors from other regions within, and outside of, the European Union compels a continuous effort to adopt competitive measures which add value to the sector and make it possible to respond to consumers' demands, to face foreign competition, to maintain the leadership of the Spanish sector and to increase its market share by introducing new products, and new ways of presenting them [6].

Spanish exportation of fruit and vegetables in recent campaigns has totalled more than 9 million tons. The main countries of destination are other member countries of the European Union, which receive more than 87% of these exports. Most of these shipments are dispatched by land, especially by road, using refrigerated vehicles to transport loads at a controlled temperature.

Analysis of Spanish production areas, trends in consumption and markets; experience in distribution and logistics; even the expansion to 27 European Union member states, with a market of 500 million consumers, all seems to confirm an increase in the demand of transport by trucks at controlled temperatures (refrigerated lorries), for shipments of fruit-and-vegetable produce and other logistic services associated to it [6,8].

However, the sector must also confront a number of problems, both internal (precarious generational relief, progressive decrease of resources such as water and land, etc.) and external (production from third countries at lower costs and less Customs control, etc.).

A conclusion can be drawn from all the above: by trying to balance market preferences and agricultural reality, the fruit-and-vegetable sector faces constant challenge. For the transformation of this sector the development of innovative solutions will be of great importance to keep its leadership positioning. This goal can be achieved by primarily focusing on aspects which enable producers to have an advantageous position over large distribution chains.

4 The PROCONET Project

When analyzing the fruit-and-vegetable marketing process as a whole, from the point where the decision is made to grow a certain kind of product to the stage when it reaches the final consumer, a wide range of innovations are used as a response to demands from markets and consumers, as well as new proposals in production, distribution and transport.

In this process, relations are established among the agents involved in the food supply chain: producers, growers, exporters, importers, haulers, etc., which must be adapted and managed from a collaborative business model.

The organizational model "Collaborative Network" is composed of a variety of entities (organizations and individuals) largely autonomous, geographically distributed, all collaborating to better achieve common / compatible goals, with the interactions among them supported by computer networks; and with common patterns, such as autonomous entities from varied locations, driven by common goals/intentions to be achieved by collaboration, and operationally based on agreed principles and inter-operable infrastructures which allow them to cope with their heterogeneity [3,5].

As aforementioned, internal and external competition in the fruit and vegetable industry obliges those companies involved to continually innovate in terms of range of products, growing techniques and product presentation, and to improve in such aspects as food handling, storage systems, loading and unloading techniques, etc. There are various reasons behind all these innovations, but they are mainly determined by consumers and food safety rules, and must respond to the different problems posed by the agents/companies in the sector.

The pursuit of the PROCONET Project research team may be defined as "comprehensive traceability of agri-food road transport at controlled temperature", which, on the basis of logistic processes (either full loads or groupages) may grant access to experimenting with electronic CMRs by means of controlling technological variables involved in the said logistical processes.

Today's existing traceability models for the food sector focus on certain products (milk, eggs, beef, transgenic products, etc.). The food safety and traceability model presented in this paper results from the lack of legislation in the agri-food sector and also from recommendations issued by both Spanish and European organizations during the last decade [1,7,11].

The PROCONET Project focuses on the construction of a prototype for strategic design of nodes in a logistics network. It incorporates the necessary concepts, models and supporting tools related to the design of the process flow and the choice of technology. The operation of the prototype will be validated with global supply chain processes for perishable products. Global supply chain processes will consider both full loads and groupages. Special attention will be given to the impact of INCOTERM agreements. The prototype will support intermodal logistics processes as an added value.

The project will develop a platform for knowledge management in a collaborative fruit-and-vegetable network, which supports the communication processes within that network (see Figure 1). Connected to the Operations Planning and Control System application run by each of the member companies in the collaborative network, this platform will design and manage such crucial elements as:

(a) Route maps (scheduled departures and arrivals, checkpoints, etc.) linked to existing applications may display real-time information on the location of transport units and related data (dispatch time, average speed, cargo temperature, etc.).
(b) Route maps connected with invoicing systems in such a way that the logistics company may invoice for the service given at the time of collection / delivery.
(c) Transport management and management of fleet condition, resource utilization, reduction of polluting emissions, data control.

The PROCONET platform, or integrated model for communication between transport systems and logistics companies, will allow, through GPS (Global Positioning System), to know where the merchandise is at any given time, facilitating its transport and delivery in terms of traceability and food safety.

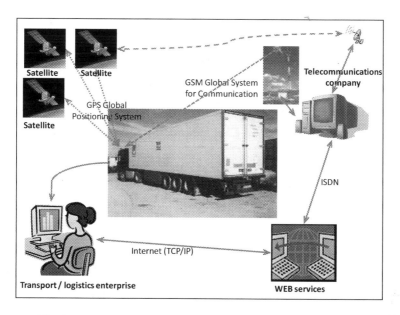

Fig. 1. Interconnected electronic information PROCONET platform

4.1 Technical Objectives of the PROCONET Project

The technical objectives targeted by this project form a continuum from business requirements up to evaluation of alternatives:

1. To inventory systems and equipment being used, likely to be used or likely to be developed for the Cold Supply Chain.
2. To design the necessary processes required for handling of loads in the groupages storage node for transportation by the Cold Supply Chain.
3. To define a model for traceability and food safety of fruit-and-vegetable products in the transport process of the cold supply chain.
4. To define a methodology which relates business decisions on transport (inventory records, suppliers' orders records and customers' orders records) with the technical requirements of the technology used in the Cold Chain.
5. To Identify and parameterize those variables likely to be present in a cold supply chain and their interaction with other agents in the chain.
6. To develop an initial traceability and food safety prototype for fruit-and-vegetable products in the logistic processes of the cold supply chain.
7. To develop a second transport safety prototype, based on INCOTERMS and demonstrate the feasibility of an electronic CMR.
8. To integrate both prototypes in such a way that a small transport business may evolve into a logistics company.
9. To assess and evaluate the developed prototypes.
10. To diffuse the conclusions of the completed prototyping work.

4.2 Methodology for the PROCONET Project

As stated by several authors [4,5], in Collaborative Networks there is not a single formal modelling methodology, tool or approach that may adequately cover all perspectives (no universal language for all problems).

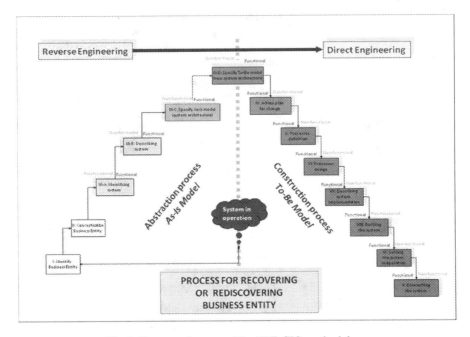

Fig. 2. Phases and stages of the ERE-GIO methodology

Therefore, for the development of a fruit-and-vegetable collaborative network which allows an appropriate paradigm and approach for different enterprise information systems of cold chain integration and collaboration, the research team are working with the ERE-GIO methodology [10], based on Integrated Information Architectures, and also on their own experience in designing and managing different enterprise information systems. The ERE-GIO methodology will allow the establishment of a modelling framework for CNs which integrates multiple perspectives, because this methodology presents a life cycle approach based on the "As-is" model as well as on the "To-be" model (Figure 2).

This model will be used to develop an approach to the cold supply chain from an endogenous CN perspective, made and mapped into different dimensions (structural, functional, etc.). This double-model methodology will also be used to integrate the GPS system and the platform that will support cold chain processes, whilst analyzing the performance and constraints of the traceability and safety prototype, and further implementation in the collaborative network.

4.3   Innovation in the Cold Supply Chain

Innovation is a complex and diversified activity involving many components interacting and acting as sources of new ideas. The PROCONET project is focused on incremental technological innovations, i.e. improvements that are made to a service or an existing process in order to increase the benefits for the chain or the network.

In this project, innovation is oriented towards four large areas (see Table 1), which for the fruit-and-vegetable collaborative network translates into the following factors: renewal and expansion of the productive processes and the range of services, changes in organization and in management, and consequences of the feasibility of the electronic CMR.

Table 1. Technological innovation of the PROCONET project

Fruit-and-vegetable Sector	• Traceability control of fruit-and-vegetable products during the transport and handling phases. • INCOTERM-based improvements in CMR application.
Cold Supply Chain	• Transport model in Cold Supply Chain, definition of indicators, implementation, measuring, evaluation and development of scoreboard. • Development of a prototype that allows and enables traceability of fruit-and-vegetable products whilst on route and its interaction with logistical companies.
Storage Nodes	• Design of processes that allow small farmers' groupages to access Cold Supply Chain transport services in the best conditions.
ICTs	• Application in the traceability of fruit-and-vegetable products. • Application in transport safety. • Application in the fruit-and-vegetable sector and cold chain. • Development under open systems.

5   Conclusions

Alongside the main objective of the PROCONET project, to achieve comprehensive traceability of fruit-and-vegetable transport with controlled temperature (in a collaborative network organization), the research team is pursuing a set of long-term goals which, once the project is completed, may be applied to different areas, depending on the type of enterprise and the business sector addressed:

- The project's consortium has established as a challenge to demonstrate the feasibility of the electronic CMR and its legal implications. If it proves to be feasible, the challenge is to propose the different Spanish institutions the modification of the current European normative and INCOTERMS agreements.
- Road export companies would be greatly interested in the results of the prototyping oriented to "on-route transport" because it is a constant source of conflict between logistic operators, customers and insurance companies.
- Logistics companies in the fruit-and-vegetable sector and in other sectors also working in the cold supply chain will have a great interest in the results of the parameterization of traceability, motivated by option to know the actual characteristics of how their transport has been carried out.

- Small farmers, the most common users of groupages, will be supplied the possibility to incorporate the added value of traceability of their products, which is usually restricted to and monopolized by large companies.
- National transport companies will be motivated to incorporating the technology involved in the prototype, to be developed in this project. This technology will initially involve investment in equipment and facilities, but it will mean an added value and differentiating feature against competition from foreign transport.

References

1. Benner, M., Geerts, R., Linnemann, A., Jongen, W., Folstar, P., Cnossen, H.: A chain information model for structured knowledge management: towards effective and efficient food product improvement. Trends. Food. Sci. Tech. 14, 469–477 (2003)
2. Camarinha-Matos, L., Pantoja-Lima, C.: Cooperation coordination in virtual enterprises. J. Intell. Manuf. 12, 133–150 (2001)
3. Camarinha-Matos, L., Afsarmanesh, H.: Collaborative networks: a new scientific discipline. J. Intell. Manuf. 16, 439–452 (2005)
4. Camarinha-Matos, L., Afsarmanesh, H.: A comprehensive modeling framework for collaborative networked organizations. J. Intell. Manuf. 18, 529–542 (2007)
5. Camarinha-Matos, L., Afsarmanesh, H., Galeano, N., Molina, A.: Collaborative networked organizations – Concepts and practice in manufacturing enterprises. Comput. Ind. Eng. 57, 46–60 (2009)
6. Gómez-Espín, J.M.: Estrategias de innovación en el sector hortofrutícola español y en las empresas encargadas de la logística y transporte de estos productos perecederos. Papeles de Geografía 39, 81–117 (2004)
7. Moe, T.: Perspectives on traceability in food manufacture. Trends. Food. Sci. Tech. 9, 211–214 (1998)
8. Luengo, G.: El sector hortofrutícola español: a la espera de su racionalización (2003), http://www.frutas-hortalizas.com
9. Pereira, A., Rabelo, R., Campos, A., Spinosa, L.: Managing distributed Business processes in the virtual enterprise. J. Intell. Manuf. 12, 185–197 (2001)
10. Ros, L., de la Fuente, M.V., Ortiz, A.: Enterprise Engineering versus Cycle Re-Engineering Methods. In: Proceeding of the 13th IFAC Symposium on Information Control Problems in Manufacturing, INCOM 2009 (2009)
11. Sarkar, S., Costa, A.: Dynamics of open innovation in the food industry. Trends. Food. Sci. Tech. 19, 574–580 (2008)

Enterprise Architecture Framework with Early Business/ICT Alignment for Extended Enterprises

Llanos Cuenca, Andres Boza, and Angel Ortiz

Research Centre on Production Management and Engineering (CIGIP)
Universidad Politécnica de Valencia, Camino de Vera s/n, 46022 Valencia, Spain
{llcuenca,aboza,aortiz}@cigip.upv.es

Abstract. Incorporating information and communication technology (ICT) is strongly necessary in extended enterprises. To do this, enterprise engineering approach has important benefits; however, there is not a complete framework to model ICT components and ICT/business alignment. This paper presents an enterprise architecture framework for extended enterprises. The main aim enclosed in this paper is to provide a modeling framework from enterprise engineering approach which including ICT. A comparative analysis has been conducted in life cycle phases, modeling views and strategic alignment between different enterprise architectures. Next, the required building blocks have been proposed: ICT conceptualization, application portfolio, maturity model, alignment heuristics and strategic dependencies. This proposal has been applied in the collaborative order management process of a ceramic tile company.

Keywords: Enterprise Engineering, Business and ICT Strategic Alignment, Enterprise Architecture Framework.

1 Introduction

The current economic conditions and the high level of market uncertainty, forces the companies to be in a continuous adaptation to respond constant changes. The competitive advantages in the changing business environment have moved organizational structures from single enterprises to extended or virtual enterprise networks. The collaboration of enterprises requires that all of the enterprise elements should interact efficiently with each other based upon a complete framework [1]. Information technology allows making better the value chain (improving the enterprise processes and defining new processes) changing the way companies do business. In this sense, it is important to define a framework to model business and information and communication technology components, and its alignment, in an extended enterprise.

In this paper we propose a modeling framework from an enterprise engineering approach identifying views, life cycle and building blocks to model extended enterprises. This framework incorporates in early life cycle phases the required elements for business and information technology alignment.

Á. Ortiz Bas, R.D. Franco, P. Gómez Gasquet (Eds.): BASYS 2010, IFIP AICT 322, pp. 11–18, 2010.
© IFIP International Federation for Information Processing 2010

2 Extended Enterprises and Enterprise Architecture

Nowadays many industrial organizations are focusing specifically on linking and unifying supply chains. This linking process leads to the synchronized behavior of all participants [2]. They form entities, commonly called extended enterprises (EE). Extended Enterprise has been defined as: "Individual companies work together to form inter-enterprise networks across the product value chain in order to survive and achieve business success" [3]. The Extended Enterprise follows a philosophy where people throughout the business supply chain participate in the decision-making process [4].

In the modern global competitive environment, manufacturing enterprises need active co-operation with a large network of suppliers and customers to form extended enterprises [5]. With inter-organizational networks, firms begin to perceive the benefits derived from a vertical disintegration process which enables them to concentrate on their distinctive capacities, while identifying and developing mechanisms which boost the rapid configuration of operative structures that are quick to reconfigure and to adapt to rapidly changeable environments [6]. Creating new organizational forms requires the intense use of information and communication technology (ICT).

Enterprise architecture is a key issue in the development of enterprises supporting by technology. Enterprise architecture should have addressed more on how to align of business strategy to technology for implementation, and not just focused on business or IT with separated research and development [7].

3 Enterprise Architectures and Modeling Frameworks Review

Enterprise engineering (EE) concerns the analysis, optimization and re-engineering of all or part of business processes, information systems and organization structures in an enterprise or in an enterprise network [8].

According to Hoogervorst [9] this engineering approach has important benefits such as: 1) the formal approach for addressing organized complexity and the realization of a unified and integrated design, 2) the formal identification of all coordination actions makes clear responsibilities. These benefits generally do not appear with other types of business process modeling. To ensure that this design is carried out coherently the concept of enterprise architecture arises. Enterprise architecture (EA) is defined as a way to structure and design the company's organization and operations. Enterprise architecture is a coherent whole of principles, methods and models that are used in the design and realization of an enterprise's organizational structure, business processes, information systems, and infrastructure [10].

The framework, as it applies to the enterprise, is a logical structure for classifying and organizing the descriptive representations of an enterprise that are significant to the management of the enterprise as well as to the development of the enterprise systems [11]. An enterprise architecture framework is applied to describe both the current (as-is) and future (to-be) states [12]. The framework should also simplify the enterprise architecture development, since it helps to articulate how the different components of the architecture relate to one another. A framework should provide a general mechanism for defining views. Views are used in modeling because the complexity of an enterprise makes it unfeasible for a single descriptive representation to be comprehensible in its entirety [13].

Another adjacent concept to EA is Enterprise Modeling (EM). EM describes the EA from various viewpoints in detail to allow specifying and implementing the systems [7]. The use of these models in enterprise engineering can shorten design times and increase modeling consistency [14].

Enterprise models have a life cycle that is related to the life cycle of the modeled entity. EM uses modeling languages, methods and tools chosen according to the life cycle phase (or life cycle activity) of the enterprise. Several architecture frameworks exist today and they all have a modeling framework organizing enterprise model that may have to be created during the life of a business entity [15].

All the enterprise architectures contain views in their frameworks, however, life cycle, building blocks, and how the building blocks fit together, is not defined by all of them [16].

3.1 Comparative Analysis between Enterprise Architecture Frameworks

The Enterprise architectures analyzed have been: TOGAF [17], GERAM [18], IE-GIP [19], Zachman [20] and EAP [21]. The comparative analysis has been conducted in life cycle phases (Identification, Conceptualization, Requirements Definition, Design, Implementation Description, Construction, Operation and Decommission) and modeling views (Business view, Information view, Data view, Application view, Technological view, Organizational view and Resource view).

We can summarize that some modeling views are included with the same name in the enterprise architecture frameworks analyzed. In other cases, the modeling views are included but with a different name, finally other views are not explicitly included but can be complemented from other views. Similar conclusions were obtained from life cycle analysis.

The next figure shows the relationships between modeling views and life cycle phases. The identification and conceptualization phases, do not take into account the information, resources, data, applications and technology views.

The requirements definition phase incorporates the information, resources and data views. Only from design specification are considered the applications and technology views (To abbreviate the figure 1 does not include operation and decommission phases).

As discussed earlier, ICT is very important for the extended manufacturing and its alignment with business process and business strategies. The figure above shows that it is not possible to define aspects of information, resources, data, application and technology in early stages of life cycle. Incorporating information systems and information technology in the organizations have considerable risks, and these risks are increased when a strategic plan for its incorporation is not done.

There are a number of proposals that relate the alignment models with enterprise architectures [22] [23] [24] 25]. In most of cases, the strategic alignment is conducted from business strategy to organizational infrastructure. ICT strategy is hardly defined and when it is done, it does not influence in business strategy. So, it is necessary to improve the definition of ICT strategy and its alignment with business strategy in enterprise architecture.

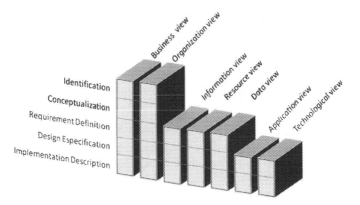

Fig. 1. The incorporation of modeling views in life cycle phases of enterprise architectures

According [26] in the enterprise architecture approach is not defined how to align and what to align. It is necessary identify what elements must be included in the enterprise architecture framework. The table 1 shows these elements and checks if they are included or not in the enterprise architectures framework analyzed. In some cases, this elements are mentioned in the enterprise architecture but it is not identified how to define them (this case has been labeled as "Limited" in the table).

Table 1. ICT and alignment components

	Togaf	Geram	IE-GIP	Zachman	EAP
ICT strategy	Yes	No	No	Limited	Limited
Business and IT alignment assessment	Limited	No	Limited	Limited	Limited
Incorporating IT definition in earlier life cycle phases	Limited	No	No	Limited	Limited
Incorporating application and services portfolio	Limited	No	No	Limited	Limited
Incorporating business and IT alignment maturity model	No	No	No	No	No

4   Enterprise Architecture Framework for Extended Manufacturing

The identified ICT and alignment components must be incorporated in the enterprise architecture framework in order to facilitate ICT strategic definition and alignment with business strategy in extended manufacturing.

We propose new building blocks according to ICT strategy components: 1) ICT conceptualization, 2) application portfolio and 3) maturity model. Other building blocks are proposed in order to promote strategic alignment between business and ICT: 4) alignment heuristics and 5) strategic dependencies.

1) ICT Conceptualization: The purpose of this building block is that the company validates whether the ICT strategy is fully established for the company and business entity. ICT conceptualization is a checklist to indicate what documents have been completed. Finally, it must also carry out a joint analysis with the business strategy. The ICT objectives may precede the formulation of business objectives and will be used as input to their development.

2) Application portfolio: 2.1) As-Is portfolio: The purpose of the as-is portfolio is to support the information associated with each application and its relationships with as-is business objectives. 2.2) To-Be portfolio: The purpose of the to-be portfolio is to support the information associated with each application and its relationships with to-be business objectives. There must be at least a relationship with a business objective. 2.3) Application and services portfolio: The applications and services portfolio include those that have been identified in the to-be portfolio and those who remain in the as-is portfolio. Each one can be associated with business objectives and business process that execute them.

3) Maturity Model: It is based on the maturity models of [27] and [28] and allows you to define the maturity level of strategic alignment. The building block maturity model allows identifying the maturity level reached by the business entity. It is important to define the revision date and the last level assigned to analyze the alignment evolution.

4) Alignment heuristics: Alignment heuristics are used in this case to detect weakness in business and ICT alignment. By using this building block, different views are related by an alignment question. The company will react with improvement actions depending on the answer.

5) Strategic dependencies: The strategic dependencies model is based on i * framework [29]. The strategic dependency building block represents the resource, task or

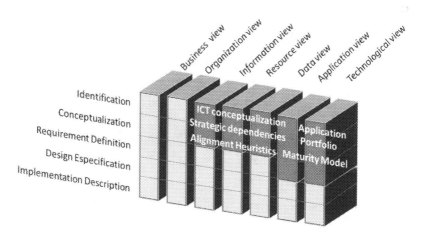

Fig. 2. Enterprise architecture framework for extended manufacturing

goal dependencies among different actors (roles, organizational units, organization cells or set of roles). It also indicates whether or not dependency is critical for the business entity. The purpose is to detect dependencies between actors.

The figure 2 shows as the modeling views have been extended in the enterprise architecture framework proposed.

The relations between new elements described above, and its location in each view and modeling phase can be found in [16].

5 Case Study

This proposal has been applied in a ceramic tile company. It was necessary to identify the components of extended manufacturing process and several interviews with the managers appointed by the company. The business entity selected was the collaborative order management because is a critical process for the company. Information systems and information technology are essential to support this process.

The business and ICT conceptualization was carried out after identifying the business entity. With the definition of the alignment heuristic at this stage, was possible to identify aspects that had not been well resolved in the conceptualization.

The strategic dependencies model helped to identify the dependencies between actors, and allowed detecting bottlenecks and vulnerabilities. First, the actors involved were identified: suppliers, manufacturers, wholesalers and customers (bringing together retailers and end customers). Besides these actors, we propose a new one to be modeled, the computer system, which includes the information system and technology to use, in this way, strategic relationships with it can be modeled.

The application and services portfolio has enabled the company to link the enterprise business processes to applications and services at the macro level through goals. Also, it has allowed a prioritization of the applications.

The maturity model has allowed a detailed analysis of the alignment between business and ICT, with an allocation of values from one to five, where one represents the lowest value. For the company, the result was a low value which represents an emerging alignment. This encouraged the company to improve some alignment aspects.

The table 2 shows an example of strategic dependency identified in the company.

Table 2. Strategic dependency

Type: Name: Facilitating coordination and collaboration between wholesalers Identification: SD-4 Design responsible: U-13
Participants: Enterprise Integration Team Depender actor: wholesalers Dependee actor: ICT Dependum: Objective, improving coordination and collaboration Dependency type: critical Chart: 1.1

6 Conclusion

This paper set out the needs for a modeling framework to include information and communication technology in early life cycle phases in extended enterprises. Traditionally, business strategy is the driver of organization and IT infrastructure. The alignment it is not concerned with the exploitation of emerging IT capabilities to impact new products and services; technology is not seen as competitive advantage. Hence it is necessary to extend all modeling views to all life cycle phases and to define the strategic alignment components.

The proposed framework allows defining ICT strategy, business and IT alignment assessment, incorporating IT definition in earlier life cycle phases, incorporating application and services portfolio and incorporates business and IT alignment maturity model by the following blocks: ICT conceptualization, application portfolio, maturity model, alignment heuristics and strategic dependencies.

Its application to an extended process, (collaborative order management), has allowed validating the usefulness of the framework.

References

1. Choi, Y., Kang, D., Chae, H., Kim, K.: An enterprise architecture framework for collaboration of virtual enterprise chains. Int. J. Adv. Manuf. Technol. 35, 1065–1078 (2008)
2. Vasiliu, L., Browne, J.: An integrated modeling approach of the Extended Enterprise using fractals, game theory and neural networks structure. In: The Proceedings of the 9th International Conference of Concurrent Enterprising, Espoo, Finland, June 16-18 (2003)
3. Zhang, J., Browne, J.: Extended and Virtual Enterprises – Similarities and Differences. International Journal of Management Systems (1999)
4. O'Neill, H., Sackett, P.: The Extended Manufacturing Enterprise Paradigm. Management Decision 32(8), 42–49 (1994)
5. Cheng, K., Popov, Y.: Internet-enabled modelling of extended manufacturing enterprises using process-based techniques. Int. J. Adv. Manuf. Technol. 23, 148–153 (2004)
6. Camarinha-Matos, L.M., Afsarmanesh, H.: Collaborative networks: a new scientific discipline. J. Intell. Manuf. 16(4), 439–452 (2005)
7. Chen, D., Doumeningts, G., Vernadat, F.: Architectures for enterprise integration and interoperability: past, present and future. Computers in Industry 59, 647–659 (2008)
8. Vernadat, F.: Enterprise Modeling and Integration. In: Principles and Applications. Chapman & Hall, Boca Raton (1996)
9. Hoogervorst, J.: Enterprise Governance and Enterprise Engineering. Springer, Heidelberg (2009)
10. Lankhorst, M.M.: Enterprise Architecture Modeling - the Issue of Integration. Advanced Engineering Informatics. Engineering Computing and Technology 18(4), 205 (2004)
11. Inmon, W.H., Zachman, J.A., Geiger, G.J.: Data stores, data warehousing and the Zachman framework. McGraw-Hill, New York (1997)
12. Tang, A., Han, J., Chen, P.: A Comparative Analysis of Architecture Frameworks. Technical Report SUTIT-TR2004.01, Swinburne University of Technology (2004)
13. Martin, R., Robertson, E.: Architectural principles for enterprise frameworks (2004)
14. Chen, D., Vernadat, F.: Standard on enterprise integration and engineering-state of the art. Int. J. Computer Integrated Manufacturing 17(3), 235–253 (2004)

15. Bernus, P., Nemes, L., Schmidt, G.: Handbook on enterprise architecture. Springer, Berlin (2003)
16. Cuenca L.l., Ortiz A., Boza A.: Business and IS/IT Strategic Alignment Framework. DoCEIS 2010, IFIP AICT, vol. 314, pp. 24–31 (2010)
17. TOGAF The Open Group Architecture Framework, http://www.opengroup.org/togaf
18. IFIP-IFAC Task Force: Generalized Enterprise Reference Architecture and Methodology, Version 1.6.2, Annex to ISO WD15704, IFIP-IFAC Task Force (1999)
19. Ortiz, A., Lario, F., Ros, L.: IE-GIP. A proposal for a Methodology to Develop Enterprise Integration Program. Computers in Industry 40, 155–171 (1999)
20. Sowa, J., Zachman, J.: Extending and formalizing the framework for information-systems architecture. IBM Systems Journal 31(3), 590 (1992)
21. Luftman, J.: Assessing business-it alignment maturity. Communications of the Association for Information Systems 4(14) (2000)
22. Spewak, S.: Enterprise Architecture Planning: Developing a Blueprint for Data, Applications, and Technology. Wiley, Chichester (1993)
23. Wegmann, A., Balabko, P., Le, L., Reveg, G., Rychkova, I.: A Method and Tool for Business-IT Alignment. In: Enterprise Architecture Proceedings of the CAISE. Porto Univ., Porto, Portugal (2005)
24. Pereira, C., Sousa, P.: Enterprise Architecture: Business and IT Alignment. In: ACM Symposium on Applied Computing (2005)
25. Plazaola, L., Flores, J., Silva, E., Vargas, N., Ekstedt, M.: An Approach to Associate Strategic Business-IT Alignment Assessment to Enterprise Architecture. In: Conference on Systems Engineering Research, Stevens Institute of Technology Campus, USA (2007)
26. Wang, X., Zhou, X., Jiang, L.: A method of business and IT alignment based on enterprise architecture (2008)
27. Chen, H.M.: SOA, Enterprise Architecture, and Business-IT Alignment: An Integrated Framework. In: Proceeedings of the 6th International Workshop on System/Software Architectures (2007)
28. Santana, R.G., Daneva, M., van Eck, P.A.T., Wieringa, R.J.: Towards a business-IT alignment maturity model for collaborative networked organizations. In: Proceedings of the International Workshop on Enterprise Interoperability Munich, Germany, pp. 70–81 (2008)
29. Yu, E.: Modeling Strategic Relationships for Process Reengineering. PhD thesis (1995)

Evaluation of Collaborative Enterprises Networks: Case Study of Brazilian Virtual Enterprises

Antonio José Cauliraux Pithon, Alessandro Garcia de Castro,
Paulo Enrique Stecklow, and Ralfh Varges Ansuattigui

CEFET-RJ
{caulliraux,garciadecastro,paulo.stecklow}@gmail.com,
varges@globo.com

Abstract. The emergency of the so called new digital economy, with intense diffusion of the information and telecommunication technologies, has provoked a revolution in the business world through the last years, changing the companies' paths and strategies, despite the nature of its products, markets and processes. Thus, the organizational networks become an alternative way of organizing the production of goods and services and may be used by the companies to improve its competitive position. This article's objective is to show the concept of virtual enterprises as dynamic collaborative networks by presenting some cases in other countries, to study the collaborative networks behavior and to compare the experience of foreign virtual companies with some Brazilian ones.

1 Introduction

The collaborative networks consist of a variety of entities (for instance, organizations and people) that are widely autonomous in terms of operating environment, organizational culture, social capital and goals. Nevertheless, these entities collaborate to achieve better objectives and goals, whose interactions are supported through computer networks [1].

The process of framing companies under pre-established perspectives demand a preliminary planning, focused on what is intended from the classification of these companies, whatever nature they are. This article qualifies virtual enterprises under criteria defined by students of the discipline Collaborative Networks taught in CEFET-RJ (Celso Suckow da Fonseca Technologic Educational Federal Center) in the first semester of 2009, following a preliminary planning.

1.1 Concept

For a better understanding on the concept, we may see how some authors defined Collaborative Networks. According to Olivieri [2] "Networks are organizational systems capable of putting individuals and institutions together, in a democratic and participatory manner, around common goals and/or themes. Flexible structures, the networks are set up by horizontal relationships, dynamically interconnected,

Á. Ortiz Bas, R.D. Franco, P. Gómez Gasquet (Eds.): BASYS 2010, IFIP AICT 322, pp. 19–27, 2010.

foreseeing the collaborative and participatory work. The networks are supported by its members will and affinity, characterized as a meaningful organizational resource for personal relationships as well as to social structuring".

Castells [3] states that "networks are the new social morphology of our societies, and the diffusion of networking logic substantially changes the operation and performance of productive processes, of experience, power and culture. Although the form of social organization in networks existed in other times and spaces, the new paradigm of information technology (IT) provides the material basis for its pervasive expansion throughout the social structure. Moreover, it can be said that this logic of networks generates a social determination at a higher level than the specific social interests expressed through networks: the power of the flows is more important than the flows of power".

According to the above concepts, we understand that Collaborative Networks are a set of bodies that connect to each other with common goals and affinities in an open system in constant interaction.

1.2 Methodology

The methodology adopted in this work was based on literature review in order to contextualize criteria to the qualifying of virtual enterprises. The survey-listed companies of all kinds of business, and the selection criteria was that each of them should be mandatorily a virtual enterprise and, also, their information would be investigated in the World Wide Web (WWW). Thus, six enterprises of different sizes were chosen and the analyzed period started from March up to June 2009.

The virtual enterprises listed in the survey were classified by their adherence to the chosen evaluation criteria. Each criterion was developed to classify the virtual enterprise on a scale of HIGH (H), MEDIUM (M) and LOW (L) and theirs criteria definitions is described ahead.

2 Virtual Enterprise

Virtual Enterprises (VE) are seen as an innovative form of management, a new model created to meet the expectations of an increasingly demanding and competitive market. Mowshowitz [4] first presented the concept of virtual enterprise in 1986 and, as joint ventures, virtual enterprises were created based on the theory of cooperation, as dynamic networks of companies.

There is not a consensus in the literature about the concept of virtual enterprise, but the ones that meet most of the concepts for this work agreed that VE consist in a temporary network of independent companies - suppliers, customers, even competitors - linked by IT to share skills, costs and to allow common access to their same markets [4]. Fuehrer [5] considers a VE a temporary network of independent institutions, businesses or specialized individuals, working together in a spontaneous way through TI in order to achieve a gain in a demanding competitive market, as well as Travica [5] affirms that VE is a new organizational form characterized by temporary or permanent grouping of geographically dispersed individuals, groups or organizational departments not belonging to the same organization, which are dependent on IT to maintain their production processes.

Exploring these definitions we can assume some VE features, like "temporality", that means that It is created to last only the necessary time to meet a specific demand (However, there is no impediment as to its perpetuation and structure reconfigurations), "meeting skills" by improving the synergy among network agents, massive use of IT, "Cooperation" among members in a synchronous or asynchronous way and "confidence" based on the mutual confidence between the members to allow the best accomplishment of the work.

3 Case Study

Based on literature review, some criteria have been developed in this study to evaluate companies. They are Sustainability, Communicability, Flexibility, Coverage, Correctness, Stability, Awareness And Technological Infrastructure. Each criterion is defined as follows:

3.1 Sustainability

According to the United Nations Organization (UN) sustainability is defined as "meeting the needs of present generations without compromising the ability of meeting the needs of future generations" [6]. Sustainability means survival of natural resources, enterprises and the society itself. It is based on the so-called Triple Bottom Line, consisting of three pillars: economic, social and environmental. This means that for any development survives, it will have to be socially fair, environmentally responsible and economically profitable. Thus, to promote the continuity of business, these three components should be necessarily present [7].

As the sustainability rating in this study, the scoring of certain criteria indicates the degree of sustainability of the considered companies. Each criterion evaluates to 2 points when it clearly applies to a company, one point when it applies but with a lesser degree of strength and zero point when it does not apply. The criteria to measure sustainability are customer loyalty marketing strategy, corporate image and brand enrichment, crisis management and public opinion control, scored accordingly to the score set in the Table 1.

Table 1. Sustainability level score classification (H – High, M – Medium and L - Low)

Sustainability Level Score Classification		
0-2 $\rightarrow$ L	3-5 $\rightarrow$ M	6-8 $\rightarrow$ H

3.2 Communicability

Communicability is the quality of the optimized communicative act, in which the message is fully, accurately, quickly and economically delivered. The integral transmission assumes that there are not suppressive, distorting or concurrent noises. The correct transmission implies identity between the message delivered by the sender and the received one by the receiver. The speed assumes that the message follows by the shortest way. The economy assumes that returns, efforts to decode and understand are not necessary.

Virtual communicability can be defined as the possibility of anyone using any kind of communication access (graphical browsers, textual, special for the blind or for mobile computing systems) to getting a complete understanding of the information contained in it, beyond having full and complete ease to interact with it. Thus, the communicability proposed refers to the possibility of the virtual space being accessed by anyone, regardless of situation, limitations or applied tool.

For qualifying the virtual enterprise in the context of communicability we considered the quality of oral communication optimized for pronounceability, audibility, readability, processability and accessibility, by summing the score applied to every criteria (Table 2).

Table 2. Sustainability level score classification (H – High, M – Medium and L - Low)

Communicability Level Score Classification		
0-3 $\rightarrow$ L	4-7 $\rightarrow$ M	8-10 $\rightarrow$ H

3.3 Flexibility

Considering flexibility as a set of features that allow an enterprise to face unplanned situations [8], it is easy to see that some capabilities enable the company to deal with variations in demand for its products.

Indicators for assessing a virtual enterprise for flexibility are plan of positions consistent with the work activities, providing training courses in the business, access to quality internet, human resources policies and availability of software tools and hardware. Each criterion evaluates to 3 points when it applies in a formal and efficient way, two points when it applies informally and one point when it does not apply. Considering the score of each indicator, the enterprise can obtain a final score ranging from five to fifteen, qualifying it for flexibility (Table 3).

Table 3. Flexibility level score classification (H – High, M – Medium and L - Low)

Flexibility Level Score Classification		
5-7 $\rightarrow$ L	8-11 $\rightarrow$ M	12-15 $\rightarrow$ H

3.4 Coverage

The use of IT, according to [9], allows the cooperation established between the partners in a virtual organization to assume a global dimension, exceeding the limits of time and distance between the corporation and its customers as a strategic way of increasing competitiveness and coverage.

The coverage as an attribute of a virtual organization has the meaning of range or maximum reachable geographical limit of operation and this can be dynamic to the extent of the variations in the resulting logistics due to organization and type of product or service offered, scored as follows (Table 4):

Table 4. Coverage Level Score Classification (H – High, M – Medium and L - Low)

Coverage Level Score Classification					
Local coverage (city/state)	→ L	National coverage	→ M	International coverage	→ H

3.5 Correctness

Correctness refers to the quality of management, characterized by inter-elements processes that support the sharing, integration and access to resources necessary to achieve their goals. The degree of importance to this criterion is established as Low (lack of or without business processes of any kind), Medium (a combined arrangement of formal with non-formal business processes) and High (formal business processes fully spread among the VE).

3.6 Stability

This criterion is based on the financial stability, characterized by the rational use of financial resources that support the production system. The liquidity attempts to measure the stability of the financial foundations of the company [10]. We consider stability as the property of maintenance and regulation of aggregation and dynamic balance of the networked organization, by means of internal mechanisms.

Based on programs and projects performance scores lead by the networked organization, the stability was classified as High (it is fully perceived), Medium (it is moderately perceived) and Low (there is no relevant perception of stability).

3.7 Awareness

According to [11], the awareness by consumers can be tangible (are those easily measurable) and intangible (have the task of showing the customer that the company is unique). This work proceed to the analysis of the criterion based on the analysis model [12], to assess customer satisfaction. So it is considered as the dependent variable for this analysis the perceived degree of satisfaction of customers, based on the overall perceived user satisfaction, content relevance of the system, speed of the system, format of the system, usability of the system and timeliness of the system.

The evaluation of the criterion was made by scoring the sub-groups of the variables described above, assigning two points when the criterion is identifiable and expressed in a formal way, one point when there is no strength at the observation of the criterion and zero point when the criterion is not observed at all (Table 5).

Table 5. Awareness Level Score Classification (H – High, M – Medium and L - Low)

Awareness Level Score Classification		
0-3 → L	4-9 → M	10-12 → H

3.8 Technological Infrastructure

Infrastructures operate as the basis on which things are added in order to generate value, production or service. Karl Marx, in 1847, said that the social forces are linked to the productive forces, which in turn, change the social relations [13], has conceptualized these infrastructures.

From the 1960's, with technology previously driven by the Second World War, new management theories emerging and with industrialization almost like we know today, the concept of infrastructure started to be employed in matters hardware infrastructure. This designation, when expressed by means of computing infrastructure weakens the semantic definition of infrastructure, which now does not express only hardware but also software, standards and procedures [14].

An adapted model choice of methods and techniques for evaluating information systems [15] and [16] was used, and because of lacking of available enterprises information, was considered only the context of programmed decisions, in which are represented by the repetitive and ordinary decisions and that do not require a different treatment for each time they occur, whereas non-programmed decisions require a more invasive approach to the organizations studied.

Custodio [15] represents the three levels of classification - "high", "medium" and "low" considering communication between groups, control of routines, project management and production planning. The total score is the result of the sum of the scores given to each of the four structured decisions listed above and adapted for this study (Table 6).

The structured decision is equivalent to the sum of their parts, which are worth 1 (one) point when they are identified within the virtual enterprise and 0 (zero) point if not observed in the virtual enterprise, resulting in the following rating scale:

Table 6. Technological Infrastructure Level Score Classification (H – High, M – Medium and L - Low)

Technological Infrastructure Level Score Classification		
0-3 → L	4-8 → M	9-12 → H

4 Criteria versus Enterprise

The six enterprises chosen to this study was Virfebrás [17], Cederj [18], Informaker [19], CVRD [20], Prodweb [21] and NOGI Fightwear [22] and will be shortly described above. Note that it was chosen a heterogeneous type of companies for this analysis, instead of narrowing the sample space of this study.

Virtual Organization of Tools of Brazil – VIRFEBRAS – is a group of companies of tooling organized as a cooperative in the production of die and mold, where each of them maintains its own identity. Distance Learning Center on Higher Education – CEDERJ is a consortium of public universities, created in 2000 by the Rio de Janeiro Government, with the explicit aim of promoting continuing education to university graduates, with special attention to upgrading teachers in the public high school. InforMaker is an Information Technology company, which operates in the IT market since 1988 in various segments of which we can highlight the Virtual Software Factory. Companhia Vale do Rio Doce – CVRD is one of the largest mining companies in the world, but to maintain its leadership position has been forming alliances and networks with customers and suppliers to further strengthen their trade relations. Prodweb is a virtual enterprise that provides software solutions (websites development, e-commerce and systems development) and operates under a model based on the network integration with its clients, thus achieving the optimization of targets and deadlines to meet. NO GI Fightwear is a manufacturer of clothing and accessories for martial arts practice, that operates in domestic and international markets. Its production process is based on a strong alliance with suppliers and garments, integrated through IT.

Table 7 shows the classification of companies based on criteria developed. The classification of HIGH, MEDIUM and LOW represents the analysis of each criterion, based on specific rules for each one of them.

Table 7. Enterprise Classification versus criteria (H – High, M – Medium and L - Low)

	Virfebrás	Cederj	Informaker	CVRD	Prodweb	NOGI Fightwear
Sustainability	H	H	H	H	M	H
Communicability	H	H	H	H	M	H
Flexibility	H	M	H	H	H	M
Coverage	M	L	M	H	H	H
Correctness	L	H	H	H	M	M
Stability	H	H	M	H	H	L
Awareness	M	H	M	H	H	M
Infrastructure	M	M	M	H	L	M

Considering that as much "H" given to a company, as much virtual it is, these companies can be classified according to the level of virtuality, from the more virtual to the less virtual as follows: CVRD, Cederj, Informaker, Virfebrás, Prodweb and NOGI Fightwear. These companies, when they are analyzed under the level of development and considering how formal the enterprises in the net are, the results are very similar, comparing with the virtuality level shown on Table 7.

5 Conclusion

The process of qualifying enterprises for selected parameters to evaluation of virtual enterprises in Brazil based on the concepts of the discipline of Collaborative Networks of The Master Course in Technology, CEFET-RJ has to be done with careful planning and by preliminarily establishing goals that this classification seeks. One of the biggest challenges of this work was to obtain data so that the qualification could be done in the most assertive way.

For a more accurate classification of the enterprises, it's necessary to establish mechanisms more focused on obtaining data such as interviews and questionnaires, prepared according to the need of the classification criteria. When the criteria for the studied enterprises are solely for virtual enterprises, the situation gets complicated: It is difficult to identify the character of "virtuality" of companies, because as the concept of "virtual company" is still elusive, with different definitions between authors, the company itself ends up complicating the access to data classification from the perspective of "virtual company".

Realized the difficulty of performing more complex activities in a network without hierarchy, which confirms the need to have a business articulator of virtual enterprise. It will not be stated that there is a need for a broker, since there is no systematic and definitive studies on the function and role of brokers in business networks.

The articulator is responsible for making the business processes of the network be followed, that goals are achieved without unnecessary redundant activities, maintaining the synergy between the actors of the network and taking a holistic approach that optimizes the network to achieve efficiency and pursue new opportunities.

References

1. Camarinha-Matos, L., Afsarmanesh, H.: Journal of Intelligent Manufacturing 1(Ed. 16), 439–452 (2005)
2. Olivieri, L.: A importância histórico-social das redes (2002)
3. Castells, M.: A sociedade em rede (A era da informação: economia, sociedade e cultura). Paz e Terra, São Paulo (1999)
4. Corrêa, G.: Proposta de Integração de parceiros na formação e gerência de Empresas Virtuais (Tese de Doutorado). Escola de Engenharia de São Carlos, Universidade de São Paulo – USP, São Paulo, Brasil (1999)
5. Pithon, A.: Projeto Organizacional para a Engenharia Concorrente no Âmbito das Empresas Virtuais, Minho, Portugal (2004)
6. ONU - Organização das Nações Unidas: Relatório Brundtland (1987)
7. Credidio, F.: Sustentabilidade – Você sabe o que significa essa palavra? In: SINPRORP, http://www.sinprorp.org.br/Jornais/filantropia170.htm (accessed Outubro 2008)
8. Corrêa, H.L., Slack, N.: Flexibilidade estratégica na manufatura: incertezas e variabilidade de saídas. Revista de Administração 29 (1994)
9. Tröger, A.: Um Estudo Sobre Organizações Virtuais (1997)
10. Schvirck, E., Giasson, O.: Diferenças nos indicadores de desempenho de empresas que fazem e que não fazem reavaliação de ativos (2006)
11. Munhoz, C.: O Marketing de Relacionamento para Pequenas Empresas. In: Portal do Marketing, http://www.portaldomarketing.com.br/ Artigos/Marketing%20de%20Relacionamento%20para%20pequenas% 20empresas.htm (accessed 2003)
12. Senger, I.: Gestão de Sistemas de Informação Acadêmica: um estudo descritivo da satisfação dos usuários, Lavras (2005)
13. Marx, K.: Miséria da Filosofia. Centauro (2004)
14. Ambrosi, A., Pimienta, D., Peugeot, V.: Enjeux de mots: Regards multiculturels sur les sociétés de l'information. C & F Éditions (2004)
15. Custódio, I.: Avaliação de Sistemas de Informação: um modelo para auxiliar na escolha de métodos e técnicas. Revista de Administração 18(4) (1983)

16. Gorry, A., Morton, M.: A Framework for Management Information Systems. Alfred P. Sloan School of Management - Massachussets Institute of Technology (1971)
17. Virfebrás - Organização Virtual de Ferramentarias do Brasil, http://www.virfebras.com.br/
18. Governo do Rio de Janeiro - Secretaria de Ciência e Tecnologia: Fundação CECIERJ. In: Consórcio CEDERJ, http://www.cederj.edu.br/fundacaocecierj/exibe_artigo.php
19. InforMaker: Quem Somos. In: InforMaker, http://www.informaker.com.br/QuemSomos.asp
20. Tauhata, T., Macedo-Soares, D.: Redes e Alianças Estratégicas no Brasil: caso CVRD. RAE-eletrônica 3(1) (2004), http://www.rae.com.br/eletronica/index.cfm?FuseAction=Artigo&ID=1811&Secao=ESTRATGIA&Volume=3&Numero=1&Ano=2004
21. In: Prodweb - Soluções de Software para a Web, http://www.prodweb.com.br/
22. In: NO GI Fightwear web site, http://www.nogi.com.br/site-ptbr/index.php

ICT for Sustainable Manufacturing:
A European Perspective

Erastos Filos

European Commission, Information Society and Media Directorate-General
erastos.filos@ec.europa.eu

Abstract. The challenges associated with environmental sustainability and greenhouse gas emissions are increasingly affecting policy making and global economic activity. Since energy use accounts for eighty percent of all greenhouse gas emissions in Europe, the European Union is determined to fight against climate change and reduce emissions by at least twenty percent in 2020. Although information and communication technologies (ICT) account for approximately two percent of global CO_2 emissions, they can significantly contribute to reducing the ninety-eight percent of CO_2 emissions caused by other activities. This requires the ICT sector to lead developments towards environmental sustainability. The paper provides an overview of the European policy landscape (regulations, incentives) with a particular emphasis on issues pertaining to the role of ICT in reducing the CO_2 footprint of manufacturing.

Keywords: ICT, sustainable manufacturing, CO_2 emissions.

1 Introduction

One of the major challenges for industry today is to be competitive in global markets whilst also being conscious of achieving environmental objectives. Sustainability considerations regarding the development, manufacturing, distribution and maintenance of industrial products not only determine the environmental footprint of manufactured products but increasingly contribute to industrial competitiveness.

In May 2008, the European Commission presented a policy paper "Addressing the Challenges of Energy Efficiency through Information and Communication Technologies" [1] underlining the role of ICT as enabler of energy efficiency across the economy. It was accompanied by a stakeholder consultation investigating opportunities for energy efficiency. An ICT-enabled systems approach, transcending process and sector boundaries, seems to offer significant potential for savings.

2 Environmental Policies and Legislation

The key objectives of European environmental legislation are to lay down rules aimed at preventing pollution and repairing damages caused to the environment. European policies however, also foresee measures that promote the development of environmentally friendly industrial activity.

Á. Ortiz Bas, R.D. Franco, P. Gómez Gasquet (Eds.): BASYS 2010, IFIP AICT 322, pp. 28–35, 2010.

Article 174 of the Lisbon Treaty [2] sets out the basic principles of European policy action on the environment, in particular the precautionary principle and the 'polluter pays' principle. These general principles are implemented by specific legislation applicable to industrial activities in Europe [3]. The Treaty also requires environmental protection to be integrated into European policies with a view to promote sustainable development.

To prevent or to minimise the amount of pollutants and waste from industrial plants being released into air, water and soil, the *Integrated Pollution Prevention and Control* Directive establishes a procedure for authorising activities with a high pollution potential and sets minimum requirements to be included in all permits, particularly in terms of pollutants released [4].

Waste management [5] is increasingly seen as one key stage in the lifecycle of resources and products. Thematic strategies on preventing and recycling waste focus mainly on ways to promote sustainable waste management, by reducing the amount of waste produced, by minimising its environmental impact or by reducing resource use. This lifecycle-based approach obligates businesses to manage natural resources and their products in a sustainable way.

In their conclusions in May 2001, ministers of the European Council stated that an effective strategy for integrating sustainable development into industrial policy should not be based on legislation alone, but should to a large extent also come from *market-based and voluntary approaches*. While this mainstreaming of sustainable development is a challenge, it should also be seen as an opportunity to stimulate innovation and to create new economic prospects and a competitive advantage for European business.

The European Commission has put instruments in place that favour the development of environmentally friendly economic activity. Businesses are offered funding in the form of co-financing or loans through various financial instruments and programmes, such as the LIFE+ programme [6] or successive Framework Programmes for research and development [7], or support through other financing institutions such as the European Investment Bank or the Structural Funds [8]. Other incentives focus on improving business visibility and image. Main examples are the 'Ecolabel' and the Community Eco-Management and Audit Scheme (EMAS) [9]. Instruments to improve regulatory management include an action plan in favour of eco-technologies, the EMAS system and the promotion of voluntary agreements.

Activities also aim to spread best practices from instruments such as integrated pollution prevention and control, integrated product policy and standards. Integrated product policy [10] is the main policy for promoting sustainable production and consumption.

Energy accounts for 80 % of all greenhouse gas emissions in the EU. Determined to fight against climate change, the EU is committed to reducing its own emissions by at least 20 % until 2020. Reducing greenhouse gas emissions involves using less energy and more clean energy.

In its *Action Plan for Energy Efficiency* [11], the European Union sets out ways to achieve its 20 % objective by 2020. Efforts include in particular energy saving measures for the transport sector, the development of minimum efficiency requirements for energy-using appliances [12], awareness-raising measures targeting consumers with respect to sensible and economic energy use, improving the efficiency of production, transport and distribution of energy (heat and electricity), improving the energy performance of buildings and also developing energy technologies.

3   Towards Sustainable Manufacturing: The Role of ICT

A report published by the European ICT Industry Association (EICTA) [13] highlights efforts of the electronics industry to reduce waste and energy use in manufacturing as well as efforts focused on *eco-design*, i.e. to reduce energy use and packaging waste of modern electronics devices.

As an example of a voluntary agreement, the Energy Star programme [14] sets minimum standards for energy efficiency. Products that comply can display an appropriate logo. Other agreements involve the application of standards – e.g. a group of mobile phone manufacturers under the auspices of the International Telecommunications Union have recently agreed to standardise the charging system for mobile phones so that in the future all chargers will work from the same kind of USB connection [15].

Gartner estimates that ICT accounts for approximately 2 % of global CO_2 emissions [16]. The industry is focused on constantly delivering products that provide increased functionality alongside improved energy performance. However, since there are substantial inefficiencies in technology use and in human behaviour, ICT may significantly contribute to reducing the 98 % of CO_2 emissions caused by non-ICT activities. A smart implementation of ICT therefore requires policy support as well as standardisation efforts, e.g. for the adequate measurement of energy consumption.

3.1   Resource Use Efficiency in Semiconductor Manufacturing

The unprecedented success of CMOS technology - offering more functionality in an ever more affordable manner - accounts for almost all recent developments in ICT. But, even if Moore's law reduces power consumption with each CMOS generation, the sheer number of proliferating semiconductor-based devices and increase of demand for computing and storage functionality ultimately leads to an overall increase in ICT-induced electricity consumption.

The industry represented in the meeting of the Smart Manufacturing Consultation Group [17] includes the process industries, discrete manufacturing sectors as well as the semiconductor manufacturing sector. The statements and the figures presented below are summarised in the report of this Consultation Group [18].

Energy efficiency and energy productivity in semiconductor manufacturing is continuously improving. The World Semiconductor Council has set up a common global metric for relevant electricity parameters and has agreed on a global definition of expectation levels for the reduction of electricity consumption in semiconductor manufacturing. The expectation level for a normalised reduction in electricity consumption between 2001 and 2010 has been set to 30 %.

The productivity of the manufacturing line as a whole within a wafer fabrication line is increased by using complex ICT systems that improve and automate manufacturing decisions in situ, on the basis of previously gathered data that is stored in ever growing databases, e.g. the automated precision manufacturing system that was developed by AMD and is used in its fabrication sites in Dresden. Infineon reported that through consistent efforts to cut down energy consumption at front end manufacturing sites, the cumulative non-used energy (measured in 'negajoules') in the period 2002-2007 exceeded the output of the coal-fired power plant in Goldenhagen, Germany: more than 1.5 TWh in 2007. IBM reported having implemented numerous measures for energy conservation and resource use efficiency in its semiconductor manufacturing facilities. Intel reported having reduced energy consumption in its operations by 20 % per production unit over the last three years (equal to a saving of 160 million kWh in 2006).

3.2 Research and the Role of Standards

Research is needed to model complex manufacturing lines with respect to tool energy consumption. Breakthroughs are needed to maximise the utilisation of the tools and for load management in a way that the sensitive fabrication process is not disrupted. Techniques have been developed in different industries that could have applicability across sectors. To be able to drive improvements, it is critical to be able to measure the current state and to understand what an achievable value should be. All levels of a factory ecosystem need to become measurable. Sensors do exist to measure energy use of components and subsystems, but not of all of them.

Smart power electronics components and systems are a prerequisite to energy saving in all ICT application areas [19]. The total savings due to the use of smart power electronics components and systems within the whole power generation chain can amount to 50 %. Therefore, the need for R&D in smart power electronics is outlined in the strategic research agendas of the SmartGrids [20] and the ENIAC [21] Technology Platforms.

The link between nanoelectronics and energy efficiency has been addressed by the 7th European R&D Framework Programme, and has been put forward in both, the ICT Work Programme 2009-10 and the Annual Work Programmes 2009 and 2010 of the ENIAC Joint Undertaking. Within the nanoelectronics part of the ICT Work Programme 2009-10 one objective has focused on 'design' and another on 'technology' aspects. The microsystems part addressed energy efficiency under 'autonomous energy efficient smart systems'. Energy efficiency will continue to be a focus area in the 2011-12 Work Programme of the ICT Theme.

Some equipment suppliers, such as vacuum pump and point of use abatement vendors, have made significant improvements with energy consumption. Examples of this are the introduction of high efficiency motors, lower cooling water flow, higher temperature gradients, and utility consumption control.

Regarding the characterisation of tool energy consumption, SEMI has developed an international industry standard, the SEMI S23 Guide for Conservation of Energy, Utilities and Materials Used by Semiconductor Manufacturing Equipment [22]. An example of a regional, sector-independent, standard is the Irish Energy Management System Standard IS 393 [23]. It is a standard that enables companies to engage in, to document their energy management systems and to drive continuous improvement at a pace appropriate to the company's size. The rules facilitate and enable widespread engagement. Intel Ireland has been certified according to this standard.

3.3 Resource Use Efficiency in Discrete Manufacturing

The experts involved in the Smart Manufacturing Consultation Group assessed the potential for energy efficiency also in the other manufacturing sectors and provided detailed recommendations [18]. Savings potentials for discrete manufacturing are seen in the following areas:

Process stability: Achieving energy and material efficiency through better process stability. "Zero waste production" avoids the manufacturing of defective parts. 100 % quality control can help achieve this goal. ICT-driven control systems can considerably reduce unproductive time during ramp-up. Operation and maintenance cycles can be optimised.

Rethinking production process technology: Mechanical, thermal and chemical processes and production systems overall have to be reconsidered with respect to their energy savings potential, which can be estimated to 25 %. Processes which lead to changes in the state of materials, such as heat treatments, lead to high material losses. Sensor-based ICT-infrastructures should be used to monitor and analyse energy-relevant parameters. Detection of the beginning and end of down times, intelligent monitoring, system diagnosis and auto-correction should be implemented. The base load on machine tools is responsible for up to ¾ of the total power consumption, while ¼ is used for the process itself. An optimisation of waiting/start-up times has a savings potential of 10-25 %. For example, coating of sheets before forming results in less energy consumption, less loss of lacquer or powder in the process and less time for the process.

Lossless infrastructure operations in manufacturing plants and factories: This production area, including the transportation of goods, accounts for more than 40 % of energy consumption in discrete manufacturing.

Intelligent motor drives: Technologies to increase energy efficiency are readily available: motors are installed in all manufacturing plants; 88 % of the motor drives today are not electronically controlled. Out of these, an estimated 50 % can be equipped with variable speed drives to achieve energy savings, during partial load, of up to 50 %. The savings potential from the use of power electronics is estimated as follows: 20-30 % traction drives using power semiconductors, e.g. through the recuperation of braking energy; 30-40 % motor control using inverters; 30-40 % air conditioning, using intelligent compressor control. There is a lack of information about energy consumption of motor systems and where savings can be made within a factory. The main role of ICT in the short term will be to monitor energy use and provide data for decision making on energy and cost reduction. Wireless networks that allow inter-machine and inter-system communication would help improve energy efficiency across the entire factory.

Energy savings in the use of compressed air: In case studies of compressed air technology it was found that energy savings are achievable in the range of 10-50 %.

3.4 Energy Efficiency and the Process Industries

Almost all options identified in the section on discrete manufacturing are also applicable to the process industries. The estimated savings potential in this industry domain is as follows:

The *steel industry* has reduced its energy consumption and CO_2 generation by 50-60 % respectively over the past 40 years. Steel can be generated from an integrated route or from a recycling route. To use the integrated route means to start with ore. The recycling route makes use of shredded material. The integrated route needs 18 GJ per ton of slab while the recycling route needs about 2.5 GJ per ton of steel. The share of the recycling route has risen from 25 % in the eighties to 41 % today. The recycling route will be further increased as steel is fully recyclable. Further savings lie in the continuous improvement in heat recovery and waste steam utilisation, and through the use of ICT.

The *chemical industry* sees in the improvement of reaction and process design a direct relevance for more energy efficient chemical production. Recent accelerating developments in high performance computing, process systems engineering, chemical sensing technology and distributed process control will ensure that 'in silico' techniques have a revolutionary impact on the way chemical industries will operate in the next twenty years. Model-based catalysis can theoretically lead to improvements up to 50 % if fundamental process improvements can be achieved. Model-based synthesis concepts (excluding catalysis) can lead to improvements of 20 %.

3.5 The Factories of the Future Initiative

The Economic Recovery Plan proposed by the European Commission on 26 November 2008 [24] includes measures for research and innovation, in particular through public-private partnerships 'Factories of the Future', 'Energy-Efficient Buildings' and 'Green Cars'. There is a clear shift towards 'green' technologies associated with this Plan. The Factories of the Future initiative in particular, aims at improving manufacturing enterprises' technological capability of adapting to environmental pressures and of adequately responding to increasing global consumer demand for greener, more customised and higher quality products. It is expected that these accelerated research and innovation efforts will lead to a paradigm shift towards a demand-driven industry with lower waste generation and less energy consumption. In the Recovery Plan, ICT is seen as an enabling technology.

In July 2009, the first call for proposals was launched under this initiative with an available funding of € 95 million, addressing the topics (a) Smart Factories: ICT for agile and environmentally friendly manufacturing; (b) Plug-and-produce components for adaptive control; (c) Supply-chain approaches for small series industrial production; (d) Intelligent, scalable, manufacturing platforms and equipment for components with micro- and nano-scale functional features. The Work Programme related to these activities was inspired by the expert recommendations given in the report regarding ICT for energy efficiency in manufacturing [18]. The response to this first call was high. Twenty-five out of a total of ninety-seven R&D proposals were selected for support. The success rate was about one in four. Industrial participation was at nearly 50 %, with 31 % being small and medium-size enterprises.

4 Conclusions

The paper highlighted the importance of ICT as an enabler of sustainable manufacturing. However, ICT and automation may not be sufficient to bring about the required paradigm shift away from 'maximum gain out of minimum capital' towards 'maximum added value with minimal resources'. A holistic perspective of manufacturing is needed with specific measures targeting resource use efficiency of factories, but also of related supply chains and of distribution and use patterns.

Like many high-tech branches, the ICT sector, and in particular the semiconductor industry, consists of a complex arrangement of various processes and technologies requiring meticulous optimisation and control to achieve sustainable and competitive manufacturing yields. The sector appears ever more conscious of its own environmental footprint and has already established sophisticated methodologies and processes in a self-regulatory manner at international level. The strategic importance of the sector for the whole economy makes energy efficiency considerations both, at product (development) and at manufacturing level, ever more important.

Acknowledgements. The views expressed in this paper are those of the author and do not necessarily reflect the official view of the European Commission on the subject.

References

1. COM (2008) 241 final of (May 13, 2008)
2. On the Treaty of Lisbon,
   http://europa.eu/lisbon_treaty/full_text/index_en.htm
3. Environment legislation,
   http://europa.eu/legislation_summaries/environment/
   general_provisions/,http://europa.eu/legislation_summaries/
   environment/index_en.htm
4. Directive 2008/1/EC, http://ec.europa.eu/environment/air/
   pollutants/stationary/ippc/summary.htm
5. E.g. the Directive 2002/96/EC on Waste Electrical and Electronic Equipment (WEEE); the Directive 2002/95/EC on the Restriction of the Use of Certain Hazardous Substances in Electrical and Electronic Equipment (RoHS); and the Regulation EC 1907/2006 on Chemicals and their Safe Use dealing with the Registration, Evaluation, Authorisation and Restriction of Chemical substances (REACH). This law entered into force on (June 1, 2007)
6. LIFE+ is the successor programme to LIFE - (Legal scheme of the) Financial Instrument for the Environment. The programme has a funding envelope of € 2.14 billion for 2007-13 co-financing environmental schemes in the European Union and in certain other countries. Details under, http://europa.eu/legislation_summaries/
   environment/general_provisions/l28021_en.htm
7. Decision No. 1982/2006/EC of the European Parliament and of the Council of 18 December 2006 concerning the Seventh Framework Programme of the European Community for research, technological development and demonstration activities (2007-2013), Official Journal of the European Union, L 41 2/1 (December 30, 2006),
   http://cordis.europa.eu/fp7/home_en.html
8. For information on European Investment Bank programmes, http://www.eib.org/; for an overview of the Structural Funds,
   http://ec.europa.eu/regional_policy/funds/prord/sf_en.htm
9. EMAS is a management tool for organisations to evaluate, report and improve their environmental performance, http://ec.europa.eu/environment/emas/

10. Integrated Product Policy Green Paper,
    http://europa.eu/legislation_summaries/consumers/
    consumer_safety/l28011_en.htm
11. Action Plan on Energy Efficiency, http://ec.europa.eu/energy/
    action_plan_energy_efficiency/doc/com_2006_0545_en.pdf
12. Energy Using Products Directive 2005/32/EC, http://ec.europa.eu/
    enterprise/policies/sustainable-business/documents/
    eco-design/index_en.htm
13. High-Tech: Low Carbon. The Role of the European Digital Technology Industry in Tack-
    ling Climate Change (2008), http://www.digitaleurope.org/
    index.php?id=242&id_article=223
14. The Energy Star programme was originally launched by the US Environmental Protection
    Agency, http://www.energystar.gov/; An initial agreement was signed in De-
    cember 2000 between the US government and the European Union and intended to coordi-
    nate energy-efficient labelling programmes for office equipment in two major global mar-
    kets for office products. The programme aims at fostering energy efficiency without creat-
    ing barriers to trade. The new EU-US Energy Star Agreement for office equipment which
    came into force in December 2006 is valid for five years. The criteria cover energy con-
    sumption in standby and use phase, and are being further developed and adapted to future
    technology and market evolution. Energy Star is part of the European strategy to better
    manage energy demand, contribute to security of energy supply and mitigate climate
    change, http://www.eu-energystar.org/.
15. Universal phone charger standard,
    http://www.itu.int/newsroom/press_releases/2009/49.html
16. Gartner, Green IT: The New Industry Shockwave, presentation at Symposium/ITXPO
    Conference (April 2007), Relevant Climate Group study "SMART 2020" under,
    http://www.smart2020.org/publications/
17. Meeting held in Brussels on (July 3, 2008), For contributions,
    http://cordis.europa.eu/fp7/ict/programme/
    events3-20080703_en.html
18. ICT and Energy Efficiency. The Case for Manufacturing, Recommendations of the Con-
    sultation Group chaired by Professor Reimund Neugebauer, European Commission, Lux-
    embourg (2009), ISBN 978-92-79-11306-2,
    ftp://ftp.cordis.europa.eu/pub/fp7/ict/docs/
    micro-nanosystems/smart-manufacturing_en.pdf
19. Zobel, R., Filos, E.: The Impact of ICT on Energy Efficiency. In: Cunningham, P., Cun-
    ningham, M. (eds.) eChallenges 2006 Conference, Barcelona, October 25-27. Exploiting
    the Knowledge Economy: Issues, Applications and Case Studies, pp. 139–146. IOS Press,
    Amsterdam (2006)
20. European Technology Platform for Electricity Networks of the Future (SmartGrids). De-
    tails, http://www.smartgrids.eu
21. European Nanoelectronics Initiative Advisory Council (ENIAC),
    http://www.eniac.eu
22. For details, http://www.powerstandards.com/SEMIS23.htm
23. Energy Agreements Programme of Sustainable Energy Ireland, http://www.sei.ie
24. A European Economic Recovery Plan, COM (2008) 800 final of (November 26, 2008),
    http://ec.europa.eu/commission_barroso/president/pdf/Comm_20
    081126.pdf; The Factories of the Future initiative, as a research and innovation public-
    private partnership, has a total budget envelope of € 1.2 billion, from 2010 to 2013, with
    half of the funds from industry

Research Issues on Customer-Oriented
and Eco-friendly Networks
for Healthy Fashionable Goods

Rosanna Fornasiero[1], Andrea Chiodi[2], Emanuele Carpanzano[1], and Luis Carneiro[3]

[1] ITIA-CNR, Via Bassini, 15
20133 Milano-Italy
{rosanna.fornasiero,emanuele.carpanzano}@itia.cnr.it
[2] Synesis Consortium
Milano-Italy
andrea.chiodi@synesis-consortium.eu
[3] Inesc Porto-FEUP campus, Rua Dr. Roberto Frias, 378
4200 - 465 Porto-Portugal
luis.carneiro@inescporto.pt

Abstract. Needs and expectations of specific target groups - such as elderly, obese, disabled, or diabetic persons- are arising as challenging opportunities for European companies which are asked to supply small series of functional and fashionable goods of high quality, affordable price and eco-compatible. In order to design, develop, produce and distribute such products, a new framework and related components of collaborative networking need to be developed, enabling the product to stay as long as digital to produce on-demand. Research is necessary in many topics like: a) consumer integrated collaborative eco-oriented design, b) radical renewal by the adoption of Rapid Manufacturing technologies; and c) the overall integration and co-ordination of business processes and information exchange by a set of new (web)services for network design and ad-hoc (re-)configuration, for real-time planning, forecasting and replenishment, d) tracking and tracing of ecology and quality.

Keywords: supply chain, consumer goods, sustainability.

1 Introduction

In recent years, it is emerging at industrial level that full adoption of methodologies and technologies for collaborative production of small series are of decisive importance for European Manufacturing Industry, SMEs in particular, to proactively respond to the high variability of consumers demand and expectations. This will help reducing the risks of following fast changing trends without appropriate tools, causing serious limits in terms of both customer satisfaction and enterprise competitiveness and sustainability.

This is especially true in consumer goods sectors, where customer's tastes change very quickly, especially in the current economic situation of downturn, where the

Á. Ortiz Bas, R.D. Franco, P. Gómez Gasquet (Eds.): BASYS 2010, IFIP AICT 322, pp. 36–44, 2010.

purchase capability of customers has sharply decreased and companies need to strongly focus on high value products.

In this work, consumer goods and in particular shoes are considered. In the last years, in footwear industry, on one hand, the number of seasonal collections has been increasing, enlarging the offer in terms of models along the year, and on the other hand the number of products per model has been decreasing in major markets, leaving best opportunities only for companies producing value added and wide range of products.

Moreover, social phenomena like ageing, increase of obese and disabled people [1] and major sensitivity versus eco-friendly products are also key challenges to be faced by the considered consumer sectors, with reference to healthcare and sustainability [2]. As a matter of fact, today consumers demand for personalization and value adding of harmonized footwear products, as well as in the textile and clothing industry, is not only in terms of aesthetics, but also in terms of health, innovative functionalities and environmental sustainability. Consumers want to know where the product comes from, how it has been created and how it will satisfy his needs and provide health and well being.

There is a clear need for health fashionable consumer goods, since customers today want to be fully satisfied both in their look and their health, but also demand for personalized solutions for their individual needs. The compromise that fashion products may not be healthy and that healthy products may not be fashionable is not going to be accepted anymore by a changing society with increasing needs and expectations and there is a niche market especially for categories like the one mentioned before (seniors, disables, obese people) where European companies can find their way to better satisfy the customer.

This implies small series production with fast delivery which cannot face long waiting time for materials, components and manufacturing services, and a new way to structure the supply network is needed [3]. Production lines and equipments need to be changed to meet such challenging requirements [4].

Open research issues need to address the design, production as well as supply and distribution of small series of health fashionable goods for specific target groups of wide impact in terms of market for the European industry as elderly, disables, diabetics and obese people through personalized and comfortable shoes (e.g. anallergic and bio materials, reduced stitching, flexible and light components) with dedicated medial insoles for foot measurement. Solutions should be based on cost, social compliance and eco-efficient design and production of customised products that fully satisfy the customers considering their health as well as their desire for fashionable products.

2   State of the Art

There are different categories of research topics to be investigated to offer a complete solution to support companies in answering and/or anticipating customer needs. Dimensions to be considered cover many different aspects of production management from organizational changes, to ICT for design and production collaboration, to new production systems and to Supply Chain management.

2.1 Frameworks for Sustainable Networks

From the organizational point of view, companies are facing a new level of complexity, given by the fact that competition as well as collaboration schemes are transitioning from among companies to among supply networks.

In literature, different forms and specifications of business networks are discussed. They are distinguished for example by value chain orientation (horizontal, vertical, lateral), life span duration (long-term vs. short-term), degree of virtualization or hierarchical structure (hierarchical vs. non-hierarchical networks) [5]. While most real-life business networks are formed along the value chain and for long-time purpose, the current market asks for flexible organizational structures which can quickly adapt to new prerequisites and challenges.

The new paradigm of Demand-driven supply networks is emerging in literature as a collaborative scheme in response to consumers direct signals and needs [6] and [7]. This implies different approaches to the market based not only on traditional sales channels (shops, retailers) but more and more on an Internet mediated direct contact with consumers both for product conception and for product sales.

For production aspects, as partners are locally dispersed, and processes are knowledge-intensive, the paradigm of Smart Organizations [8], which is based on concepts like the Extended Enterprise, (Dynamic) Virtual Organization and Virtual Breeding Environment, need to be transferred to hybrid and disomogeneuos networks where footwear companies integrate their production with other companies to offer to the customer solutions embedded with high tech devices [5]. Collaboration will not only be regarded in the perspective of organizational networking, but also in terms of networking ICT support to achieve strategic goals like resource optimization, synergy creation, the achievement of a critical mass and increased benefit for all partners [9], [5].

2.2 Knowledge Management in Networks

Recent literature on knowledge sharing in networks is based on:

- hybrid centralized-decentralized models for data and services to allow private confidential data (like Design data) to be kept by the owner and less private, commercial and collaboration data, to be stored in third party data-service centers, thanks to the new IoS technologies of ICT resources virtualization (i.e. Cloud Computing);
- value added services provided by reliable service centers set up and maintained by IT professionals, while Utility Services (like interoperability and collaboration services) offered by distributed service centers based on the existing infrastructure (like COIN[1] proposes);
- real time data capture from the field provided by Open Source platforms (like ASPIRE) also to allow the acquisition of eco-compatible data series.

---

[1] Collaboration and interoperability for networked enterprises, FP7-ICT-2007.1.3-216256, http://www.coin-ip.eu

2.3 Co-design and Sustainability

Today product co-design tools commercially available do not either encapsulate customer orientation as a common feature or foresee real interoperability for an effective distribution of the design phase along the chain. Considering solutions developed within past and ongoing projects, only some steps within customization domain are covered (see for example EUROShoE project[2] and CEC-made-shoe project[3] results for CAD).

Another aspect to be considered during design phase is the evaluation of environmental impact of products and processes for each shoe model to be developed and for each collection. Shoes are complex products in terms of their environmental impacts: combination of constituting materials and short use time lifecycle result as critical factors able to increase dramatically the environmental burden. Every year nearly 12 million of shoes are sent in landfill with minimal possibilities of recovery contributing to increase the whole amount of not recyclable waste.

At present, a number of environmental standards provide partial information on process related to product (ISO labels, Ecolabel and Environmental Product Declaration) with a common weak point, such as lack of adequate quantitative information in order to compare different products identified as environmental friendly, or possible hidden steps in product conditions.

Designers suffer from a scarcity in tools and methodologies in order to evaluate easily the impact related to design choices in advance. Current tools are frequently too expensive and not suitable for the use within firms especially within SMEs. The main barrier is the high level of customization and changeability of such products. For each firm, the whole portfolio may include several hundred of models each requiring specific materials and modifications. The introduction of new advanced materials in place of traditional materials introduces a further complexity in impact assessment.

2.4 Methods and Tools for Co-planning Production and Distribution

Small series and personalized products require totally different supply network structures, having to be configured for each customer order and including small number of companies chosen in a large number of accredited potential partners. In practice scenarios will be characterized by a very large number of small orders, each of them having different partner companies, based on their availability and capabilities. In this context, new co-planning systems will be required to optimize the production plans that result, on a first iteration, from the configuration (or set up) of the supply network for each order. Distribution emerges to be different from the one for traditional products and has to be faster and more flexible, assuring that each product is mainly directed to the sales point where best fits the local customer preferences.

---

[2] EUROSHOE project, EU VFP.
[3] CEC-made-shoe project, EU VIFP mass-customization.blogs.com/.../the-cec-co-design-contest-open-innovation-in-the-footwear-industry.html

The complex planning problems arising in the context of collaborative networks is based on the broad class of "Combinatorial Optimization" and for tackling hard problems, it is possible to use state-of-the art metaheuristics. These are reasonably simple and flexible optimization algorithms based on local search procedures, and in general quite easily adaptable to cope with new problem configurations.

The "classical metaheuristics" (Simulated Annealing, tabu search and Genetic Algorithms) have evolved to more refined methods, and also have given rise to new methodologies like Variable Neighbourhood Search (VNS), Greedy Randomized Adaptive Search Procedure (GRASP), Ant Colonies Optimization, etc. [10], [11].

A recent, extension of these approaches is on the design of multi-objective metaheuristics, thus incorporating some critical requirements of practical problems. These approaches are presenting very promising results in several areas and expected to be key in the successful resolution of optimization [12], [13], [14].

3   The Proposed Approach

Future research for healthy fashionable products need to be based on the following pillars:

P1. Reference Framework for Collaborative Supply Networks
The reference framework model for collaborative supply networks shall address, orientate and integrate all aspects both at organizational and technological level concerning interaction of organizations, business processes, considering co-ordination and synchronisation of contents, as well as information exchange and software application modularity for improvements in data management, in order to create a seamless flow of information from market to design and development, to production and distribution.

From the organizational point of view the following topics will be considered to implement an innovative model for footwear collaborative supply networks:

- Hierarchical vs. not-hierarchical supply chains
- Business ecosystems vs. smart organizations
- Agile and proactive Virtual Organisations creation, management and governance
- Social networking, Consumer Communities and Living Labs as vehicles for customer/consumer integration in the context of OpenInnovation.

From the technological point of view, the reference data model shall be based on service interoperability defined as a backbone for the development of the related applications in the following pillars. Particular attention will be given to the integration of the new services in already existing solutions in order to avoid replication and overlapping with existing systems.

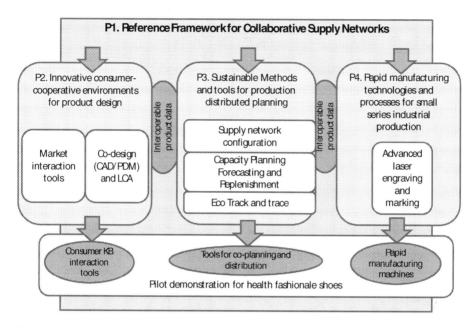

Pilot demonstration for health fashionale shoes

P2. Innovative consumer-driven environments for product design

This pillar will address the implementation of innovative environments for consumers and suppliers collaboration and knowledge management. The goal is to create a novel concept that enables the vision of an "empowered-to-design" consumer from one side, and the creation of market and design knowledge within a social network environment [15].

This pillar aims thus to achieve cutting edge innovation along the following lines:

- Collaborative design tools, empowering the consumers to design their own products by providing them the ability to collaborate in an informed design process not only regarding aesthetics, prices and delivery times, but also regarding resources consumption and social responsibility, implementing sustainability parameters in the design phase and relying on the synchronization of the design along the supply chain;
- A new model of market information sourced from the unstructured information from consumers, designers and suppliers interaction, within a social network/virtual community environment and relying upon the use of semantic technologies for knowledge extraction and pattern matching [16], [17].

Multifunctional design need to be supported by an event driven tool for the coordination of design and industrialization phases with production process. Intelligent tools for product and components design is necessary to plan the ecological, economical and social sustainability of each model based on innovative approach to LCA-Life Cycle Analysis. All of these should be developed as plug-ins and additional services for existing enterprise applications (CAD-PDM solutions).

This pillar need to study how to manage market and product data to define not only "customer-" but also "market virtual profile" and how to use this data during design process. Information on consumers to capture requirements on style preferences, physical measure, health needs and feedback on product previous versions, through implementation of consumer communities, web spaces for customers feedback, "point of opinion" at retailers stores, configurators capable of managing personalized data.

P3. Methods and tools for supply network configuration and distributed production planning

In this pillar, innovative and adaptive services for production process modeling and supply networks formation and management shall be based on a distributed interaction system to integrate different actors (components suppliers, outsourcers, service providers, retailers, customers) of different sectors collaborating in dynamic networks. Moreover product and process quality control based on environmental impact parameters shall be developed through a shared platform for eco-monitoring.

Main contribution in this pillar shall be based on developing innovative services for supply network management based on existing technologies like SOA, EDA, Product Tracking & Tracing, web2.0, semantic web[4] and existing commercial applications.

In particular it will be important to develop the following three services:

- Easy-to-use Supply & Distribution Network Design (SDND) Service for configuring supply networks, based on full sustainability parameters. Life Cycle Costing tool for supply networks can be used to evaluate the sustainability impact of each of the possible network configurations according to a peer-to-peer distributed data set published autonomously by each potential supplier. Particular attention need to be paid to cross-domain collaborative processes support and fast changing networks. Companies need to share a reference and extensible competences model, which captures comprehensive relevant information and knowledge to maximize end-to-end visibility related to suppliers, distributors, third party logistics providers, based on Availability-to- promise and Capacity-to-promise data.
- User-friendly Collaborative Planning Forecasting and Replenishment (CPFR) Service, based on ad-hoc combinations of optimization algorithms shall be studied and implemented to guarantee on-time delivery based on optimization of the trade-off between minimization of cost and lead time, quality and customer service. The systems shall be based on real-time product tracking and tracing data, captured from distribution centers, from third party logistics providers and data from producers. Supply and Distribution processes will be managed in a decentralized way allowing the partners of the value network to choose the best option for on-time delivery. New models shall be studied to merge delivery from different producers.
- A web- and wireless- enabled Eco- and Quality- Monitoring service on product/process quality and eco-sustainability along the value chain, to collect information for producers and customers on who, how, where, when, the product was produced and delivered indicating a level of sustainability and product quality.

Such services will be made available for integration into state-of-the-art existing SCM systems, either as plug-ins or as external services to be called on-demand.

---

[4] Under development in ICT projects like COIN (IP www.coin-ip.eu) and iSURF (STREP http://www.srdc.com.tr/isurf/)

P4. Rapid manufacturing technologies for small series industrial production
Rapid manufacturing technologies shall enable the flexible, energy and eco-efficient production of specific added value components/parts of consumer personalized goods [18]. In particular reduction of set-up time is crucial in the production of small series in order to avoid loss of time when changing models. Cutting-edge technologies for developing a multi-process machine based on laser decoration and engraving for production of small series specifically developed as a unique integrated unit coping with high speed laser cutting, laser engraving, laser marking for personalized shoes.

These four pillars should be integrated in a unique solution and demonstrators need to be implemented to test and validate pilot collaborative supply network offering integrated small series of personalized shoes to target groups. Pilot demonstrators shall be composed of manufacturing companies collaborating with technologies providers along product lifecycle where coordination has to be managed at supply chain level.

4 Conclusions

The proposed approach to support footwear companies in the implementation of new models for small series production for health and fashionable goods follows the Competitive Sustainable Manufacturing (CSM) paradigm [19] and current initiatives of European Technological Platforms like Manufuture [20] and Footwear [21] asking to join forces for strengthening the European manufacturing sectors for the benefit of the European industry and of the final customer.

This means that sustainability is interpreted in the European STEEP (Social Technological Economical Environmental Political) sense to include in strategy definition: globalisation of the economy, climate change, ageing population, public health for all, poverty and social exclusion, loss of biodiversity, increasing waste volumes, soil lost and transport congestion [19].

In this context, the specific objective of new research shall be to increase significantly the sustainability of value creation of small series health fashionable consumer goods and in particular of footwear products, for emerging social by systemic/coordinated intra- and inter-sector networking of producers/service providers using cutting-edge (digital and) production technologies and as well as innovative organizational models based on cross-supply network integration through major complementary breakthrough innovations.

References

1. DG Employment: Europe's demographic future: Facts and figures on challenges and opportunities, European Commission, DG for Employment, Social Affairs and Equal Opportunities (2007), http://ec.europa.eu/employment_social/spsi/docs/social_situation/demo_report_2007_en.pdf
2. EU Commission White Paper on Health Together for Health:A Strategic Approach for the EU 2008-2013 (2007), http://ec.europa.eu/health/ph_overview/strategy/health_strategy_en.htm

3. Fornasiero, R., Tescaro, M., Scarso, E., Gottardi, G.: How to Increase Value in the Footwear Supply Chain. In: Camarinha-Matos, L.M., Paraskakis, I., Afsarmanesh, H. (eds.) Leveraging Knowledge for Innovation in Collaborative Networks, Proceedings of the 10th IFIP WG 5.5 Working Conference on Virtual Enterprises, PRO-VE 2009, IFIP Advances in Information and Communication Technology, Greece, October 7-9, vol. 307, pp. 527–536 (2009)

4. Carpanzano, E., Ballarino, A.: Collaborative networked enterprises: a pilot case in the footwear value chain. In: Azevedo, A. (ed.) Innovation in Manufacturing Networks. IFIP. Springer Series in Computer Science, pp. 57–66 (2008)

5. Camarinha-Matos, L.M., Picard, W.: Pervasive Collaborative Networks. In: IFIP TC 5 WG 5.5 Ninth Working Conference on Virtual Enterprises, IFIP Advances in Information and Communication Technology, vol. 283 (2008), ISBN: 978-0-387-84836-5

6. Childerhouse, P., Aitken, J., Towill, D.R.: Analysis and design of focused demand chains. Journal of Operations Management 20(6), 675–689 (2002)

7. De Treville, S., Shapiro, R.D., Hameri, A.-P.: From supply chain to demand chain: the role of lead time reduction in improving demand chain performance. Journal of Operations Management 21(6), 613–627 (2004)

8. Filos, E.: Smart Organizations in the Digital Age. In: Integration of Information and Communication Technologies in Smart Organizations, pp. 1–38. Hershey Idea Group Publishing (2006)

9. Camarinha-Matos, L.: Virtual Enterprises and Collaborative Networks, Boston (2004)

10. Resende, M.G.C., Sousa, J.P.: Metaheuristics: Computer Decision-Making. Kluwer, Dordrecht (2004), ISBN 1-4020-7653-3

11. Glover, F., Laguna, M.: Tabu search. Kluwer Academic Publishers, Boston (1997)

12. Azevedo, A.L., Toscano, C.A.M., Sousa, J.M.P., Soares, A.L.: An Advanced Agent-Based Order Planning System for Dynamic Networked Enterprises. Production Planning & Control, special issue on Management of Operations 15(2), 133–144 (2004)

13. Blum, C., Roli, A.: Hybrid Metaheuristics: An Introduction. Studies in Computational Intelligence, vol. 114. Springer, Heidelberg (2008), ISSN 1860-9503

14. Siarry, P., Michalewicz, Z. (eds.): Advances in Metaheuristics for Hard Optimization. Natural Computing Series. Springer, Heidelberg (2008), ISBN 978-3-540-72959-4

15. Hendrickson, M.: TechCrunch. Nine Ways to Build Your Own Social Network (July 2007), http://www.techcrunch.com/2007/07/24/9-ways-to-build-your-own-social-network/

16. Lea, B., Yu, W., Maguluru, N., Nichols, M.: Enhancing business networks using social network based virtual communities. Industrial Management & Data Systems 106(1), 121–138 (2006)

17. Boulton, C.: eWeek.com. Consolidation Time for White-label Social Networks (2008), http://www.eweek.com/c/a/Messaging-and-Collaboration/Consolidation-Time-for-Whitelabel-Social-Networks/

18. Carpanzano, E., Ballarino, A., Jovane, F.: Towards the New Mass Customisation and Personalisation Paradigm: Needed Next Generation Manufacturing Technologies. In: Proc. 40th Cirp International Seminar on Manufacturing Systems, Liverpool, May 30-June 1 (2007)

19. FoF-PPP: Factories of the Future: Public, Private Partnership, Strategic Multi-annual Roadmap (2009)

20. Manufuture, Strategic Research Agenda (2006)

21. ETP-Footwear: Vision and Strategic Research Agenda of the European Footwear Products and Processes Technology Platform (2006)

Part II
Industry Ecosystems and Emergent Business Models

A Multi-criteria Approach to Select Suppliers Based on Performance

María José Verdecho, Juan José Alfaro-Saiz, and Raúl Rodríguez-Rodríguez

Department of Business Organization, CIGIP (Research Centre on Production
Management and Engineering), Universidad Politécnica de Valencia, Camino de Vera, s/n,
46022, Valencia, Spain
{mverdecho,jalfaro,raurodro}@cigip.upv.es

Abstract. Selecting suppliers is a multi-criteria decision-making problem involving both qualitative and quantitative factors. The aim of this paper is to propose a multi-criteria approach that aids to select suppliers based on two interrelated inputs: overall system performance and supplier performance. With this model, enterprises that are collaborating will have a tool to select suppliers not only based on supplier performance but also aligned with their own strategy increasing the quality of the supplier selection process and, therefore, improving the sustainability of the partnership and their competitiveness.

Keywords: performance measurement, collaboration, supplier selection.

1 Introduction

One of the strategies most used to increase/maintain enterprise competitiveness is to establish collaboration relationships with suppliers. Congruent with the need to integrate multiple linked processes in the supply chain, theoretical research advocate that early and extensive supplier involvement results in many benefits, e.g. faster development process, reduced costs, etc. [1]. In this context, selecting suppliers becomes a crucial process for manufacturers.

Various studies about customer-supplier relationships point out the importance of considering the performance measurement of the entire supply chain in order to provide products and services that meet the expectations of end customers and promote improvement and innovation of the whole processes. In [2], Mentzer defines supply chain collaboration (SCC) as *'a means by which all companies in the supply chain are actively working together towards common objectives, and is characterized by sharing information, knowledge, risk and profits'*. For that reason, it is important to define common performance indicators for all the enterprises that are collaborating as they will aid to focus their efforts towards strategic aspects of their business and, therefore, they will support their competitiveness. In fact, it is acknowledged that the way enterprises measure performance shows the organizational culture and the formulation and deployment of their strategy [3]. Thus, it is important for those enterprises to define and use a structured performance measurement framework that allows managing performance under various perspectives or dimensions that provide a relevant

Á. Ortiz Bas, R.D. Franco, P. Gómez Gasquet (Eds.): BASYS 2010, IFIP AICT 322, pp. 47–55, 2010.

overview of their performance status. One of the most important performance frameworks developed in the academic literature and business applications is the Balanced ScoreCard (BSC) by Kaplan and Norton [4]. In fact, possibly due to this acceptance, the BSC developed initially for managing performance of enterprises has been extended by different authors for interorganizational performance management such as the works by Brewer and Speh [5], Bititci et al. [6], Folan and Browne [7] and Alfaro et al. [8].

In addition, the muti-criteria nature of the process of supplier selection has been widely studied in the literature focusing attention on two main issues: the identification of criteria for the assessment and the application of multi-criteria techniques to pass from the initial criteria to an overall ranking of suppliers [9]. Besides, supplier selection involves considering both qualitative and quantitative criteria [10]. Therefore, selecting suppliers can be defined as a multi-criteria decision-making (MCDM) problem involving both qualitative and quantitative factors.

In this context, it seems reasonable that enterprises that desire to select suppliers need to make their decision based on two main inputs: performance of the enterprises that are collaborating and supplier performance. On the one hand, the enterprises that are collaborating pursue the improvement of the overall system. For that purpose, they should define performance elements (such as performance objectives, performance indicators, etc.) for the whole interorganizational context and select the new supplier that better match those performance elements. In addition, these performance elements are better managed under a structured framework such as the BSC. On the other hand, enterprises need to identify relevant criteria for supplier assessment based on supplier performance as not all the suppliers excel at the same characteristics.

The purpose of this paper is to propose a multi-criteria decision-making approach that aids to select suppliers according to both inputs: overall system performance and supplier performance. With this model, enterprises will have a tool to select suppliers not only based on supplier performance but also aligned with their own strategy increasing the quality of the supplier selection process, its long-term partnership and improving the competitiveness of the whole enterprise association.

The structure of this paper is as follows. First, a literature review of multi-criteria decision analysis methods applied for supplier selection is presented focusing attention on the Analytic Hierarchy Process (AHP) method. Then, the multi-criteria approach to select suppliers is described. Finally, conclusions are exposed.

2   Literature Review

Several methods have been proposed for solving the supplier selection problem such as vendor profile analysis (VPA), multi-objective programming (MOP), data envelopment analysis (DEA) and analytic hierarchy process (AHP) [10]. Evaluation and ranking of potential suppliers involves both tangible and intangible criteria. This is because overall assessment of suppliers should not only consider quantitative performance data but also some other criteria that are critical for successful partnerships and are not directly quantifiable, e.g. trust and commitment [11]. Therefore, the AHP method developed by Saaty [12] is a useful method to select suppliers as it deals with both types of criteria. In addition, AHP aims at integrating different measures into a single overall score for ranking decision alternatives [13].

The AHP method has been previously used for supplier selection under a wide variety of applications [14]. In [15], it is presented an integrated AHP and linear programming method for choosing the best suppliers and placing the optimum order quantities among them. In [9], it is proposed four different vendor selection systems (VSSs) depending on the time frame (short-term versus long-term) and the content (logistic versus strategic) of the co-operative customer/supplier relationships using an AHP framework. In [16], it is proposed an AHP model for casting supplier assessment based on four groups of criteria: product development capability, manufacturing capability, quality capability, and cost and delivery. In [17], it is applied AHP in the field of project management to select the best contractor to perform the project based on six criteria: experience, financial stability, quality performance, manpower resources, equipment resources, and current workload. In [18], a multi-criteria group decision making model for supplier ranking based on AHP is developed by combining group member's preferences into one consensus ranking. The criteria used to rate suppliers are quality, delivery, price, technical capability, financial position, past performance attitude, facilities, flexibility and service. In [19], an AHP model to structure SCOR (Supply Chain Operations Reference) model metrics to evaluate overall supplier efficiency is proposed. In [20], it is developed a selection model for supplier selection process using AHP. In [21], a multi-criteria supplier selection procedure using AHP is presented. The first level criteria used to compare suppliers involve: supplier, product and service criteria. In [22], it is developed an AHP approach for virtual enterprise partner selection using the SCOR model and the AHP method. In [10], it is presented an AHP approach to select global suppliers according to five criteria: cost, quality, service performance, supplier profile and risk factor.

Regarding the combination of AHP and BSC, in [23], it is developed a model to implement a BSC framework. In [24], it is proposed a model to align the BSC and a firm's strategy using the AHP. In [25], a model for long-term vendor selection based on vendor performance is presented. In [26], a model for selecting performance indicators for supply chain management is presented. In [27], an approach for evaluating performance of IT department in the manufacturing industry in Taiwan is exposed. In [28], it is proposed a decision support system for selecting ERP systems in textile industry by using the BSC.

However, there is not a specific model developed for selecting suppliers that integrates performance information of suppliers as well as the overall system performance. For this reason, the purpose of the remaining of this paper is to present a multi-criteria BSC-AHP model for supplier selection that fills this research gap. With this approach, enterprises that are collaborating and have defined a BSC framework (or desire to do it) will have a tool to select suppliers based not only on specific performance data of suppliers but also aligned to their common strategy and, therefore, have a tool to improve their competitiveness. In addition, supplier performance and overall performance are interrelated as there is probably a supplier that can contribute more than the other suppliers to enhance overall efficiency. With this approach, both inputs are connected to provide an overall rating of suppliers for decision-makers.

3 The Proposed Multi-criteria Approach for Supplier Selection

3.1 Description of the Model

The AHP method structures the decision problem in a hierarchy of levels. These levels are linked by unidirectional dependence relationships. In the upper level of the hierarchy, it is defined the ultimate goal of the decision problem. Then, the criteria that contribute to achieve the goal stand in the second level. In the next levels, intermediate subcriteria and attributes that compose the hierarchical structure are located. Finally, in the last level, the decision alternatives are established. Using levels allows decision makers to focus on a small set of decisions [12]. By making pairwise comparisons and using the fundamental scale of Saaty [12], the AHP method provide relative weights to each element within a level depending on its contribution to an element linked to it that is located on the immediate upper level.

In order to apply AHP, we have defined four phases. In the first phase, the criteria and attributes to improve overall efficiency are defined and the AHP model is composed. Once the AHP model is obtained, the second phase consists of making pairwise comparisons within each level and obtaining the relative priorities. The third phase aims at calculating the overall priorities of the decision alternatives. Finally, the fourth phase deals with sensitivity analysis of the solution provided. It has to be noted that this paper deals with the description of the phase 1.

The multi-criteria model developed for selecting suppliers is founded on two main interrelated inputs: overall performance and supplier performance. Figure 1 shows the hierarchical structure of the BSC-AHP model. The main goal is to select a supplier to improve overall interorganisational efficiency so that this goal stands on the top of the hierarchical structure. In order to manage this goal, different performance indicators are defined. The performance indicators that are to be monitored by the partners are the main criteria of the model as the achievement of the objectives related to these performance indicators will benefit the overall performance. Thus, at this phase, it is suggested to define performance objectives and indicators according to the four performance perspectives of the BSC [4]: financial perspective, customer perspective, internal business process perspective and innovation & learning perspective. In order to support these performance indicators, supplier performance information has to be evaluated under different supplier dimensions. Therefore, there is a direct link between the performance of the supplier and the performance of the overall system. That is the reason why supplier dimensions stand on a layer below overall performance indicators as the performance of the supplier has to contribute to the consecution of the performance of the overall system. In order to define the supplier performance data, the model uses the conceptual framework by Croom [29] for supplier involvement which considers both operational and relational competencies and comprises three dimensions: product, structure and interaction dimensions. Finally, the last level is composed of the potential suppliers (1, 2, ... n). Suppliers will be pairwise evaluated to know which one best performs on the performance dimensions previously defined. Thus, the BSC-AHP model is composed by these four main components: overall goal, performance perspectives, supplier attributes and potential suppliers.

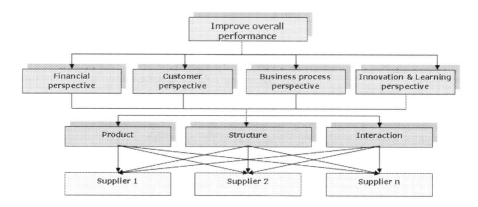

Fig. 1. BSC-AHP model: main components

Figure 2 shows an example of a detailed BSC-AHP model for partner selection. As can be observed, the second level (performance perspectives) is further deployed to show their performance indicators within each performance perspective. Similarly, the supplier attributes within each dimension are also shown. Based on Croom's work, the attributes comprising the dimensions (product, structure and interaction) are described as follows.

The *product* criterion comprises the main attributes that are to be addressed when assessing the product dimension of the supplier. Some relevant attributes of the product dimension include [10, 16, 21]: quality, price, development time, flexibility, and research and development (R&D) initiatives. Quality is one of the most important product attributes. It relates to the historical rejection rate during a period of time of the products delivered by the supplier. Rejection is due to deviations from specifications in the design, manufacturing, or packaging of the product. It also considers deviations from the specified quantities or delivery dates in the customer order. The second attribute is the price of the product as it affects to the bottom-line. Development time refers to the competence of the supplier to design, develop and launch products within the agreed period of time according to the product specifications. Flexibility involves the response time of the supplier when product changes are needed. It also considers the response time to new orders or order modifications during the development and manufacturing stages. Finally, R&D initiatives measure the ability of the supplier to provide support during product development and manufacturing. It is an important attribute as most products, after launching, demand continuous improvement to remain competitive.

The second criterion is *structure*. Structure comprises the capabilities/procedures for developing products and processing materials/components as well as the systems to facilitate control, co-ordination and communication through organizational and interorganizational systems [29]. The first attribute within the structure criterion is dedicated cross-functional team which assesses the human compromised capabilities of the supplier into the relationship. The second attribute is project management methodology which measures the degree of knowledge and implementation of project management practices in the supplier organization as well as the compatibility with the project management practices of the rest of enterprises. The third attribute is quality methodologies. The fourth attribute is Information Technology and Information Systems (IT & IS). It assesses the extent of technology implementation and interoperability of supplier information systems in order to send/receive and use the information exchanged with the rest of enterprises. The role of the technology is an important attribute as effective collaboration it is highly influenced by seamless communication between supplier and manufacturer. The fifth attribute is process alignment. It evaluates the extent of business process interoperability defined as the *"ability of different processes to work together and exchange information, data, control information, etc."* [30]. The sixth attribute is complementary capabilities. It measures the degree of interdependence on assets as well as the capacity on development/manufacturing so that the collaborative relationship can develop and manufacture higher variety/amount of products to increase the market share. Finally, the financial profile attribute assesses the past and current financial condition of the supplier in order to support/invest in the long-term [10].

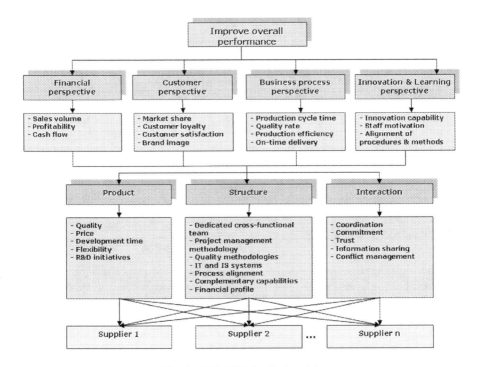

Fig. 2. BSC-AHP detailed model.

The third criterion is the *interaction* criterion which deals with the relational side of collaboration. Based on [11], the relational attributes considered in the AHP model are: coordination, commitment, trust, information sharing, and conflict management. Coordination involves the tasks that are to be taken for linking activities performed by the different members in a seamless manner. Commitment refers to the willingness of the supplier to perform effort on behalf of the relationship. It is the establishment of the foundation of the relationship and it is based on being supportive in solving problems together. A high level of commitment provides the context for the achievement of individual and mutual goals. Trust is based on the belief that the partner is reliable and will fulfil its responsibilities acting fairly. A partner trusts another partner if considers that decisions made by this last one will be in the interest of both parts. Information sharing considers the timeliness, accuracy, adequacy and completeness of the relevant information exchanged. Finally, conflict management measures the degree of intensity and conflict resolution mechanisms that exist between manufacturer and supplier.

4   Conclusions

This paper introduces a multi-criteria approach to select suppliers for collaborative relationships based on two types of performance information: supplier performance information and overall performance of the collaborating enterprises. Performance data of the suppliers is the common performance information considered in the literature for supplier selection problems. In addition, we have introduced the BSC of the whole collaborative enterprises as it is important that the supplier selected should contribute the most to the overall efficiency improvement. Therefore, in our approach, supplier performance information is linked to the common performance indicators defined by all the enterprises that are collaborating. With this approach, enterprises will have a tool to select suppliers aligned with their own strategy increasing the quality of the supplier selection process, its long-term partnership and improving the competitiveness of the whole enterprise association.

Acknowledgments. This work has been developed within the framework of a research project funded by the Polytechnic University of Valencia, titled "Design and Implementation of Performance Measurement Systems within Collaborative Contexts for aiding the Decision-making Process", reference PAID-06-08-3206.

References

1. Petersen, K.J., Handfield, R.B., Ragatz, G.L.: Supplier integration into new product development: coordinating product, process and supply chain design. Journal of Operations Management 23, 371–388 (2005)
2. Mentzer, J.: Managing Supply Chain Collaboration. Supply Chain Management. Sage Publications, Inc., Thousand Oaks (2001)
3. Pun, K.F., White, A.S.: A performance measurement paradigm for integrating strategy formulation: a review of systems and framewors. International Journal of Management Reviews 7(1), 49–71 (2005)
4. Kaplan, R.S., Norton, D.P.: The balanced scorecard – measures that drive performance. Harvard Business Review 70(1), 71–79 (1992)
5. Brewer, P.C., Speh, T.W.: Using the Balanced ScoreCard to measure supply chain performance. Journal of Business Logistics 21(1), 75–93 (2000)

6. Bititci, U.S., Mendibil, K., Martinez, V., Albores, P.: Measuring and managing performance in extended enterprises. International Journal of Operations & Production Management 25(4), 333–353 (2005)

7. Folan, P., Browne, J.: Development of an Extended Enterprise Performance Measurement System. Production Planning and Control 16(6), 531–544 (2005)

8. Alfaro, J.J., Ortiz, A., Rodríguez, R.: Performance measurement system for Enterprise Networks. International Journal of Productivity and Performance Management 56(4), 305–334 (2007)

9. Masella, C., Rangone, A.: A contigent approach to the design of vendor selection systems for different types of co-operative customer/ supplier relationships. International Journal of Operations & Production Management 20(1), 70–84 (2000)

10. Chan, F.T.S., Kumar, N.: Global supplier development considering risk factors using fuzzy extended AHP-based approach. Omega 35, 417–431 (2007)

11. Mohr, J., Spekman, R.: Characteristics of partnership success: Partnership attributes, communication. Strategic Management Journal 15(2), 135–152 (1994)

12. Saaty, T.L.: The Analytic Hierarchy Process. McGraw-Hill, New York (1980)

13. Rangone, A.: An analytical hierarchy process framework for comparing the overall performance of manufacturing departments. International Journal of Operations & Production Management 16(8), 104–119 (1996)

14. Perçin, S.: An application of the integrated AHP-PGP model in supplier selection. Measuring Business Excellence 10(4), 34–49 (2006)

15. Ghodsypour, S.H., O'Brien, C.: A decision support system for supplier selection using an integrated analytic hierarchy process and linear programming. International Journal of Production Economics, 56–57, 199–212 (1998)

16. Akarte, M.M., Surendra, N.V., Ravi, B., Rangaraj, N.: Web based casting supplier evaluation using analytical hierarchy process. Journal of the Operational Research Society 52, 511–522 (2001)

17. Al-Harbi, K.M.: Application of AHP in project management. International Journal of Project Management 19(4), 19–27 (2001)

18. Muralidharan, C., Anantharaman, S., Deshmukh, S.G.: A Multi-Criteria Group Decision making Model for Supplier Rating. The Journal of Supply Chain Management: A Global Review of Purchasing and Supply, 22–33 (November 2002)

19. Huan, S.H., Sheoran, S.K., Wang, G.: A review and analysis of supply chain operations reference (SCOR) model. Supply Chain Management: An International Journal 9(9), 23–29 (2004)

20. Chan, F.T.S.: Interactive selection model for supplier selection process: an analytical hierarchy process approach. International Journal of Production Research 41(15), 3549–3579 (2003)

21. Kahraman, C., Cebeci, U., Ulukan, Z.: Multi-criteria supplier selection using fuzzy AHP. Logistics Information Management 16(6), 382–394 (2003)

22. Bittencourt, F., Rabelo, R.J.: A systematic approach for VE partners selection using the SCOR model and the AHP method. In: Camarihna-Matos, L., Afsarmanesh, H., Ortiz, A. (eds.) Collaborative Networks and their Breeding Environments. Springer, Boston (2005)

23. Clinton, B.D., Webber, S.A., Hassell, J.M.: Implementing the balanced scorecard using the analytical hierarchy process. Management Accounting Quarterly 3(3), 1–11 (2002)

24. Searcy, D.L.: Aligning the balanced scorecard and a firm's strategy using the analytic hierarchy process. Management Accounting Quarterly 5, 1–10 (2004)

25. Chiang, Z.: Decision Approach for Long-Term Vendor Selection Based on AHP and BSC. In: Huang, D.-S., Zhang, X.-P., Huang, G.-B. (eds.) Advances in Intelligent Computing. Springer, Heidelberg (2005)
26. Bhagwat, R., Sharma, M.K.: Performance measurement of supply chain management using the analytical hierarchy process. Production Planning & Control 18(8), 666–680 (2007)
27. Lee, A.H.I., Chen, W.C., Chang, C.J.: A fuzzy AHP and BSC approach for evaluating performance of IT department in the manufacturing industry in Taiwan. Expert Systems with Applications 34(1), 96–107 (2008)
28. Cebeci, U.: Fuzzy AHP-based decision support system for selecting ERP systems in textile industry by using balanced scorecard. Expert Systems with Applications 36, 8900–8909 (2009)
29. Croom, S.R.: The dyadic capabilities concept: examining the processes of key supplier involvement in collaborative product development. European Journal of Purchasing & Supply Management 7, 29–37 (2001)
30. Interop. Interoperability ontology. Interop-vlab platform,
    http://interop-vlab.eu/

COL-PMS: A Collaborative Performance Measurement System

María José Verdecho, Juan José Alfaro-Saiz, and Raúl Rodríguez-Rodríguez

Department of Business Organization, CIGIP (Research Centre on Production
Management and Engineering), Universidad Politécnica de Valencia, Camino de Vera, s/n,
46022, Valencia, Spain
{mverdecho,jalfaro,raurodro}@cigip.upv.es

Abstract. Enterprises look for new strategies to increase/maintain their
competitiveness. One of these strategies consists of establishing collaboration
relationships with other enterprises. Collaborating enterprises need tools and
methods that facilitate the management their performance. Performance Measurement Systems developed in the literature have overlooked the development
of frameworks that include the social side of collaboration relationships under
an integrated and structured approach. The purpose of this paper is to introduce
the COLlaborative Performance Measurement System (COL-PMS) framework
which overcomes this gap.

Keywords: performance measurement system, collaboration, interorganizational relationships.

1 Introduction

Global competition, higher specifications of products/services, and fast technological
changes are some of the factors that are boosting enterprises to adopt new business
models to remain competitive in the marketplace. In this context, some enterprises
that traditionally operated with their suppliers under a transactional approach, have
shifted their strategy and adopted collaborative initiatives. Collaboration involves two
or more independent enterprises working together to align their processes with the
goal of creating value to end customers and stakeholders with greater success than
acting alone [1]. It implies sharing information, resources, responsibilities, knowledge, risk and profits among the partners [2]. In addition, in the current business environment, information and communication technologies play a fundamental role
increasing the interoperability among the different enterprises and supporting the
different processes and activities developed by the collaborating enterprises.

Performance measurement is 'a process of quantifying the efficiency and effectiveness of pass action' [3]. The complexity of collaboration environments requires
new tools that aid to define and collect the necessary information for measuring the
performance of enterprises. For that reason, Performance Measurement Systems
(PMSs) should include in their structure special characteristics to support this issue. In

Á. Ortiz Bas, R.D. Franco, P. Gómez Gasquet (Eds.): BASYS 2010, IFIP AICT 322, pp. 56–63, 2010.

supply chain management, interorganizational relationships rely on 'hard' (techno-logical and infrastructural) and 'soft' (social and behavioural) aspects [4, 5]. Around 50% of interorganizational performance drivers are considered to rely on people fac-tors while process and technology factors represent 30% and 20% respectively [6]. In fact, in real assessments of business relationships, 'hard' aspects have been addressed while 'soft' aspects appear to be overlooked [7]. For that reason, one of the lacks of PMS for collaborative contexts is the inclusion of mechanisms and elements that aid to manage jointly hard and soft aspects under an integrated framework.

The purpose of this paper is to introduce a PMS for collaborative contexts, called (COLlaborative Performance Measurement System (COL-PMS)), that fills this gap by including both (hard and soft) aspects within its structure in order to provide a tool for managing the performance of collaboration relationships more efficiently and effectively.

The structure of this paper is as follows. First, a literature review of PMS for inter-organizational contexts is presented. Then, the COL-PMS framework is described. Finally, conclusions are exposed.

2 Background

The behavioral, social or relational side of collaboration consists of a set of aspects or elements that describe the interaction among the different partners. In [8], it is sug-gested that successful partnerships rely on three types of characteristics: attributes of the partnership (commitment, coordination, trust, etc.), communication behavior (such as information sharing) and conflict management techniques.

Based on [8], a literature review regarding PMS for interorganizational environ-ments is performed to analyze if PMS developed support the behavioral side of col-laboration. In [9], a PMS is proposed using the Balance Scorecard (BSC) [10] to measure supply chain (SC) performance. Their work presents the classical four per-spectives (business process, customer, financial, and innovation and learning), generic goals of the SC and examples of performance indicators for these goals. Regarding the social elements, two of the goals to accomplish within the innovation and learning perspective are 'partnership management' and '(shared) information flows'. For these goals, the performance indicators 'product commitment ratio' and 'number of shared data sets with respect to total data sets' are defined. However, other aspects could be included to manage SC performance such as trust and commitment.

In [11], it is presented a framework for supply chain performance measurement that classifies metrics within three levels of management: strategic, tactical and opera-tional. The authors also indicate the importance of measuring partnerships and present a list of partnership evaluation parameters such as 'level and degree of information sharing' and extent of 'mutual assistance in problem solving'. Nevertheless, the framework could be extended by considering other elements such as trust, coordina-tion and conflict management.

In [12], it is developed a process-based PMS for supply chains. The work estab-lishes a set of steps to decompose the core supply chain processes into lower level processes. The PMS associates goals, responsibility and function, and their respective performance measurements to each level and each element within each level (subprocesses, activities). It identifies that the strategy of the supply chain should be defined to identify the core processes. Nevertheless, social collaborative elements (information sharing, trust, etc.) can be intuited to be within the subprocesses and activity borders, but they are not explicitly defined.

In [13], it is proposed a PMS for Extended Enterprises (EEs). The PMS comprises three levels: enterprise, business unit and extended processes. The work considers strategic and operational coordinating measures which should include collaboration measures. The authors present a case study where the performance measurement of 'number of inter-partner strategic conflicts' is included in the EE scorecard. However, the work does not detail the extent of collaborative elements to be measured through the coordinating measures.

In [14], it is presented a PMS for EE. The PMS consists of two frameworks: a structural and a procedural framework. The structural framework comprises two levels: individual enterprise and EE PMS. At the individual level, each node PMS is composed of four perspectives: internal, supplier, customer and EE perspectives. However, the PMS could be further detailed by considering the social elements.

In [15], it is developed a PMS methodology for virtual enterprises. It defines two levels: virtual and individual enterprise. The work exposes the necessity to assess relationships within the PMS. The authors present a case study where the elements 'culture' and 'interpersonal relationships' are included in the 'virtual enterprise' and 'learning and growth' perspectives respectively but they do not specify how they are to be measured.

In [16], it is presented a PMS for supply networks composed of a methodology and a framework. The work identifies that equity and trust have to be maintained through the functional levels, perspectives and performance structure. However, the PMS does not consider how to integrate and measure these collaborative elements.

In [17], it is presented an audit model to assess an enterprise readiness for collaboration. Although the model is not structured as a PMS, it is considered within this group of the typology because it intends to evaluate the antecedent stage of a collaboration relationship. The model comprises four perspectives: strategic, operational, cultural and commercial. The cultural and commercial perspectives pursue to assess the compatibility of culture (trust, management style, information sharing, etc.) and commercial position (risk, investments, etc.) among enterprises. The work could be further extended by considering other social aspects (cooperation, coordination, conflict management, etc.).

In [18], it is developed a PMS for Virtual Organizations Breeding Environments (VBEs). The objective of a VBE is to prepare its member's organizations for their potential involvement in a collaborative opportunity-based virtual organization. The PMS is based on the four perspectives by Kaplan and Norton [19]. Collaboration elements are incorporated in all four PMS perspectives such as developing collaborative opportunities (outcome perspective), partnership development (stakeholder perspective), trust and relationship management (internal perspective), and culture, alignment of goals and collaboration (learning and growth perspective). However, although the work exposes the strategic map and performance indicators for measuring collaborative elements, a PMS structure is not explicit.

In [20], it is proposed a PMS for measuring collaboration performance in virtual organizations. The PMS is based on the four perspectives by Kaplan and Norton [10] and a fifth perspective for measuring collaboration that comprises five subperspectives: reliability, flexibility, responsiveness, commitment and communication. However, it would be necessary to explain further the extent of the five subperspectives and how these subperspectives are related to the rest of perspectives in order to define an integrated and solid PMS.

As a conclusion, it can be stated that although some of the PMSs reviewed include the measurement of some social elements in their structure, there is a clear lack of a collaborative PMS that considers the social side of the collaboration that allows managing the performance of collaborating enterprises under a solid performance structure. The framework proposed on this paper aims to fill this research gap.

3 COL-PMS Framework

3.1 Description of COL-PMS

From the literature review, it can be observed that there is a need of methods, systems and procedures that establish the steps to be followed to manage performance within collaborative contexts considering the social side of collaboration and following an integrated approach. The COL-PMS framework introduces these characteristics based on the PMS developed by Alfaro et al. [16] which is founded on three phases: 1) definition of the strategic framework, 2) definition of the process framework and 3) monitoring. The characteristics of a PMS for collaborative environments are related to the requirements that should be covered by the PMS in order to be considered solid and integrated. This implies that the PMS should provide all the necessary functionalities to approach the context for which it was developed. Additionally, this PMS should support the decision-making process of the enterprises and entities that collaborate. For that reason, it is necessary that the PMS considers two levels: interorganizational level (where collaboration takes place) and individual enterprise level. Both levels should be aligned in order to keep traceability among the performance elements that are to be defined.

At the individual enterprise level, COL-PMS derivates from the vision and strategy and reflects the most important aspects of the business. If this concept is extended within the interorganizational context, it can be said that it is a process of strategic planning for all the partners and implies a common understanding of their aims what facilitates the evaluation and degree of success reached in their objectives and strategies. Thus, COL-PMS starts with a strategic approach for its adequate interpretation and application. Therefore, the starting point of COL-PMS is the definition of the strategic framework (phase 1).

Figure 1 shows the composition of the COL-PMS generic framework which distinguishes between two types of frameworks: strategic and process framework. In detail, the definition of the strategic framework needs to incorporate all the performance elements (philosophical planning (mission and vision), stakeholder requirements, objectives, strategies, critical success factors and key performance indicators (KPIs). All these elements at defined for the four performance perspectives [10]: financial, customer, process and learning & growth. These perspectives aid to structure performance measurement following relationships of cause-effect.

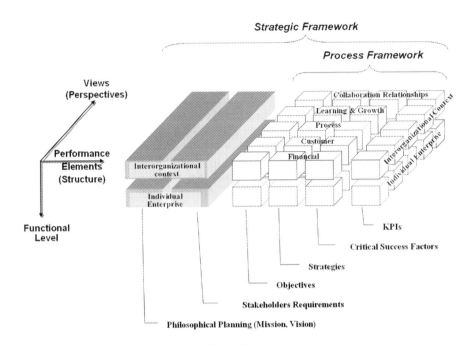

Fig. 1. COL-PMS Framework

In addition, it is necessary to introduce one perspective oriented to manage collaboration relationships that covers the social side of collaboration. This perspective supports the consecution of the other four perspectives, due to the fact that is related to the aspects of the collaborative culture which provides a mediator effect or social climate above the components of the rest of perspectives. Therefore, this perspective will consist of a set of objectives, strategies, critical success factors and KPIs related to relational characteristics such as the ones described by [8]: relationship attributes (trust, commitment, cooperation, etc.), communication behaviour (information sharing) and conflict resolution techniques. The descriptions of these characteristics are as follows (Boddy et al., 2000; Hanfield and Betchel, 2004; Lejeune and Yakova, 2005):

Commitment refers to the willingness of the supplier to perform effort on behalf of the relationship. It is the establishment of the foundation of the relationship and it is based on being supportive in solving problems together. A high level of commitment provides the context for the achievement of individual and mutual goals. There are different types of commitment depending on the effort (to continue the relationship), loyalty, contract duration or their combination.

Coordination involves the tasks that are to be taken for linking activities performed by the different members in a seamless manner. The coordination degree between manufacturer and supplier is an important attribute of the relationship as it allows moving together towards the achievement of mutual objectives.

Trust is based on the belief that the partner is reliable and will fulfill its responsibilities acting fairly. A partner trusts another partner if considers that decisions made by this last one will be in the interest of both parts. There are different types of trust depending if they are founded on deterrence, reliability, competence, goodwill, loyalty or their combination.

Information sharing considers the timeliness, accuracy, adequacy and completeness of the relevant information exchanged. It is the degree of private information that enterprises share in order to perform their activities and make decisions. It is one of the main flows through the companies and it defines the depth and width of the other two main flows (material and monetary) and develops the flow of social relationships.

Finally, *conflict management* measures the degree of intensity and conflict resolution mechanisms that exist between manufacturer and supplier. The existence of conflict is inherent to interpersonal as well as interorganizational relationships. However, the manner this conflict is managed is essential to the long-term and stability of the relationship.

It is not the purpose of this paper to provide a full overview of social characteristics of collaboration relationships but to present the elements that a PMS should have to manage them. For that reason, the social characteristics described are only given as examples that are to be considered but do not conform a definitive list.

In addition, it has to be noted that collaboration relationships perspective is mainly related to the interorganizational functional level as it is the level in which interorganizational collaboration takes place. However, social aspects between companies are not isolated from the individual enterprise level as it happens with the other four perspectives. Therefore, the consecution of the interorganizational level is linked to the individual enterprise level.

On the other hand, in the definition of the process framework (phase 2), it is not required to incorporate the philosophical elements (mission and vision) or the stakeholder requirements, excepting special circumstances that require it. Once the strategic framework is obtained, performance elements of the process framework (objectives, strategies, critical success factors and KPIs) are defined for those key business processes associated to the collaborative context. These key processes are processes directly linked to a common product/service produced by the partners or processes that support the success of the production of those products/services.

In the previous phases, all the performance elements have been defined. This last phase aims at monitoring of all those elements in order to know which are the most important elements, what levels are the most relevant from a performance management point of view and where are located special indicators for a specific partner. For that reason, it is convenient show graphically the deployment of all the elements by elaborating two types of diagrams: graphics of global deployment and graphics of partial deployment.

The graphics of global deployment represent the deployment of the basic performance measurement elements for all the functional levels (interorganizational context level and individual enterprise level). Consequently, there will be one graph for the objectives, another for the strategies, another for the critical success factors and, finally, another for the key performance indicators. Then, such graphics will also be constructed for both the strategic and the process framework. Figure 2 shows an example of graphic of global deployment for the objectives.

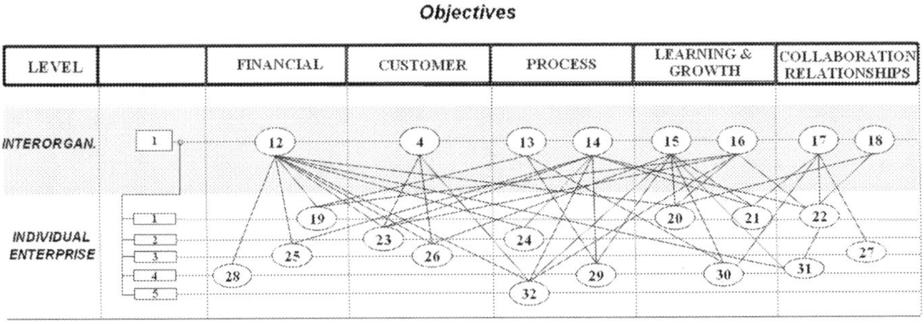

Fig. 2. Graphic of Global Deployment: Objectives

The graphics of partial deployment complements the graphics of global deployment providing the combination of elements necessary for measuring performance for each level (interorganizational level and individual enterprise level).

4   Conclusions

This paper has reviewed the literature regarding interorganizational PMSs in order to analyse if the social aspects of collaboration are managed through a solid and integrated PMS structure. Based on the gaps coming from the literature review, we have introduced a new collaborative PMS, called COL-PMS, which includes the social side of collaboration within its structure in order to provide a tool for managing the performance of collaboration relationships more efficiently and effectively.

This framework considers five performance perspectives in order to manage collaborative performance. In fact, there is a need to consider a specific perspective for managing the relational aspects of collaboration relationships as they act as a mediator element for reaching the elements that compose the other performance perspectives. In addition, we have described the elements that integrate the COL-PMS framework so that enterprises that desire to collaborate or are collaborating have a tool for aiding to define and collect performance management information.

Acknowledgments. This work has been developed within the framework of a research project funded by the Polytechnic University of Valencia, titled "Design and Implementation of Performance Measurement Systems within Collaborative Contexts for aiding the Decision-making Process", reference PAID-06-08-3206.

References

1. Simatupang, T.M., Wright, A.C., Sridharan, R.: Applying the theory of constraints to supply chain collaboration. Supply Chain Management: An International Journal 9(1), 57–70 (2004)
2. Mentzer, J., Min, S., Zacharia, Z.G.: The Nature of Interfirm Partnering in Supply Chain Management. Journal of Retailing 76(4), 549–568 (2001)
3. Neely, A., Adams, C., Kennerley, M.: The Performance Prism: The Scorecard for measuring and managing business success. Financial Times Prentice Hall, London (2002)

4. Harland, C.M.: Supply Chain Management: Relationships, Chains and Networks. British Journal of Management 7, 63–80 (1996)
5. Burgess, K., Singh, P.: A proposed integrated framework for analysing supply chains. Supply Chain Management: An International Journal 11(4), 337–344 (2006)
6. Zaklad, A., McKnight, R., Kosansky, A., Piermarini, J.: The social side of the supply chain. Industrial Engineer 36(2), 40–44 (2004)
7. Staughton, R., Johnston, R.: Operational performance gaps in business relationships. International Journal of Operations & Production Management 25(4), 320–332 (2005)
8. Mohr, J., Spekman, R.: Characteristics of partnership success: Partnership attributes, communication. Strategic Management Journal 15(2), 135–152 (1994)
9. Brewer, P.C., Speh, T.W.: Using the balanced scorecard to measure supply chain performance. Journal of Business Logistics 21(1), 75–93 (2000)
10. Kaplan, R.S., Norton, D.P.: The balanced scorecard – measures that drive performance. Harvard Business Review 70(1), 71–79 (1992)
11. Gunasekaran, A., Patel, C., Tirtiroglu, E.: Performance measures and metrics in a supply chain environment. International Journal of Operations & Production Management 21(1-2), 71–87 (2001)
12. Chan, F.T.S., Qi, H.J.: Feasibility of performance measurement system for supply chain: a process-based approach and measures. Integrated Manufacturing System 14(3), 179–190 (2003)
13. Bititci, U.S., Mendibil, K., Martinez, V., Albores, P.: Measuring and managing performance in extended enterprises. International Journal of Operations & Production Management 25(4), 333–353 (2005)
14. Folan, P., Browne, J.: Development of an Extended Enterprise Performance Measurement System. Production Planning and Control 16(6), 531–544 (2005)
15. Chalmeta, R., Grangel, R.: Performance measurement systems for virtual enterprise integration. International Journal of Computer Integrated Manufacturing 18(1), 73–84 (2005)
16. Alfaro, J.J., Ortiz, A., Rodríguez, R.: Performance measurement system for Enterprise Networks. International Journal of Productivity and Performance Management 56(4), 305–334 (2007)
17. Bititci, U.S., Turner, T., Mackay, D., Kearney, D., Parung, J., Walters, D.: Managing synergy in collaborative enterprises. Production Planning & Control 18(6), 454–465 (2007)
18. Romero, D., Galeano, N., Molina, A.: A conceptual Model for Virtual Breeding Environments Value System. In: Camarihna-Matos, L., Afsarmanesh, H., Novais, P., Analide, C. (eds.) Establishing the Foundation of Collaborative Networks. Springer, Boston (2007)
19. Kaplan, R.S., Norton, D.P.: Strategy maps: converting intangible assets into tangible outcomes. Harvard Business School Publishing Corporation, Boston (2004)
20. Westphal, I., Thoben, K.D., Seifert, M.: Measuring collaboration performance in virtual organizations. In: Camarihna-Matos, L., Afsarmanesh, H., Novais, P., Analide, C. (eds.) Establishing the Foundation of Collaborative Networks. Springer, Boston (2007)
21. Boddy, D., Macbeth, D., Wagner, B.: Implementing collaboration between organizations: an empirical study of supply chain partnering. Journal of Management Studies 37(7), 1003–1018 (2000)
22. Handfield, R.B., Bechtel, C.: Trust, power, dependence, and economics: can SCM research borrow paradigms? International Journal of Integrated Supply Chain Management 1(1), 3–32 (2004)
23. Lejeune, M.A., Yakova, N.: On characterizing the 4 C's in supply chain management. Journal of Operations Management 23(1), 81–100 (2005)

Forest Fire Evolution Prediction Using a Hybrid Intelligent System

Aitor Mata[1], Bruno Baruque[2], Belén Pérez-Lancho[1] Emilio Corchado[1],
and Juan M. Corchado[1]

[1] Department of Computing Science and Automation, University of Salamanca, Spain
{aitor,lancho,escorchado,corchado}@usal.es
[2] Department of Civil Engineering, University of Burgos, Spain
bbaruque@ubu.es

Abstract. Forest fires represent a quite complex environment and an accurate prediction of the fires generated is crucial when trying to react quickly and effectively in such a critical situation. In this study, an hybrid system is applied to predict the evolution of forest fires. The Case-Based Reasoning methodology combined with a summarization of SOM ensembles algorithm has been used to face this problem. The CBR methodology is used as the solution generator in the system, reusing past solutions given to past problems to generate new solutions to new problems by adapting those past solutions to the new situations to face. On the other hand, a new summarization algorithm (WeVoS-SOM) is used to organize the stored information to make it easier to retrieve the most useful information from the case base. The developed system has been checked with forest fires historical and experimental data. The WeVoS-CBR system presented here has successfully predicted the evolution of the forest fires in terms of probability of finding fires in a certain area.

1 Introduction

A hybrid artificial intelligence system [1], [2] is presented in this study. It is applied to generate predictions about the evolution of forest fires. That kind of systems combines symbolic and sub-symbolic techniques to construct more robust and reliable problem solving models. In this study a system based on *Case-Based Reasoning* (CBR) [3] and *Topology Preserving Models* [4] is presented and successfully applied.

Case-Based Reasoning systems have the potential to use past information in order to generate useful knowledge that may be used to solve new problems. Those systems should organise the information handled in order to improve the way that information is used. When the amount of information stored in a CBR system grows, the results obtained are normally better. But the growth of the *case base* (internal structure where the data is accumulated) also implies a more difficult retrieval process, where more information has to be considered in order to obtain the best possible collection of data.

The summarization algorithm presented here, WeVoS-SOM (Weighted Voting Summarization of SOM ensembles) [5] represents the organizing system of the internal structure of the data in the CBR system. With such an inner organization, it is

Á. Ortiz Bas, R.D. Franco, P. Gómez Gasquet (Eds.): BASYS 2010, IFIP AICT 322, pp. 64–71, 2010.

easier to locate the new data that is introduced in the system and to retrieve the needed information to solve new problems.

The combination of both, the generalization power of the CBR methodology and the organizational capabilities of the WeVoS-SOM algorithm generates a system that has been used to generate predictions in a natural environment such as forest fires. Historical data have been used to check the correction of the system, where the predictions generated were compared with the actual past data.

This paper is organized as follows. In the second section the Case-Based Reasoning methodology is introduced and briefly explained. In the third section, the novel summarization algorithm presented in this paper is explained and analyzed. Next, WeVOS-CBR, the developed system is described, and its main phases are detailed. Finally, some results of the application of the system to the forest fire case study and some conclusions are shown.

2   Introducing the CBR Methodology

Case-Based Reasoning [3] origins are in knowledge based systems. CBR systems solve new problems acquiring the needed knowledge from previous situations [6]. The main element of a CBR system is the case base, a structure that stores the information used to generate new solutions.

The learning capabilities of CBR systems are due to its own structure, composed of four main stages [7]: *retrieve, reuse, revision* and *retain*. The first stage is called *retrieve*, and consists in finding the cases (from the case base) that are most similar to the new problem. Once a set of cases is extracted from the case base, they are *reused* by the system. In this second stage (*reuse*), the selected cases are adapted to fit in the new problem. After applying the new solution to the problem, that solution is *revised* to check its performance. If it is an acceptable solution, then it is *retained* by the system and could eventually serve as a solution to future problems.

As a methodology [3], CBR has been used to solve a great variety of problems [8],[9]. It is a cognitive structure that can be easily applied to solve problems such as those related with soft computing, since the procedures used by CBR are quite easy to assimilate by soft computing approaches. CBR has also helped to create applications related to quite different environments. Different kinds of neural networks such as ART-Kohonen [10] or Growing Cell Structures [11] have been combined with CBR to automatically create the inner structure of the case base. Some effort has also been devoted to the case-based maintenance issue [12].

It is easy to understand that the case base is one of the key elements of a CBR system. It is crucial to dispose of a great amount of data, but properly organized. The quantity is important, but if there is no order within the stored cases, it could become impossible to obtain all the knowledge that such an accumulation of data may offer. This is why an algorithm like the WeVoS-SOM that is going to be explained next, is so useful to CBR systems.

3   Explaining the WeVoS-SOM Algorithm

Case-Based Reasoning systems are highly dependent on stored information. The new algorithm presented here, Weighted Voting Summarization of SOM ensembles

(WeVoS-SOM) (Baruque *et al.*) is used to organize the data that is accumulated in the case base. It is also used to recover the most similar cases to the proposed problem.

The main objective of the new fusion of an ensemble of topology preserving maps [4] algorithm presented here, WeVoS-SOM, is to generate a final map processed unit by unit. Instead of trying to obtain the best position for the units of a single map trained over a single dataset, it aims to generate several maps over different parts of the dataset. Then, it obtains a final summarized map by calculating by consensus which is the best set of characteristics vector for each unit position in the map. To do this calculation, first this meta-algorithm must obtain the *"quality"* [13] of every unit that composes each map, so that it can relay in some kind of informed resolution for the fusion of neurons.

The final map obtained is generated unit by unit. The units of the final map are first initialized by determining their centroids in the same position of the map grid in each of the trained maps. Afterwards, the final position of that unit is recalculated using data related with the unit in that same position in every of the maps of the ensemble. For each unit, a sort of voting process is carried out as shown in Eq. 1:

$$V(p,m) = \frac{|x_{p,m}|}{\sum_1^M |x_p|} \cdot \frac{q_{p,m}}{\sum_1^M q_p} \tag{1}$$

where, $V_{p,m}$ is the weight of the vote for the unit included in map m of the ensemble, in its position p; M is the total number of maps in the ensemble; $x_{p,m}$ is the binary vector used for marking the dataset entries recognized by the unit in position p of map m; and, $q_{p,m}$ is the value of the desired quality measure for the unit in position p of map m.

The final map is fed with the weights of the units as it is done with data inputs during the training phase of a SOM, considering the *"homologous"* unit in the final map as the BMU. The weights of the final unit will be updated towards the weights of the composing unit. The difference of the updating performed for each *"homologous"* unit in the composing maps depends on the quality measure calculated for each unit. The higher quality (or the lowest error) of the unit of the composing map, the stronger the unit of the summary map will be updated towards the weights of that neuron. The summarization algorithm will consider the weights of a composing unit *"more suitable"* to be the weights of the unit in the final map according to both the number of inputs recognized and the quality of adaptation of the unit (Eq. 1). With this new approach it is expected to obtain more faithful maps to the inner structure of the dataset.

This algorithm generates a structure where similar data is placed close together, with a clear relationship between the distribution of the initial data and the structure obtained by the algorithm. This relation between reality and inner structure is quite useful to a CBR system, where the stored information must be used in future situations to obtain future solutions.

Next, the system developed combining the CBR methodology and the WeVoS-SOM algorithm is explained, focusing on the main phases of the CBR cycle.

4   An Hybrid Forecasting System

CBR have already been used to generate predictions in complicated environments where different parameters were involved [14]. In this occasion, the CBR methodology is used in combination with a summarization of SOM ensembles algorithm, in order to improve its results. The WeVos-CBR system presented here is able to generate predictions using past information as a source of knowledge to solve new problems. The available information is divided into cases that are stored in the case base. Those cases are structured, using the WeVoS-SOM algorithm.

When a new problem should be solved by the system, then the most similar data to the problem is retrieved from the case base. Then, the inner organization generated by the WeVoS-SOM algorithm is useful to recover those elements more similar to the one that is introduced in the system as a problem. The retrieved cases are used to generate the new solution, by feeding a neural network, trained to generate solutions. If the solution generated is good enough to be proposed to the user, then it is also stored in the case base, to serve as new data to solve new problems. All this process, covering the four main phases of the CBR cycle explained before, is covered by the next sub-sections.

4.1   Creating the Case Base and Retrieving the Most Similar Cases

When the case base is created the WeVoS-SOM algorithm is used to structure it. The graphical capabilities of this novel algorithm are used in this occasion to create a model that represents the actual variability of the parameters stored in the cases. At the same time, the inner structure of the case base will make it easier to recover the most similar cases to the problem cases introduced in the system.

The WeVoS-SOM algorithm is also used to recover the most similar cases to the problem introduced in the system. The case base is organized by using the WeVoS-SOM algorithm. This organization keeps similar values stored close one to another. When a new problem comes into the system, then its virtual position into the inner structure of the case base is calculated. The system tries to store the problem into the case base like if it was a solution. That virtual allocation serves to calculate the position of the problem into the case base, and to recover those elements that are located close to that virtual position. Those retrieved cases are used in the next stage to generate the solution.

4.2   Adapting the Retrieved Cases to Generate a New Solution

After recovering the most similar cases to the problem from the case base, those cases are used to obtain a solution. Growing RBF networks [15] are used to generate the predicted solution corresponding to the proposed problem. The selected cases are used to train the GRBF network. This adaptation of the RBF network lets the system grow during the training phase in a gradual way increasing the number of elements (prototypes) which work as the centres of the radial basis functions. The error definition for every pattern is shown below:

$$e = \frac{1}{n} \sum\nolimits_{k=1}^{p} \|t_{ik} - y_{ik}\|$$
(2)

where t_{ik} is the desired value of the kth output unit of the ith training pattern, y_{ik} the actual values of the kth output unit of the ith training pattern. After the creation of the GRBF network, it is used to generate the solution to the introduced problem. The solution will be the output of the network using as input data the retrieved cases.

4.3 Revising and Retaining the Proposed Solution

In order to verify the precision of the proposed solution, Explanations are used [16]. To justify and validate the given solution, the retrieved cases are used once again. The selected cases have their own future associated situation. Considering the case and its solution as two vectors, a distance between them can be measured by calculating the evolution of the situation in the considered conditions. If the distance between the proposed problem and the solution given is smaller than the distances obtained from the selected cases, then the proposed solution is considered as a good one.

Once the proposed prediction is accepted, it can be stored in the case base in order to serve to solve new problems. It will be used equally than the historical data previously stored in the case base. The WeVoS-SOM algorithm is used again to introduce new elements in the case base.

5 Case Study and Results

Forest fires are a very serious hazard that, every year, cause significant damage around the world from an ecological, social, economical and human point of view [17]. These hazards are particularly dangerous when meteorological conditions are extreme with dry and hot seasons or strong wind. For example, fire is a recurrent factor in Mediterranean areas.

Table 1. Variables that define a case in the *WeVoS-CBR* system

Variable	Definition	Unit
Longitude	Geographical longitude	Degree
Latitude	Geographical latitude	Degree
Date	Day, month and year of the analysis	dd/mm/yyyy
Temperature	Celsius temperature in the area	°C
Bottom pressure	Atmospheric pressure in the area	Newton/m^2
Area of the fires	Surface covered by the fires present in the analyzed area	Km^2
Meridional Wind	Meridional component of the wind	m/s
Zonal Wind	Zonal component of the wind	m/s
Wind Strength	Wind strength	m/s

Fires represent a complex environment, where multiple parameters are involved. In this sub-section, a series of applications and possible solutions are explained. There are different approaches to the forest fire problems [18], [19], [20] and [21], including all the main phases existing in the evolution of this kind of problem.

The WeVoS-CBR system presented here has been applied in this study to generate predictions in a forest fire scenario. Forest fires represent a great environmental risk. The main approaches that have been used to solve this problem come first from the detection of the fires [18], where different techniques have been applied. Once the fire is detected, it is important to generate predictions that should help to take decision in those contingency response situations [22].

The data used to check the WeVoS-CBR system was a subset of the available data that has not been previously used in the training phase. The predicted situation was contrasted with the actual future situation as it was known (historical data was used to train the system and also to test its correction). The parameters taken into account to create the cases stores in the system are listed in *table 1*. The proposed prediction was, in most of the variables, close to 90% of accuracy. To create the cases, the geographical area analyzed was divided into small squares, each of which were considered a case, with all its associated parameters (longitude, latitude, wind, pressure, temperature, etc.). The squares determine the area to be considered in every case. The problem is represented by the current situation of the area (all its parameters and the presence or not of fire). The solution is represented by the situation in that area in a future moment (same location but parameters changed to next day, or next step –if less than a day is considered in every step-).

In *table 2* a summary of the results obtained is shown. In this table different techniques are compared. The table shows the evolution of the results along with the increase of the number of cases stored in the case base. All the techniques analyzed improve its results when increasing the number of cases stored. Having more cases in the case base, makes easier to find similar cases to the proposed problem and then, the solution can be more accurate.

The *"RBF"* column represents a simple Radial Basis Function Network that is trained with all the data available. The network gives an output that is considered a solution to the problem. The *"CBR"* column represents a pure CBR system, with no other techniques included, the cases are stored in the case bases and recovered considering the Euclidean distance. The most similar cases are selected and after applying a weighted mean depending on the similarity, a solution is proposed. The *"RBF + CBR"* column corresponds to the possibility of using a RBF system combined with CBR. The recovery from the CBR is done by the Manhattan distance and the RBF network works in the reuse phase, adapting the selected cases to obtain the new solution. The results of the *"RBF + CBR"* column are, normally, better than those of the *"CBR"*, mainly because of the elimination of useless data to generate the solution. Finally, the *"WeVoS-CBR"* column shows the results obtained by the proposed system, obtaining better results than the three previous analyzed solutions.

Table 2. Percentage of good predictions obtained with different techniques

Number of cases	RBF	CBR	RBF + CBR	WeVoS-CBR
100	36 %	38 %	41 %	44 %
500	40 %	44 %	47 %	51 %
1000	48 %	51 %	59 %	65 %
2000	52 %	58 %	66 %	73 %
3000	56 %	62 %	70 %	78 %
4000	61 %	66 %	73 %	85 %
5000	66 %	70 %	78 %	90 %

6 Conclusions

The comparison of the WeVoS-CBR system with other techniques and systems has shown its advantage in terms of efficiency and quality of the provided results. The performance of the WeVoS-CBR system was also compared with a previous local version of the system, with the same artificial intelligence techniques implemented, but without the use of agents and services. The tests performed consisted of the execution of the same series of predictions in both systems. There were 50 different prediction requests to be generated by the system. It was shown that, the current system was faster than previous versions (a 70% faster in answering 50 successive requests)and the number of crashes produced when the load of work was increased, was quite lower (80% less crashes when using the current system).

With the optimistic results obtained after applying the presented system to the forest fires scenario, a future line of investigation will be the application of this system to other complex environments where its predicting and generalizing capabilities could be successfully applied.

Acknowledgments

This research has been partially supported through projects of the Junta of Castilla and León BU006A08; project of the Spanish Ministry of Education and Innovation CIT-020000-2008-2 and CIT-020000-2009-12. The authors would also like to thank the vehicle interior manufacturer, Grupo Antolin Ingenieria S.A., within the framework of the project MAGNO2008 - 1028.- CENIT Project funded by the Spanish Ministry.

References

1. Abraham, A., Corchado, E., Corchado, J.M.: Hybrid learning machines. Neurocomputing 72, 2729–2730 (2009)
2. Herrero, Á., Corchado, E., Pellicer, M.A., Abraham, A.: MOVIH-IDS: A mobile-visualization hybrid intrusion detection system. Neurocomputing 72, 2775–2784 (2009)
3. Watson, I.: Case-based reasoning is a methodology not a technology. Knowledge-Based Systems 12, 303–308 (1999)
4. Kohonen, T.: The self-organizing map. Neurocomputing 21, 1–6 (1998)
5. Baruque, B., Corchado, E.: A weighted voting summarization of SOM ensembles. Data Mining and Knowledge Discovery, 1–29
6. Aamodt, A.: A Knowledge-Intensive, Integrated Approach to Problem Solving and Sustained Learning. In: Knowledge Engineering and Image Processing Group. University of Trondheim (1991)
7. Aamodt, A., Plaza, E.: Case-Based Reasoning: Foundational Issues, Methodological Variations, and System Approaches. AI Communications 7, 39–59 (1994)
8. Baruque, B., Corchado, E., Mata, A., Corchado, J.M.: A forecasting solution to the oil spill problem based on a hybrid intelligent system. Information Sciences 180, 2029–2043 (2010)

9. Mata, A., Corchado, J.M.: Forecasting the probability of finding oil slicks using a CBR system. Expert Systems With Applications 36, 8239–8246 (2009)
10. Yang, B.S., Han, T., Kim, Y.S.: Integration of ART-Kohonen neural network and case-based reasoning for intelligent fault diagnosis. Expert Systems With Applications 26, 387–395 (2004)
11. Diaz, F., Fdez-Riverola, F., Corchado, J.M.: Gene-CBR: A case-based reasoning tool for cancer diagnosis using microarray data sets. Computational Intelligence 22, 254–268 (2006)
12. Liu, C.-H., Chen, L.-S., Hsu, C.-C.: An Association-based Case Reduction Technique for Case-based Reasoning. Information Sciences 178, 3347–3355 (2008)
13. Pölzlbauer, G.: Survey and Comparison of Quality Measures for Self-Organizing Maps. In: Rauber, J.P. (ed.) Fifth Workshop on Data Analysis (WDA 2004). Elfa Academic Press, London (2004)
14. Corchado, J.M., Fdez-Riverola, F.: FSfRT: Forecasting System for Red Tides. Applied Intelligence 21, 251–264 (2004)
15. Karayiannis, N.B., Mi, G.W.: Growing radial basis neural networks: merging supervised andunsupervised learning with network growth techniques. IEEE Transactions on Neural Networks 8, 1492–1506 (1997)
16. Sørmo, F., Cassens, J., Aamodt, A.: Explanation in Case-Based Reasoning–Perspectives and Goals. Artificial Intelligence Review 24, 109–143 (2005)
17. Long, D.G.: Mapping fire regimes across time and space: Understanding coarse and fine-scale fire patterns. International Journal of Wildland Fire 10, 329–342 (2001)
18. Mazzeo, G., Marchese, F., Filizzola, C., Pergola, N., Tramutoli, V.: A Multi-temporal Robust Satellite Technique (RST) for Forest Fire Detection. Analysis of Multi-temporal Remote Sensing Images (2007)
19. Arrue, B.C., Ollero, A., Matinez De Dios, J.R.: An intelligent system for false alarm reduction in infrared forest-fire detection. Intelligent Systems and Their Applications 15, 64–73 (2000)
20. Muñoz, C., Acevedo, P., Salvo, S., Fagalde, G., Vargas, F.: Forest fire detection using NOAA/16-LAC satellite images in the Araucanía Region. Chile. Bosque 28, 119–128 (2007)
21. Rodríguez, R., Cortés, A., Margalef, T., Luque, E.: An Adaptive System for Forest Fire Behavior Prediction. In: 11th IEEE International Conference on Computational Science and Engineering (2008)
22. Iliadis, L.S.: A decision support system applying an integrated fuzzy model for long-term forest fire risk estimation. Environmental Modelling and Software 20, 613–621 (2005)

Modelling Human Resource Systems in Support of Efficient Production

S.N. Khalil and R.H. Weston

Manufacturing System Integration (MSI) Research Institute, Wolfson School,
Loughborough University, Leicestershire United Kingdom, LE11 3TU

Abstract. Resource systems in manufacturing businesses need to be managed innovatively particularly when a range of products and services needs to be realized with minimum investment in resource systems. In this research, the primary form of active resource system, namely people, will be modelled with a view to facilitating efficient production. Humans play the key role in organising manufacturing businesses and contribute greatly towards competitive production performance. Enterprise Modelling is use to create static models that capture key organisational relationships in a manufacturing business and transformed into equivalent structures within Simulation Models that enable dynamic analysis. This provides both graphical and computer executable models of people and facilitates quantitative analysis and comparison of different human system configurations that suit various manufacturing workplaces. The paper illustrates the application of the modelling approach and observes advantages gained through using coherent sets of enterprise and simulation models.

Keywords: Human system, manufacturing enterprise, simulation modelling, process-oriented enterprise modelling.

1 Introduction

To be able to design an efficient production system, designers and managers of Manufacturing Enterprises (MEs) need to be able to reason about the assignment of persons to production activities such that key performance measures (like lead-time, quality and cost targets) are met. Typically in industry this is done *implicitly* with regard to 'abilities' (of alternative candidate resources (including people, semi- automated machines and supporting IT systems) to fulfill a given set of product realising roles with respect to specific case performance measures. When assigning production operatives to roles, production system designers and managers use their experience and knowledge about abilities of the people involved and makes judgments about their individual and collective abilities to accomplish predicted patterns of upcoming work. However often production systems, and/or the products they make, can be complex. Indeed when production systems need to share human and technical (machine and IT) resources amongst a changing mix of multiple value streams, frequently designers/managers may make poor people and machine assignment decisions, which will lead to poor attainment of production targets that causally may result in poor competitive performance of the manufacturing business as a whole. In such case

Á. Ortiz Bas, R.D. Franco, P. Gómez Gasquet (Eds.): BASYS 2010, IFIP AICT 322, pp. 72–79, 2010.

managers/designers can gain significant competitive advantage from the ongoing re-use of an effective decision-support tool which will help them make better informed decisions about how and when to allocated a finite production resource in response to any given customer induced dynamic.

This paper researches a new means satisfying this requirement for decision support. The approach taken is to deploy a synergistic combination of:

- *Enterprise Modelling*, which *explicitly* describes organisational structures related to a particular parent manufacturing business; so that process-oriented structural relationships inter-connecting production systems are uniquely defined, and
- *Simulation Modelling*, which is capable of simulating time-based behaviours of alternative production system configurations of people and technical resource; thereby potentially enabling production system designers and managers, in a virtual environment, to experiment within systematic changes to organisational structures and production system parameters so as to predict changes in production system behaviours and therefore performance outcomes in respect of new work scenarios.

The modelling approach taken has potential within dynamic production systems environments to much improve the deployment of a constrained set of people and machine resources and further by predicting change outcomes prior to making physical production system change the costs and benefits of changes trial can be assessed, thereby protecting risk associated with production system investments and potentially extending the economic life-time of production systems. This paper describes how an enterprise model can be used to capture a big picture of the organisational structures of a case study Manufacturing Enterprise (ME). The approach being researched has potential to form the basis of a decision support tool, which can repetitively, quantitatively and explicitly inform production system designers/manager about the suitability of different assignments of human and technical resources, given a set of changing work. Therefore this paper is design to aid the efficient deployment of human systems in MEs by:

- Proposing a human system modelling technique which can be used on an ongoing and systematic basis to model, understand and engineer human systems that satisfy dynamic production system requirements;
- Analyzing key aspects of human system dynamics by developing static and dynamic models of human systems.

The paper will discuss the background of the research work. It will also explain how Enterprise (static) and Simulation (dynamic) modelling can be used in a complementary fashion to visualise and computer executes alternative possible human system deployments.

2   Manufacturing Complexity

Over many years great interest has been placed in managing complexity in manufacturing organizations. Siemieniuch and Sinclair[1] defined manufacturing complexity from an organisational perspective. They state that if interactions between entities of

an organisation give rise to unpredictable organisational performance then that organisation is complex. Common entities in manufacturing organisations comprise
human resources, electromechanical and IT machines which typically are organised to
realise customer related processes and infrastructure services [2].

When seeking to manage complexity, various approaches and manufacturing paradigms have been introduced. For example the Group Technology (GT) has widely
been used in industry to improve manufacturing processes by means of grouping and
coding. GT types of activities are also referred as classification and clustering: of
parts that are similar in nature; or parts that require operations of similar machinery
and processes[3]. Advantages of deploying GT philosophy are (1) to simplify the flow
of parts and tools, (2) to reduce set-up times, (3) reduce throughput time, (4) reduce
work-in-process inventory and (5) maximize design and manufacturing efficiencies.
However according to name Kusiak and Heragu, the use of a clustering method may
not be efficient because of constraints from needed information flows in the processes; such as if data related to material, geometry and tolerances is not available.

The average lifetime of products has shortened dramatically in the last 10 years.
Product variations have increased and this requires MEs to be more flexible and responsive towards their customer demands. But current trends in global demand mean
that more products are now produced in low quantities, with high variety amongst
demand patterns. This is because increasingly products are highly customised and/or
their underlying technologies and components are subject to increased rates of
change. Richards states that being responsive and agile is as being able to respond to
sophisticated customer requirements when subject to persistently changing competitive processes and success factors [4].

3 Trends and Needs to Model Human Systems

3.1 Currents Trends in Manufacturing Industry

The new millennium has seen rapid change in many aspects and segments of manufacturing industries. Some factors contributing towards this change are:

- Intense global competition.
- Mass markets fragmenting into niche markets.
- Customers expecting low volume, high quality, custom products.
- Seemingly ever shortening product life-cycles, development times, and pro-
  duction lead times are required.
- Customers want to be uniquely treated, i.e. as individuals

In an attempt to address these factors, organisations need much more frequently to be
re-configured. This for example may require some form of change in human oriented
organisational structures. Manufacturing organisations, basically comprise human
resources, and electromechanical and IT machines; and in general systematic use of
these 'active' resources (i.e. resources that can perform required ME actions) are
commonly organised so that they systematically achieve value adding processes and
related infrastructure support and engineering developmental activities (Pandya et al
1997). Earlier in this paper, the literature focussed on the paradigms and approaches

that industry is adopting to improve manufacturing processes. However these paradigms were mainly discussed in respect of their mechanistic aspects rather than their behavioural aspects and how such behaviours can impact on MEs. However the functional aspects of human-related processes still requires further study. As the prime ME resource, there is a great need for humans to know about the 'how', 'what' and 'do' (BS ISO 14258:1998) activities in a given ME and the related roles that they and other humans can play with respect to manufacturing activities. The literature reviewed in this paper illustrates that there is a gap in quantitative understandings about potential roles of technical (electromechanical and IT) resources and related roles that human resources can play with respect to engineering, infrastructural and direct value adding manufacturing activities.

3.2 Needs to Model Human System

As yet there is no widely accepted (by industry or academia) systematic way to qualitatively and quantitatively model ME process oriented roles; and how such roles may function over time under differing production demand patterns should they be resourced by humans and machines or by humans or machines. In general it is observed that addressing this deficiency requires effective models of relationships between human/human and human/machine, which may be uncertain in nature. Therefore it is observed that great advantage could be gained by having a 'simulation tool' to model alternative combinations of resource entities; so as to inform 1) managerial aspects of human/machine resource allocation, by providing support for planning decisions and determining suitable resource system reconfigurations based on predictions about organisational behaviours and 2) design aspects of production systems, associated with mid to long term investment decision making.

4 Human System Modelling in Manufacturing Enterprise

Humans are unique and their behaviour can be difficult to predict. Thus it may be almost impossible to model the unconstrained human due to these complexities. On the other hand, potentially human systems can be modelled from more constrained viewpoints. Example viewpoints include: psychology, physiology, culture, structure, dynamic, roles and attribute. Researchers in the MSI (Manufacturing System Integration Institute) have focused their human systems modelling efforts on modelling people roles (i.e. organised sets of activities that people perform) and to consider how the abilities and behaviours of potential human role holders impact on achieving production targets. The approach being taken is therefore based in process oriented modelling. One thread of top-down modelling followed is centered on ME process decomposition into hierarchy/levels for action taking and information sharing. Here processes are explicitly and graphically modelled as related sets of enterprise activities (EAs) which identify possible sets of explicitly defined roles that can be resourced by alternate groups of people competent to perform the role sets defined. Here role sets essentially specify a process oriented organisational structure. This is illustrated by figure 1. The activities are defined in terms of unitary functional operations (FO) that require unitary functional entities (FE) which can be possessed by human and/or machine holders of those roles. In a second thread of modelling candidate human (and machine) holders of roles are described in a tabular fashion, in terms of the competencies they can bring to bear on defined role sets (which can be matched to FE) and likely behavioural performances they can achieve (which can be linked to FO sequence models). A third thread of modelling is centered on simulation of alternative candidate configurations of roles and role holders, which provides a tool for comparing throughputs, utilisation, cost and value generation abilities of those alternative configurations.

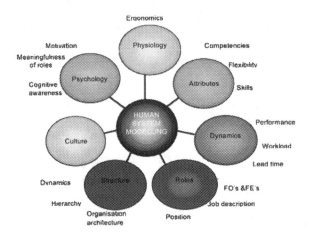

Fig. 1. Human system entities

5   Modelling Concepts and Research Methods

MSI researchers have been using enterprise engineering and simulation modelling technique to aid decision-making. Enterprise modelling is used primarily to (1) externalizing enterprise knowledge about case study MEs, and can add value to the enterprise by enabling knowledge sharing and (2) to provide a process-oriented decomposition mechanism, so that high levels of complexity can be handled and it becomes possible to break down the barriers in organization that hinder productivity by synergizing the enterprise to achieved better understandings about how business goals can be achieved in an efficient and productive way[5].

The enterprise modelling (EM) technique used in this study is known as CIMOSA. CIMOSA is an acronym derived from CIM Open System Architecture and this acronym was introduced by the AMICE consortium. In CIMOSA the user representation and system representation, and related function information and control perspectives are decomposed. The associated decomposition and isolation of different modelling concepts and viewpoints enables an organization to be represented in a flexible fashion, so as to realise changing requirements for functional and facilities integration. Generic graphical representation of CIMOSA models is illustrated in figure 2. CIMOSA modelling enables ME decomposition into the following:

- Domains (DM)
- Domain Processes (DP)
- Business Processes (BP) and

- Enterprise Activities (EA)
- Functional Operators (FO)
- Functional Entities (FE)

This case study modelling is supported by simulation models (dynamic models) that are in part derived from (and hence are consistent with) selected segments of the CI-MOSA static model. CIMOSA graphical models are static in the sense that they only encode relatively enduring properties of MEs and cannot be computer executed to show ME behaviours over time. The simulation models are capable of modeling queues, stochastic events, product flows, process routes, resource utilisation, break-downs and absence, exception flows and etc. Enterprise and simulation modeling (SM) techniques can mutually support analysis of human system roles in a manufacturing enterprise.

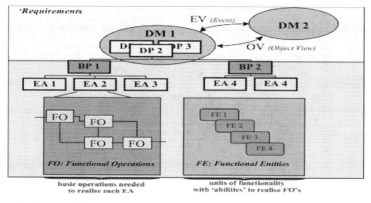

Fig. 2. CIMOSA static model

6 Research Domain, Integration of Enterprise and SM

Chosen case study company is an air conditioning company, LS a privately owned Chinese manufacturing company located in Shun De in the Guangdong province of South China. Since 1988 when it came privately owned, it has expanded its manufacturing and supply scope and is currently specialised in the 'engineering to order' of customised industrialised air conditioners. Their unique expertise is demonstrated in their competence in meeting varying customer needs. On the average LS employs about 1000 staff of which 60 are mainstream Engineers. Most of the staff is young graduates from universities and colleges and hence the company exhibits high level of exuberance in terms of its personnel. The assembly shop 2 has been chosen as the case study for this research. The shop floor assembly held in five stages:1)general assembly, 2)pipes and tubing and hydraulic tests, 3)electronic control installation and side panels assembly, 4) testing and lastly 5)packaging. Each stages of the assembly work is supported by 66 staff that is grouped into 5 sets of different teams. Each team are trained and specialised in each stages. The process that took place during the assembly is described in CIMOSA enterprise activity diagram BP 6.3.1 as referred in figure 3.

The simulation modelling (SM) of these workstations is as described in figure 5. The simulation modelling is held using Teknomatix Plant Simulation Modelling software tool. The software is a custom made tool for users that specifically designed to model the performance of a manufacturing plant. The SM is capable of modelling human resources hierarchically. The broker or acting as supervisor worked by assigning workers in the workpool to perform activities/processes at the workstations. Workstations are the places where worker is assigned to do their work assigned at each stage and the performance is affected by i.e. workers efficiency, dynamic input etc.

In this case the efficiency of the workers are set to 60% efficient in the first experiment and the other is set 80% efficient in the second experiment. Thus is done to compare the performance of the production line when workers efficiency is changed.

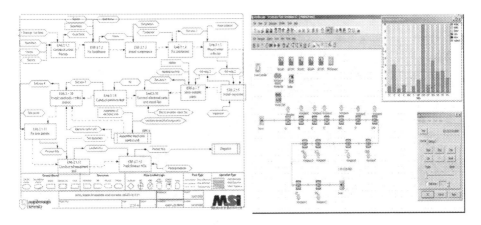

Fig. 3. Activity Diagram-Assembly shop 2   **Fig. 4.** SM of AC assembly

The chart of the overall performance of the work centers is shown in figure 4. The column in the chart shows the pattern of working and blocked processes taking place during the simulation is done. The simulation throughput results showed that there is a 30% increase of production throughput i.e. from 1 AC unit per day to 1.3 AC units per day when the efficiency of workers increased from 60% to 80%. When the number of workers in Team 1 is reduced by half, the simulation results showed that the throughput remained to 1 per day when the resource efficiency is set to 80%. The results showed there is potential for the production system design to reduce the amount of workers when the workers are working at higher efficiency.

7   Further Work in Human System Modelling in Manufacturing Enterprise

Current modelling is based on the 'as is' model, i.e. the current process carried out in the particular bearing manufacturing system. Improvements that will be performed in later stages include:

1) Improving matching roles to role holders in Static Model for modelling and allocating the right worker for the right processes according to different competency levels of workers.
2) Enhancing the current team with abilities to perform multiple processes and able to work in cross-team assembly work. This will improve the throughput of the process line due to increase of shared-knowledge and information flow in the assembly line.

8 Summary and Conclusions

This approach has developed new understandings about different types of model that can be used to characterize human system dynamics. This characterization is based on a job order specification at which influenced by multiple variances i.e. product specification variances. At this stage of experimentation the author has not yet been able to find out whether these models can usefully predict the impact of the overall performance of manufacturing enterprise due to product variance. But early results are encouraging.

Acknowledgments

The principal researcher is currently a PhD researcher in Loughborough University and sponsored by the Malaysian Ministry of Higher Education/ Universiti Teknikal Malaysia Melaka.

References

1. Siemieniuch, C.E., Sinclair, M.A.: On complexity, process ownership and organisational learning in manufacturing organisations, from an ergonomics perspective. Applied Ergonomics 33(5), 449–462 (2002)
2. Pandya, K.V., et al.: Towards the manufacturing enterprises of the future. International Journal of Operations & Production Management 17(5), 502–521 (1997)
3. Kusiak, A., Heragu, S.S.: Group technology. Computers in Industry 9(2), 83–91 (1987)
4. Richards, C.: Agile manufacturing beyond lean. Production and Inventory Management Journal, 60–64 (1996)
5. Vernadat, F.B.: Enterprise Modelling and Integration. Chapman and Hall, London (1996)

Open Services Ecosystem Supporting Collaborative Networks

A. Luis Osório[1,2], Hamideh Afsarmanesh[2], and Luis M. Camarinha-Matos[3]

[1] Instituto Superior de Engenharia de Lisboa, Lisboa Portugal
aosorio@deetc.isel.pt
[2] University of Amsterdam, Amsterdam Netherlands
h.afsarmanesh@uva.nl
[3] Faculdade de Ciências e Tecnologia, Universidade Nova de Lisboa, Portugal
cam@uninova.pt

Abstract. The growing complexity of the information and communication technologies when coping with innovative business services based on collaborative contributions from multiple stakeholders requires novel and multidisciplinary approaches. Service orientation is a strategic approach to deal with such complexity, and various stakeholders' information systems. Services or more precisely the autonomous computational agents implementing the services, provide an architectural pattern able to cope with the needs of integrated and distributed collaborative solutions. This paper proposes a service-oriented framework, aiming to support a virtual organizations breeding environment which is the basis to establish short or long term goal-oriented virtual organizations. The notion of integrated business services, where customers receive some value developed through the contribution from a network of companies is a key element.

Keywords: Collaborative Networks, Virtual Organizations, Service Oriented computing, Service Oriented Architecture.

1 Introduction

Service oriented architecture (SOA) and service oriented computing (SOC) are concepts that have been developed both by research community and industry as innovative patterns to structure the growing complexity of computational infrastructures needed to cope with complex integrated solutions. One main motivation has been the risks of increased dependency of the complex integrated solutions on the proprietary approaches, which in turn make them too dependent on specific suppliers. From the engineering viewpoint, existing integrated solutions tend to follow a "one-of-a-kind" approach making them too expensive not only at the development phase but also along its overall life cycle. In line with service oriented architecture, an initiative such as the service component architecture (SCA) proposes a strategy to develop assemblies of distributed and heterogeneous autonomous components from the same or different providers. Another contribution comes from the open services gateway initiative (OSGi) that proposes a framework to add agility to the development of applications based on loosely coupled components, even though they are too close to

Á. Ortiz Bas, R.D. Franco, P. Gómez Gasquet (Eds.): BASYS 2010, IFIP AICT 322, pp. 80–91, 2010.

the Java technology. The proposed SCA framework is an interesting approach for combining distributed heterogeneous and autonomous computational entities into integrated solutions. Nevertheless the simple combination of heterogeneous and autonomous components originated from different suppliers is not enough to cope with the growing complexity and needs of collaborative networks. Especially when considering the complete life cycle - from, development, deployment, operations management and evolution.

While SOA and SOC tackle complexities in distributed systems, it is fundamental to establish a clear semantics for the concept of services. The organization for the advancement of structured information standards (OASIS) suggests a holistic approach to SOA systems, as networks of a number of entities including service providers, individuals (acting at different roles), machines, suppliers, entities that directly or indirectly establish a system's behavior [1]. More conservative approaches point to an enterprise service bus (ESB) as a structured evolution from enterprise application integration (EAI), where message oriented middleware and data/information transformations play a major role, while they do not present significant innovations. Even when a *service wrapper* layer is proposed to transform legacy applications/systems into more *normalized* components, we can question whether this is the right strategy to cope with the requirements of more complex integrated systems.

As pointed out by the IEEE Transactions on Services Computing initiative, a necessary convergence of semantics around service oriented computing is expected to bring some clarity to the currently dispersed contributions. This new body of knowledge is organized around four main areas: i) services and service systems; ii) service technologies; iii) services consulting and delivery; and vi) services applications and management [2]. This and other complementary initiatives are being pushed by a class of new business services offering people new facilities, and involving contributions from different stakeholders, while making the underlying business arrangements transparent to clients. A paradigmatic example is the utilization of a unique business card (or business nomadic card) that can be used by an individual to pay for public transports, newspapers, street parking, and shopping in stores, based on a unique contract with an integrated service provider. These new collaborative business scenarios, where critical processes rely on a number of diverse information systems, require an innovative distributed computational infrastructure closer to the notion of *service ecosystem* or *service park*.

This paper proposes a strategy for creation of a service ecosystem integrating multi-cultural technical systems through declarative semantics (ontology) in order to make such ecosystem sufficiently agile to cope with the emerging collaborative business scenarios offering integrated value-added services to the customers. For instance, when considering integrated solutions for many different running services at a large complex building, a large shopping centre, a hospital or a public services building, there is also a need for an integrated management and supervision solution to support interoperation among these services. The needed solution must support and shall span over the basic subsystems, e.g. programmable logic controllers (PLC), video camera infrastructures with video server recorders (VSR), heating, ventilation, and air conditioning systems (HVAC), and many other specialized subsystems, which are provided by different technological stakeholders. The open question is how to model and effectively support a network of stakeholders, with offering a single integrated holistic approach to the end-users, while keeping the independence among the service providers.

2 Balanced Approach for Integration of Business Services

The notion of integrated business service is not an entirely new concept, as it can be perceived whenever business challenges require a multidisciplinary approach for service provision or the complexity and the need to reduce operational risks requires the participation of more than one company in a given business opportunity. Such services require a balanced approach considering the need for the participation of technology, process, and business expertise. The integrated business service can be linked to the collaborative network (CN) concept as it results from the contribution of heterogeneous and autonomous distributed entities (e.g. organizations, people, software agents) that collaborate to achieve common objectives through sharing their resources and capabilities and thus jointly creating new values [3]. Integrated business services are much more efficiently grounded if they are established within a long-term business alliance that can serve as the breeding environment for formation of business-based collaborations; namely within a virtual organizations breeding environment (VBE) [4]. The concept of VBE has been proposed to guarantee a minimum collaboration preparedness state for its members, as a pre-condition to participate in collaborative business opportunities, i.e., as the ground for supporting the complete lifecycle of virtual enterprises/ virtual organizations (VE/VO) [5].

Establishing an integrated business service (IBS) also requires an adequate preparedness state from its candidate stakeholders in line with the VO concept. From the ICT development point of view, the requirements identified in [6] for a collaborative network, namely: i) ICT-I reference framework; ii) ICT-I business models; iii) Security framework; and iv) ICT SOA-based infrastructure for collaboration, represent an important basis for the definition of a generic ICT infrastructure for integrated business services. Similar requirements come from other domains as the ePAL/BRAID roadmaps [16] on ICT and ageing.

At present some IT supplier companies tend to offer some integrated platforms in response to the increasing needs for integrated solutions. As identified in [7], this implies that then the complementary networked stakeholders shall negotiate long term service level agreements (SLA) with the IT provider company in order to jointly develop an IBS and establishing their collaborative business relations. Nevertheless, such IT suppliers typically tend to promote monolithic closed solutions, and find it very difficult to cope to the CN requirements of providing an open infrastructure. The open approach is even seen as a threat by some market players.

While most proposed research in the area of CN is centered on identifying the dynamics of business ecosystems involving producers, service providers, consumers, certification bodies, and regulators, with a focus on the business patterns, our research follows a complementary approach to the proposed integrated business service concept. In our approach IBS emerges from collaborative network ecosystems – VBEs - made of complementary autonomous stakeholders which possess their own heterogeneous information systems. Therefore, the discussion is centered on the networked integration perspective, i.e. an integration of contributions (services) linked to diverse IT systems, held by the participating stakeholders. As such, an integrated business service can be defined as a service provided by a network of stakeholders, which are transparent to the subscribing end-user, namely under the assumption that the service subscriber assumes only one contractual relation. In this

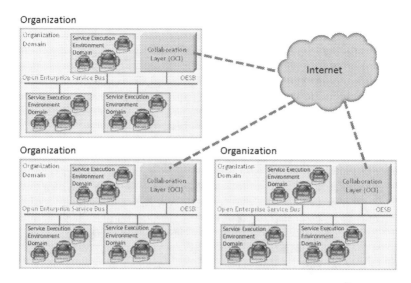

Fig. 1. Collaborative networks formed by multiple organization domains

way, an integrated business service establishes a virtual provider that might be operated and coordinated by a new organizational entity (a new company, a temporary legal entity, or an association where one participating company leads and supports the collaboration). Furthermore, the supporting persons and IT resources are spread over a network. Each participating stakeholder in such collaborative network has its own information system related to its specific organization domain (Fig. 1). Organization domains (OD) establish a trusted execution context under a unified organization's intra-enterprise information system with its associated collaboration layer.

Provision of an integrated business service requires an extended cooperative space beyond the intra-organization domain. Nevertheless, a key requirement is the need for some unified platform even considering that each participating organization has its own IT system relying on some specific architecture and technology bindings. Furthermore, each organization has its own specific business process framework(s) adapted to its internal process models. On the one hand it is advisable to promote a tight integration between intra organizations' processes and the collaborative processes, those contributing to the realization of the integrated business services. But on the other hand, establishment of strong dependencies among stakeholders when participating in the processes that support integrated business services is against the openness approach and is not desirable or even realistic in time. This situation points to the need for a strategy that can preserve organization's autonomy while coping with collaboration contractual agreements that underlie integrated business services. As an example, an evolution in one stakeholders' information system should not affect the behavior of the running processes and services participating in collaborative IBPs [8]. Our proposed strategy considers existence of a collaboration layer (CL) at every participating stakeholder, thus providing a separation of contexts between the domain of intra-enterprise information systems, and that of the network collaboration domain (Fig. 1).

For instance, in an intelligent transportation network, an integrated business service can offer an innovative insurance model based on drivers' behavior, which can be identified through the data collected from an enhanced on-board unit, similar to the one nowadays used for tolling (on-board dedicated short range communication transponder). This gives an example of the need for the participation (cooperation) of several systems that can be managed by: a tolling service provider, multiple highway operators (multiple concessionaires) and an insurance company. When a vehicle crosses a tolling infrastructure, the needed information collected from vehicle bus (CAN bus) is sent to the tolling stakeholder in conjunction with the tolling transaction data. As such, within the same contract that was initially exclusively related to highway tolling, the above insurance company, in cooperation with the business integrated service provider, can now offer an innovative insurance fee calculation for customers. Therefore, the extracts (cost statements for customers) can be enhanced with the insurance payments when presented to subscribers, depending on the agreed payment periods (e.g. daily, weekly, monthly or yearly). The example of the Spanish insurance company Mapfre that has developed a pay-as-you-drive (PAYD) model, based on a specialized on-board system, is discussed in [9]. Another similar example is the integrated business service offered by the Portuguese Via-Verde company, which in the same contract covers both the tolling and car parking payments. It is a running example where collaboration among the involved organizations follows a specific IT infrastructure design and developed mechanisms [10], even though the information systems of some of the involved stakeholders has evolved to a service oriented culture.

A similar situation can be foreseen for the provision of care services to elderly, in which different entities e.g. care centers, health centers, social security, leisure centers, etc., can contribute to provide integrated services under a single contract. These examples suggest the need for a balanced approach where VBEs might need to involve members at different IT development stages, motivating the proposal of introducing the collaboration layer.

3   Cooperative Open Service Infrastructure

The integrated business services often require the involvement of a grid of diverse resources, including the computational services, persons interacting through multiple communication channels (human machine interaction channels), and devices (also represented by services), which are able to participate in different collaborative processes. Such resources need to all be represented as adaptive entities or components, embedding meta-information, and able to be managed in different lifecycle phases of the IBSs. In such an environment, collaborative processes can be provided, realizing integrated business services, through the composition of a hierarchy of processes, each one relying on the composition of other already defined simple or composite services.

In this framework the finest grained entity is a simple service seen as an autonomous computational entity, implemented in some technology (e.g. Web Services, JINI, WCF, Multi-agent framework, grid-services). Here, the entire computational logic, even if associated to monolithic systems such as a classic enterprise resource planning (ERP) application, is abstracted as services that are supported through wrappers, according the proposed framework. Motivated by the need to increase reutilization of computational logic, services can be organized in two main classes: i) *system services*, and ii) *application services*. The system services are those autonomous computational entities, possibly from different suppliers, that are part of the organization's open service bus. They contribute to establish the ICT *culture* of the organization, i.e. providing a kind of organization's signature. The planned strategy is to encourage (or force) new service suppliers to reutilize as much as possible the existing resources, instead of developing from scratch. As an example, a new application service for managing human resources (or simply to add a new service to the human resource management facilities) must use the already existing and documented identity management system service. Therefore, a system service is part of the organization's open service bus. On the other hand, an application service is not conditioned to offer services to other peer services and thus it is not part of the organization's open service bus.

The logical structure of an application or system service, while prepared to be involved in collaborative processes, involves four primary aspects:

1. A *functional interface* making available a number of operations under some predefined semantics (implicit or explicit semantics through the association of an ontology). A functional interface can include operations like add (op1, op1), multiply (op1, op1), as part of a calculator service.
2. *Event infrastructure* responsible to manage asynchronous relationships among services. Consider a subscription of an event signaling the subscriber each time a functional operation is called in the calculator;
3. *Instrumentation port* to integrate a monitoring infrastructure based on specialized diagnostic and prognostic services (agents);
4. *Meta-data* embedding the necessary parameters to support service client's adaptation. This can be done through implicit semantics, data structures and semantics resulting from a normalization process or adopting an ontology, thus offering dynamic adaptability to potential clients.

The functional interface establishes a number of operations to be accessed by other services (clients) according their functional needs.

The *events* infrastructure makes it possible to subscribe to certain events, thus providing an asynchronous access to service relevant information. A client service can subscribe to relevant events directly from their originating services or can access the generated events through a tuple space (in this case shared by all other services in the collaboration network). The utilization of a tuple-space avoids the need for services to know the event ports for each event originating service.

The *instrumentation port* aims at establishing an open monitoring infrastructure based on coordinated monitoring agents which are specialized to guarantee the correct operation of the running services. This strategy is inspired by the existing monitoring infrastructures for communication systems, like the routers and switches. Network management applications can monitor system's behavior by accessing a management information base through the single network management protocol or using other open standards like the Java management extensions protocol and the corresponding managed Beans.

The associated *meta-data* is organized under two main groups: i) the information related to the infrastructure, and ii) the information related to the collaboration in the context of a collaborative network (Fig. 2). Both service information (meta-data) groups are organized in two sub groups: i) the acquaintance information holding the knowledge required by potential service clients and market-place to discover and select decision support, and ii) the self information addressing the infrastructure configuration requirements.

The open service framework (OSF) for collaboration among organizations is made of cooperative enabled services (CES) which are available from a market place. One important difference from existing approaches namely the cooperative processes defined by business process modeling notation (BPMN) where collaboration is associated to exchange of messages among organizations, is that the proposed framework considers the CES as public services available to participate in collaborative processes. A collaborative process is enacted on a collaborative network infrastructure, established by the proposed OSF. Furthermore, any service in one organization can access a CES in any other organization within the same collaborative network (CN). This means that all CESs, provided by different service providers within a CN, establish a basis for design of new specialized services, which can be developed and deployed as compositions of the base services available in the network. If the collaboration layer of a service has no defined information, it is considered a private service and as such it is not visible at the collaborative network level.

In such a service space at least one service must play the role of service repository, which might be implemented as an LDAP, JINI/Reggie, UDDI, ActiveDirectory or other directory service. To cooperate with other services, a service first looks up at the repository and selects the needed subset of services that are needed in order to generate a cooperative integrated solution (Fig. 2).

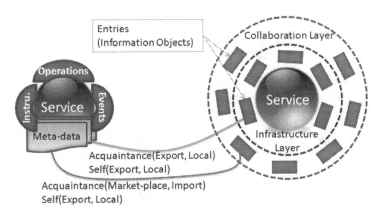

Fig. 2. Model of a service in a collaborative network

4   Open Collaborative Business Framework

Most existing ICT solutions are so far developed without embedding any capabilities to support their potential future integration with other solutions. This means that existing systems/applications are developed in response to specific functional and/or other requirements, following a software development process considering the completeness of the developed solution against the expected results. Even when solutions are based on open source, their considered criteria and advantage is on an eventual reduction of the total costs by significant reduction in their development-time and complexity as well as the run-time costs. Nevertheless, the costs associated to the extra development and configuration required for open source components may generate expensive solutions.

What is expected to contribute to the reduction of the total cost of ownership of integrated solutions is the approach of grounding the development of complex integrated solutions on a multi-vendor computational autonomous market place. This requires a new approach to service development and establishing a high level language able to abstract a multi-technology and multi-supplier computational infrastructure. In this line, the enterprise generation language (EGL) from IBM [11] is an example of the market recognition of the fact that something new is needed to cope with the complexity associated to the development of integrated solutions made of an evolving diverse set of resources, e.g. hardware, operating environments, specialized frameworks and systems. There is an ongoing discussion on the need for an additional language, however one thing has become accepted - there is a need for a new strategy to cope with the development of integrated solutions.

Beyond the shift to a model-driven development with or without a new language, the proposed service orientation can provide a strategic approach to evolve to *multi technology and multi-supplier integrated solutions*, as for example demonstrated in practice by the new service-oriented toll management system developed by the Portuguese Brisa company [12]. The Brisa's experience however has shown that so far software development companies are not yet prepared to develop solutions under a cooperation approach. Furthermore, the pressure for rapid innovation does not give enough time to consolidate approaches for complex critical systems, where the risks are a strong inhibitor to the adoption of open software development patterns.

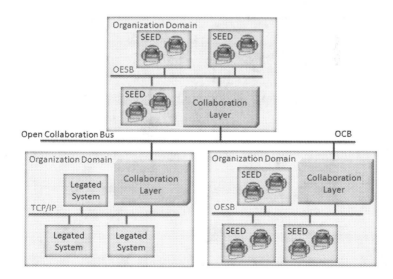

Fig. 3. The Collaboration Layer abstracting internal network organization's architecture

Therefore the proposed separation of contexts through collaboration layer, which was introduced above and illustrated in (Fig. 1), is important, considering that not all organizations are expected to internally evolve to adopt a uniform open enterprise service bus (Fig. 3).

While such evolving strategy is important for an increasing reutilization of already existing computational resources, it is up to the collaboration layer to establish the required collaborative ecosystem, making it possible to offer the integrated business services.

This above scenario suggests the assumption that an enterprise's information system might be at one of the following four possible stages: i) it presents a clear service oriented strategy considering it publishes its internal service through the OESB bus as a set of reusable resources (system and application services) to be considered by suppliers / developers of new services; ii) the enterprise is in the migration process and the enterprise service bus (OESB) only partially integrates its application systems, and thus through this bus it is not possible to access all the internal enterprise's systems; and iii) the enterprise is already organized in "islands of automation" while integrated applications are constructed on one-to-one specific protocols; a service bus was not introduced yet as a strategy to get integrated solutions on an open basis (Fig. 3). However the focus of this research is not the intra-enterprise information systems but rather its involvement in collaborative networks [4], [5] offering the integrated business services (Fig. 4).

The proposed strategy illustrate in (Fig. 4) above is to abstract the internal diversity of enterprises' information systems by considering only what is shared with others through the organizations' cooperation layer (CL). Therefore, the collaboration layer aims to play a proxy role, hiding the complexity of dealing with intra-enterprise systems and more important it is responsible to present a uniform view of each enterprise

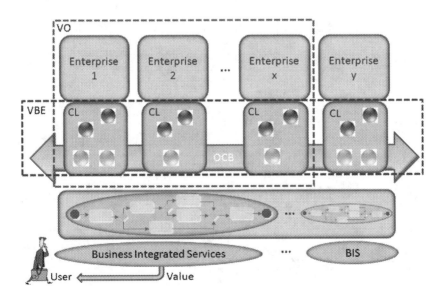

Fig. 4. Business Integrated Services Framework Reference Architecture

to all other participating organizations. It is clearly expected that a CL for a company that has not yet adopted the SOA approach is much more complex to develop than that for a company already owing an open service bus. For the SOA based company, the services in the CL might mainly address security issues and the management of resources needed to support the CN. On the other hand, for the monolithic systems company, there is a need for the services to implement proprietary protocols and interfaces to make the necessary resources available through the CL to the collaborating community. The CL is also an important element for the realization of the open collaboration bus (OCB) concept, considering that all published systems and application services are implemented into the CL of the participating companies (Fig. 4). In short, the collaboration layer (CL) of an enterprise is mainly responsible for the following:

i.   It manages all enterprise resources that are shared within the virtual organization breeding environment (VBE) of which the enterprise is a member, and which can be employed through the life cycle of virtual organizations (VO). Availability of these resources through the CL is a part of each enterprise's participation preparedness;

ii. All services that an enterprise publishes in the OCB are implemented in its collaboration layer, even if a simple forwarding to the effective service provider inside the company is necessary. The CL implements both the system services and the application services. As stated above, the system services are part of a specific OCB signature while the application services do not follow so rigid rules considering that they are not part of the OCB.

The integrated services offered by a collaborative network establish a number of new challenges from the ICT viewpoint considering their intrinsic complexity. On one hand, there is a need for holistic approaches - one collaborative process might require the involvement of systems from different organizations - and, on the other hand, the important requirement to maintain solutions as much as possible independent from a specific supplier is an important pre-condition for the success of such collaborative businesses.

5 Related Work

The definition of an ICT infrastructure able to support the complexity associated to the CNs is an open research topic. Research projects from diverse areas have attempted to tackle this problem but there is not yet a definite approach that can be considered agile and adaptive enough to receive a consensus as a reference strategy. The European integrated project ECOLEAD proposes that developing a plug-and-play horizontal ICT infrastructure (ICT-I) based on an open platform-independent specifications and ICT standards [13] can address this problem. With this approach potentially a collaborative business infrastructure (CBI) can be derived as an open service oriented infrastructure to support the collaborative tasks of CN members in the context of collaborative processes. The proposed approach lacks however a clear strategy on how to cope with the complexity associated to the distribution and vulnerabilities (fault-tolerance, reliability, security, coordination) considering that organization's information system infrastructures follow different development and operation cultures. Our proposed collaboration layer aims to concentrate on the same reference architectural entity to resolve such diversities and embed the necessary coordination mechanisms, able to answer scalability and dependability requirements.

Other works more centered in the area of computer science and computer engineering, are focused on developing an open ICT infrastructure for the inter-organizational space, and can be exemplified by the case of NESSI, the European Technology Platform dedicated to Software and Services [14]. Another common strategy is to consider a centralized architecture as it can be exemplified by the case of the collaborative infrastructure for collaborative genetics experiences; the e-infrastructure to support collaborative embryo research [15]. The strategy might be acceptable for collaborative research and some other application domains but the integrated business service concept requires a federated approach considering that each organization holds its own culture, processes and technology, and thus the collaboration layer proposed in our research work is grounded on the participation of diverse independent and autonomous nodes. Strategic roadmaps on ICT and ageing as those being developed by the ePAL and BRAID projects [16] also require a new approach for service integration.

5 Conclusions

This paper proposes a collaborative network approach to the development of the integrated business service concept. The research work is grounded on the acquired experience with already deployed business solutions requiring the participation of multiple stakeholders considering a single contract for the end users. The case of the Portuguese Via-Verde, initially developed for the tolling service and now extended to payments in parking areas and gas stations, provides a practical guiding background. Another important example is the provision of care services to elderly by multiple stakeholders.

One important aspect is the federative characteristic considering that organizations have their own process and technological culture what recalls for a strategy that guarantees their independence while committed to the collaborative network. In our proposed approach, it is up to the collaboration layer to support and implement mechanisms able to execute the collaborative processes underlying the business models associated to the offered integrated business services. One additional complexity addressed by our approach is the need for global coordination of the participating autonomous computational services which run on distributed and heterogeneous computational platforms. This second complexity is outside the scope of this paper and will be addressed in forthcoming papers. Furthermore, dependability considering security, reliability, fault tolerance, scalability from other quality issues, are complex requirements that need to be addressed in future and guaranteed in such federated collaborative network. The solution approach, must be balanced considering key issues from technology to process and the business levels, and requires a clear modeling framework and innovative mechanisms contributing to the development of collaborative solutions for collaborative network businesses.

Acknowledgements

This work was partially supported by BRISA Innovation and Technology company through a research and development project, and by the European Commission through the FP7 BRAID (grant agreement ICT-2009-7.1 2484852) project.

References

1. Laskey, K., et al.: Reference Architecture Foundation for Service Oriented Architecture Version 1.0. Public Review Draft 2 (October 14, 2009)
2. Zhang, L.-J.: IEEE EIC Editorial: Introduction to the Body of Knowledge Areas of Services Computing. IEEE Trans. on Services Computing 1(2) (April-June 2008)
3. Camarinha-Matos, L.M., Afsarmanesh, H., Ollus, M.: ECOLEAD And CNO Base Concepts. In: Methods and Tools for Collaborative Networked Organizations, May 9, pp. 3–32. Springer, Heidelberg (2008)
4. Afsarmanesh, H., Camarinha-Matos, L.M.: A Framework for Management of Virtual Organization Breeding Environments. In: Collaborative Network and Their Breeding Environments, vol. 186, pp. 35–48. Springer, Heidelberg (2005)
5. Camarinha-Matos, L.M., Afsarmanesh, H.: The Emerging Discipline of Collaborative Networks. In: Virtual Enterprises and Collaborative Networks, vol. 149, pp. 3–16. Springer, Heidelberg (2004)
6. Afsarmanesh, H., Camarinha-Matos, L.M.: Ermilova, Ekaterina: VBE Reference Framework. In: Methods and Tools for Collaborative Networked Organizations, pp. 35–68. Springer, New York (2008)
7. Nikolaou, C., Marina, B.: Towards a Theory of Emergent Service Value Networks - and an Application, in an e-Learning Service Economy in FET Proactive Workshop on Objective IST-2007.8.4. In: The Science of Complex Systems for Socially Intelligent ICT Complexity Research Projects Forum, ECCS 2007 Dresden, October 6 (2007)
8. Rolland, C., Nurcan, S., Grosz, G.: A unified framework for modeling co-operative design processes and co-operative business processes. In: The Proceedings of the 31st Annual Int. Conf. on System Sciences, Big Island, Hawaii, USA, January 6-9 (1998)
9. Troncoso, C., Danezis, G., Kosta, E., Preneel, B.: PriPAYD: Privacy Friendly Pay-As-You-Drive Insurance in Workshop on Privacy in the Electronic Society - WPES 2007, Alexandria, VA, USA, October 29 (2007)
10. Osório, A.L., Camarinha-Matos, L.M., Gomes, J.S.: A Collaborative Networks case study: The extended "ViaVerde" toll payment system. In: PRO-VE 2005 Valencia – Spain, Collaborative Networks and their Breeding Environments, September 26-28, pp. 559–568. Springer, Heidelberg (2005)
11. Margolis, B.: IBM Rational Business Developer with EGL. MC Press (June 2008)
12. Osório, A.L., Camarinha-Matos, L.M.: Towards a Distributed Process Execution Platform for Collaborative Networks. In: 7th IFIP Int. Conf. on Information Technology for Balanced Automation Systems in Manufacturing, Ontario, Canada, September 4-6 (2006)
13. Rabelo, R.: Advanced Collaborative Business ICT Infrastructures. In: Methods and Tools for Collaborative Networked Organizations, pp. 337–370. Springer, Heidelberg (2008)
14. Nikolov, R., Ilieva, S.: Building a research university ecosystem: the case of software engineering education at Sofia University. In: Proceedings of the the 6th Joint Meeting of the European Software Engineering Conference and the ACM SIGSOFT Symposium on The Foundations of Software Engineering, pp. 491–500 (2007)
15. Barker, A., Hemert, J.I., van Baldock, R.A., Atkinson, M.P.: An Infrastructure to Support Collaborative Embryo Research. In: Proceedings of the 2009 9th IEEE/ACM Int. Symposium on Cluster Computing and the Grid, pp. 520–525 (2009)
16. Camarinha-Matos, L.M., Afsarmanesh, H.: The Need for a Strategic R&D Roadmap for Active Ageing. In: Proceedings of PRO-VE 2009, Thessaloniki, Greece, Leveraging Knowledge for Innovation in Collaborative Networks, October 7-9, pp. 669–680. Springer, Heidelberg (2009)

Service Entities
in Manufacturing Networks

Rubén Darío Franco, Rosa Navarro Varela,
Angel Ortiz Bas, and Pedro Gomez-Gasquet

Research Centre on Production Management and Engineering
Universidad Politécnica de Valencia
{dfranco,ronava,aortiz,pgomez}@cigip.upv.es

Abstract. Service Entities have been proposed as a relevant approach that may help to support structural and functional Collaborative Networks modeling and deployment, especially when they are engineered inside Virtual Breeding Environments. This work is intended to explore the suitability of such approach to next-generation manufacturing networks. By means of a supporting case, the paper identifies main service entities of the problem domain, exemplifies how service interfaces can be defined and how can they be used to compose abstract collaborative processes definitions.

Keywords: Service Entities, Collaborative Manufacturing Networks.

1 Introduction

Virtual Breeding Environments enhance the effectiveness and rapidness of Virtual Organizations creation and operation [4]. In achieving such goals, it is necessary to design and implement a new kind of systems which can be able of managing both VBE and VO Life Cycles in a consistent and integrated way. The so-called **VBE Management Systems** are expected to fully support the creation, operation and dissolution of Virtual Organizations, by defining a set of reference models (at structural, functional or behavioral level, to name few of them) that must be adopted by VBE/VO participants when they are willing to be involved in emerging collaboration opportunities [9].

Manufacturing networks are clear manifestations of those VBEs where spot collaboration opportunities may usually appear. But, in order to fully take advantage of them, next-generation management systems need to be designed and implemented, by combining relevant previous developments [5] with most recent technological developments.

This work represents the first step in building that kind of systems since the approach here introduced is intended to combine architectural principles of Enterprise Integration [6] with fundamental principles of Service Oriented Architectures.

The work has been structured as follows. In Section 2, a short introduction to basic concepts is given; Services Entities concepts and their life cycle are also briefly described. In Section 3, supported by a running case, suitability of Service Entities

Á. Ortiz Bas, R.D. Franco, P. Gómez Gasquet (Eds.): BASYS 2010, IFIP AICT 322, pp. 92–99, 2010.

approach for manufacturing networks is analysed. Finally, in Section 4, main conclusions and further research needs are envisioned.

2 Main Concepts and Motivation

2.1 Virtual Breeding Environments and Virtual Organizations

Collaboration between partners is a preferred way to ensure optimal resource balance and to get perdurable benefits [1]. Time of preparation and difficulty of launching a Virtual Organization will increase in the same proportion as the number of potential partners and complexity of collaborative processes to be carried out.

Virtual Breeding Environments [2] are intended to harmonize the preparedness level of involved organizations while, at the same time, a collaborative infrastructure is deployed in order to deal with interoperability problems at different levels: communications, data, services, processes or business [3].

In VBEs, the main idea is to restrict the number of potential participants by drawing a border to the open universe and allowing some partners to come inside. Those partners have to agree on common operating principles: business semantics, strategies or goals, distributed business processes management practices or even common ICT tools. Being inside the border reduces uncertainty between partners, basic to share information and to reach their common objectives. Rapidness and flexibility in VO preparation and launching are requirements that any VBE management system must accomplish.

2.2 Service Entities

Service Entities (SE) have been defined as the result of logically grouping a finite series of web-oriented business services interfaces which, given its functionality and performance, enable interaction (making requests) with a specific conceptual entity (e.g., bank, supplier, factory, etc.) from an interorganizational network or a working team [7].

SEs have been proposed as basic modelling constructs for Collaborative Networked Organizations [8], for both the Structural and Functional dimensions. As they have been defined, a single Service Entity is the result of logically tying together:

- A finite set of business services interfaces which jointly defines the expected behaviour of those conceptual entities involved into the domain being modelled and,
- A finite set of attributes which will allow characterize and distinguish between them.

2.3 Abstract Service Entities (ASEs)

Abstract Service Entities are generic constructive blocks used to model different 'types' of entities that are present in the problem domain under study. For example, in manufacturing networks context, the ASE concept may be used to define and represent the generic characteristics and services of: factories, suppliers, plants, warehouses, subcontractors, transport companies, lines, sections, or, in general, the different types of resources that will be part of the final model.

ASEs are not associated with any specific instance of the entity defining it. They not only represent the abstract definition of the series of attributes which may characterize the Entity, but also the specifications of the electronic services interfaces which are defined by each Entity.

If Transport entities, like trucks, are identified within the problem domain to be modeled, they could be defined as an Abstract Services Entity named as Truck which contemplates the attributes and services required to identify them and to discover their electronic behavior.

2.4   Concrete Service Entities (CSE)

ASEs may be used in the Design Specification phase to model the problem, but without referring any specific resource to be used. However, as for wishing to support the execution, it is necessary to consider that the activities involved in the processes are carried out by specific requests from the various entities that have been modeled.

These requests are provided by Concrete Service Entities (CSE). The CSE creation process is known as Instancing and leads to specific occurrences of a particular ASE. This explicitly implies that the new entity created must have values which fill the empty ASE structure from which it originates: that is, to give values to the attributes and implementations to their network services.

Therefore, the attributes defined in the ASE will now take the specific values of that particular entity (a machine number, a warehouse identifier, etc.), and the corresponding electronic services will also have an implementation that is typical of the Entity; access to these services, and the request for them to be executed, will be via web.

2.5   Service Entities Life Cycle

As defined, Service Entities will also have their own lifecycle. In Figure 1, it is possible to identify some of their main activities.

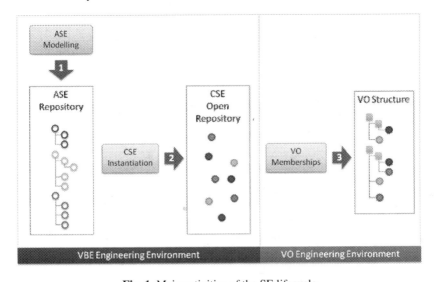

Fig. 1. Main activities of the SE lifecycle

At their first stage, ASE must be modelled into the VBE Engineering Environment (Figure 1, Step 1). At this stage, and as in the object orientation paradigm, ASE may be refined or generalized as needed. In this way, each specific VBE will count with a repository of ASE that will be used during the instantiation process (Figure 1, Step 2). During the instantiation process, CSE are registered in an Open Repository which can be, later on, accessed from the VO Engineering Environment. This instantiation process provides the membership applicants with the service interfaces that they ought to locally deploy and integrate at level.

From now on, they are prepared to be involved into as many VOs as they can be granted to be (Figure 1, step 3).

3   Service Entities Modeling in Manufacturing Networks

An experiment carried out for the purpose of applying the ASE and CSE concepts to the modeling and coordination of manufacturing network processes is now introduced.

First, a description of the manufacturing network and the main manufacturing process characteristics will be given. Then, how modeling the SEs has been done in this scenario will be shown. Finally, a component of the Technological Platform which will support the network Production Planning process will be described, this being a ASE/CSE-based manufacturing processes editor.

3.1   Description of a Manufacturing Network

The Manufacturing/Supply Network on which this study is based is made up of a series of actors from the automobile sector. The company with which the case is developed (a manufacturer) is, at the same time, a first-tier supplier as it directly supplies the OEM, and is also a second-tier supplier as it supplies components to the second-tier suppliers. Both the OEM and the first-tier suppliers, and in some cases other end clients, are those which generate demand for the manufacturer and, for the purposes of this case, they only play this role with which the references made to finished products, half-finished products, or raw materials actually refer to those originating from the manufacturer (in this case, Molding).

At the same time, the manufacturer not only relates to suppliers of raw materials (RM), which are other second-tier (or third-tier) suppliers, but also to subcontractors to manufacture the ordered products. Finally, the network counts on various logistics operators to move the RM, half-finished products, and finished products.

The manufacturing process starts by receiving RM (spools of steel) in the manufacturer's warehouse. According to the Production Plan, the spools of steel are transported (internally) to the Molding area where a first operation is carried out. There are two possibilities at this stage: a readily available finished product (which will be sent to the Client and, also in accordance with the Production Plan), or a half-finished product, in which case it will remain in the warehouse until required. Once again in accordance with the Production Plan, and for this particular case, the process requires a welding operation which is subcontracted. The Logistics Operator is in charge of transporting the half-finished products between the manufacturer and the subcontractor.

Once this part of the process has been completed, the half-finished product returns to the manufacturer's warehouse where other operations are carried out (washing, oiling, labeling, etc.) until the finished product is made which the Logistics Operator is in charge of transporting to the client's facilities.

From the planning and control perspective of the Manufacturer's Production Department operations, internal processes could be efficiently monitored. However, when the manufacturing process would need to mobilize half-finished products (WIP) to subcontractors, difficulties would arise in the visibility and control of the operations. Furthermore, the company would be starting to increase its production volume and, as a result, would also increase the need to resort to contracting additional productive capacity.

3.2 Modeling Service Entities

The following approach has been based on the use of Service Entities as constructive elements which could provide solutions to this kind of problems from an integrated business and technology point of view.

After first analyzing the Manufacturing/Supply Network, three types of main ASE were identified (see Fig. 2):

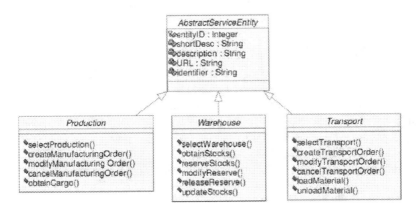

Fig. 2. Main ASEs in a manufacturing network

– **Productive** entities: those in charge of totally or partially transforming some reference. In the case of this network, both the Molding section and the subcontractor are examples of productive entities.

– **Warehouse** entities: destined to store both finished and half-finished products in the network domain. In the example, even though others existed, only the stocks of one warehouse belonging to the manufacturer would be considered.

– **Transport** entities: these are in charge of moving materials from any possible combination of the two aforementioned entities both internally and externally.

In this case, there are two transport entities: the Logistic Operator and Internal Transport. For each of these entities, the main attributes were defined and a preliminary design of their services was done.

If we start with this ASE definition, it is possible to rapidly define the manufacturing network structure by making a request (CSE, Concrete Service entities) for each node by assigning values to its attributes. By way of example:

- ASEProductive = {''Molding'', ''Subcontractor''}
- ASEWarehouse = {''WarehouseManufacturer''}
- ASETransport = {''LogisticOperator'', ''InternalTransport''}

One direct benefit that this approach offers is that it is possible to vary the network structure, if it were necessary. For example, should the idea be to incorporate new subcontractors, suppliers of RM or Logistics Operators, all that needs to be done is to use the same request process and register for each new node.

Having defined the structural aspects, we now go on to analyze how ASEs contribute to facilitate the interoperability in the extended processes domain.

As previously mentioned, each ASE possesses a ''homogenized'' series of services interfaces, $S = \{s1, s2,..., sn\}$, which may encompass different business activities (or processes) when they are called upon. These services interfaces are defined generically for the ASEs and they are specified for each CSE, depending on each node's requirements.

In the example, the ''Logistics Operator'' and the ''Internal Transport'' transport entities, which are requests of the same Transport ASE, share the same service interface (s = ''createTransportOrder()'') intended to receive the order to organize the transport of the materials involved. What varies in each case is the **implementation** of this service, that is, the way in which each implementation is carried out. For one entity it will mean a simple internal warehouse operation to the Molding section, while for the other it will involve transferring half-finished products from the Manufacturer to the Subcontractor.

Having defined the entity's services, the interfaces are implemented in a corporate computer (or similar) with Web capacities. At this stage, the link with the internal information systems of each node is created.

With a subsequent request, the extended processes are modeled as an orchestration of the activations of the services which the various participating ASE/CSE may supply. For instance, Fig. 3 depicts a simplified representation of the reserveStocks() service of a warehouse-type entity.

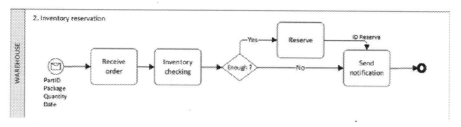

Fig. 3. Business service example of inventory reservation in Warehouse ASEs

After the extended processes model has been created, the interface may be used to define, for example, that a Productive Entity requests a Warehouse to reserve the stocks of a given material. In this way, the following representation would be obtained (see Fig. 4):

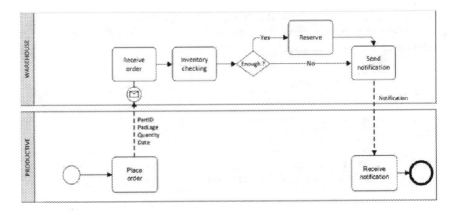

Fig. 4. Process models in manufacturing networks may use ASE Services

From the network processes management viewpoint, the second interesting aspect of this study, this approach is also very useful for solving the interoperability problems at this level.

If the process has been modeled with the services of an ASE, any of the concrete requests of this type (CSE) which was registered **could provide the network with the execution of this service**.

4   Conclusions and Further Research

The main goal of this study has been to explore the suitability of the Service Entities approach for manufacturing networks support.

As it has been presented, service entities modeling seems to be a promising approach when engineering next-generation manufacturing ecosystems. By means of abstract service entities and concrete instances implementing each business service interface, partners involved in a manufacturing network can be easily integrated into the collaborative processes execution.

Since ASEs modeling and CSE intantiation is just a first step in the whole process of creating manufacturing ecosystems, next research actions will cover a fully implemented scenario where collaborative manufacturing processes can be tested and validated.

Additionally, authors are working in a fully functional platform that will be used as ecosystem management system for those manufacturing networks.

References

[1] Jagdev, H.S., Thoben, K.: Anatomy of enterprise collaborations. Production Planning & Control 12, 437–451 (2001)
[2] Camarinha-Matos, L.M., Afsarmanesh, H.: Collaborative networks: a new scientific discipline. Journal of Intelligent Manufacturing 16, 439–452 (2005)
[3] Ruggaber, R.: ATHENA-Advanced Technologies for Interoperability of Heterogeneous Enterprise Networks and their Applications. In: Interoperability of Enterprise Software and Applications, pp. 460–463. Springer, London (2006)

[4] Camarinha-Matos, L., Afsarmanesh, H.: A comprehensive modeling framework for collaborative networked organizations. Journal of Intelligent Manufacturing 18, 529–542 (2007)
[5] Ni, Q., Lu, W.F., Yarlagadda, P.K., Ming, X.: A collaborative engine for enterprise application integration. Computers in Industry 57, 640–652 (2006)
[6] Kosanke, K., Vernadat, F., Zelm, M.: CIMOSA: enterprise engineering and integration. Computers in Industry 40, 83–97 (1999)
[7] Franco, R., Ortiz Bas, Á., Lario Esteban, F.: Modeling extended manufacturing processes with service-oriented entities. Service Business 3, 31–50 (2009)
[8] Franco, R., Ortiz Bas, Á., Prats, G., Navarro, R.: Supporting Structural and Functional Collaborative Networked Organizations Modeling with Service Entities, IFIP Advances in Information and Communication Technology. In: Leveraging Knowledge for Innovation in Collaborative Networks, vol. 307, pp. 547–554 (2009)
[9] Ecolead, D21.1 Characterization of Key Components, Features and Operating Principles of the Virtual Breeding Environments (2005), http://www.ve-forum.org/projects/284/Deliverables/d21_1_vbe.pdf

Towards Eco-efficient Lean Production Systems

Francisco Moreira, Anabela C. Alves, and Rui M. Sousa

Production and Systems Engineering Department
University of Minho, Campus of Azurém, 4800-058 Guimarães, Portugal
fmoreira@dps.uminho.pt, anabela@dps.uminho.pt, rms@dps.uminho.pt

Abstract. Lean Production has proved itself a worthwhile production strategy in many distinct industries across all regions of the planet by achieving higher levels of production efficiency. Several authors identified that Lean inadvertently has had significant environmental gains. Such achievements are considered of special relevance in a global and highly competitive economy which is progressively both tied-up and driven by an environmental agenda. The main goal of the present study is to enlighten the contribution of Lean for achieving a better environmental performance of production systems and identify this as an emergent business model for supporting eco-efficiency.

1 Introduction

Lean is a world leading production strategy that has proved its worthiness in industrial environments over a long period of time. It worked well when mass production was predominant by delivering goods in an affordable way. Lean ultimately outpaced it when costumers begun to change their needs and demanded increasingly customized and high quality products at competitive costs. More recently, new issues have been raised to the agenda and companies begun to rethink their purpose and strategies, so that more value could be added while contributing to social equity and preventing environmental burdens. Lean is a production strategy whose fundamental principles drive the industry towards a more effective production of goods and services. The eco-efficiency concept is primary to sustainable development and intends to provide more value with less environmental impact. This could be regarded, as "doing more with less" which is a well known saying in Lean Thinking. This is translated into operational terms by a systematic and continuous elimination of waste. However, Lean methods seem not to explore nor put much emphasis on environmental gains, nor in quantifying them. Does Lean make in fact a positive contribution towards greener production of goods and services? Could Lean Production benefit from a more clear endorsement of environmental issues?

The aim of this study is to identify and explore the contributions of Lean to reduce environmental impacts that naturally result from industrial activity. This is accomplished through a literature review followed by a critical discussion.

2 Literature Review

2.1 Lean Production

The Lean Production concept was coined in 1988 by Krafcik [1], based in TPS-Toyota Production System [2] and was widely disseminated by several projects of the

Á. Ortiz Bas, R.D. Franco, P. Gómez Gasquet (Eds.): BASYS 2010, IFIP AICT 322, pp. 100–108, 2010.

IMVP-MIT program [3], [4, [5]. The reason for this interest in the Japanese automotive industry was the excellent set of results achieved by the Toyota factories, since the oil crises in 1973, in designing and building cars in less time with fewer people and lower inventories. TPS is based on principles and techniques of Just-in-Time (JIT) production and on continuous improvement - "Kaizen" [6], [7]. Lean Production aims to achieve, for a large diversity of products, high productivity and, simultaneously, synchronization of production and demand. To attain these objectives, five principles were established: (i) create value for the customer, (ii) identify the value stream, (iii) create flow, (iv) produce only what is pulled by the customer, and (v) pursuing the perfection by continuous identification and elimination of waste. These principles are part of the Lean Thinking concept [4] which is focused on waste, or "muda", elimination. Waste is everything that does not directly contributes for adding value to a product, under the perspective of customers' needs and requirements, being identified seven main types: defects, inventory, over-processing, waiting, motion, transportation and overproduction. Overproduction means produce more than the demand, and, probably, is the worst waste due to its implications, e.g. overstaffing and excessive inventory, along with the associated costs. Due to their visibility, usually the defects are easily identified (by inspection) within the manufacturing process. They are the major concern of any quality department and may imply rework (if the defective parts can be fixed) or disposal (if the defects are unrecoverable). Inventory means raw material, WIP (Work In Process), or finished goods spread all over the shop-floor and warehouses, frequently hiding real problems like production imbalances, suppliers that do not accomplish the deliveries' due dates, long setup times, defects and machines breakdowns. This causes longer lead times, risk of obsolescence and/or deterioration of goods, transportation and storage costs, and delays. Over-processing, or incorrect processing, is another kind of waste, resulting from unnecessary or incorrectly processed operations due to wrong methods or inadequate tools. The main consequences are the potential occurrence of defects and the waste of time and material. The waiting waste happens when operators are stopped waiting for parts, machines or other colleagues. Motion and transportation are associated to operators' movements and transport of materials, respectively. Besides the previously referred wastes, Liker [8] considers an additional type: unused operators' creativity. When properly stimulated, operators can improve, better than anyone, the process they are working on. In fact, the creative thinking was pointed out by TPS as one of its pillars [2].

2.2 Eco-efficiency

Back in 1991, the Business Council for Sustainable Development (BCSD) coined the term eco-efficiency while preparing a document that would serve as an input for the Earth Summit held in Rio de Janeiro in 1992. The eco-efficiency concept was first published in 1992 by Stephan Schmidheiny and BCSD in the book "Changing Course". The World Commission on Environment and Development (WCED) refers that eco-efficiency was sought to encapsulate the business goal of promoting sustainable development, i.e. a development model that meets present human needs without compromising wealth of future generations [9]. According to BCSD, eco-efficiency is "The delivery of competitively priced goods and services that satisfy human needs and bring quality of life, while progressively reducing ecological impact and resource intensity throughout the life cycle, to a level at least in line with the Earth's estimated carrying capacity." [10]. The concept was envisaged after recognition that the growth in human population, associated with the strong environment impact of their activity, threatens the future of new generations of human beings and of other species. Eco-efficiency concept translates the simple idea of "creating more with less" by: (i) reducing materials intensity; (ii) minimizing energy intensity in both products and services; (iii) reducing the quantity and the dispersion of toxic substances and decreasing the level of toxicity of such substances; (iv) promoting recycling and the use of renewable energy; (v) extending the durability of products, and; (vi) increasing service intensity. Akin to eco-efficiency is the need to provide genuine goods and services that consumers truly treasure and fully benefit while minimizing the full environmental impact, i.e. the impacts resulting from resources origins to product disposal. This might be regarded as a full perspective of the impact of such goods and services, from a cradle-to-grave perspective [11]. Eco-efficiency uses both a recurrent step-by-step process improvement and a radical innovation process, and can be applied to products and processes. Industrial symbiosis is also stimulated so that aggregated impacts (multiple companies) are lowered. Eco-efficiency concept has been disseminated through the works of the WBCSD (World Business Council for Sustainable Development). This coalition gathers contributions from about 200 international companies from about 20 major industrial sectors.

Several other contributions, akin to eco-efficiency concept, have been made in the past by many other individuals and organizations. For the purpose of this paper, those contributions were considered to be aligned to eco-efficiency goals, and, should be regarded as an aggregated body of concepts that push forward the vision of progressing mankind footprint. These other contributions, such as works and concepts, will be shortly referred and presented next.

United Nations Environment Programme (UNEP) launched their Cleaner Production Programme in 1989, and intended "the continuous application of an integrated preventive environmental strategy applied to processes, products and services to reduce risks to humans and the environment" [12]. This was partnered by United Nations Industrial Development Organization (UNIDO) from 1994 onwards and has resulted in the establishment of multiple country-wide Clean Production Programmes. WBSCD and UNEP recognize that eco-efficiency and cleaner production programme are complementary, and reinforce mutually while sharing the same goal of sustainable development [13].

Weizsäcker [14] describe a world of waste and propose an efficiency cure. McDonough and Braungart [15], authors of the Cradle-to-Cradle concept, expressed the need for an emerging and novel industrial revolution, one that might be grounded on both human creativity and cooperation, and on natures' design effectiveness. According to these authors, consumers, environmentalists and industry, have long time antagonistic perspectives: conventional industrial processes (extraction, production, disposal), along with a never ending demand for economic growth, have been regarded as highly damaging to the ecosystems; environment defenders represent often an obstacle to production and growth; consumers have difficulty to restrain their increasing consumption behavior. They acknowledge that "most industrial processes are unintentionally depletive" and that *crude products,* i.e. "...products that are not designed particularly for human and ecological health are unintelligent and inelegant", persist in our daily life as outcomes of outdated and unintelligent design. These authors propose a new eco-effectiveness concept for, more than progressing present status, making a radical change in the way products are designed, produced and used.

Other concepts, such as: Industrial Ecology, Green Production, Sustainable Engineering, Design for the Environment, Industrial Metabolism, among others, seem targeted at making a positive contribution to sustainable development.

2.3 Lean and Green

The creativity stimulus and the continuous improvement have an important role in promoting a culture of pursuing perfection. The companies that embrace this culture

Table 1. Publications about Lean and Green relationship

Date	Authors	Publication title
1993	Maxwell et al.	"Does lean mean green?: The implications of lean production for environmental management"
1996	Florida, R.	"Lean and green: the move to environmentally conscious manufacturing"
1997	Helper et al.	Can Green be Lean?
1998	Maxwell et al.	Case study: Honda of America Manufacturing, Inc.: Can lean production practices increase environmental performance?
1999	Pojasek, R.	Quality toolbox: Five S's: A tool that prepares an organization for change.
1999	Pojasek, R.	Quality toolbox: Poka-yoke and zero waste
1999	Pojasek, R.	Quality toolbox: Zeroing in
1999	Waldrip, G.	Integrating the Elements of Sustainable Manufacturing
2000	Wlodarczyk et al.	Using a systems approach to improve process and environmental performance
2000	U.S. EPA	Pursuing perfection: Case studies examining lean manufacturing strategies, pollution prevention, and environmental regulatory management implications.
2000	Klassen, R.D.	Just-in-time manufacturing and pollution prevention generate mutual benefits in the furniture industry.
2001	Rothenberg et al.	Lean, green, and the quest for superior environmental performance.
2002	Soltero and Waldrip	Using Kaizen to Reduce Waste and Prevent Pollution
2003	U.S. EPA	Lean manufacturing and the environment: Research on advanced manufacturing systems and the environment and recommendations for leveraging better environmental performance.
2004	Larson and Greenwood	Perfect Complements: Synergies between Lean Production and Eco-Sustainability Initiatives
2007	U.S. EPA	The Lean and Environment Toolkit
2008	U.S. EPA	The Lean and Energy Toolkit
2008	Pojasek, R. B.	Quality Toolbox: Framing your Lean-to-Green effort
2009	Found, P.	Lean and Low Environmental Impact Manufacturing
2010	Yang et al.	Mediated effect of environmental management on manufacturing competitiveness: An empirical study

are always aware to find the wastes referred in section 2.1, in all their activities. So, it is natural that besides these wastes several others had been identified, such as excessive use of energy and materials [16], and emissions of pollutants into the air, water and land [17]. Nevertheless the efforts to reduce waste should be associated not only to the production process, but also to the product design "...a vehicle that can make the air cleaner than it is..." *and* "In my vision for the future, the most important themes are the environment, energy,..." (Toyota president, cited in [18]. According to the literature, Lean implementations seem to, unintentionally, reveal interesting environmental performances, while its methods resemble environmental management systems [17] which have been published at least since 1993, as shown in Table 1.

Several individual authors and organizations have researched the relationship between Lean and environmental performance - eco-efficiency, as the authors put it - starting in 1993, just a year after the eco-efficiency concept was disseminated. The issue was therefore subject of reflection for about two decades. The 1990s is not as much as rich on publications on the subject as it is the second decade of 2000s. Lean paradigm concept dissemination to Western economies had a great impulse after the first IMVP publications on the subject after 1990. This explains the early works, published not long time after, which attempted to relate Lean to environmental impacts. Some other publications about Lean Production, like [16], even without formally address the mentioned relationship, refers the energy waste as something to eliminate. On the other hand, publications in journals like Business Strategy and Environment [19], [20], [21] or Corporate Social Responsibility and Environmental Management, have appealed to a urgent need to implement management policies or to create sustainable supply chains that promotes best practices in environment [22].

3 Discussion

Based in Lean industrial case studies and in principles and methods akin to Lean Production, most studies refer that Lean continuously improves resource productivity, therefore decreasing products' intensity in both materials and energy (two fundamental aspects of eco-efficiency). Although not specifically addressed, it seems rather logic that dispersion of toxic substances is generally improved, deriving from lower use of raw materials. In terms of improvements in the levels of toxicity of substances used, the review is not conclusive. The EPA (Environmental Protection Agency) report, dated 2003 [17], suggests that Lean might not be addressing adequately such issue. Design for manufacturing method was spotted a potential source for improving recyclability levels, since it normally results in lower number of different materials used. Along with materials type identification and marks to facilitate dismantling, this would easy materials separation and dismantling tasks at end-of-life.

Overall, there is strong evidence that the scientific community holds a positive opinion on the real impact of Lean on improved environmental performance of production systems. This is particularly truth for continuous improvement culture and waste reduction. Figure 1 illustrates, by way of a cause-effect diagram (Ishikawa diagram), the origins and implications of waste within production systems.

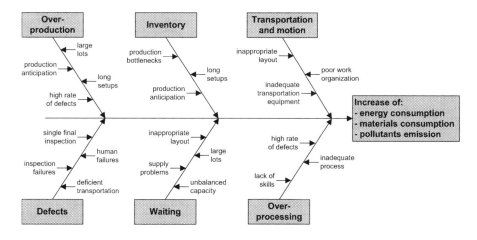

Fig. 1. Production wastes as causes of weak environmental performance

This diagram (Figure 1) includes the main causes of each type of waste providing thus valuable hints on how to reduce them. For example, the reduction of equipments' setup time (by applying the SMED methodology – Single Minute Exchange of Die) contributes to reduce both overproduction and inventory. These reductions naturally lower the energy and materials consumption while reducing the emissions. Figure 2 show the main effects of each production waste.

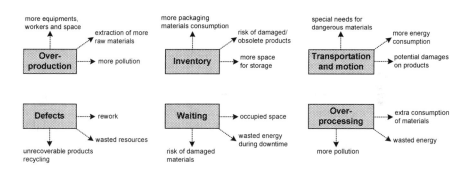

Fig. 2. Effects of the production wastes

All the consequences resulted from the 6 waste types, illustrated in figure 2, can be detailed within the previous classes of environmental impact, namely: energy use, materials consumption and emissions (Figure 1). For example, supplementary energy is required to produce the extra products which are above the required quantity (overproduction), thus resulting in added energy for: (i) extraction and conversion of natural resources into raw material; (ii) transportation of the raw materials to the shop floor; and, (iii) processing of the raw materials into the extra products at the shop floor. While the third consequence is positioned at the second stage of the products' life-cycle (production) and derives directly from overproduction, the first two are secondary (or indirect) consequences to the problem of overproduction, and are positioned within the first stage of products' life-cycle (extraction and processing of raw materials). Naturally most of environmental effects are consequence of more than one production waste. In fact, all production wastes have a direct or indirect impact on each of the three sub-classes of effects represented in Figure 1. In order to map such impacts and to improve the environmental performance some authors have been adapting some Lean Production tools, such as Five S, Poka-Yoke mechanisms, Kaizen, Visual Stream Mapping [23], [24], [25], US-EPA, 2007, US-EPA, 2008.

Some examples have been found that negatively contrast Lean against environmental performance, namely by improved quality and durability by way of using more toxic chemicals to ensure higher rust-proofing [26], and the use of more frequent trips for delivery of materials [27] which result in increased Greenhouse Gas (GHG) emissions. Wider implications of Lean improvements within full products' life-cycle seem not yet fully studied and understood. LCA impact assessment is for that purpose suggested [28].

4   Conclusion

A literature review has been conducted to investigate the causal relationship between Lean Production and eco-efficiency, i.e. the use of a specific production strategy for achieving superior environmental performance. Several individual authors and organizations have researched this relationship in the last two decades. The studies are essentially based on industrial case studies and on conceptual relationships given Lean principles and methods. Few environmental drawbacks that can be attributed to Lean production were found in literature. On the other hand, most of the studies that found a causal relation between Lean and Eco-efficient production systems are highly positive in their findings, resulting in strong evidence that Lean has in fact a positive contribution in the improvement of the environmental performance. This contribution is done in a multitude of aspects, both in direct and secondary forms. Although relevant, the positive contribution was identified to be non-intentional or at least not strategic, since the DNA pattern of Lean methods was not identified within this contribution, i.e. it is not reported, neither clearly measured nor specifically addressed. In terms of future research, the authors intend to progress further the research on the Lean-to-Green relationship and to adapt Lean Production tools to promote production cleanliness.

References

1. Holweg, M.: The genealogy of Lean Production. Journal of Operations Management 25(2007), 420–437 (2007)
2. Monden, Y.: Toyota Production System - an integrated approach to just-in-time, 3rd edn. Engineering and Management Press, Institute of Industrial Engineers (1998)
3. Womack, J., Jones, D., Roos, D.: The machine that changed the world. Rawson Associates (1990)
4. Womack, J., Jones, D.: Lean Thinking. Siman & Schuster, New York (1996)

5. Womack, J.: Lean solutions: how companies and costumers can create value and wealth together. Simon & Schuster, London (2005)
6. Imai, M.: KAIZEN - the key to Japan's Competitive Success. McGraw-Hill, Irwin (1986)
7. Imai, M.: Gemba Kaizen: a common sense low-cost approach to management. McGraw-Hill, New York (1997)
8. Liker, J.: The Toyota Way: 14 Management Principles from the World's Greatest Manufacturer. McGraw -Hill, New York (2004)
9. WCED, Our Common Future. Report of the World Commission on Environment and Development, United Nations (1987),
   http://worldinbalance.net/intagreements/1987-brundtland.php
   (accessed February 20, 2010)
10. WBCSD, Eco-Efficiency and Cleaner Production: Charting the course to sustainability (1996)
11. Hendrickson, C., Lave, L., Matthewsal, S.: Environmental Life Cycle Assessment of Goods and Services: An Input-Output Approach, Resources for the Future (2006)
12. UNEP, Cleaner Production: a training resource package, first edition (1996), http://www.uneptie.org/shared/publications/pdf/WEBx0029xPA-CPtraining.pdf (accessed February 20, 2010)
13. WBCSD/UNEP, Cleaner Production and Eco-efficiency: Complementary approaches to sustainable development. WBSCD and UNEP edition (1998)
14. Weizsäcker, E., Lovins, A., Lovins, L.: Factor Four: Doubling Wealth-Halving Resource Use. Earthscan Publications Ltd. (1997)
15. McDonough, W., Braungart, M.: Cradle to cradle: Remaking the way we make things. North Point Press (2002)
16. James-Moore, S.M., Gibbons, A.: Is lean manufacture universally relevant? An investigative methodology. International Journal of Operations and Production Management 17, 899–911 (1997)
17. U.S. EPA, Lean manufacturing and the environment: Research on advanced manufacturing systems and the environment and recommendations for leveraging better environmental performance. United States Environmental Protection Agency (2003)
18. Stewart, T.A., Raman, A.P.: Lessons from Toyotas's long drive. Harvard Business Review (2007)
19. Bragd, A., Bridge, G., Hond, F., Jose, P.D.: Beyond Greening: New Dialogue And New Approaches For Developing Sustainability. Business Strategy and the Environment 7, 179–192 (1998)
20. Korhonen, J., von Malmborg, F., Strachan, P.A., Ehrenfeld, J.R.: Management and Policy Aspects of Industrial Ecology: An Emerging Research Agenda. Business Strategy and the Environment 13, 289–305 (2004)
21. Anttonen, M.: Greening from the Front to the Back Door? A Typology of Chemical and Resource Management Services. Business Strategy and the Environment (2008)
22. Gold, S., Seuring, S., Beske, P.: Sustainable Supply Chain Management and Inter-Organizational Resources: A Literature Review. Corporate Social Responsibility and Environmental Management (2009)
23. Pojasek, R.B.: Quality toolbox: Five S's: A tool that prepares an organization for change. Environmental Quality Management 9(1), 97–103 (1999a)
24. Pojasek, R.B.: Quality toolbox: Poka-yoke and zero waste. Environmental Quality Management 9(2), 91–97 (1999b)

25. Soltero, C., Waldrip, G.: Using kaizen to reduce waste and prevent pollution. Environmental Quality Management 11(3), 23–38 (2002)
26. Helper, S., Rozwadowski, H., Clifford, P.G.: Can Green Be Lean? Academy of Management Annual Meeting, Organizations and the Natural Environment (1997)
27. Katayama, H., Bennet, D.: Lean production in a changing competitive world: a Japanese perspective. International Journal of Operations & Production Management 16(2), 8–23 (1996)
28. Hollie, S.: Solutions to Health Care Waste: Life-Cycle Thinking and "Green" Purchasing. Environmental Health Perspectives 109, 205–207 (2001)

Understanding Social Capital in Collaborative Networks

António Abreu[1,2] and L.M. Camarinha-Matos[2]

[1] ISEL, Polytechnic Institute of Lisbon, Lisbon, Portugal
[2] CTS – Uninova and Faculdade de Ciências e Tecnologia, Universidade Nova de Lisboa,
2829-516 Caparica, Portugal
ajfa@dem.isel.ipl.pt, cam@uninova.pt

Abstract. The characterization and assessment of the social capital of a member in collaborative networks is an important element to help promoting the success of collaborative networks. However, models to measure the social capital are lacking. Applying some concepts from social networks theory, this paper discusses some perspectives and criteria to identify and measure the value of social capital of a member in the context of a Virtual organization Breeding Environment (VBE).

Keywords: Social Capital, Social Network, Collaborative Networks.

1 Introduction

According to various authors on Collaborative Networks (CNs), as well as reports from a growing number of practical case studies, the involvement in a collaborative network is commonly assumed to bring valuable (potential) benefits to the involved entities [1, 2], [3]. These benefits include an increase of the "survival capability" in a context of market turbulence, but also the possibility to better achieve common or compatible goals. On the basis of these expectations are, among others, the following factors: joining of complementary skills and capacities, access to new / wider markets and new knowledge, etc [4].

However, it is important to realize that, when an enterprise is a member of a long-term networked structure, for instance a Virtual Breeding Environment (VBE), its value is not given only by its tangible assets – economic capital (such as: cash, resources, and goods). In this context, the existence of cooperation agreements, norms, reciprocal relationships, mutual trust, common infrastructures and common ontologies, allows members to operate more effectively in pursuit of their goals. In other words, there is an intuitive assumption that a VBE structure represents a group of organizational entities that have developed intangible assets of "social capital" that bring added value to its members. However, in spite of this assumption, it is, in fact, difficult to prove its relevance due to the lack of objective measurements, clearly showing the social capital value for each member [5], [6], [7].

Social capital metrics tailored to collaborative networks or even an adequate conceptual basis for social capital analysis is not available yet and might be an obstacle for a wider acceptance of this paradigm.

Á. Ortiz Bas, R.D. Franco, P. Gómez Gasquet (Eds.): BASYS 2010, IFIP AICT 322, pp. 109–118, 2010.

Nevertheless, in recent years some preliminary studies have explored the importance of social capital in the context of networked organizations [8], [9], [10], however none of them proposed methodologies, approaches or support tools to help managers of enterprises to analyze and measure their social capital in a Virtual organizations Breeding Environments (VBE) context.

This paper introduces some discussion of the nature of social capital as a contribution to a future identification of a set of indicators that are suitable for collaborative networks. This work aims at contributing to answer the following main questions:

- What are the main components that contribute to the formation of social capital of each member in a VBE context?
- How can social capital be measured in a VBE context?

2 Some Background

Although capital social is not new concept, its definition is not consensual among the various main disciplines that have addressed this topic (e.g. economy, sociology) and therefore several definitions can be found in the literature [11]. This problem results in part from the fact that the social capital needs to be analyzed from a multi-dimensional approach which has not occurred. For instance, the diversity of the perspectives on social capital varies according to this being focused on: the relationships that an actor has with other actors, the structure of relations among actors within a network, or both types of relationships [12].

As mentioned above, social capital has been defined from multiple and separated perspectives or for different purposes. From a sociological perspective, Bourdieu [13] defined social capital as "the aggregate of the actual or potential resources which are linked to possession of a durable network of more or less institutionalized relationships of mutual acquaintance and recognition," while for Portes [14] capital social is "the ability of actors to secure benefits by virtue of membership in social networks or other social structures". On the other hand, from an economic perspective Nahapiet and Ghoshal [15] defined social capital as "the sum of the actual and potential resources embedded within, available through, and derived from the network of relationships possessed by an individual or social unit. Social capital thus comprises both the network and the assets that may be mobilized through that network". For Fukuyama [16] "social capital can be defined simply as the existence of a certain set of informal values or norms shared among members of a group that permit cooperation among them".

Nevertheless, taking into account the above definitions, it is possible to conclude that social capital is a valuable asset which has some typical characteristics of economic capital such as: It can be invested with the expectation of future benefits [17] and, is convertible [13]. But, on the other hand, it is different, since its existence lies in the relationships that are established within the network while economic capital can exist at the member level [18]. In other words, social capital cannot be traded by entities on an open market like as economic capital, but exclusively within a network [19].

In order to categorize the components associated with the concept of social capital, several authors have proposed a multi-dimensional approach (see eg [15]). However, the current limitations of existing methods and a poor understanding of the components that are the source of social capital have acted as a barrier to the development of this concept in other fields of application such as the collaborative networks. Therefore, identifying and characterizing the components that make up the social capital tailored to collaborative networks, is a necessary first step. Based on the literature, and taking into account the context of collaborative networks, the most relevant components, as a first approach, include:

- Type of interaction among members – related to the forms of interrelationship that can occur between enterprises within a network. For instance, the following types of relationships can be identified:
    o Subordinate relationships – which characterize the authority and/or dependence structure within a network.
    o Peer relationships – which characterize the friendly relations within a network.
- Frequency of contact – related to the number of contacts between network members.
- Intensity of contact – related to the strength and nature of relationship in terms of potential benefits or losses.
- Geographical dispersion of network members – related to the geographical distance among members.
- Values – related to the behaviour of members, such as: trust, solidarity, reciprocity, values systems alignment, rules and norms of governance.
- Resources – related to the number and type of resources that can be mobilized through the network. Such as: capital, raw-material, workforce, energy, goods, services, etc.
- Knowledge - related to the type of knowledge that can be made available through the network, such as: skill, markets information, lobbying information, etc.

3   A Model to Analyze Social Capital

As mentioned above, one of the main weaknesses in this area in terms of social capital is the lack of appropriate formal methods to analyze social capital in the context of the networked organizations paradigm. We depart from the assumption that, the capital social of an enterprise is related to the "level of health" of the relationships that it establishes with other enterprises within a network.

In order to analyze the social capital of each member in a collaborative network, it is necessary to develop a model that supports the analysis of the relationships among members and the assets that may be accessed through the network of contacts.

Therefore, as a first approach, these relationships are modelled using graphs, as illustrated in Figure 1. The main objective is to represent a network in symbolic terms from the perspective of analysis, abstracting reality through a set of connecting nodes.

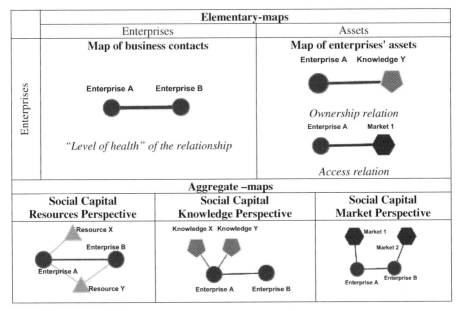

Fig. 1. Simple model to analyze Social Capital in CN's

The proposed model considers elementary-maps and aggregate-maps. The elementary maps are:

Map of business contacts - A graph showing the network of contacts among members belonging to the network. In this case, the link's width represents the "level of health - LH" of the relationship between two enterprises, and its value is given by the following equation:

$$LH_{ij} = w_1 \times SRFC_{ij} \times SRIC_{ij} + w_2 \times PRFC_{ij} \times PRIC_{ij} + w_3 \times VS_{ij}$$
$$\sum_{j=1}^{n} w_j = 1 \text{ and } w_j > 0 \tag{1}$$

Where:

LH_{ij} - Level of health of the relationship between enterprise i and enterprise j

$SRFC_{ij}$ - Frequency of contact between enterprise i and enterprise j, based on subordinate relation.

$SRIC_{ij}$ - Intensity of contact between enterprise i and enterprise j, based on subordinate relation.

$PRFC_{ij}$ - Frequency of contact between enterprise i and enterprise j, based on peer relation.

$PRIC_{ij}$ - Intensity of contact between enterprise i and enterprise j, based on peer relation.

VS_{ij} - Value systems alignment between enterprise i and enterprise j.

However, the main difficulty is naturally the determination of each of the five components mentioned above. To collect and record those values without being intrusive in the network members' "life" requires further research and development.

Combining these notions with concepts from the Social Network Analysis area, a useful tool to analyze in detail the map of business contacts can be obtained, as illustrated in Table 1.

Table 1. Mapping between SNA and Map of Business contact

Social Network Analysis (SNA)	Map of Business Contact
Key concepts	
Node - A social discrete entity such as: enterprises, actors, corporate or collective social units	Enterprises, organizations, people
Relational tie - Type of ties or links between nodes	Subordinate relation Informal relation
Dyad – consists of a pair of actors and the possible ties between them	Subordinate relation Peer relation
Structural Variables – measure ties of a specific kind between pairs of actors.	Frequency of contact Intensity of contact Value systems alignment
Composition variables – are measurements of actors' attributes.	Geographical localization Number of assets
Basic Analysis	
Nodal Degree – is a measure of the activity of the actor. Define indicators in order to measure: - Actor degree centrality - Group degree centralization - Actor closeness centrality - Group closeness centralization - Actor betweenness centrality - Group betweenness centralization - Degree of prestige - Proximity prestige - Status or Rank prestige	Measures the ability to have access to others nodes through the network
Network Size	Number of members of the CN
Density of network	Level of contacts
Connectivity of network - Cutpoints - Bridges - Walks - Trials - Tours - Cycles	Measures the concept of reachability between pairs of nodes.
Cohesive Subgroups - Clique - n-cliques - n-clans - n-clubs	Identification of subsets of actors among whom there are relatively strong, direct, intense and frequent ties

Map of enterprises' assets - This graph shows the assets held by each enterprise and how they are shared. In this case, there are two sets of nodes: enterprises and assets. The nodes are connected by ownership/access relations.

Aggregate-map – Graph showing how an enterprise may have access to assets held by another enterprise. It results from the aggregation between the map of business contacts and map of enterprises' assets. Based on this map, it is now possible to analyze the social capital of each enterprise through a visual representation of the components that make up the social capital. Therefore, this map will be composed of two sets of nodes (enterprises and assets), and two types of links.

Assuming that the assets are classified into classes in accordance with their purposes, then, in this context it becomes possible to analyse the social capital of an enterprise according to different perspectives, such as:

- Capacity perspective – related to the ability of accessing to external resources.
- Innovation perspective – related to the ability of accessing to external knowledge.
- Market perspective – related to the ability of accessing to new markets.

Therefore, it is possible to define three notions of social capital that can be measured using a quantitative or a quantitative scale. However, in this discussion social capital is assumed as an abstract quantifiable value with the same meaning as utility concept.

Partial Social Capital (PSC) – Corresponds to the social capital of an enterprise under a single perspective. Its value is given by the following equation[1]:

$$PSC_{ik} = \sum_{j=1}^{n} LH_{ij} \times (v_{A1i} + v_{A2i} + ... + v_{Ani}) \quad i \neq j \tag{2}$$

Where:

PSC_{ik} - Partial social capital of enterprise i according to perspective k

LH_{ij} - "Level of health" of the relationship between enterprise i and enterprise j

v_{Ani} - Value assigned to asset An. The worth of the asset An is decided by enterprise i and depends on the relative importance/utility of each asset.

Effective Social Capital (ESC) – corresponds to the social capital that an enterprise uses in carrying out its activities. Its value is given by the following equation:

$$ESC_{il} = \sum_{k=1}^{n} PSC_{ikl} \tag{3}$$

Where:

ESC_{il} - Effective social capital of enterprise i to perform an activity l

PSC_{ikl} - Partial social capital of enterprise i according to perspective k to perform an activity l

---

[1] It shall be noted however that this equation does not properly capture all situations. For instance, it does not cover the cases in which an enterprise has relationships with two or more enterprises that hold identical assets.

Total Social Capital (TSC) – corresponds to the maximum social capital that an enterprise can get from the network. Its value can be obtained through the sum of partial social capital. Its value is given by the following equation:

$$TSC_i = \sum_{k=1}^{n} PSC_{ik} \tag{4}$$

Where:

TSC_i - Total social capital of enterprise i

PSC_{ik} - Partial social capital of enterprise i according to perspective k

4 Potential Application

In order to analyze and measure the social capital of members in a collaborative network, the following example illustrates how the proposed approach can be used.

Let us consider a scenario, where we have a *VO breeding environment* (VBE) which contains seven organizations, as illustrated in Figure 2. Please note that the purpose of this example is only to illustrate the potential of this analysis, and in the network of business contacts, the "level of health" of the relationship among enterprises (LH_{ij}) (see, Equation 1) is identical for all enterprises.

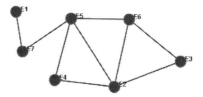

Fig. 2. Map of business contacts

Let us suppose the existence of three distinct classes of assets (Knowledge, Market, and Resources), as illustrated in Figure 3. Analyzing the graphs of enterprises' assets, it is possible to identify that in terms of knowledge (graph 3A) enterprise E4 does not have any asset while enterprise E7 has an exclusive asset K4. On the other hand, according to the analysis of resources (graph 3C), it is possible to verify that resource R2 is shared by both enterprises E4 and E7.

In order to analyze the social capital of an enterprise according to different perspectives, the following graphs are generated (Figure 4). From the perspective of innovation (graph 4A), it is possible to verify that enterprises E5 and E1 might have access to knowledge K4 (exclusive in this network) via the enterprise E7. On the other hand, from the perspective of market (graph 4B) enterprise E7, through enterprise E1, might access to market M1.

From the perspective of resources (graph 4C) enterprise E4 might have access to all available resources within the network through enterprise E2 and E5.

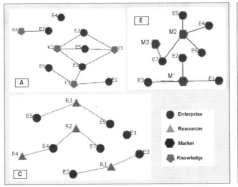 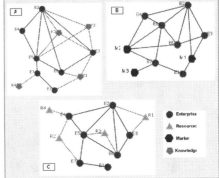

Fig. 3. Map of enterprises' assets - (A) Knowledge (B) Market and (C) Resources

Fig. 4. Social Capital Analysis - (A) Innovation (B) Market, and (C) Capacity perspective

In order to illustrate how to estimate the social capital in a VBE context, let us make the following assumptions:

- There are records of the enterprises' past involvement in collaboration activities at the VBE management level, which makes possible to quantify the *"level of health"* of the relationship between enterprises (LH_{ij}), such as: type of interaction among enterprises, number of contacts between members, value system alignment indicators, strength and nature of relationships in terms of potential benefits or losses.
- There are records of the type of assets that can be mobilized through the network at the VBE management level, and each enterprise decides on the relative importance/utility of each one of those assets.

In this scenario, let us suppose that enterprise E4 needs to have access to some assets in order to accomplish two business opportunities, as illustrated in the table 2. Table 3 shows the relative importance of each asset regarding the increase of the "survival capability" according to enterprise E4 perspective.

Considering that the "level of health" of the relationships among enterprise is identical and equal to 1 (LH_{ij}=1), table 4 shows the effective social capital for each business opportunity and the total social capital for a radius of 1 around enterprise E4 (see, Figure 2). For instance, in order to achieve the Partial Social Capital (PSC) value for business opportunity 1, applying Equation 2, we get the following equation: $PSC_{4k} = LH_{42} \times v_{Ak_2} = 1 \times 9 = 9$, where: PSC_{4k} - Partial social capital of enterprise E4 according to the knowledge perspective, LH_{42} - "Level of health" of the relationship between enterprise E4 and enterprise E2 and, v_{Ak_2} - Value assigned to asset k_2 (see, Table 3). Based on Equation 3, the Effective Social Capital (ESC) is worth 9 units in this case ($ESC_{41} = PSC_{4k1}$), where: ESC_{41} - Effective social capital of enterprise E4 to perform the business opportunity 1 and PSC_{ikl} - Partial social capital of enterprise E4 according to the knowledge perspective to perform business opportunity l.

Table 4 shows that for business opportunity 1 the effective social capital that enterprise E4 can get from the network is greater than for business opportunity 2, despite the amount of assets involved being smaller (table 2). Furthermore, as the effective social capital is positive for both business opportunities (table 4) means that enterprise E4 can operate more effectively compared to a scenario of working alone out of this VBE. On the other hand, based on this model, it is possible to analyse the potential maximum of social capital that an enterprise may have access through the network. As an example, by applying the Equation 4, the Total Social Capital value (TSC) for a radius of 1 around enterprise E4, is given by the following equation:

$$TSC_4 = PSC_{4k} + PSC_{4R} + PSC_{4M} = 11 + 5 + 3 = 19,$$ where: TSC_4 - Total Social Capital of enterprise E4, and PSC_{4x} - Partial Social Capital of enterprise E4 according to perspective x, where x is knowledge, resources, and markets.

In this example, as the worth of effective social capital is lower than the total social capital, it means that E4 is not extracting all advantages of belonging to this community.

Table 2. Assets required   **Table 3.** Assets utility   **Table 4.** Social capital as an abstract value

Business Opportunity	Assets required
1	K2
2	K3, R3, R1

Asset (An)	Value assigned to asset An (Van)
R1	3
R3	2
K2	9
K3	2
M1	3

Business Opportunity	Effective Social Capital	Total Social Capital
1	9	19
2	7	

5   Conclusion

Reaching a better characterization and understanding of the role of social capital in collaborative processes is an important element for a better understanding of the behavioural aspects in the collaborative networks paradigm in its various manifestation forms.

The definition of a set of indicators to capture and measure the capital social can be a useful instrument to the VBE manager, as a way to support the promotion of collaborative behaviours, and for a VBE member as a way to extract the advantages of belonging to a network. Using simple calculations as illustrated above, it is possible to extract some indicators. Some preliminary steps in this direction, inspired by the Social Networks analysis, were presented. The proposed model, although simplistic, has the advantage of providing a visual/graphical representation which is easy to understand.

However, the development of practical indicators and a software tool to analyze the social capital in collaborative networks still requires further work.

Acknowledgments. This work was supported in part by the FCT-MCTES – "Fundação para a Ciência e Tecnologia" (CTS multiannual funding) through the PIDDAC Program funds".

References

1. Beckett, R.C.: Perceptions of value that sustain collaborative networks. In: Camarinha-Matos, L.M., Afsarmanesh, H., Ortiz, A. (eds.) Collaborative Networks and Their Breeding Enviroments. Springer, Heidelberg (2005)
2. Afsarmanesh, H., Marik, V., Camarinha-Matos, L.M.: Challenges of collaborative networks in Europe. In: Camarinha-Matos, L.M., Afsarmanesh, H. (eds.) Collaborative Networked Organizations: A research agenda for emerging business models. Kluwer Academic Publishers, Dordrecht (2004)
3. Tenera, A., Abreu, A.: A TOC perspective to improve the management of collaborative networks. In: Camarinha-Matos, L.M., Picard, W. (eds.) Pervasive Collaborative Networks, pp. 167–176. Springer, Boston (2008)
4. Camarinha-Matos, L.M., Abreu, A.: A contribution to understand collaboration benefits. In: Camarinha-Matos, L.M. (ed.) Emerging Solutions for Future Manufacturing Systems. Springer, Heidelberg (2004)
5. Durlauf, S.N.: Symposium on social capital: Introduction. The Economic Journal 112, 417–418 (2002)
6. Adam, F., Roncevic, B.: Social Capital: Recent Debates and Research Trends. Social Science Information 42, 155–183 (2003)
7. Sabatini, F.: The Empirics of Social Capital and Economic Development: A Critical Perspective,
   http://www.feem.it/Feem/Pub/Publications/WPapers/default.htm
8. Yu, K.: A new idea for the research on cluster innovation network system model-based on the view of the use and creation of social capital. In: Sun, L., Wang, C.B. (eds.) Proceeding of China Private Economy Innovation International Forum, pp. 129–140. American Scholars Press, Marietta (2007)
9. Molina-Morales, F.X., Martines-Fernandez, M.T.: Does homogeneity exist within industrial districts? A social capital-based approach. Papers in Regional Science 88(1), 209–229 (2009)
10. Francis, J., Mukherji, A., Mukherji, J.: Examining relational and resource influences on the performance of border region SMEs. International Business Review 18(4), 331–343 (2009)
11. Bankston, C.L., Zhou, M.: Social Capital as a Process: The Meanings and Problems of a Theoretical Metaphor? Sociological Inquiry 72(2), 285–317 (2002)
12. Adler, P.S., Kwon, S.-W.: Social Capital: Prospects for a new concept. The Academy of Management Review 27, 17–40 (2002)
13. Bourdieu, P.: The Forms of Capital. In: Richardson, J.G. (ed.) Handbook of Theory and Research for Sociology of Education, pp. 241–258. Greenwood Press, New York (1986)
14. Portes, A.: Social Capital its origins and applications in modern sociology. Annual Review of Sociology 24, 1–25 (1998)
15. Nahaiet, J., Ghoshal, S.: Social Capital, Intellectual Capital, and the organizational advantage. Academy of Management Review 23(2), 242–266 (1998)
16. Fukuyama, F.: Social Capital and the modern capitalist economy: Creating a high trust worplace. Stern Business Magazine (1997)
17. Camarinha-Matos, L.M., Abreu, A.: Performance indicators based on colaborative benefits. In: Camarinha-Matos, L.M., Afsarmanesh, H., Ortiz, A. (eds.) Collaborative Networks and Their Breeding Enviroments. Springer, Heidelberg (2005)
18. Robison, L.J., Schimid, A., Siles, M.E.: Is social capital really capital? Review of Social Economy 60, 1–24 (2002)
19. Gant, J., Ichniowski, C., Shaw, K.: Social capital and organisational change in high involvement and traditional work organisations. Journal of Economics and Management 11, 289–328 (2002)

Part III
Advanced Production Engineering

A Framework for Developing a Web-Based Optimization Decision Support System for Intra/Inter-organizational Decision-Making Processes

Andrés Boza, Angel Ortiz, and Llanos Cuenca

Research Centre on Production Management and Engineering (CIGIP)
Universidad Politécnica de Valencia. Camino de Vera s/n, 46022 Valencia, Spain
{aboza,aortiz,llcuenca}@cigip.upv.es

Abstract. The evolution in information technology has allowed the development of new DSS architectures. This paper presents a framework for developing a web-based optimization decision support system for intra/inter-organizational decision-making processes. Data exchange in inter-organizational decision, separate decision and data models, and web services technology have been raised. Considering these factors a framework for developing a DSS with web services have been defined. In a business context, these web services could be offered for different web services provider companies and used by the different participants in an intra/inter-organizational decision-making process. In order to contextualize this framework, three scenarios have been defined and different relationships have been identified between the participating enterprises.

Keywords: Decision Support Systems, optimization, web services.

1 Introduction

Decision Support Systems (DSS) have been used to help in a wide range of enterprise decision-making processes. The evolution in information technology has allowed the development of new DSS architectures, from stand-alone DSS to Group Decision Support Systems, OLAP and data warehouse technology in DSS, agent-based DSS or Web-based DSS [1][2][3]. Power [4] defined the expanded DSS framework with five categories: data-driven, model-driven, knowledge-driven, document-driven and communication-driven DSS.

A new generation of web-based model-driven DSS is beginning to emerge [3]. These systems take advantage of the web services concept. A single DSS problem may be solved using multiple modelling or solution paradigms developed by different sources as separate web services and the results are then presented to the user in an aggregated or summarized form. Developing a web-based model-driven DSS requires identifying its components and describing their functionalities.

This paper presents a web-based optimization DSS framework for intra and inter-organizational decision-making processes in order to be used in the early design stages of a DSS. The framework is focused on service-oriented architectures (SOA)

Á. Ortiz Bas, R.D. Franco, P. Gómez Gasquet (Eds.): BASYS 2010, IFIP AICT 322, pp. 121–128, 2010.

using web services. This paper deals with the model-driven DSS, specifically about optimizations models, and increasing their potential by means of web technology.

2   Data Exchange in Inter-organizational Decisions

Huxham [5] defines inter-organizational collaboration as a "process in which organizations exchange information, alter activities, share resources and enhance each other capacity for mutual benefit and a common purpose by sharing risks, responsibilities and rewards". Relationships among trading partners in a supply network have been categorized as [6]: 1) Transactional (automation of buyer-seller EDI-based transactions), 2) Information-Sharing (the partners are given access to a system that has the shared information in it, or one partner transmits shared information to the other partner), and 3) Collaborative (information is not just exchanged and transmitted, but it is also jointly developed by the trading partners working together). According to Vernadat [7] in enterprise interoperability the main challenge is operations optimization via these co-decision, co-ordination, and even negotiation mechanisms.

DSS in inter-organizational systems have been defined for SCM [8], X-networks [9], Extended Enterprise [10], Virtual Enterprise [11] or in the broad area of distributed decision making contexts [12]. European initiatives have been elaborated to develop interoperability of enterprise (decision) applications [13] and will be elaborate in future internet enterprise systems to support inter- and intra- organisational collaboration [14].

The internal/external enterprise decision structures are changing. For example, planning collaboration cannot be just a solution between close partners, but needs to be implemented with a large number of different business partners [15]. The goal today must be solutions that enable mass collaboration. In the Virtual Enterprise (VE) paradigm, enterprises must share and exchange a part of their internal local information in order to interact and cooperate with each other towards the achievement of the global VE goals [16]. A member of the VE may decide to give access to its partners, with different levels of visibility according to their cooperation agreements, to part of the information it owns [17]. About technological aspects, the major principles and technological waves that have prevailed in building integrated or interoperable enterprise systems so far have been [7]: 1) Data integration, 2) Object-oriented approaches and object request brokers (ORBs), 3) Business process modelling (BPM) and process-oriented approaches, 4) Enterprise application integration (EAI), 5) Web services and service-oriented architectures (SOAs). The architectural style of next generation technological platforms intended to support design, deployment, and execution of extended business processes inside organizational networks, must be guided by interoperability principles at the processes, services, or data level, and service-oriented architectures attempt to address these issues [18]. Web Services are a key component of the emerging, loosely coupled, web-based computing architecture. Other systems may interact with a web service in a manner prescribed by its definition, using XML based messages conveyed by Internet protocols. The web services specifications offer a communication bridge between the heterogeneous computational environments used to develop and host applications [19]. The web environment is emerging as a very important DSS development and delivery platform [2]. DSS built for this environment, named web-based DSS [4], use different technologies [20][21]. Among these technologies, web services are considered a viable technological platform for web-based optimization [22].

3   DSS with Separate Decision and Data Models

Data Modelling, Decision Modelling, and Model Analysis and Investigation, are logical constructs, which play a leading role both in the interaction of information systems and decision technologies, as well as in rational decision making [23]: 1) Data Modelling refers to the 'structured' internal representation and external presentation of recorded facts. Broadly speaking this provides the decision-maker with information about their decision problem. 2) Decision Modelling is the development of a model, or a range of models that captures the structure as well as the decisions in respect of a given problem. These models are used to evaluate possible decisions in a given problem domain, and the probable outcomes. 3) Model Analysis and Investigation refers to the instantiation of the model with data, and the evaluation of the model parameters as well as the results in order to gain confidence and insight into the model. This separation between data and models, already included in [24], has been used in multiple DSS designs [25][26][27][28]. [10] proposes a framework for a decision support system in a hierarchical extended enterprise decision context. Figure 1 illustrates, in a simplified form, some of the components defined and its relationships without include hierarchical decision details.

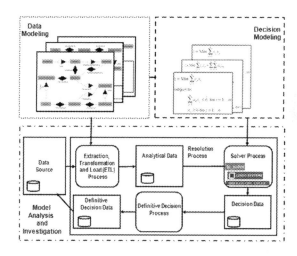

Fig. 1. Separate decision and data models (adapted from [10])

[22] shows this separation in web-based environments for optimization. A web enabled system for optimization should aim at: a) Providing each single optimisation tool as an independent service, b) Enabling remote interaction between the optimization components to provide a complete problem solving environment, c) Combining the provision of the tools with the provision of user support and security. This can be

achieved by adopting an IT architecture based on web services, so we propose to use this technology.

4   A Framework for Developing a DSS Using Web Services for Separate Intra/Inter-organizational Data and Decision Models

The components have been identified and classified as Web Services, Data exchange, Roles and Organization's Data Sources (figure 2).

Web Services
Models Manager: Makes possible the definition and links of Decision Models and Data Models. *Decision Models Manager:* Enables the definition and storage of Decision Models. *Data Models Manager:* Enables the definition and storage of Decision Data Models. *Model Analysis and Investigation:* Makes possible the instantiation of the Decision Data Model to solve Decision Models and obtain a Definitive Decision Data. *Decision Data Model Instantiation:* Carries out the extraction and transform of data from Organization's Data Sources to instance a Decision Data Model with organizations' data. *Solver Process:* Performs the resolution process which is capable of understanding a Decision Model Instance to solve and obtain the Decision Data. *Definitive Decision Process:* Allows decision-makers to consider additional factors in order to make its definitive decision.

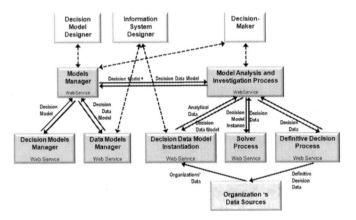

Fig. 2. A framework to developing a DSS using web services for separate intra/inter-organizational data and decision models

Data exchange
Decision Model: A mathematical representation of a decision problem to find the best solution. The decision model uses components of a Decision Data Model as index, data entries, decision or bounds variables for its definition, but not their values. *Decision Data Model:* A formal definition and format of data, compressible by computer systems, used in decision models. These decision data models will be instanced with organizations' data for a decision model in the Model Analysis and Investigation.

Analytical Data: Organizations' data obtained from the Organizations' Data Sources according to a Decision Data Model. *Decision Model Instance:* A Decision Model instanced with Analytical Data. *Decision Data:* Data obtained by a Solver Process with a Decision Model Instance. *Definitive Decision Data:* Data about the definitive decision taken by the decision-maker in a Decision Model. Decision Data obtained by the solver can be updated by the decision-maker in function of their judgments and choices.

Roles
Decision-Maker: Person(s) in charge of a decision making for a decision problem. *Decision Model Designer:* Person(s) in charge of constructing the suitable Decision Models. *Information System Designer:* Person(s) in charge of constructing the suitable Information System to give service to the information necessities

Organization's Data Sources
Data bases, files or spreadsheets in organization information systems where the data of a Decision Data Model are located.

5   The Proposed Framework in Three Scenarios

In order to contextualize the framework in an intra/inter-organizational environment, three scenarios has been defined (figure 3): *Scenario 1:* Intra-organizational data and decision model. There is not information or decision model sharing between organizations. *Scenario 2:* Inter-organizational data and intra-organizational decision model. There exists information sharing between organizations but not a joint decision model. *Scenario 3:* Inter-organizational data and decision model. There is information sharing and joint decision model between organizations.

5.1   Intra-organizational Data and Decision Model

In this context, Decision Model Designers and Decision-Makers interact with the Model Manager Web Service in order to define Decision Models and Decision Data Models, which will be later instanced. Defining separate Decision Models and Decision Data Models allows Decision Model Designer and Decision-Makers to define some Decision Models that use a same Decision Data Model.

Information System Designer interacts with the Data Models Manager web service and Decision Data Model Instantiation web service in order to define the instantiation process to obtain Analytical Data. Decision-Maker use Model Analysis and Investigation web service in order to instance a Decision Model with a data set, resolve it and make a decision. In this sense, Decision-Makers could resolve different previously defined Decision Models, and these could be instanced with different data sets (different companies, departments or simulations data) that fit with its Decision Data Model.

It is possible to implement a DSS platform in the organization with all these web services, but using the web services technology facilitates that they can be provided by web services provider companies. In this sense, a web services provider company with mathematical model specialized staff could advice on model definitions and host the defined models, another provider could offer web services for data management and a third could provide solver web services. Therefore, the main advantage of the framework in this scenario for the organizations is reuse decision models, and from a technological perspective, the main advantage is to build a DSS with components provided for different web services companies.

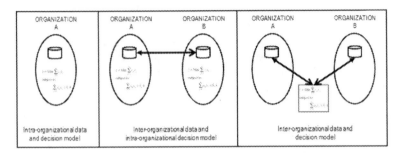

Fig. 3. Three inter/intra-organizational DSS scenarios

5.2 Inter-organizational Data and Intra-organizational Decision Model

In this scenario, there is information-sharing between organizations but not joint decision models. Besides the features included in the previous scenario, additional features can be identified: Participating organizations must work jointly in the data model definition that each organization shares with the other. Also, it is necessary to define a Decision Data Model Instantiation in order to retrieve data, not for its DSS but for the partner organization. In these sense, the participating organization require establishing the data exchange periodicity in order to orchestrate the web services.

An advantage in this case is to use web services technology to exchange data between DSS web-based or uses a common data-manage web services provider company.

5.3 Inter-organizational Data and Decision Model

There are decision models defined jointly by the participating organization and information sharing. Besides the features included in the previous scenarios, additional features can be identified:

In this scenario, the Models Manager web service is a common tool to jointly define share Decision Models and Decision Data Models. Each organization must define its Decision Data Model Instantiation web service in order to retrieve its data subset that participates in the joint Decision Data Model. The participating organizations require establishing a common schedule in order to resolve its share Decision Models and the necessary mechanisms to define a definitive decision in function of the (inter-organizational) decision-makers judgments and choices.

A DSS developed from the framework for this scenario allows defining decision models, share data and solve shared decisions with a web-based technology to be used in intra/inter-organizations decision-making processes.

6 Conclusions

DSS for intra and inter-organizational decision have been defined in a wide range of decision making situations. The technological advances in the Internet make available new DSS advances. In this sense, service-oriented architectures using web services allow defining new web-based DSS. The proposed framework for developing DSS using web services for separate intra/inter-organizational data and decision models draws on web technology to design Decision Models and Decision Data Models which will be later instanced and solved to make a decision. Its components have been identified and classified as web services, data exchange, roles and organization's data sources. Designing a DSS with web services allows splitting its functionality using these web services. Different web services providers can offer these and can be used by the different participants in an intra/inter-organizational decision-making process. Contextualizing the proposed framework using three scenarios has allowed identifying different aspects of the proposal with the participating enterprises in an intra/inter-organizational decision process and web services providers companies.

References

1. Carlsson, C., Turban, E.: DSS: directions for the next decade. DSS 33, 105–110 (2002)
2. Shim, J.P., Warkentin, M., Courtney, J.F., Power, D.J., Sharda, R., Carlsson, C.: Past, present, and future of decision support technology. DSS 33, 111–126 (2002)
3. Power, D.J., Sharda, R.: Model-driven decision support systems: Concepts and research directions. DSS 43, 1044–1061 (2007)
4. Power, D.J.: Supporting Decision-Makers: An Expanded Framework. In: Informing Science Conference, Krawkow, Polonia, June 19-22 (2001)
5. Huxham, C.: Creating Collaborative Advantage. Sage Publishers, London (1996)
6. AMR: Are we moving from buyers and sellers to collaborators? SCM Report. American Manufacturing Research Inc. (July 1998)
7. Vernadat, F.B.: Interoperable enterprise systems: Principles, concepts, and methods. Annuals Reviews in Control 31, 137–145 (2007)
8. Julka, N., Srinivasan, R., Karimi, I.: Agent-based supply chain management-1: framework. Computers and Chemical Engineering 26, 1755–1769 (2002)
9. Alix, T., Zolghadri, M., Bourrieres, J.P.: A DSS for production and procurement planning of enterprises X-networks. In: IEEE Int. Conf. on Systems, Manufacturing and Cybernetics (2004)
10. Boza, A., Ortiz, A., Vicens, E., Poler, R.: A Framework for a DSS in a Hierarchical Extended Enterprise Decision Context. LNBIP, vol. 38, pp. 113–124 (2009)
11. Zhou, Q., Ristic, M., Besant, C.B.: An Information Management Architecture for Production Planning in a Virtual Enterprise. IJAMT 16, 909–916 (2000)
12. Shneeweiss, C.: Distributed decision making—a unified approach. European Journal of Operational Research 150, 237–252 (2003)
13. Chen, D., Doumeingts, G.: European initiatives to develop interoperability of enterprise applications-basic concepts, framework and roadmap. Annual Reviews in Control 27, 153–162 (2003)
14. FInES: Future Internet Enterprise Systems Cluster. Position Paper, Version 3.0 (2009)

15. Holmström, J., Främling, K., Kaipia, R., Saranen, J.: Collaborative planning forecasting and replenishment: new solutions needed for mass collaboration. Supply Chain Management: An International Journal 7(3), 136–145 (2002)
16. Frenkel, A., Afsarmanesh, H., Garita, C., Hertzberger, L.O.: Supporting information access rights and visibility levels in virtual enterprises. In: IFIP Conf. on Infrastructures for Virtual Organisations (2001)
17. Camarinha-Matos, L.M., Pantoja-Lima, C.: Cooperation coordination in virtual enterprises. Journal of Intelligent Manufacturing 12, 133–150 (2001)
18. Franco, R.D., Ortiz, A., Lario, F.C.: Modeling extended manufacturing processes with service-oriented entities. Service Business 3, 31–50 (2009)
19. W3C, Web Services Choreography Description Language Version 1.0 (2005)
20. Power, D.J., Kaparthi, S.: Building Web-based decision support systems. Studies in Informatics and Control 11(4), 291–302 (2002)
21. Bhargava, H.K., Power, D.J., Sun, D.: Progress in Web-based decision support technologies. Decision Support Systems 43, 1083–1095 (2007)
22. Valente, P., Mitra, G.: The evolution of web-based optimisation: From ASP to e-Services. DSS 43, 1096–1116 (2007)
23. Dominguez-Ballesteros, B., Mitra, G., Lucas, C., Koutsoukis, N.-S.: Modelling and solving environments of mathematical programming (MP): a status review and new directions. Journal of the Operation Research Society 53, 1072–1092 (2002)
24. Geoffrion, A.M.: An introduction to structured modelling. Management Science 33(5), 547–588 (1987)
25. Dolk, D.R.: Integrated model management in the data warehouse era. European Journal of Operation Research 122, 198–218 (2000)
26. Lee, K.W., Huh, S.Y.: A model-solver integration framework for autonomous and intelligent model solution. DSS 42, 926–944 (2006)
27. Liew, A., Sundaram, D.: Flexible modelling and support of interrelated decision. DSS 46, 786–802 (2009)
28. Liu, S.F., Duffy, A.H.B., Whitfield, R.I., Boyle, I.: Integration of decision support systems to improve decision support performance. In: Knowledge and Information System (2009)

An Expert System for Inventory Replenishment Optimization

Ander Errasti[1], Claudia Chackelson[1], and Raul Poler[2]

[1] Industrial Organisation, Tecnun-School of engineering, University of Navarra, Spain
[2] CIGIP, Universidad Politécnica de Valencia, Spain

Abstract. Companies survive in saturated markets trying to be more productive and more efficient. In this context, to manage more accurately the finished goods inventories becomes critical for make to stock production systems companies. In this paper an inventory replenishment expert system with the objectives of improving quality service and reducing holding costs is proposed. The Inventory Replenishment Expert System (IRES) is based on a periodic review inventory control and time series forecasting techniques. IRES propose the most effective replenishment strategy for each supply classed derived of an ABC-XYZ Analysis.

1 Introduction

Some authors argue that Operational Research could contribute by developing models that link the effectiveness of new forecasting methods to the organizational context in which the models will be applied [1].

Even if future demand information is scarce, Make to Stock Production systems needs more accurate demand forecasting in order to improve quality service and reduce holding costs.

This paper explores the development of a expert system based on a periodic review inventory control, which forecast future demands more accurately beneath the time series techniques with less forecast error and proposing the most effective replenishment strategy for each supply classed derived of an ABC/XYZ analysis.

This research has also conducted a case study from Original Equipment Manufacturers (OEM) point of view answering the difficulties mentioned above.

The research methodology behind the work presented in this paper, consists of a theory-building phase, a theory-testing phase and a synthesis phase:

-   Theory-building: started with an extensive literature review to identify the issues/factors to be considered in the implementation of an inventory management optimization based on time series forecasting.
-   Theory-testing: designed around action research principles. Action Research can be seen as a variation of case research [2], in which the action researcher is not an independent observer [3].
-   Conclusions/Synthesis: in the synthesis phase the conclusions of the case study and the findings are shown, which increase the understanding of the reengineering process and the techniques based on time series forecasting techniques.

Á. Ortiz Bas, R.D. Franco, P. Gómez Gasquet (Eds.): BASYS 2010, IFIP AICT 322, pp. 129–136, 2010.

2   Literature Review

2.1   Supply Chain Management

Companies have to survive in saturated markets through competitiveness, trying to be more productive, more efficient or more innovative [4]. The APICS Dictionary [5] describes the supply chain as the processes from the initial raw materials to the ultimate consumption of the finished product, via different agents (suppliers, manufacturing plants, warehouses, customers, etc,). Supply Chain Management coordinates and integrates all activities of planning, sourcing, manufacturing and delivery. Some authors [6] classify and define the production strategies as make-to-order (MTO), make-to-stock (MTS) and assemble-to-order (ATO). They relate these approaches to choosing the master production scheduling (MPS) approach. Other authors [7] add the engineer-to-order production strategy and state that the decoupling point is a key issue [8]. The decoupling point concept is also known as order penetration point [9]. The customer order decoupling point decouples operations in two parts. Upstream this point the activities are performed to forecast and downstream they are performed to customer order (see Figure 1). The product differentiation point is the point where the firm's product is configured and it takes on specific features.

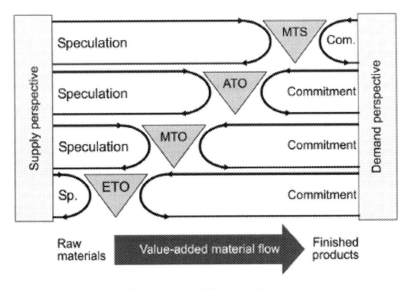

Fig. 1. MTS, ATO and ETO production strategy

In make-to-stock (MTS), the MPS is based on end items, and these end products are produced to meet forecast demand. Li [10] cited by Van Donk [11] states that competition can breed a demand for MTS, just as other economic phenomenon such as economies of scale, uncertainty and seasonality. Competitive pressure have shortened the life cycles for many products and increased the penalty of holding obsolete finished goods inventories. Standard planning methods lead to high forecasting errors and-as a consequence-to high safety inventories.

Demand information and accuracy is a critical factor for achieving end product lower inventory levels and providing better customer service [12], [13] and [14]. This issue could be essential to improve customer service and warehousing costs in make to stock production systems.

2.2 ABC/XYZ Analysis

The Pareto principle (also known as the 80-20 rule, the law of the vital few, and the principles of factor sparcity) serves as a baseline for ABC-analysis and XYZ-analysis. The ABC/XYZ Analysis is used to generate the supply and inventory control and production strategy. Rushton et al [15] state that it is useful in logistics and procurement for the purpose of optimizing stock of goods. The analysis consists of a procedure of stock management with which on the basis empirical experiences, results are usually assigned to a classification by the determination by variation and/or fluctuation coefficients of goods concerning its turnover regularity (consumption and its predictability). Items with high sales are called A-articles, while C-articles have low consumption. Articles which are sold very regularly and in some extent constant are called X-Articles, while Z-class runs very irregularly or even stochastically (see Figure 2).

ABC/XYZ Analysis would be automatically generated by means of a tool, and finished goods would be checked and then assigned to the proper supply classes. After that, for each supply classes the most effective replenishment strategy is settled to increase service and optimize stock.

2.3 Demand Forecasting

Demand forecasting qualitative and quantitative methods can aid in establishing the right replenishment strategy [16]. To sort out the adequate qualitative and/or quantitative method some authors propose selection decision trees [17].

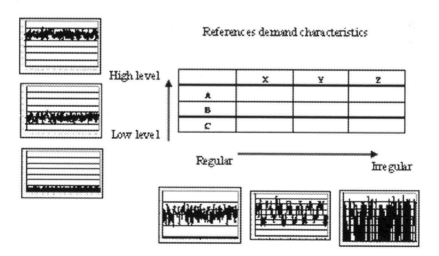

Fig. 2. ABC/XYZ References demand characteristics chart

In recent decades, numerous time series forecasting models have been proposed. De Gooijer and Hyndman [18]performed a review of the last 25 years. Time series forecasting software tools usually offer a variety of techniques, some of which provide the user the possibility to automatically define parameters or, even, to select the best forecasting method.

Model predictive inventory control systems have been previously applied to supply chain problems with promising results [19], however most systems that have been proposed so far possess no information on future demand. The incorporation of a forecasting methodology for individual item forecasts could promote the efficiency of control actions by providing insight in the future. This efficiency would be based on more accurate predictions to forecast demand extrapolating historical data aided on time series forecasting.

Demand is one of the greatest sources of uncertainty and, selecting the best time series forecasting model for each time series to be dealt with is still a complex problem [20]. This could be the reason why only 2% of 120 interviewed companies a forecasting system based on forecasting software [21].

According to Shah [22] the sense in which accuracy is defined may vary. Examples include the mean square error (MSE) and the mean absolute deviation (MAD) as two possible ways of stating the forecast accuracy. The main advantage of those measures is that could be used for intermittent demand, while others have problems.

Commercial software packages often report the mean absolute percentage error (MAPE) distinguishing between in-sample and out-of-sample evaluations. But there are special cases, e.g. intermittent demand, in which these error measures are not appropriate [23].

In-sample and out-of-sample errors have been used for time series forecasting model selection. In-sample tests are used when the real values are known and out-of-sample test when the real values are unknown. However, some authors use out-of-sample simulation [24]. Makridakis [25] used this procedure with a rolling temporal horizon as a selection method for estimation of parameters.

Makridakis et al [26] applied out-of-sample simulation on time series, and demonstrated that forecast accuracy improves when forecasting parameters were defined out-of-sample errors rather than in-sample ones.

An alternative model selection method is the so-called cross validation method [27]. Data is partitioned into subsets in such a way that the analysis is initially performed on a single subset, while the other subset(s) is/are retained for subsequent use in confirming and validating the initial analysis. The mean squared prediction errors in the subsets left out defines the cross validation error.

Forecast accuracy can be improved by the consideration of relevant information beyond historical data. Collaborative forecasting is based on the fact that each inter-related company (customers and suppliers, or nodes in an enterprise network) has relevant information available to forecast what the rest do not have. It is a question of managing all sources of relevant information and of eliminating "analysis islands". Poler et al. [28] proposed a structured model for the collaboration among firms of a network in the demand forecast and production planning settings and analysed the impact of collaboration mechanisms on forecast accuracy.

3 The Inventory Replenishment Expert System

The Inventory Replenishment Expert System (IRES) is composed by four main modules (see Figure 3).

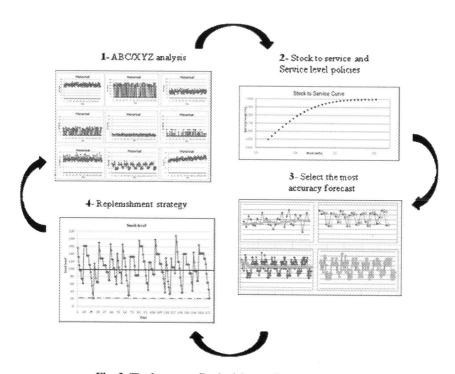

Fig. 3. The Inventory Replenishment Expert System (IRES)

The first module performs ABC/XYZ analysis for each reference type. All types of references, according to this analysis, are sorted out taking into account the demand behavior for a given past horizon.

The second module simulates possible service policies aided with Stock to Service curves, which relate service and stock level, and allow comparing service level policies with performance rates such as stock turnover and stock out.

The third module selects the most appropriate time series forecasting model. Depending on the pattern of time series, different forecasting models might be used. The selection of the most accurate forecasting method among a set of forecasting methods is made. The selection criteria pursue to minimize a concrete forecast error measure (MSE, MAD, MAPE, etc.), which depends on each particular case, using an out-of-sample simulation with rolling time horizon was carried out.

The fourth module proposes the best replenishment strategy taking into account the demand forecasts obtained by the selected method.

4 Empirical Study

The OEM, which led the supply chain improvement, was a Washing Machine Business Unit devoted to design, production and distribution of washing machines on the European market.

In order to ease the comprehension of the case study, the main characteristics of the external supply chain (distributors or customers and suppliers network) and the internal supply chain (finished product warehouse and manufacturing plant) are presented (see Figure 4).

The Spanish Household Appliances Sector is a saturated market, with an increasing number of multinational competitors. Besides, there has been a process of concentration

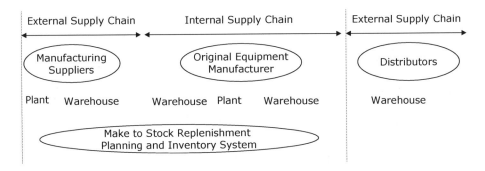

Fig. 4. Internal and external supply chain considered in the case study

Table 1. Recommended Forecasting methods and Replenishment strategies depending on make to stock references ABC/XYZ classification

		X: Regular	**Y: With Trend (T) or Seasonality (S)**	**Z: Irregular**
A: High	Replenishment Strategy:	Variable lot size based on Forecasts	Variable lot size based on Forecasts	Safety stock equal pick consume
	Forecasting method:	Moving Average	(T) Exponential Smoothing with trend	Moving Average
B: Medium	Replenishment Strategy:	Variable lot size based on Forecasts	Variable lot size based on Forecasts	Safety stock equal pick consume
	Forecasting method:	Moving Average	(S) Exponential Smoothing with Seasonality	Exponential Smoothing
C: Low	Replenishment Strategy:	Variable lot size based on Forecasts	Variable lot size based on Forecasts	Safety stock equal pick consume
	Forecasting method:	Exponential Smoothing	(T) + (S) Exponential Smoothing with Trend and Seasonality	Exponential Smoothing

of Retailers and Wholesalers, which has caused loss of margins to the OEM and the stock ownership has passed to the OEM. In this context, the Washing machine Business Unit tried to gain a sustainable competitive advantage.

The goal of the research was to reduce the total cost of the supply chain and increase the customer service, through the implementation of an expert system for inventory management.

The implementation of the new production system was monitored with key performance indicators related to cost (stock) and customer service (order fulfillment). The results obtained are shown at Table 1.

The recalculation of safety stocks considering pick consume, and the assumption of a variable lot size replenishment strategy based on forecasts, was effective in reducing up to an 88% the number of stock-out.

5   Conclusions

This paper present a new Inventory Replenishment Expert System (IRES) based on the combination of ABC/XYZ analysis, Stock to Service curves, Time Series Forecasting and Replenishment Strategies.

The multidisciplinary team involved in the reengineering project has found that IRES is useful for minimizing inventory level and increasing service quality.

Future research could be done in the following areas: a) increasing the forecasting techniques of the expert system; b) analyzing the impact of different forecasting methods selection criteria; c) improving the forecasting model selection module by integrating qualitative methods such as judgmental and statistical methods; d) testing IRES in supply chains of different sectors.

References

1. Fildes, R., Nikolopoulos, K., Crone, S.F., Syntetos, A.A.: Forecasting and operational research: a review. Journal of the Operational Research Society 59(9), 1150–1172 (2008)
2. Voss, C., Tsikriktsis, N., Frohlich, M.: Case research in operations management. Int. J. Oper. Prod. Manage. 22(2), 195–219 (2002)
3. Westbrook, R.: Action Research: a new paradigm for research in production and operations management. International Journal of Operations and Production Management 15(12), 6–20 (1995)
4. Lummus, R., Vovurka, R.: Defining supply chain management: a historical perspective and practical guidelines. Industrial Management and Data Systems 99(1), 11–17 (1999)
5. Blackstone, J., Cox, F.: APICS Dictionary, 11th edn., CFPIM, CIRM, Alexandria (2004)
6. Vollmann, T.E., Berry, W.L., Whybark, D.C.: Manufacturing Planning and Control Systems, 4th edn. McGraw-Hill, Irwin (1997)
7. Rudberg, M., Wikner, J.: Mass customization in terms of the customer order decoupling point. Production Planning & Control 15(4), 445–458 (2004)
8. Hoekstra, S., Romme, J.: Integrated Logistics Structures: Developing Customer Oriented Goods Flow. McGraw-Hill, London (1992)
9. Olhager, J.: Strategic positioning of the order penetration point. International Journal of Production Economics 85(3), 319–329 (2003)

10. Li, L.: The role of inventory in delivery-time competition. Management Science 38(2), 182–197 (1992)
11. Van Donk, D.P.: Make to stock or make to order: The decoupling point in the food processing industries. International Journal of Production Economics 69(3), 297–306 (2001)
12. Buffa, E.S., Miller, J.G.: Production Inventory Systems: Planning and Control, 3rd edn., Homewood, IL, Irwin (1979)
13. Hax, A.C., Candea, D.: Production and Inventory Management. Prentice Hall, Englewood Cliffs (1984)
14. Silver, E.A., Pyke, D.F., Peterson, R.: Inventory Management and Production Planning and Scheduling. John Wiley and Sons, Inc., New York (1998)
15. Rushton, A., Croucher, P., Baker, P.: The handbook of logistics and distribution management. Kogan Page Publishers (2006)
16. Makridakis, S., Wheelright, S.C., Hyndman, R.J.: Forecasting: methods and applications. Wiley, Chichester (1998)
17. Armstrong, J.S., Green, K.C.: Demand Forecasting: Evidence-based Methods. In: Strategic Marketing Management: A Business Process Approach edited by Luiz Moutinho and Geoff Southern, September 14 (2005)
18. De Gooijer, J.G., Hyndman, R.J.: 25 Years of IIF Time Series Forecasting: A Selective Review. Tinbergen Institute Discussion Paper (2005)
19. Doganis, P., Aggelogiannaki, E., Sarimveis, H.: A combined model predictive control and time series forecasting framework for production-inventory systems. International Journal of Production Research 46(24), 6841–6853 (2008)
20. Poler, R., Mula, J., Peidro, D.: Parameterisation of demand forecasting models through out-of-sample errors on a rolling horizon. Dirección y Organización 37, 76–82 (2009)
21. Errasti, A.: Proyecto: Sistemas de previsión de la demanda y su aplicación a la gestión de almacenes, Cluster de Transporte y Logística de Euskadi (2009)
22. Shah, C.: Model Selection in Univariate Time Series Forecasting Using Discriminant Analysis. International Journal of Forecasting 13(4), 489–500 (1997)
23. Syntetos, A.A., Boylan, J.E.: The accuracy of intermittent demand estimates. International Journal of Forecasting 21, 303–314 (2005)
24. Coccari, R.L., Galucci, C.: Average two best forecasts can reduce forecasting risk. Journal Business Forecasting (Fall 1984)
25. Makridakis, S.: Sliding simulation: a new approach to time series forecasting. Management Science 36, 505–512 (1990)
26. Makridakis, S., Andersen, A., Carbone, R., Fildes, R., Hibon, M., Lewandowski, R., Newton, J., Parzen, E., Winkler, R.: The accuracy of extrapolation (time series) methods: results of a forecasting competition. Journal of Forecasting 1, 111–153 (1982)
27. Stone, M.: Cross validation choice and assessment of statistical predictions. Journal of the Royal Statistical Society B36, 111–147 (1974)
28. Poler, R., Hernandez, J.E., Mula, J., Lario, F.C.: Collaborative forecasting in networked manufacturing enterprises. Journal of Manufacturing Technology Management 19(4), 514–528 (2008)

A Threshold Based Dynamic Routing
for Jobs with QoS Ranking

Seyed Behrouz Khodadadi and Jafar Razmi

Department of Industrial Engineering, College of Engineering,
University of Tehran, Iran
{jrazmi,bkhodadadi}@ut.ac.ir

Abstract. We consider a set of n heterogeneous servers which differ in processing time and Quality of Service (QoS). Jobs are divided into m levels with regard to their service ranks. We present a Threshold Policy (TP) depending on number of different jobs in the queues as a practical and flexible dynamic routing policy to control the QoS. Two performance measures are discussed: the QoS and the Average Waiting Time (AWT) in the queues. The TP is compared with both a static routing policy which maximizes the QoS level and the Minimum Expected Delay (MED) policy which minimizes the AWT. Numerical example validate that the proposed TP is more effective when both measures are considered. The TP balances the trade-off between QoS and AWT and therefore it is superior to the MED policy and any static routing which keeps the QoS in a certain level.

Keywords: Dynamic Routing, Quality of Service, Heterogeneous Servers, Threshold Base Policy.

1 Introduction

Routing policies have widely used to control queuing systems and they can highly improve the system performance. The application of routing policies arise in several areas such as manufacturing industries, computer and communication systems. We deal with dynamic routing of jobs among heterogeneous parallel servers which are ranked by their QoS. Jobs are also divided into several levels of service. Jobs of different quality levels enter to the system with different stream of arrivals and a router must dispatch the jobs to one of the servers immediately after their arrival. Service times are independent of arrival process and job's level.

Routing policies are concerned with the assignment of arrived jobs to the queues of machines. Mostly the assignment decision should be made immediately after job arrival and it is a routing decision based on number of jobs in each queue [1]. Obviously there is no routing policy which can optimize various performance measures all together. There has been presented variety of policies by investigators, which each of them has its own performance measures and cost functions and is appropriate for specific problems. One common objective function which is frequently discussed by researchers is waiting time minimization. In this direction, the JSQ policy for identical

Á. Ortiz Bas, R.D. Franco, P. Gómez Gasquet (Eds.): BASYS 2010, IFIP AICT 322, pp. 137–144, 2010.

parallel machines has been investigated by Winston [2] and Nelson and Philips [3],[4]. The performance of the Minimum Expected Delay (MED) policy which is derived from JSQ policy and is appropriate for non-identical parallel machines - also called heterogeneous servers - is analyzed by Lui et al. [5].

Routing policies are divided into static policies and dynamic policies. In static scheme no information exchanges are used at decision epoch. Static policies are appropriate when all jobs are available at time zero or situations in which the system characteristics are under the control. For instance the Joining-Shortest-Queue (JSQ) policy assigns each job to the machine with the minimum number of waiting jobs.

Threshold-based policies, which are a kind of dynamic routing, are frequently used to control queuing systems. In this mode, the analysis of heterogeneous servers is mainly limited to two servers because of high complexity of such systems. ([6], [7], [8], [9], [10] and [11]). In this paper we consider several streams of arrivals, parallel queues and several heterogeneous servers.

It is common in manufacturing, service and computer systems to categorize jobs or customers and rank them in order of their importance. Usually the QoS is not at the same level for different servers. In this scheme, more valued jobs are processed by higher quality machines. On the other hand, it is a common practice to provide high quality services even for the low graded jobs as much as possible. An example of this situation is dispatching automobile bodies to paint shops in Iran Khodro Company (IKCO) - the biggest car producer factory in the Middle East. Each paint shop has a specific production rate and QoS due to its technology specifications. Different model of automobiles can be painted in any of paint shops but usually the capacities of higher quality paint shops are assigned to higher valued automobiles. Each automobile body is released from its own body shop. Conveyors carry automobile bodies from body shops to White Body Stocks. Finally automobile bodies are dispatched to paint shops regard to their quality level. To the best of our knowledge, analysis of QoS performance measure has not been studied in dynamic routing policies. Most of researches are focused on AWT and utilization balancing analysis.

The presentation of the rest of this paper is organized as follows. In section 2 we present the problem statement. Section 3 contains the proposed algorithm and the development process. Numerical examples are presented in section 4 and conclusions are stated in section 5.

2 Problem Statement

The problem regarded in this paper consists of a set of n parallel heterogeneous servers and m level of jobs. All servers can perform the same operation, but with different performances i.e. they have different service time and QoS. Servers are arranged in order of their quality ranking. The quality ranking is in increasing order from 1 to n whereby top ranked server indicates that the server has greater quality. In the same manner jobs are ranked in order of their quality level from 1 to m. There is a separate stream of arrivals for each level. Arrivals of each level of jobs are independently distributed. The arrival of a new job occurs only after the current job is dispatched. The dispatched job waits in the queue of corresponding server until the server becomes idle. Queues are assumed to have infinite capacity and their discipline is FCFS. No preemption or jockeying is allowed. Each job is processed in only one server. The service times are independently distributed and they are also independent of the job's quality level. Table 1 summarizes the main parameters of the model.

Table 1. Model parameters

Parameter	Description	Range
i	Job rank	1,2..m
j	Server rank	1,2..n
t_i	Inter arrival time of jobs with rank i	> 0
T_i	Service time of server j	> 0
T	Processing period	> 0
P_i^T	Total number of processed jobs with rank i in period T	$0,1..\infty$
$p_{i,j}^T$	Processed jobs with rank i in server j in period T	0,1..Pi
$q_{i,j}$	Number of jobs with rank i waiting in queue of server j	$0,1..\infty$

The necessary condition for stability is as follows ([12]).

$$\sum_{j=1}^{n} \frac{1}{T_j} > \sum_{i=1}^{m} \frac{1}{t_i} \tag{1}$$

3 Proposed Method

3.1 Threshold Policy

We propose a TP based on the number of jobs with different levels in each queue. When a job with quality level i arrives, the number of jobs with levels 1 to i which currently await service in the queue of the first ranked server are counted and the summation is compared with a predefined threshold. If the summation is smaller than the threshold, then the job is dispatched to the server; otherwise the summation of jobs with levels 1 to i await service in the queue of the second ranked server is compared with its corresponding threshold. The above routine continues until a server is selected and the job is dispatched. The procedure of the proposed threshold routing is depicted in procedure 1.

```
Procedure 1
                        S = Ø
For j = 1 to n-1
        If   Σ₁ⁱ qᵢ,ⱼ < cᵢ,ⱼ  then  S=j  and break
End for
If S = Ø then S=n
```

Where S denotes the selected server. $c_{i,j}$ is a constant threshold and it is a cell of matrix C. Note that the last machine is a reserved machine in case of heavy traffic conditions. If none of $j=1$ to $n-1$ servers are selected for a job then the job is dispatched to the last server. Thus we have excluded the last column of matrix C. If we consider $c_j=(c_{0,j},\ c_{1,j},\ ...,\ c_{m,j})^T$ then $c_{i,j}$ values are integer and c_j is in non-increasing order. Our main idea to find effective thresholds is to solve the problem for deterministic situation and use the same solutions for stochastic model. In this section we present an algorithm for the deterministic model which determines the thresholds so that the total QoS is maximized. In this direction the following statement determines a feasible solution.

$$\forall\{j,j' < j\}\ if\ \lim_{T\to\infty} utilization(j) > 0\ then\ \lim_{T\to\infty} utilization(j') = 100\% \qquad (2)$$

Statement (2) denotes that the lower quality machines should not be used unless the higher quality ones are completely utilized. In deterministic model, t_i and T_j are assumed to be constant values. Using the Kendall [13]'s notation the model can be described as $D/D/n$ with m arrival streams. The following statement represents an optimal assignment for the deterministic model.

$$\forall i,j,T\ if\ p_{i,j}^T > 0\ then\ \sum_{x=i+1}^{x=m}\ \sum_{y=1}^{y=j-1} p_{x,y}^T = 0 \qquad (3)$$

Statement (3) implies that the high ranked jobs should be prior in assigning to higher quality machines. In the other word, if a server with a short service time has low quality, it is not allowed to dispatch any jobs to it unless constraint (2) is satisfied. Thus, statement (3) is sufficient to consider a solution as optimal. It is noteworthy that an easy way to reach optimal solutions is to use zero or big integer values for the thresholds to force the system to dispatch jobs to a specific server or avoid dispatching to some other servers. Such thresholds actually function like static rules and therefore reduce the flexibility of the routing method. The main reason for development of the proposed threshold policy is to construct a flexible routing policy for stochastic situation. Therefore it is not appropriate to use extreme values.

3.2 Initial Solutions

By solving a variety of problems, we concluded a general initial solution for threshold values which has advantages over random ones. Procedure 2 shows the initialization procedure. The proposed initial solution not only makes the algorithm reaching the optimal solution earlier, but also increases the flexibility of routing policy under uncertainty.

```
Procedure 2
For x = 1 to m
  For y = 1 to n-1
       If x <= m-n+j then cx,y = n-j+1 else cx,y = m-x+1
  End for
End for
```

3.3 Objective Function Value

We carried out a simulation model to evaluate the performance of the proposed routing policy against the optimal assignment. The simulation model evaluates the OFVs and indicates the critical servers which have discrepancies in relation to optimal ones. The OFV is defined for each machine as stated in procedure 3. The routine counts the number of discrepancies between the optimal assignment and the dynamic routing policy for each server. The objective of the proposed algorithm is to minimize the discrepancies of all servers ($\sum_{j=1}^{n} OFVc_j=0$). The simulation model also determines the critical jobs for each critical server. Jobs which are assigned wrongly to a critical server are called excessive jobs. Jobs which are not assigned to the correct server are called lacking jobs.

```
Procedure 3
For i=1 to m
```

$$\text{if } p_{i,j}^T > 0 \text{ then } OFVc_j = OFVc_j + \min \left(\sum_{x=i+1}^{x=m} \sum_{y=1}^{y=j-1} p_{x,y}^T , p_{i,j}^T \right)$$

```
End for
```
if $OFVc_j > 0$ then $j \in \{\text{critical servers}\}$

3.4 Performance Measures

Two performance measures are considered, first the percentage of incorrect assignments to total assignments which is denoted by $FV = 100 \times \sum_{j=1}^{n} OFVc_j / \sum_{i=1}^{m} P_i^T$, and second the AWT. The proposed threshold policy tends to maximize the QoS but it does not deal with other performance measures such as waiting time. Thus, a policy should be developed to reach a desirable level for both QoS and AWT.

3.5 Tune-Up

An algorithm is developed to tune up the threshold policy. The algorithm consists of an initialization stage and four repetitive steps. The proposed algorithm is as follows.

Step 0: procedure initialization
Step 1: if the solution is feasible and $\sum_{j=1}^{n} OFVc_j = 0$ then C is an optimal solution, stop. Else if the solution was infeasible go to step 2. Else go to step 3
Step 2: select server $y=\{\min(j)|j\neq n$ and utilization$(j)<100\%\}$. select job $x=\{\min(i)|p_{i,y+1}>0\}$. Make an increase of 1 in cell $c_{x,y}$ of matrix C. update values of $c_{i,y}$ for $i<x$ and go to step 1.
Step 3: select the first critical server ($y=\min\{\text{critical servers}\}$). For the selected server select the first lacking job ($x=\min\{\text{lacking jobs of server } y\}$). make an increase of 1 in cell $c_{x,y}$ of matrix C. if the OFVc$_y$ is decreased update values of $c_{i,y}$ for $i>x$ so and go to step 1 else $c_{x,y}$-- and go to step 4.
Step 4: select the first critical server ($y=\min\{\text{critical servers}\}$). For the selected server select the last excessive job ($x=\max\{\text{excessive jobs of server } y\}$). make a decrease of 1 in cell $c_{x,y}$ of matrix C. if the OFVc$_y$ was decreased update values of $c_{i,y}$ for $i<x$ and go to step 1 else $c_{x,y}$++ and go to step 1.

In the first step the OFVs are calculated and the critical servers and critical jobs are determined. If the current solution is both feasible and optimal the algorithm is stopped and the current solution is regarded as optimal solution, otherwise the algorithm tries to overcome the discrepancies of job assignment in a top-down order. If the current solution is not feasible (i.e. there is at least one server that its utilization is not equal to 100% excluding the last server), then step 2 aims to reach a feasible solution by increasing the corresponding thresholds. There are two reasons that may cause a solution not to be optimal. First, a job with a low quality level has been wrongly assigned to a high quality server and second, a job with a high quality level has been wrongly assigned to a low quality server. To resolve these mismatches, the algorithm decreases/increases the threshold of corresponding jobs (step 3 and 4).

4 Numerical Examples

To evaluate the performance of the justified TP presented in section 3.3, it was compared with a static routing policy, the modified version of static policy and the MED policy. The static routing policy maximizes the quality of service whereas the MED policy minimizes the AWT. The modified static policy keeps the quality in a lower level in comparison with the static policy. Instead, in stochastic models the system is stable by using the modified version. We consider three types of uncertainty: *stochastic arrivals*, *stochastic service times* and *unexpected breakdowns*. To put it more clearly, a numerical experiment is addressed as follows

Table 2. Simulation results

Policy	D/D/n		M/D/n		D/M/n		M/M/n		M/M*/n	
	OFV	AWT	OFV	AWT	OFV	AWT	OFV	AWT	OFV	AWT
Static	0	274.8	0	55280.2	0	40214.2	0	98901.7	0	∞
MS	8.1	551.53	8.1	1308.06	8.1	1638.68	8.1	2556.6	8.1	11553.8
TP	0	641.4	11.7	742.4	11.6	828.4	17.1	1236.7	23.8	3931.8
MED	16.3	233.0	26.6	428.4	28.9	453.9	28.4	775.4	32.4	1893.0

As it is shown in table 2, five different systems are considered. The exponential distribution is used for stochastic systems. m, n and $E(T_j)$ are identical in each of five systems. To keep the traffic volume in a constant level while a variety of problems to be evaluated, ten random combinations of arrival times were generated so that $\sum_{i=1}^{m} \frac{1}{E(t_i)}$ was considered fixed. The system parameters are $(m,n)=(4,3)$, the deterministic Tj is $\{288,576,432\}$, the stochastic Tj is $\{expo(288), expo(576), expo(432)\}$, $\{mttf, mttr\} = \{expo(7200), expo(600)\}$ and $\sum_{i=1}^{m} \frac{1}{E(t_i)} = 6.366 \times 10^{-3}$. The simulation model was run for each of five systems for 10000 hours with 2 hours warm-up period. The average OFVs and the average of AWTs for four policies are shown in table 2.

As it has been mentioned before, the static routing is suitable for the deterministic situation. Although in the MED policy the AWT is about 15% smaller than the static policy but the OFV is about 16% greater. In contrast, the static policy is not appropriate for stochastic models. Because the servers are planned to be fully utilized the system becomes unstable and therefore modifications are needed if intended to be used in such systems. In the modified static (MS) policy, the assignment is scheduled with 90% of capacity of each server to prevent instability. However, in this paper we focus on the dynamic routing policies. A Wilcoxon signed rank test for ten samples of each group shows that the TP in average provides jobs with higher QoS in comparison with the MED policy. For example in the M/M*/n model which arrival times of jobs and the s times, mean time to failure (MTTF) and mean time to repair (MTTR) of servers are exponentially distributed, the hypothesis $\mu_{TP} = \mu_{MED}$ is rejected with P-value 0.005 against $\mu_{TP} < \mu_{MED}$. The TP is superior to MED policy in QoS level and it is superior to static routing policies in AWT. Table 2 also implies that if the average waiting time is decreased, some quality priorities would be ignored.

Table 3. Variation of thresholds with different mean of arrival time

	$t_2=125$		$t_2=150$		$t_2=175$		$t_2=200$		$t_2=225$		$t_2=250$		$t_2=275$	
	j=1	j=2	j=1	j=2	j=1	j=2	j=1	j=2	j=1	j=2	j=1	j=2	j=1	j=2
i=1	3	2	3	2	3	2	3	2	3	3	4	4	3	3
i=2	3	2	3	2	3	2	3	2	3	3	4	4	3	3
i=3	2	2	2	2	2	2	2	2	2	3	2	3	2	2
i=4	1	1	1	1	1	1	1	1	1	1	1	1	1	1

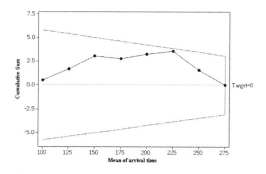

Fig. 1. Cumulative-sum control chart with two-sided V-mask (h:4.0, k:0.5) for OFV

Table 3 shows the threshold variation in response to changes in its mean arrival time of a level of jobs in a 4×3 M/M/n system. The corresponding cumulative-sum control chart with two-sided V-mask for OFV of this system after 10000 hours simulation is illustrated in figure 1. V-masks are used to warn about abnormal conditions. The sensitivity analysis implies that algorithm 3.3 justifies thresholds so that the QoS is kept under the control.

5   Conclusions

A threshold policy was presented for dynamic routing of jobs with service ranking among servers with different QoS. In contrast with traditional dynamic routing policies which have not considered the QoS, the proposed policy assigns jobs to servers with QoS considerations. The algorithm, which is developed on the basis of deterministic situation, tunes-up the thresholds in order to increase the QoS. The tune-up procedure is simple to implement and it reaches certain thresholds for each set of input parameters. Numerical experiments show that the adjusted TP keeps the QoS in a high level while maintains the stability of system. A sample problem was solved by the proposed algorithm to compare it with other policies. The TP balances the trade-off between QoS and AWT and therefore it is more effective than the MED policy which only minimizes the AWT and any static routing which keeps the QoS in a certain level. The proposed method is useful to control the QoS in production, service and communication systems. Distinguished advantages of the threshold policy are simplicity and flexibility. The decision maker can change the thresholds manually to change the utilization of servers or to root a level of jobs in a specific way. Mathematical analysis of the system is a problem yet to be resolved.

References

1. Down, D.G., Lewis, M.E.: Dynamic load balancing in parallel queueing systems: Stability and optimal control. European Journal of Operational Research 168, 509–519 (2006)
2. Winston, W.: Optimality of the shortest line discipline. J. Appl. Prob. 14, 181–189 (1977)
3. Nelson, R.D., Philips, T.K.: An approximation for the mean response time for shortest queue routing with general interarrival and service times. Perform. Eval. 17, 123–139 (1993)
4. Nelson, R.D., Philips, T.K.: An approximation to the response time for shortest queue routing. Perform. Eval. 17, 181–189 (1989)
5. Lui, J.C.S., Muntz, R.R., Towsley, D.: Bounding the mean response time of a minimum expected delay routing system: an algorithmic approach. IEEE Trans. Comput., 1371–1382 (1995)
6. Lin, W., Kumar, P.R.: Optimal control of a queueing system with two heterogeneous servers. IEEE Trans. Automat. Control 29, 696–703 (1984)
7. Koole, G.: A simple proof of the optimality of a threshold policy in a two-server queueing system. Systems & Control Letters 26, 301–303 (1995)
8. The, Y.C.: Critical Thresholds for Dynamic Routing in Queueing Networks. Queueing Systems 42, 297–316 (2002)
9. Feng, W., Adachi, K., Kowada, M.: A two-queue and two-server model with a threshold-based control service policy. European Journal of Operational Research 137, 593–611 (2002)
10. Sun, W., Guo, P., Tian, N.: Equilibrium threshold strategies in observable queueing systems with setup/closedown times. Springer, Heidelberg (2009), doi:10.1007/s10100-009-0104-4
11. Altman, E., Nain, P.: Optimality of a Threshold Policy in the M/M/1 Queue with Repeated Vacations. Mathematical Methods Operations Research 44, 75–96 (1996)
12. Thomas, M.U., Wilson, G.R.: Applications of queuing theory, Industrial engineering handbook, 5th edn., vol. 2, pp. 11.67–11.99. Mc-Graw-Hill, New York (2001)
13. Kendall, N.K.: Stochastic processes occurring in the theory of queues and their analysis by the method of imbedded Markov Chains. Annals of Mathematical Statistics 24, 360–369 (1953)

Collaborative Distributed Computing in the Field of Digital Electronics Testing

Eero Ivask, Sergei Devadze, and Raimund Ubar

Tallinn University of Technology, Department of Computer Engineering, Raja 15,
12618 Tallinn, Estonia
{ieero,serega,raiub}@pld.ttu.ee

Abstract. Computation tasks used in digital design flow for test quality evaluation can require a lot of processor and memory resources. To speed up execution and to overcome memory restrictions, a collaborative computing approach was proposed in this paper. Web-based system architecture allows seamlessly aggregate many remote computers for one application. Efficient collaboration requires credit based priority concept, issues of task partitioning, task allocation, load balancing and model security must be handled. Experimental results show feasibility of proposed solution and gain in performance.

Keywords: collaboration, distributed computing, task partitioning, task scheduling, load balancing, priorities, fault simulation, model security.

1 Introduction

Today, sizes of digital electronic circuits are still increasing dramatically according to Moore's law, which states that transistor density on integrated circuits doubles about every two years. This trend is predicted to continue at least for another decade, posing serious problems for test engineers.

To ensure fault-free products, devices must be carefully tested with appropriate test inputs during manufacturing. Widely used process in test engineering is fault simulation: it is used to evaluate the fault coverage of the test sets, it is often required for automatic test pattern generation, fault diagnosis, test compaction, built-in-self-test optimization, etc. For some computation intensive tasks, like test generation, fault simulation step is carried out many times, making simulation speed one of the key issues for overall task performance.

One solution to meet the time-to-market for larger circuits could be the improvement of the fault analysis algorithms. However, plentiful of different methods proposed during last decades leaves little room for improvement. Another way to solve the problem is to divide computation tasks and combine available computer resources. In this paper, we focus on collaborative computing. We assume that participants have computers that are not fully loaded and this load is rather uneven in time. Working is more efficient when every participant has the possibility to run his tasks using collective resources. Effective collaboration requires credit based priorities, good task scheduling and load balancing.

Á. Ortiz Bas, R.D. Franco, P. Gómez Gasquet (Eds.): BASYS 2010, IFIP AICT 322, pp. 145–152, 2010.
© IFIP International Federation for Information Processing 2010

Concept of infrastructure of the current solution was initially inspired from MO-SCITO [1], [2] used for example in European VILAB cooperation project. Original system was implemented as client-server Java application. It allowed invoking single work tools remotely and organizing them into predefined automated workflows. Users in different locations cooperated via sharing their software tools in joint workflows. However, task partitioning and parallel execution was not supported. Major limitation for extensive Internet based use was TCP/IP socket based communication that required dedicated communication ports in firewalls on server side and also on the client side for each application and for end users.

More flexible web-based solution for remote tool usage following some key ideas of MOSCITO was proposed in [3]. Socket communication was replaced with HTTP, Java Servlets were used on server side and Applets along with Java applications were used on client side, also database was introduced. In current paper, this concept is revised and improved to support distributed computing and collaboration via effective resource sharing.

There exist also some general-purpose frameworks for distributed computing. BO-INC [4] for example, built with PHP scripts and AliCE [5] that uses Java based Jini technology. Both have drawback of relying on remote procedure calls, which is restriction in firewall-protected networks.

The paper is organized as follows: web-based infrastructure is described in section 2. In section 3 priorities concept is explained. Task partitioning and task allocation are handled in sections 4 and 5. Section 6 discusses model security problems. Section 7 presents workflow with distributed computing. Experimental results are presented in section 8 and conclusions are given in section 9.

2   Distributed Environment

We have used Web-based client-server concept in our solution. There is Master server, several workstations and arbitrary number of users (Figure 1). Each user is associated with certain workstation, he is owner or he belongs to the team. Simulator application instances run on workstations. Simulator is provided with network communication abilities, it is wrapped with additional software layer – agent is created. For each simulator there is dedicated agent. Agent and simulator reside on the same computer. User accesses only Master. Users and Agents work in "polling" mode, Master is working in "answering" mode. Master and Agents must be started by administrators first. Thereafter, user can initiate a task, which is passed to Master where it is stored until a free Agent is asking for a new task. Each user has its own server-side workspace in the database. When task is complete, Agent passes results to Master where results are assembled and stored again until user will ask for results.

2.1   Implementation

Infrastructure of the system is built with Java applet/servlet technology. Communication flow between system components can be seen in Fig. 1. Tomcat is a servlet container that is used in the official reference implementation for the Java Servlet and JavaServer Pages technologies. Tomcat and servlets running on it play important role in order to access intranet resources on workstations and MySQL database. Simulator tool is implemented in C language. Wrapper agent for simulator is written in Java, which has excellent support for network programming. System components can run on different computing platforms. Simulator instances must run on their native platform. Master servlet resides usually separately from agents, they must not reside in the same local area network. Each agent can reside on different local area network. Since accessing hard drives for Java applet is restricted for security reasons by default, then GUI applet has been signed digitally, with self-signed certificate for simplicity.

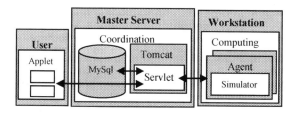

Fig. 1. System components and communication

Use of applet/servlet approach means that general communication is based on HTTP protocol. Firewall traversal is therefore no problem as only one web server port must be configured on Master server. There is no need for opening extra ports in the firewalls on the user side as it is the case with other solutions (which would be major restriction). Communication could be secured via SSL encryption, when necessary. Data passing between user and Master and between workstations is implemented following Transfer Object (TO) design practice – information is passed once as data bundle with serialized Java objects.

Data handling takes place in coordinator servlet on Master server. Problem is that web-based HTTP communication is naturally stateless. Normal HTTP session is valid only for short time, but simulation process may run much longer. We must identify users and store all their data. Users can then come back and receive their results later. Data module has three layers: presentation layer, business logic tier (data base queries, etc.) and physical database. First two layers are implemented in Java. User is accessing database via presentation layer, not directly. User tier consists of several functions to execute business layer queries. Database access is implemented using Data Access Object (DAO) design practice. Data access is using also Tomcat built-in connection pooling to speed up DB transactions.

3   Priorities

Important prerequisite for collaboration is that performance of each participant is overall enhanced; nobody should experience unfair lack of computing power, especially these participants who previously have donated most of their resources. Solution here is to introduce a priority system based on participants credit. Credit for host computer is calculated as:

$$Credit = Credit + Mode \cdot HostPerf \cdot CompTime \cdot LoadFraction . \qquad (1)$$

In formula (1), Mode equals "1" when computer is donating and "-1" when consuming; HostPerf referes to performance index of the computer, it is calculated initially after executing sample calibration task; CompTime is the time host computer has devoted to the current running task; LoadFraction is number between 0 and 1, inclusively. Credit rating of the host increases while other participants are consuming its processor time, at the same time ratings of the quests will decrease the same amount. Credit numbers can go negative, it shows who is contributing and who is not. Participant with higher credit rating will have higher priority and will be served sooner.

4 Task Partitioning

There are several methods to parallelize task execution in digital test engineering: algorithm can be parallelized, circuit model can be partitioned into separate components, fault set and test pattern data can be divided. In this paper, we rely on model partitioning, but technically it is possible to improve the overall performance by adding at the same time also test pattern parallelism concept. Faults are included already in simulation model, therefore fault list itself is not partitioned. Granularity of the task is important issue to consider. The smaller the network latency, the smaller slices of the task are useful. However, Internet has relatively big network latency, therefore larger model pieces are suitable – communication between partitions should be avoided.

Our simulation method and graph based model partitioning is described in [6]. Process of fault simulation is divided into number of parallel sub-processes. For each sub-process, a partial calculation model is constructed. In the current implementation, no analysis is conducted to find the optimal selection of partition for minimizing the size of overlapped area. Instead of that, partition is selected randomly taking into account only the required task size and amount of available memory. Algorithm uses internal memory counter to keep track of the currently allocated memory and stops the construction of partial calculation model when maximally allowed amount of allocated memory is reached. During model partitioning some overlapping likely occurs, as we want to avoid interdependences. These repetitive model parts are simulated several times, resulting some speed penalty. In fault coverage point of view results will be accumulated.

5 Task Allocation

Optimal task allocation ensures that all computers would stop computing at the same time. Several aspects have to be considered. Very slow machines should get only a small fraction of total load, workstation, which has fault, should get no load at all. Distribution of the tasks should happen within short time interval. Scheduler has to be fast not to delay the execution of the tasks. Scheduling objective is to minimize overall execution time, which is actually time of the longest executing subtask. In real-life situations tasks are accumulated and then scheduled in batches [7].

There could be possibly two goals while allocating tasks to different computers: 1) maximize the speed of particular task execution for particular user 2) maximize system overall throughput from the perspective of all users. We assume that in case of collaborative networking, the latter is more important; we can use adaptive approach depending on the situation.

5.1 Scheduling Algorithm

Initially, idle agents are polling the master server. Each agent announces its tolerated load threshold, it's current load and current performance index. Agents can determine its performance index by host profiling i.e. executing a small sample task and measuring the completion time. Thereafter, Agents prepare it's profiling message for Master server. This message includes also time stamp, so Master can measure the transfer time and determine network latency index for this particular Agent (it is assumed that clocks of both hosts are synchronized). Master collects the information initially for some predetermined time, obtained coefficients are applied later – faster machines will get larger tasks respectively.

Let us assume, that tasks are already submitted to the Master. Scheduler takes the task with highest credit rating and selects an Agent with least load index in the list, given that Agent's load is smaller than allowed threshold. Thereafter, scheduler takes the task with next highest credit rating and searches for next Agent satisfying the threshold condition above. This repetitive process continues until there are no tasks in the list.

The Agent selection idea in this intuitive scheduling strategy corresponds to Best-fit algorithm described in [8] and used for memory allocation problem. When dimension of scheduling becomes larger, i.e. number of agents and tasks grows, it is possible to switch over to a First fit algorithm also described in [8] – we look for first Agent in the list who's parameters satisfy condition above. This ensures that scheduling itself is not delayed.

When higher-priority task is submitted to scheduler, and there is no idle Agent available in the system, then scheduler has to suspend or reallocate some of the current tasks if expected completion time of the priority task is greater than migration time of the current task. Candidate task for migration is the one who has the lowest priority and longest execution time. Migration means that Agent notifies Master server and sends intermediate result of simulator tool to Master, thereafter Agent terminates the simulation task. Scheduler finds new target candidate for the task under migration. It will be the Agent with the lowest credit rating and with the best performance rating. Task must be also migrated when load on the host increases above allowable threshold, i.e. if local computing activity increases, as our goal was that participants in collaboration may not suffer. Exception is only the case, when such task belongs to the host owner. Load threshold is adjustable by each participant. Further information on load balancing can be found for example in [9], [10].

6   Circuit Model Security

In this paper, we assume that server host is trusted – circuit models must be uploaded first. Other hosts of participants can be less trusted, because to a certain extent, we can overcome model security problem automatically by partitioning the model itself - partial model is not very valuable for potential malicious agent. We may even enforce that model pieces are scheduled to the same processors during repetitive executions of the same circuit model, disabling the potential collection activity. However, identifying the right pieces of model must be handled. It is possible to compute the hash value of the model piece and save it to database. When later within limited time frame same hash value is computed for some model piece, then this task is scheduled to the same processing unit. Less limiting strategy is to ensure that not all the model pieces will be scheduled to the same processing unit. Malicious collector still will have no complete puzzle. Let us note that it is much harder to assemble the meaningful full model from pieces than just to recognize the same model piece. Computation of hash values could be performed in parallel with separate execution threads on multiprocessor computer.

7 Simulation Workflow

First, user specifies parameters and design file location (see Fig. 1). In addition, size of the simulation task can be predefined by user. Thereafter users Applet contacts with coordinating Master server and described parameters along the model are passed automatically. Task coordinator process on Master stores all requests from user(s) in the database. Simulation agents constantly poll the Master and if any subtask is scheduled by coordinator, then agents receive the appropriate parameters and design file and will start actual native simulator tool executable.

Simulator first constructs simulation model taking into account of the size limit of the subtask. While reaching the limit, it saves the breakpoint information into local file system. Simulation agent then reads the breakpoint information and passes it to the Master where it will be stored for other simulation agents. When next idle agent is polling, then it will receive the circuit file along parameters and breakpoint information. Agent starts a copy of simulator tool on the their host. Simulator first constructs simulation model again, but this time it is not starting from beginning, but restores from breakpoint up to the point when task size limit will be reached. New break point information will be again saved to local file system and later passed to Master server database by agent. Simulation agents then wait until their subtasks will be completed and report results back to Master server. Process repeats until there are no simulation sub tasks left. Note that simulators have been started subsequently, but thereafter they run concurrently. Total starting delay is small compared to runtime. Finishing order of simulators depends. It may not necessarily be the same as starting order as simulation speed depends on the piece of the circuit model - some pieces are more complicated to simulate. When all simulators are finished, then Master assembles sub results into final result and stores in database. Results are passed to user when requested.

8 Experimental Results

In experiments we measured communication overhead, memory gain by model size reduction, overall simulation speedup and scalability of the solution when processor number increases. Simulation was carried out on UltraSPARC IV+ 1500Mhz servers.

Tomcat servlet engine and MySQL database were running on two cores AMD Athlon 64 6000+ 3 GHz processor with 2 Gb memory. User applet was also running on the similar Athlon machine. Circuit file loading takes less than second for the largest 3,2 Mb size circuit file B17C on the user computer. File transfer to the database and user notification takes about 6 seconds. Thereafter, simulation agent receives circuit file from Master server 3-4 seconds later. Total communication delay was approximately 12-15 seconds (8%) in average compared to local single processor solution with current sample circuits [11]. Simulation results are presented in Table 1. B17C circuit for example contains part of the Intel 386 processor, repeated three times. In simulation experiments 100K test patterns were applied to circuits.

Table 1. Distributed simulation with model partitioning

Circuit	B17C	B21C	B22C
Number of logic gates	31008	18966	27599
Max model partitions	13	12	13
Max model build time,s	0,24	0,32	0,37
Max subtask simul. time, s	214	146	195
Model size reduction, times	4,1	2,5	2,6
Pure simulation speedup, times	3,4	2,7	3,1
Distrib. simul. speedup, times	3,2	2,5	2,9

9 Conclusions

We have presented how web-based distributed computing concept can be used collaboratively for digital circuits fault simulation. We introduced credit based priority management, addressed task scheduling and load balancing problem, handled model security issues. In experiments, web communication overhead was sufficiently small, depending on the size of the circuit and the number of test vectors simulated. In practice, circuits and vector sets may be much larger – overhead would be consequently smaller. Further improvement could be the use of compacted models.

Model partitioning allowed reducing required memory amount up to 4 times and at the same time simulation was also speed up 3,2 times (pure simulation speedup 3,4 times) compared to single processor simulation. Further speedups can be achieved by combining model partitioning and test set partitioning in the future.

Model partitioning algorithm could be possibly improved to support finer granularity. However, for moderately sized collaborative consortium, granularity might be sufficient, especially when combined with test set partitioning, since in reality there is usually more than single circuit model in use at given time – total number of tasks to be scheduled may be larger and appropriate for number of computers available. Model partitioning is useful in sense that it offers basic circuit model security since entire model needs to be handed over to central server only.

Acknowledgement

The work has been supported by Estonian SF grants 7068, 7483, EC FP7 IST project DIAMOND, ELIKO Development Centre and European Union through the European Regional Development Fund (Research Centre CEBE).

References

1. MOSCITO, `http://www.eas.iis.fhg.de/solutions/moscito`
2. Schneider, A., Ivask, E., Miklos, P., Raik, J., Diener, K.H., Ubar, R., Cibáková, T., Gramatová, E.: Internet-based Collaborative Test Generation with MOSCITO. In: Design, Automation & Test in EUROPE, DATE 2002, Paris, France, pp. 221–226 (2002)
3. Ivask, E., Raik, J., Ubar, R., Schneider, A.: WEB-Based Environment: Remote Use of Digital Electronics Test Tools. In: Virtual Enterprises and Collaborative Networks, pp. 435–442. Kluwer Academic Publishers, Dordrecht (2004)
4. Open-Source Software for Volunteer and Grid Computing, `http://boinc.berkeley.edu/`
5. Teo, Y.M., Low, S.C., Tay, S.C., Gozali, J.P.: Distributed Geo-rectification of Satellite Images using Grid Computing. In: International Parallel & Distributed Processing Symposium. IEEE Computer Society, Washington (2003)
6. Devadze, S., Ubar, R., Raik, J., Jutman, A.: Parallel Exact Critical Path Tracing Fault Simulation with Reduced Memory Requirements. In: Design & Technology of Integrated Systems in Nanoscal Era, DTIS 2009, Cairo, Egypt (2009)
7. Hwang, K., Xu, Z.: Scalable Parallel Computing: Technology, Architecture, Programming. McGraw-Hill, San Francisco (1998)
8. Donald, E.K.: Fundamental algorithms, 2nd edn., vol. 1. Addison-Wesley, Reading (1973)
9. Eager, D.L., Lazowska, E.D.: Zahorjan: Adaptive load sharing in homogenious distributed systems. IEEE Transactions on Software Engineering SE-12 (5), 662–675 (1986)
10. Shivaratri, N.G., Krueger, P., Singhal, M.: Load distributing for locally distributed systems. IEEE Computer 25(12) (1992)
11. Example circuits, `http://www.cad.polito.it/tools/itc99.html`

Context-Driven Decision Support in Flexible Networked Organisations

Alexander Smirnov, Tatiana Levashova, and Nikolay Shilov

St. Petersburg Institute for Informatics and Automation
of the Russian Academy of Sciences,
39, 14-th Line, 199178, St.-Petersburg, Russia
{smir,oleg,nick}iias.spb.su

Abstract. The paper proposes a context-driven approach to decision making in flexible networked organisations for the purpose of selecting partners for a specific task. The main idea of the approach is to represent the members of the networked organisation by services they provide. This makes it possible to replace the configuration of the networked organisation with that of services constituting it. Such representation benefits from the principles of the service-oriented architectures, such as service autonomy, abstraction, standardisation, and reusability. For the interoperability purposes the services communicate in terms of a common ontology. To improve the flexibility of the operational decision support each particular situation is described by a narrow context that contains only information that is relevant to the situation.

Keywords: Operational decision support, service network, ontology, context.

1 Introduction

Global climate changes and globalization of the world economy set new goals for the manufacturing companies. One of such new requirements is sustainability. There are several definitions for this term (e.g., [1]) but all of them refer to being environment friendly and as a result aiming at long-term competitive advantage. One of such definitions is given in [2]: sustainable manufacturing is developing technologies to transform materials without emission of greenhouse gases, use of non-renewable or toxic materials or generation of waste.

The author of [2] also identifies five major means helping to make manufacturing more sustainable. These means include:

1. Use less material and energy.
2. Substitute input materials: non-toxic for toxic, renewable for non-renewable.
3. Reduce unwanted outputs: Cleaner production, Industrial symbiosis.
4. Convert outputs to inputs: recycling and all its variants.
5. Changed structures of ownership and production: product service systems, supply chain structure.

The first four means require technological advances and fall beyond the scope of this paper. Instead, the paper concentrates on structural changes in production.

Á. Ortiz Bas, R.D. Franco, P. Gómez Gasquet (Eds.): BASYS 2010, IFIP AICT 322, pp. 153–159, 2010.

A context-driven service-oriented approach to decision support in flexible networked organisations is proposed for the purpose of selecting partners for a specific task. The approach also relies at profiling, which is important for determining members capable of carrying out a specified task with the given level of sustainability.

The paper is structured as follows. The context-driven service-oriented architecture is described in sec. 2. The application of the profiling technology is described in sec. 3. Major results are summarised in conclusions.

2 Approach

This work is a development of the idea presented in [3] aimed at knowledge management in production networks. The main idea of the developed approach is to represent the members of the flexible networked organisation by services they provide (Fig. 1). This would make it possible to replace the modelling of the networked organisation with that of services constituting it. The flexibility assumes efficient management of information and taking into account the dynamic environment. For this purpose the approach proposed actualises information in accordance with the current situation. An ontological model described by the Application Ontology (AO) is used in the approach to solve the problem of service heterogeneity. This model makes it possible to enable interoperability between heterogeneous information services due to provision of their common semantics [4]. Depending on the considered problem the relevant

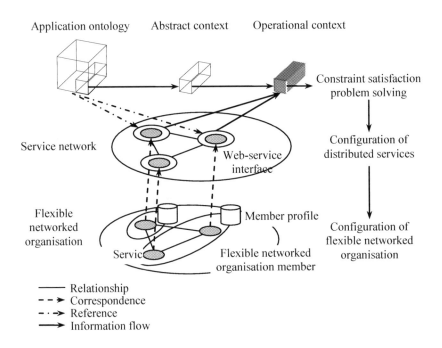

Fig. 1. Generic scheme of the approach

part of the application ontology is selected forming the abstract context that, in turn, is filled with values from the sources resulting in the operational context. Application of the context model makes it possible to reduce the amount of information to be processed. This model enables management of information relevant for the current situation [5]. The operational context represents the constraint satisfaction problem that is used during configuration of services for problem solving. The access to the services, information acquisition, transfer, and processing (including integration) are performed via usage of the technology of Web-services.

The service-oriented architecture has a number of advantages resulting from its principles [6]. Among these the following once should be mentioned (the specifics related to flexible supply network modelling are indicated with italic):

1. **Service Autonomy.** Services engineered for autonomy exercise a high degree of control over their underlying run-time execution environment. Autonomy, in this context, represents the level of independence which a service can exert over its functional logic. *With regard to networked organisations the autonomy also reflects independence of the network members, which in real life are independent companies.*

2. **Service Abstraction.** Further supporting service autonomy, service-oriented architecture advocates that the scope and content of a service's interface be both explicitly described and limited to that which is absolutely necessary for the service to be effectively employed. Beyond the service interface, abstraction applies to any information, in any form, describing aspects of the service's design, implementation, employed technologies, etc. *This principle helps to abstract from real services provided by the networked organisation members and concentrates on their modelling via Web-services.*

3. **Service Standardisation.** As services are typically distributed throughout networks, they must be easily accessible by other entities in terms of discoverability and consequential invocation. Given this requirement, service-oriented architecture recommends that services adhere to standards, including, for example, standards for the language used to describe a service to prospective consumers. *In the proposed approach the standardisation is achieved via usage of the common standards such as WSDL and SOAP as well as common terminology described by AO. As a result the services constituting the network are fully interoperable and can communicate with each other without any problems.*

4. **Service Reusability.** Reusability is a central property of any successful service. It denotes the capacity of a service to be employed in support of not just one but rather a variety of business models. Service-oriented architecture promotes such functional reuse through stipulations for service autonomy and interface abstraction. With these features, the same service can be invoked by multiple consumers, operating in various business domains, without requiring the service provider to re-code service internals for each application domain. *Service reusability significantly facilitates the modelling process and decreases the amount of work required for model building. Besides, the existing services of flexible supply network members can be used.*

In [6] two more service-oriented architecture principles are defined, namely service composability and service discovery. However, they are out of the scope of the presented approach.

3 Service-Oriented Architecture

In the proposed service-oriented architecture (Fig. 2) two types of Web-services are distinguished: *core Web-services* and *operational Web-services*.

The core Web-services are intended to create the abstract context and to monitor the business environment. The core Web-services comprise:

- **MonitoringService** monitors the environment, identifies the types of problems arising, and produces corresponding messages.
- **ManagementService** manages Web-services to create the abstract context. It operates with the service registry where the core services are registered.
- **AOAccessService** provides access to the AO;
- **AbstractContextService** creates, stores, and reuses abstract contexts;

The operational Web-services organize a service network. To make the Web-services active components capable to negotiate an agent-based service model is used. Agents are intended to negotiate services' needs and possibilities in terms of the AO and "activate" Web-services when required. The services' needs and possibilities are respectively input and output arguments of the functions that the Web-services implement. The set of operational Web-services comprises:

- **InformationSourceService** – a set of Web-services responsible for interactions with information sources of different types and for processing information provided by these sources. The following main types of information sources are distinguished: *sensors*, *databases*, *Web-sites*, and *humans*.
- **ProblemSolvingService** – a set of Web-services responsible for problem solving.
- **MemberProfileService** creates, modifies, and updates profiles of the acting resources or, in other words, the members of the networked organisation; provides

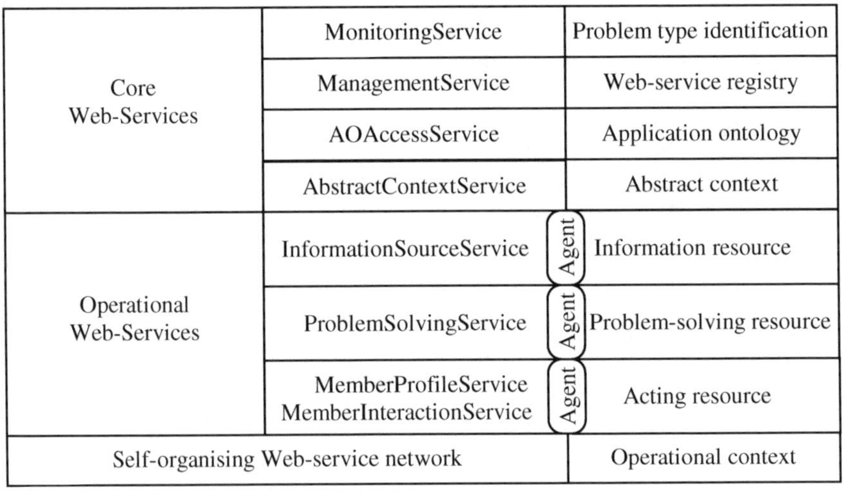

	MonitoringService	Problem type identification
Core Web-Services	ManagementService	Web-service registry
	AOAccessService	Application ontology
	AbstractContextService	Abstract context
Operational Web-Services	InformationSourceService [Agent]	Information resource
	ProblemSolvingService [Agent]	Problem-solving resource
	MemberProfileService MemberInteractionService [Agent]	Acting resource
Self-organising Web-service network		Operational context

Fig. 2. Service-oriented architecture

access to these profiles; collects information about the members; in a context-based way accumulates information about the member activities; reveals preferences of the members.

- **MemberInteractionService** – a set of Web-services responsible for support of and interactions with the members. They communicate between the system and the members (i) providing system messages, context-sensitive help, pictures of the current situation, results of problem solving to the members, and (ii) delivering information from the members to the system.

4   Profiling in Flexible Networked Organisation

Choosing the right partner in sustainable production network is essential and should be based on the potential partners' competences and sustainability. For this purpose application of the profiling technology is proposed. The structure of the networked organisation member profile is given in Fig. 3. Member competence is determined by capabilities, capacities, price-list and quickness. The network member profile comprises: *General Information, Member Information, Request History, Member Preferences.*

- The *General Information* part contains information about the member organisation, i.e. name of organisation, organization identifier in the system, date the organization was founded, and URL to the organization web page.
- *Member Information* is a set of tuples describing information about the member. Each tuple has the following properties:
  - Member Name – the name of the member;
  - Location – current geographical location of the member, it can be taken into account for estimating the speed and quality of request processing in a particular situation.
  - Time – time zone of the member;
  - List of Languages – languages for contacting the member;
  - Rights – knowledge area that the member can access;
  - Group – the member can be part of a group, based on its capabilities;
  - Phone Number, E-mail – contact information;
  - *Network Member Competence* includes the following properties:
    - Capabilities – types of operations that the member can implement;
    - Capacities – capacity of the member;
    - Prices – prices for implementing operations by the member;
    - Velocity – velocity of implementation operation by this member.
  - *Member Sustainability* describes sustainability properties of the member with regard to particular operations it can perform [1].
- *Request History* is a set of tuples. Each tuple possesses the following properties:
  - Request – a request to the member;
  - Context – is used to analyze the performance of the member (other members can see solutions generated in particular situations) and to identify detectable member preferences;

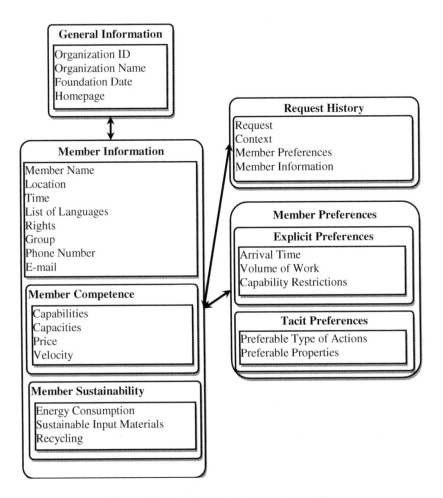

Fig. 3. Networked organisation member profile

   o   Member Preferences – stores member preferences at the moment of request initiation. They contain a snapshot of all the properties of the category "Network Member Preferences";

   o   Member Information – stores specific information about the member at the moment of request initiation. It contains a snapshot of all the properties of the category "Member Information".

• The *Member Preferences* part consists of Explicit Preferences and Tacit Preferences. Explicit Preferences describe member preferences that are manually introduced by a member. These preferences are used for choosing a member for a particular situation, and contain the member preference for arrival time, volume of work, and capability constraints. The latter stores several capabilities and logical restrictions from a list of all the capabilities for the domain. *Tacit Preferences* describe the automatically detectable member preferences.

5 Conclusions

The paper describes an approach to decision support in flexible networked organisations. The approach is aimed at achieving a higher sustainability level due to maximisation of the flexibility and taking into account the sustainability properties of the organisation members. The members are proposed to be represented via Web-services. As a result the configuration of the flexible networked organisation can be replaced with that of services. Usage of context makes it possible to reduce the search space since it narrows the domain. Profiling is important for determining, which member is capable of carrying out a specified task with the given level of sustainability and, hence, can be chosen as a team member.

Acknowledgments

Some of the results are due to research carried out as a part of the project funded by grants # 09-07-00436-a, 08-07-00264-a, and 09-07-00066-a of the Russian Foundation for Basic Research, and project # 213 of the research program "Intelligent information technologies, mathematical modeling, system analysis and automation" of the Russian Academy of Sciences.

References

1. Seliger, G. (ed.): Sustainability in Manufacturing. Springer, Heidelberg (2007)
2. Allwood, J.: What is sustainable Manufacturing?
   http://www.docstoc.com/docs/2319993/
   What-is-Sustainable-Manufacturing
3. Smirnov, A., Pashkin, M., Chilov, N., Levashova, T., Krizhanovsky, A.: Fusion-based Intelligent Support for Logistics Management. Emerging Solutions for Future Manufacturing Systems. In: Camarinha-Matos, L.M. (ed.) Proceedings of IFIP TC 5 / WG 5.5 Sixth IFIP International Conference on Information Technology for Balanced Automation Systems in Manufacturing and Services (BASYS), pp. 209–216. Springer, Heidelberg (2004)
4. Dey, A.K.: Understanding and Using Context. Personal and Ubiquitous Computing J. 5(1), 4–7 (2001)
5. Uschold, M., Grüninger, M.: Ontologies: Principles, methods and applications. Knowledge Engineering Review 11(2), 93–155 (1996)
6. CADRC. KML Sandbox: An Experimentation Facility Based on SOA Principles. CADRD Currents, Fall, Collaborative Agent Design Research Center (CADRC), California Polytechnic State University, San Luis Obispo (2009)

Creation of Robust Schedule
for Profit Based Cooperation

Jiří Hodík

Gerstner Laboratory – Agent Technology Center, Faculty of Electrical Engineering,
Czech Technical University in Prague, Technická 2, Praha 6, Czech Republic
hodik@labe.felk.cvut.cz

Abstract. Method for robust schedule preparation for domain of profit based cooperation is introduced in this paper. The method aims schedules, which are prepared and concluded step-by-step during the team formation phase. The method takes into account domain specifics, like incomplete information about the partners, and their various reputation and skill levels. The method is based on critical path dispatching rule, which is widely used in heuristics for *np* hard and continuous scheduling problems. Experimental results are presented for various workflow structures and other configurations of the domain.

1 Introduction

In the domain of profit based cooperation, the cooperators are motivated to join (and to stay in) the team (e.g. Supply Chain and some types of Virtual Organizations) by expected profit. We concentrate to teams with one leader subcontracting the other partners mutually independently. Sometimes the leader has to conclude contracts with the others without having prepared whole schedule; it is to be prepared online during the negotiation about involvement the partners. Contrary to the intra-organizational scheduling, this scheduling adds requirements and constraints to scheduling methodologies. Together with complexity of the scheduling problem it is too hard to prepare valuable estimation of schedule until it is negotiated with the partners. Moreover, the leader has limited access to information about the partners' resources and such information may be distorted either by intention of partners to improve impression about their competencies, or by inexperienced guess of them.

When any already concluded due-date is not kept and if there is not enough slack, the processing of consequent tasks is delayed. It is critical mainly when it is not possible to reschedule the consequent tasks either because of high utilization of facility, or because of high penalties for not keeping the concluded due-dates.

The targeted domain relates to the supply chain planning and scheduling models class, which includes medium planning models mainly on an entire network level (e.g., project planning and scheduling or lot sizing models), as well as detailed scheduling models mainly on work-centers levels (e.g., job shop scheduling). The features crucial for the top level schedule creation are:

Á. Ortiz Bas, R.D. Franco, P. Gómez Gasquet (Eds.): BASYS 2010, IFIP AICT 322, pp. 160–167, 2010.
© IFIP International Federation for Information Processing 2010

- *Members.* They may be autonomous, self-oriented and distributed.
- *Limited access to information.* Nobody has direct access to the partners' internal information, neither the team leader.
- *Partners with limited reliability.* Presumption about partners' trustworthiness may be helpful in negotiation about resources allocation.
- *Concluded contracts.* Withdrawing from a contract or changing it is limited by the concluded rules and the affected partner's willingness.

There are several scenarios for team creation phase; all of them provide the plan and schedule for further team operations. The schedule is pre-negotiated with the partners before its conclusion, or involvements of the partners are being concluded continuously during the scheduling process. Reasons for continuous concluding are: (i) partners provide an expected completion time of the task but they do not share knowledge about available resources; and (ii) partners' resources may be shared within the partner; once dedicated for a task they cannot be used for the other one.

The scheduling algorithm is interlinked with a protocol for negotiation about tasks processing commitments. Often, it is possible to pre-negotiate involvement of the members, or mechanisms for its update according to current state of the team exist. There are several works extending basic negotiation protocols by non-bounding offers and commitments to improve quality of the consortium and its schedule like LAP [5], C-CNP [7], RC-CNP [1], and RBVO formation protocol [8]. Although any such mechanism for involvement modification may be implemented, there is a condition of available resources. Without resources, the schedule update is excluded although the negotiation protocols would support the updating process.

2 Scheduling Methods

Many scheduling methods for (not only hard) scheduling problems are based on priority rules comparing tasks priorities from attributes of tasks, machines, and actual state of the world. The rules are *static*, or *dynamic* (time is important as well). There are several schedule measures and objectives. Example of a schedule objective is the *makespan*, which is defined as the latest completion times of mutually related tasks.

2.1 Critical Path Method

The Critical Path Method (CPM) is a common method for scheduling set of tasks with defined precedence constraints. The objective to be optimized is the makespan. The method concentrates to finding and optimization of *critical path* under these constraints: (i) the processing time of a task is fixed, (ii) no other resource than machine time is required, and (iii) there are enough of parallel machines. The CPM inspired for Critical Path dispatching rule, which employs precedence constraints and processing times of tasks. From them the strings of processing times are counted and the head of the longest one is given the highest priority.

2.2 Robustness of Schedule

The robust schedule is required when any rescheduling may negatively influence the schedule objectives (e.g., too expensive, late, or no alternate resources). The robust schedule has *"the ability to satisfy performance requirements predictably in an uncertain environment"* (Pape in [4] in [2] by Davenport et al.). Pinedo presents four examples how to create a more robust schedule [6]:

- *Inserting idle/slack times.* Depending on a rule, the idle times may be equal or depending on size/priority of foregoing task.
- *Scheduling less flexible jobs/tasks first.* Each task may be influenced by aggregated perturbations of its predecessors, for the less flexible ones this risk should be minimized.
- *Postponing the processing of an operation only if really needed.* Contrary to the inventory cost point of view it is better to start as soon as possible.
- *Bottleneck machine utilization optimization.* As the bottleneck has high impact on
- facility capacity and makespan, is should not wait for a task.

We suggest extending the Pinedo's list of potentials to increase the robustness by:

- *Reliable partners.* The ones with higher probability to keep concluded dates should be preferred.

Various method for computation of idle times is explored e.g. by Davenport et al., who concentrate to using robustness technique for scheduling of job-shops with totally ordered tasks in domain with full access to control over the machines [2].

To evaluate robustness of the schedule, the measure must be defined. The robustness may be counted from the schedule as it is prepared, or evaluated after the scheduled tasks (real or simulated) execution. Pinedo defines a concept, which evaluates robustness of the original schedule. The measure is based on the amount of weighted slacks between the tasks' completion times and due-dates [6]. Kouvelis and Yu suggest criteria to evaluated schedule robustness from simulated performance [3]:

- *Absolute robustness.* The worst scenario performance is the key.
- *Robust deviation.* Each scenario performance is evaluated against the optimal one to get the deviation. The worst deviation got is the key.
- *Relative robustness.* Similar to the robust deviation but the percentage deviation from the optimal case for the scenario is used.

3 Scheduling Process

The presented scheduling algorithm is based on CPM. The *makespan* and *schedule robustness* are the optimized objectives. The idea is that the critical tasks should be preferred during scheduling. Contrary, as the expected processing times are known after their negotiation, they may differ from the nominal ones. Therefore the critical path is not known until the whole schedule is prepared. It is being estimated and modified during the scheduling process. Simultaneously, keeping the negotiated times is not guarantied and therefore there is a request for robust schedules to be able to process whole job of the team.

3.1 Formal Description of the Scheduling Problem

From the task definition a nominal processing time is known. Actually, due to various capabilities and available resources, the processing times negotiated with the machines[1] may differ. While the capabilities are supposed to be constant during the life-cycle of the VO, the resources may vary in time.

The nominal processing time of the task[2] j is p_j. For starting time S_j, the nominal completion time is $C_j = S_j + p_j$. For processing of task j on machine i the concluded completion and processing times are C_{ij} and p_{ij}. There may be also an expected completion time C'_{ij}, which is delayed by δ_{ij}. The expected processing time is $p'_{ij} = C'_{ij}(\delta_{ij}) - S_{ij}$; relation $p'_{ij} \geq p_{ij}$ may be expected.

For estimation of the delay, only following is available: the task and its complexity (represented by p_j), concluded processing time p_{ij}, and confidence in machine (given as some reputation model R_i). The expected delay for the task j is $\delta_{ij} = f(p_j, p_{ij}, R_i)$. As the concluded processing time p_{ij} is counted from the machine's available resources, p_j may be omitted and therefore $\delta_{ij} = f(p_{ij}, R_i)$.

3.2 Algorithm Overview

Estimation of the critical path in any scheduling step is based on already concluded tasks processing (on the expected completion times), and nominal processing times (for scheduled yet part of the schedule). The following is defined:

- *JOB* is a list of all tasks, $JOB = \{t_1, ..., t_n\}$, where t_j for $(1 \leq j \leq n)$ is a task from the list, and n is number of tasks in the list. For any couple of tasks the finish-to-start transitive precedence constraint $t_1 \prec t_2$ may be defined. The precedence graph must be acyclic.
- *CLOSE* is a list of already scheduled tasks. For every t_k its starting time, and concluded and (if applied) expected completion times are known.
- *OPEN* is a list of not yet scheduled tasks. Let *OPEN'* denote a subset of tasks from *OPEN* having their precedential tasks scheduled.

For $\forall t_k \in OPEN$ the earliest possible starting time is denoted by the latest completion time from set of completion times of all predecessors: $S'_j \geq \max\{C_k : t_k \prec t_j\}$. If

---

[1] To be consistent with common terminology, the work-centers of the members are called machines.

[2] In the definitions j, k are indexes of tasks, and h, i indexes of responsible machines.

$\forall t_k \left(t_k \prec t_j \rightarrow t_k \in CLOSE \right)$ then t_j may be scheduled with starting time S'_j, otherwise S'_j denotes that final $S_{ij} \geq S'_j$.

There are various priority rules for selection of the next task to be scheduled (t_{NEXT}) from the $OPEN'$ list. We have adopted following ones:

- *Any ready task rule*, by that any task ready to be scheduled is chosen.
- *Nominal critical path rule*, the next task is chosen according to the critical path counted from nominal processing times.
- *Current critical path rule*, the next task is chosen according to the critical path, which is updated according already existing schedule fragments.
- *Longest chain of successor rules*, the next task is chosen as the head of the longest chain of not scheduled tasks yet.

When the t_{NEXT} is defined, the negotiation about its assignment and completion time is performed. We consider basic negotiation protocol which for defined starting time provides a set of completion times proposed by the interested machines. The decision process for determination of the winning proposal takes into account the proposed completion time and (if applied) reputation model of the proposer. We have adopted two rules for winning offer determination:

- The *basic rule* for offer determination: $C_{\min}\left(\forall C_{hj}\right)$, where C_{hj} is by machine h proposed completion time for task j.
- The *reputation rule* for offer determination: $C'_{\min}\left(\forall C'_{hj}\right)$, where C'_{hj} is the expected completion times counted from reputation models of the proposers ($C'_{hj} \geq C_{hj}$).

Next step to increase the schedule robustness is adding the *idle time* to the concluded completion time. The idle time $idle_j$ of the task j postpones earliest time for starting consequent tasks ($S_k - C'_{ij} \geq idle_j; t_j \prec t_k$). In this work, the rules for idle time determination do not consider whether the task is the earlier one or the latter one (such information could be also beneficial as described in [2]). Our rules are:

- No *idle time rule*, $idle_j = 0$.
- The *nominal processing time rule* based on requested robustness and nominal processing time, $idle_j = f\left(p_j\right)$.
- The *concluded processing time rule* is based on requested robustness and concluded processing time of the task, $idle_j = f\left(p_{ij}\right)$.
- The *expected processing time rule* is based on requested robustness and expected processing time of the task, $idle_j = f\left(p'_{ij}\right)$.

Algorithm 1. Process of Robust Schedule Preparation

```
OPEN and CLOSE are empty
copy ∀t_j from JOB to OPEN
for ∀t_j ∈ OPEN do
   setup S_j to S_JOB
end for
repeat
   for ∀t_j ∈ OPEN do
     for ∀t_k, where t_k takes precedence over t_j do
        if ∀t_k ∈ CLOSE then
           setup S_j to max(∀C_k'; t_k takes precedence over t_j)
           move t_j to OPEN'
        end if
     end for
   end for
   use priority rule to select t_NEXT from OPEN'
   use negotiation mechanism to get offers for of C_ij,
where t_j = t_NEXT and ∀i are machines able to process t_j
   use reputation model to get C_ij'
   select C_j' = min(∀C_ij)
   insert idle time to increase robustness
   move t_j from OPEN' to CLOSE
until OPEN' is empty
C_JOB = max(C_j'; ∀j, t_j ∈ CLOSE)
```

Formal description of process of preparation robust schedule preparation is presented by Algorithm 1. In the algorithm, the S_{JOB} is the starting time of whole operation, the C_{JOB} is its completion time.

4   Experiments

Several configurations of the algorithm were used; each configuration was run 20 times. In all of them simple CNP is used as a negotiation mechanism and 10 machines with limited resources shared across all tasks is involved, their capabilities vary from 70% to 90%. Each machine is able to process any task. Requested robustness is 5%. Number of tasks is counted as square of numbers from 1 to 7. For each task, its resources requirements are equal to 10 times the number of tasks IDs. Three different workflow structures (see Figure 1) defined by precedence constraints are used:

- *Single string*, all the tasks are in one string, which is a critical path. All priority rules provide the same t_{NEXT}.
- *All tasks in parallel*, each parallel string consists of one task. The critical path consists of the longest task(s). "Any task" priority rule provides random t_{NEXT}, the other rules provide the same one.
- *Parallel strings*, all parallel strings consist of same number of tasks and have the same starting date. The tasks are distributed by rule that the following task is added to the tail of the next string. Each of priority rule may provide different t_{NEXT}.

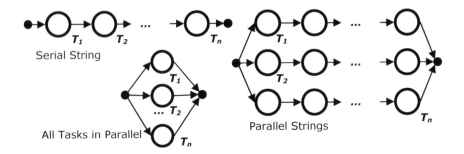

Fig. 1. Applied workflow structures

4.1 Results

Example of simulation runs is presented on Figure 2. The set of graphs presents makespan, robustness and scheduling order for number of tasks from 1 to 49 for parallel strings workflow structure and the priority rule of "Any task". The reputation is not assumed; no extra idle times are added.

In most of the results (not just this one), there is a break in results at position between 9 ($=3^2$) and 16 ($=4^2$) tasks. It is due to number of tasks that is higher than number of machines; the machines may be overloaded by already scheduled tasks.

The Table 1 presents selected results of simulations for 9 (maximum number of tasks, which is less then number of machines) and 49 tasks (maximum number of tasks in experiments, machines are overloaded). In all simulations the requested robustness was kept. The slack reserves were mainly in parallel structure on non-critical tasks if the priority rule was "Any task". For the linear-parallel structure, there is space for post-processing negotiation with partners about redistribution of slacks on the end of non-critical chains among their tasks. Also it is clear that assuming any information about the future tasks is better than scheduling any task of the ready ones. The average makespans does not differ significantly although the order of tasks

Table 1. Selected simulation results

Average robustness based on processing time:		Scheduled makespan (No. of tasks):			
		9 (more machines than tasks)		49 (more tasks than machines)	
Structure:	Priority rule:	Nominal	Concluded	Nominal	Concluded
Linear	Any task	1.12	1.18	1.11	1.17
Parallel	Any task	1.21	1.25	11.89	12.68
	CP nominal	1.11	1.56	14.74	16.13
Linear-parallel	Any task	1.12	1.17	1.21	1.28
	CP nominal	1.12	1.17	1.11	1.17
	CP current	1.12	1.17	1.11	1.17
	Longest successors	1.12	1.17	1.12	1.17

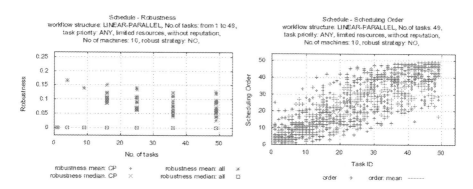

Fig. 2. Example of simulation results

scheduling varies, the main difference is in variances of robustness mainly when the reputation models are applied (not in scope of this paper).

References

1. Bíba, J., Vokřínek, J., Hodík, J.: Renegotiable competitive contract net protocol. Technical Report GL 194/08, ATG, Gerstner Laboratory, CTU (2008)
2. Davenport, A.J., Gefflot, C., Beck, J.C.: Slack-based techniques for robust schedules. In: Proc. of the Sixth European Conf. on Planning, ECP 2001 (2001)
3. Kouvelis, P., Yu, G.: Robust Discrete Optimization and Its Applications. Springer, Heidelberg (1996)
4. Pape, C.L.: Constraint propagation in planning and scheduling. Technical report, Stanford University, Palo Alto, California (1991)
5. Perugini, D., Jarvis, D., Reschke, S., Gossink, D.: Distributed deliberative planning with partial observability: Heuristic approaches. In: Proc. of the Int. Conf. on Integration of Knowledge Intensive Multi-Agent Systems. KIMAS 2007, pp. 407–412 (2007)
6. Pinedo, M.L.: Planning and Scheduling in Manufacturing and Services. Series in Operations Research and Financial Engineering. Springer, Heidelberg (2006)
7. Vokřínek, J., Bíba, J., Hodík, J., Vybíhal, J., Pěchouček, M.: Competitive contract net protocol. In: van Leeuwen, J., Italiano, G.F., van der Hoek, W., Meinel, C., Sack, H., Plášil, F. (eds.) SOFSEM 2007. LNCS, vol. 4362, pp. 656–668. Springer, Heidelberg (2007)
8. Vokřínek, J., Bíba, J., Hodík, J., Vybíhal, J., Volf, P.: RBVO formation protocol. In: 2007 IEEE/WIC/ACM International Conference on Intelligent Agent Technology (IAT 2007), pp. 454–457 (2007b)

Designing a Genetic Algorithm to Solve an Integrated Model in Supply Chain Management Using Fuzzy Goal Programming Approach

M. Rostami N. K.i[*], J. Razmi, and F. Jolai

Department of Industrial Engineering, College of Engineering, University of Tehran, Iran
{jrazmi,marostamy,fjolai}@ut.ac.ir

Abstract. Application of fuzzy goal programming and genetic algorithm is considered in this paper. We extend a multi-objective model for integrated inventory-production-distribution planning in supply chain (SC). We consider a supply chain network which consists of a manufacture, with multiple plants, multiple distribution centers (DCs), multiple retailers and multiple customers. The manufacturer produces several items. Decision maker's imprecise aspiration levels of goals are incorporated into model using fuzzy goal programming approach. Due to the complexity of problem in large size and in order to get a satisfactory near optimal solution with great speed, a new genetic algorithm is proposed to solve constrained problems. To show the efficiency of the used model and fuzzy goal programming approach and genetic algorithm for the collaborative inventory-production-distribution problem, computational experiments are performed on a hypothetically constructed case problem.

Keywords: fuzzy goal programming, supply chain management, genetic algorithm.

1 Introduction

Industries around the world are now all rushing the territory of globalization and specialization. Cooperating with good strategic partner is the sure way to tackle the potential problems arising from competition. Companies can achieve the optimum operating efficiency by working with other companies through communication and specialization which evolve a new type of relationship, the SC relationship, among these companies and further faster a new concept in management: the supply chain management (SCM). Production and distribution operations are the two most important operational functions in a SC. To achieve optimal operational performance in a SC, it is critical to integrate these two functions and plan them jointly in a coordinated way [[1],[9]]. Different aspects of integrated problems for different parts of supply chain have been considered in the literatures. Nozick and Turnquist [9] tried to integrate inventory, transportation and location functions of a supply chain. The proposed model has been confined to a single period, single echelon problem with no capacity constraint.

---

[*] Corresponding author.

Á. Ortiz Bas, R.D. Franco, P. Gómez Gasquet (Eds.): BASYS 2010, IFIP AICT 322, pp. 168–176, 2010.
© IFIP International Federation for Information Processing 2010

Some researchers have investigated fuzzy production planning problems in SC ([10], [1], [5]). Decision analysis in e-supply chain using fuzzy set approach mainly on the basis of fuzzy reasoning Petry nets has been considered by Gao et al [5]. The method proposed by Liang [8] aims at simultaneous minimization of total distribution costs and the total delivery time on the basis of fuzzy available supply, total budget, fuzzy forecast demand, and warehouse space. Chen et al. [4] suggested an approach to deriving the membership function of the fuzzy minimum total cost of the multi-period SC model with fuzzy parameters. The considered fuzzy production planning models and methods are mainly a single product type and separate production planning model without integration with distribution and inventory problems. Computational intelligence is widely used in economics and finance [Chen [3], Sheen [11], Zadro et al. [14]]. Torabi and Hassini [13] considered a supply chain master planning model consisting of multiple suppliers, one manufacturer and multiple distribution centers. They proposed a method to solve multi-objective linear programming (MOLP) models, named TH. Although many researchers have been devoted to solve production–distribution problems in SC environment, there is a few researches that integrates an aggregate inventory-production and distribution plan in a collaborative manner using fuzzy modeling approaches.

This paper contributes to the literature by presenting a multi objective model with resource constraints and lead times and considering a manufacturer with states which is near to real world rather than other models and using FGP approach for handling the collaborative inventory- production–distribution planning problems SC and presenting a new genetic algorithm approach for constrained problems. Evolutionary algorithms such as genetic algorithm were used to solve combinatorial problems. A Genetic algorithm (GA) based method has been used to develop an efficient solution algorithm by Tasan[12]. Fuzzy-Genetic approach has been proposed to aggregate production and distribution planning in supply chain management by Aliev et al [2]. Many challenges arise when the algorithm is applied to heavily constrained problems where feasible regions may be sparse or disconnected. This study proposes an approach to obtain solutions which are close to the feasible region.

2 Mathematical Model

2.1 Indices

i: index of production items (i=1,...,I)
t: index of time periods(t=1,...,T)
p: index of plants(p=1,...,P)
d: index of DC s(d=1,...,D)
r: index of retailers(r=1,...,R)
c:index of customers(c=1,...,C)

2.2 Problem Assumptions

The assumptions to model the problem are as follows:

1. It has been considered a manufacturer with p plants, d distributors, r retailers, and c customers
2. All of the decisions are made within multi-periods.

3. Customers assign cost for backorder as a penalty for retailers.
4. There is transportation capacity constraint for all echelons.
5. Delivery due dates have been assigned by distributors.

2.3 Parameters

CD_{irct} : Amount of product i demanded by customer c from retailer r in period t.
PCP_i: Unit production cost of product i.
$SPMD_{it}$: Unit sales price for product i from manufacturer to DCs in period t. This included product cost, the cost of transportation, and ordering cost.
SPD_{idrt}: Unit sales price for product i from DC d to retailer r in period t.
$TCPD_{ipdt}$: Unit transportation cost for product i from plant p to DC d in period t. DC pay it.
HCF_{ip}: Unit inventory holding cost of final product i in plant p.
HCD_{id}: Unit inventory holding cost of final product i in DC d.
$FHCP_{ipt}$: Final product i warehouse capacity in plant p in period t.
$PHCP_{idt}$: Final product i warehouse capacity in DC d in period t.
$PHCR_{irt}$: Final product i warehouse capacity in retailer r in period t.
TFP_i: Unit processing time for final product i.
TDR_{drt}: Transportation capacity from DC d to retailer r in period t.
$DUEM_{ipdt}$: Delivery due date for product i from DC d to manufacturer in period t.
TPD_{pd}: The time required to ship the products from plant p to DC d.
TCM_{pdt}: Transportation capacity from plant p to DC d in period t.

2.4 Decision Variables

PTD_{idrt}: Amount of product i to be transported from DC d to retailer r in period t.
TRC_{irct}: Amount of product i to be transported from retailer r to customer c in period t.
$PTPD_{ipdt}$: Amount of product i to be transported from plant p to DC d in period t.
ID_{idt}: Inventory of product i at the DC d in period t.
IR_{irt}: Inventory of final product i in retailer r in period t.
PQ_{ipt}: Production quantity of product i in plant p in period t.
BCR_{irct}: The amount of backorder of product i from retailer r to customer c at the end of period t.
TIP_{ipt}: The time in which final product i is maintain in plant p in period t.
FP_{ipt}: The amount of inventory of product i in plant p in period t

2.5 Objective Functions

Manufacturer Profit :(Maximization)=sales revenue-total manufacturing cost - total inventory types holding cost

$$=\Sigma_i \Sigma_p \Sigma_d \Sigma_t (SPMD_{it} * PTPD_{ipdt}) - \Sigma_i \Sigma_p \Sigma_t (PCP_i * PQ_{ipt})$$
$$- \Sigma_i \Sigma_p \Sigma_t (HCF_{ip} * FP_{ipt}) \tag{1}$$

inventory cost-total transportation cost

$$=\sum_i \sum_r \sum_t (SPD_{idrt} * PTD_{idrt}) -\sum_i \sum_p \sum_t (SPMD_{it} * PTPD_{ipdt})$$
$$-\sum_i \sum_t (HCD_{id} * ID_{idt}) -\sum_i \sum_p \sum_t (TCPD_{ipdt} * PTPD_{ipdt}) \tag{2}$$

Backorder Level For Retailer r : (Minimization)

$$=\sum_i \sum_c \sum_t (BCR_{irct}) \tag{3}$$

2.6 Constraints

$$FP_{ipt} \leq FHCP_{ipt} \qquad \forall\, i, p, t \tag{4}$$

$$ID_{idt} \leq PHCP_{idt} \quad \forall\, i, d, t \tag{5}$$

$$IR_{irt} \leq PHCR_{irt} \qquad \forall\, i, r, t \tag{6}$$

(4), (5), (6) state that inventory level in each echelon is restricted by inventory capacity.

Since, distributors set due date for delivering items from manufacturer, thus sum of production time in manufacturer and inventory holding time in plants in each period and delivery time items to distributor, should be less than product delivery due date. Thus we have:

$$\left(PQ_{ipt} * TFP_i\right) + \left(TIP_{ipt}\right) + \left(TPD_{pd} * PTPD_{ipdt}\right)$$
$$\leq DUEM_{ipdt} \qquad \forall i, p, d, t \tag{7}$$

$$\sum_i PTPD_{ipdt} \leq TCM_{pdt} \quad \forall\, d, p, t \tag{8}$$

$$\sum_i PTD_{idrt} \leq TDR_{drt} \qquad \forall\, d, r, t \tag{9}$$

(8), (9), mean that the amount of product i to be transported among echelons is limited by transportation capacity.

$$ID_{idt} = ID_{idt-1} + \sum_p PTPD_{ipdt} - \sum_r PTD_{idrt} \qquad \forall\, i, d, t \tag{10}$$

(10) is balance equation for DCs; the amount of products that enter to DC d must be equal to the amount of products that leave from and stored at this DC.

Inventory of product i in plant p in period t is equal to inventory of that product in previous period plus production quantity of product i in plant p in period t minus amount of product i transported from plant p to DCs in period t. As shown by (11):

$$FP_{ipt} = FP_{ipt-1} + PQ_{ipt} - \sum_d PTPD_{ipdt} \quad \forall\, i, p, t \tag{11}$$

Backorder level of product i incurred by retailer r in period t equals to backorder level of that product in previous period plus total demand of the product by retailer r in that period. This is shown by (12).

$$\sum_{c} BCR_{irct} = \sum_{c} BCR_{irc(t-1)} + \sum_{c} CD_{irct} - \sum_{c} TRC_{irct} \qquad \forall i, r, t \qquad (12)$$

And finally, the backorder level at the last period should be zero for fulfilling the customer demand:

$$\sum_{c} BCR_{ircT} = 0 \quad \forall i, r \qquad (13)$$

All of variables are continuous and positive.

3 Methodology

3.1 The Proposed Genetic Algorithm

In this problem we are dealing with a multiple objective possibilistic linear programming model. To solve this problem, we apply a two-step approach. In the first step, the original problem is converted into an equivalent auxiliary crisp multiple objective linear model. In the second step, a fuzzy goal programming approach which is named TH is used. In this method the crisp multi-objective model convert to a single objective model considering decision maker's imprecise aspiration levels for goals.

To solve the problem, we propose a genetic algorithm (PGA) considering constrained model and compare the results with algorithm which is proposed by Haupt and Haupt[7] (HGA). We use continuous genetic algorithm versus binary genetic algorithm, because variables are continuous. For dealing with our constrained model when model's size is large, we propose a genetic algorithm which its solutions are selected from feasible region as far as possible because it is impossible to select all members of population from feasible region. Then we compare obtained results through this method with method which is proposed by Haupt and Haupt [7] named HGA. In HGA method, constraints are added to objective function by using penalty coefficients.

A constrained model can be stated as follows:

Min f(x)   s.t

$g_j(x) \le 0 \quad j = 1, \dots, J$

$h_i(x) = 0 \quad i = 1, \dots, I$

In majority of algorithms, for generating initial population random numbers are used for generating initial population. While, in a problem which includes constraints in addition to objective functions, using this random numbers cannot imply that initial population has been selected from a feasible region or has minimum violation. Also, initial population is the base for constructing next populations. In genetic algorithm which is presented here, we consider this problem. Also initial solution is constructed with minimization of violation. We do it, using PSO algorithm which is an evolutionary algorithm similar to genetic algorithm but it have operators less than genetic algorithm. Thus, for generating initial population, we minimize below fitness function: Violation= $\sum_j \max(0, g_i) + \sum_i |h_i|$

Another difference between our proposed genetic algorithm and other algorithms is that in this algorithm fitness function is the same as objective function. The method for mating which has been proposed by Haupt and Haupt[7] is as follows:

The blending method finds ways to combine variable values from the two parents into new variable values in the offspring. A single offspring variable value, P_{new}, comes from a combination of the two corresponding offspring variable values

$P_{new} = \beta \ P_{mn} + (1-\beta)P_{dn}$ Where: β= random number on the interval [0, 1], P_{mn}= nth variable in the mother chromosome, P_{dn}= nth variable in the father chromosome. In our proposed genetic algorithm for mating, β change while the violation for new offspring is less than the average violation in initial population. Also for mutation and selecting the member which should be affected by mutation ,we continue generating random numbers while interested violation will be occurred, then replace the amount of selected member with the amount of same member in chromosome which has minimum violation.

3.2 Analysis of Variance

In addition to achievement level, another characteristic which has been considered to compare performance of HGA and PGA is violation. It has been done by analysis of variance (ANOVA). An independent t-test has been conducted to test the difference between mean of violations. It is assumed that:

M1: violation which was resulted from HGA
M2: violation which was resulted from PGA

Analysis of variance was done using Minitab. Thus following 2 tests of hypothesis were performed.

$$\begin{cases} H_0: M_1 = M_2 \\ H_1: M_1 \geq M_2 \end{cases}$$

Amount of obtained p-value for test of hypothesis 1 is 0.045. Considering, test of hypothesis is performed with 0.95 for confidence level, and p-value for test of hypothesis is less than 0.05, thus, null hypothesis is rejected. It shows that mean of violation in PGA is less than HGA (P-value<0.05).

4   Numerical Example

To demonstrate the practicality of the proposed model, we considered an assumed SC. In our hypothetically constructed SC, there is a manufacturer company consists of multiple plants, multiple DCs, retailers and customers. First, a problem with a small size has been designed and then results have been compared with Lingo's results. Both genetic algorithms run 30 times and satisfaction degree for each goal is calculated. Then we set:

w_1 (Weight of manufacturer)=0.3,w_2 (Weight of DCs)=0.3,w_3 (Weight of retailers)=0.4. Also, we set δ =0.5(δ is coefficient in TH method)

i=3, t=4, p=3, d=2, r=3, c=3. We generate all of required parameters randomly. For receiving further information about these random numbers, please contact the corresponding author. To survey the results obtained from Lingo8 and genetic algorithm, a problem with small size has been solved and results have been presented in table1. It is concluded that the average difference between PGA and HGA and lingo is 7% and 10% respectively. Obviously, difference between results obtained from PGA and HGA are not large; thus, methods can be used in problems with large size. Now, consider a large model and set: i=6, t=8, p=5, d=2, r=3, c=3. The satisfaction degree of each goal is shown in table 2; as can be seen, the satisfaction degree for goals in PGA algorithm is more than HGA, and it reveals the efficiency of proposed genetic algorithm.

Table 1. Achievement levels obtained by Lingo, HGA, PGA in small size

Achievement Level(%)	Lingo	HGA	PGA
μprofitM	0.85	0.63	0.66
μ_{DC1}profit	0.94	0.75	0.80
μ_{DC2}profit	0.92	0.72	0.76
μ_{RET1}BLG	0.95	0.75	0.79
μRET2BLG	0.75	0.61	0.69
μRET3BLG	0.87	0.65	0.71

Table 2. Achievement levels obtained by HGA, PGA in large size

Achievement Level(%)	HGA	PGA
μprofitM	0.59	0.6
μ_{DC1}profit	0.71	0.7
μ_{DC2}profit	0.68	0.69
μ_{RET1}BLG	0.72	0.74
μRET2BLG	0.6	0.62
μRET3BLG	0.67	0.69

5   Conclusions

Managing operations in today's competitive market place poses significant challenges. Based on the traditional thought there were so many conflicts in the multiple demands on the operational functions that trade-offs were made in achieving excellence in one or more of these dimensions.

This paper tackled with integrated inventory-production-distribution planning problem in SC system. A multi-objective linear programming model has been developed in this concern. Decision maker's imprecise aspiration levels for the goals have been incorporated into the model using fuzzy goal programming approach. Computational experiments have been provided from a case problem. A genetic algorithm has been proposed to solve constrained problem and results have been compared to genetic algorithm suggested by Haupt and Haupt(2004). While, in solving problems with constraints there is no guarantee that initial population is feasible or has minimum violation. Proposed Genetic Algorithm, using PSO algorithm, tries to construct initial solution with minimum violation. Also a new mating method has been proposed in our genetic algorithm. In addition we don't use penalty function as fitness function. Numerical results obtained, showed the efficiency of proposed algorithm rather than algorithm used by Haupt and Haupt[7]. The paper contributes to literature in designing a multiple objective linear model for integrated inventory-production-distribution planning which is close to real world supply chain and using fuzzy goal programming, also proposing a new genetic algorithm. Analysis of variance has been used to compare mean of violation in HGA and PGA. It is resulted that violation in PGA is less than HGA. Thus, PGA is closer than HGA to feasible solution.

References

1. Abbasbandy, S., Asady, B.: Ranking of fuzzy numbers by sign distance. Inform. Sci. 176, 2405–2416 (2006)
2. Aliev, R.A., Fazlollahi, B., Guirimov, B.G., Aliev, R.R.: Fuzzy-genetic approach to aggregate production –distribution planning in supply chain management. Information Sciences 177, 4241–4255 (2007)
3. Chen, S.-H.: Computational intelligence in economics and finance: carrying on the legacy of Herbert Simon. Inform. Sci. 170(1), 121–131 (2005)
4. Chen, S.-P., Chang, P.C.: A mathematical programming approach to supply chain models with fuzzy parameters. Eng., Optimiz. 38(6), 647–669 (2006)
5. Gao, M., Zhou, M.C., Tang, Y.: Intelligent decision making in disassembly process based on fuzzy reasoning Petri nets. IEEE Trans. Syst. Man. Cyb. B: Cyb. 34(5), 2029–2084 (2004)
6. Gottwald, S.: Mathematical fuzzy logic as a tool for the treatment of vague information. Inform. Sci. 172(1-2), 41–71 (2005)
7. Haupt, R.L., Haupt, S.E.: Practical Genetic Algorithm, 2nd edn. John Willey and Sons, Inc., Hoboken (2004)
8. Liang, T.-F.: Distribution planning decisions using interactive fuzzy multi-objective linear programming. Fuzzy Sets Syst. 157(10), 1303–1316 (2006)
9. Nozick, L.K., urnquist, M.A.: Inventory, Transportation, Service quality and the location of distribution centers. European Journal of Operational Research 129, 362–371 (2001)
10. Selim, H., Araz, C., Ozkarahan, I.: Collaborative production–distribution planning in supply chain: A fuzzy goal programming approach. Transportation Research Part E (2007)
11. Sheen, J.N.: Fuzzy financial profitability analyses of demand side management alternatives from participant perspective. Inform. Sci. 169(3-4), 329–364 (2005)

12. Tasan, A.S.: A Two Step Approach for the Integrated Production and Distribution Planning of a Supply Chain, pp. 883–888. Springer, Heidelberg (2006)
13. Torabi, S.A., Hassini, E.: An interactive possibilistic programming approach for multiple objective supply chain master planning. Fuzzy Sets and Systems 159, 193–214 (2008)
14. Zadroznya, S., Kacprzyk, J.: Computing with words for text processing: an approach to the text categorization. Inform. Sci. 176(4), 415–437 (2006)

Evaluation of Enterprise Cooperation through Information Exchange

Marcius Fabius Carvalho[1,2] and Ralph Santos Silva[1]

[1] Centro de Tecnologia da Informação Renato Archer - CTI,
Rodovia Dom Pedro I, Km 143,5
13069-901 – Campinas, SP, Brazil
[2] Assistant Professor Civil Engineering Faculty - State University of Campinas
Campinas, Brazil
marcius.carvalho@cti.gov.br

Abstract. Considering that cooperation among enterprises contributes significantly to improve the product performance in a supply chain, this work presents a method for evaluating the enterprise cooperation focused on the exchange of information among firms. Two indexes are used: the intensity, which seeks to measure the amount of information shared; and the extension, which seeks to measure how many stages of the supply chain are exchanging information both upstream and downstream. The proposed method was applied to eighteen auto part firms of Campinas region in Brazil. The intensity and the extension indexes for each enterprise were measured and some relevant conclusions regarding to information exchange for automotive sector are presented.

Keywords: Supply Chain, Enterprise Cooperation, Information Exchange, automotive industry.

1 Introduction

It is recognized that supply chain management requires the inter- and intra-organizational integration relationships and coordination of different types of flows as material, founds and information. Information technology to improve supply chain performance as point of sale scanner and electronic data interchange are available, nonetheless the performance of the supply chain has never been worse [1].

The true supply chain excellence will only come from making a digital business transformation and when done effectively, it enables companies to share information that can dramatically shorten processing time, eliminate value-depleting activities, and improve quality, all of which are fundamental to long-term success [2]. The importance of strategic collaboration and definition of supply chain integration as the degree to which a manufacturer collaborates with its supply chain partners and collaboratively manages intra- and inter-organization processes was highlighted by [3].

Despite of the importance of information flow, little attention has been given in the literature to measure the magnitude and the effectiveness of information exchange for the coordination of enterprises with their supply chain. This is a paradox since the

Á. Ortiz Bas, R.D. Franco, P. Gómez Gasquet (Eds.): BASYS 2010, IFIP AICT 322, pp. 177–184, 2010.

integration and coordination, through information technology can be largely utilized in an accessible cost.

In one of the few papers in the literature addressing the issue of information exchange among enterprises examine the relationship between the information availability and successful implementation of integrated logistics systems inside of an individual company [4]. Scales for measuring supply chain integration and five different strategies were identified was developed by [5]. Each of these strategies is characterized by a different "arc of integration", representing the direction (towards suppliers and/or customers) and degree of integration activity. There was consistent evidence that the widest degree of arc of integration with both suppliers and customer shad the strongest association with enterprise performance improvement. A Research [6] extended the work of [4] by providing a general tool that can be used for both the macro and micro levels to evaluate the relative performance of a given information flow structure. The measure, a single 2-tuple index, was derived from information about a firm's relationship with suppliers and customers. The measure encompasses both the depths of information exchanges, that is how far up or down in the supply chain a firm exchanges information as well as the intensity of the information that is exchanged and used in logistics planning. Intensity is measured by gauging the degree to which demand, inventory, and production planning is shared and used by the firms in both directions of the supply chain.

This study takes the work [6] to answer the question: What is the actual level of integration of auto parts industry sited in Campinas region? The next section presents the method to evaluate the information exchange. In the following the methodology defines the sample specification and questionnaire composition. In the section four the results are analyzed and finally in the section five the conclusion and limitation of the research are presented.

2 Supply Chain Coupling Index

The method for describing the degree to which a firm is "coupled" within its supply chain, called Supply Chain Coupling Index SCCI based on two indicators [6]: Information Extent (IE) and Information Intensity (II). IE describes how deep into the network (in either direction of customers or suppliers) the information is exchanged, whereas II describes the richness, and amount of the information used (either in the direction of customers or suppliers). Then SCCI is defined as:

$$SCCI = EI + II \qquad (1)$$

The enterprise will be less coupled within its supply chain as the value of both indexes (IE and II) approaches zero. On the other hand, the enterprise becomes more coupled as SCCI approaches unity. The ideal situation, $EI = II = 1$, means all relevant information from all members of the supply chain (customers, suppliers) are shared.

2.1 Information Extent (IE)

The EI index describes how deep the information can be seen and used into the network (in either direction of customers and suppliers). It is defined as the weighted average of two indexes: the IE toward customers (IE^d) and the IE toward suppliers (IE^u). Thus, the degree of IE is defined as:

$$I E = k_1 . IE^c + k_2 . IE^s \qquad (2)$$

Where IEc is the information extent toward customers, IEs is the information extent toward suppliers, k1 and k2 are weights toward customer and suppliers respectively. k1, k2 are between 0 and 1 and sum one.

2.2 Information Intensity (II)

The II index describes the richness, and amount of the information used (either in the customer and supplier direction)and, similarly, is composed of two indexes Eq.3.

$$II = l_1 . II^c + l_2 . II^s \qquad (3)$$

The IIc and IIs indicate the intensity of information exchange of the firm with its customer and supplier respectively and 11,12 are weights that sum equal 1. To be coordinated in an effective way a supply chain must consider at minimum the exchange of information of: demand (D), inventory (I), capacity (C), and production scheduling (P). Assuming Dc for demand information from the customer and so on, the information intensity index related to the customer can be written as:

$$II^c = w_1{}^c D^c + w_2{}^c I^c + w_3{}^c C^c + w_4{}^c P^c \qquad (4)$$

Where w1c, w2c, w3c and w4c are weights that sum equal one.

And, also assuming Ds for demand information toward suppliers and so on, the customer information intensity index related to customer can be written as:

$$II^s = w_1{}^s D^s + w_2{}^s I^s + w_3{}^s C^s + w_4{}^s P^s \qquad (5)$$

3 Methodology

The supply chain coupling evaluation was composed of three main activities: sample definition, questionnaire composition, application and analysis of results.

3.1 Sample Definition

Taking the theoretical referential it was structured and conducted a field research involving medium and large size auto parts enterprises of Campinas region, Brazil with the objective to answer the question: What is the actual level of integration of auto parts industry sited in Campinas region? This area has been chosen due to a significant number of auto parts firms in the region to be an area on vanguard in the utilization of advanced technology and methodology mainly associated to information exchange. The automotive sector has been chosen since it is one of those dependents of information exchange for the success of its supply chain. Also the automotive sector in Brazil has contributed with 18% of the Gross Domestic Product (GDP). Eighteen enterprises, representing suppliers of first and second level of final assembly plant were participating in the research and fifteen questionnaires were considered valid. Medium and large enterprises were chosen since they are those with perspective of best information technology utilization with their partners. Particularly, assembly plants were neglected since they are not accessible as auto part enterprises are.

3.2 Questionnaire Composition

The questionnaire was structured in four parts. The two initial parts was focused on qualitative and quantitative measures to identify the size, the position of the participant enterprise in the supply chain, its main suppliers and customers, and internal importance attributed to the information technology. The two last parts were dedicated to determine the Supply Chain Coupling – SCCI as a result of upstream and downstream information coupling. Due to lack of space, this work presents part1 and analyze only the results of the part 3 and part 4 of the questionnaire.

Part 1
Distribution of enterprises according to number of employees

Workers	+ 1500	751 → 1500	251 → 750	0 → 250
Enterprise	E2, E4, E9	E5, E10	E6, E8, E11, E15, E16, E17, E18	E3,E12, E14

Part 3
Four questions directed to the supplier, to the supplier of the direct supplier, to the direct customer and to the customer of the customer were defined to identify the Information extent Index (IE) as shown in Table 1.

Part 4
This part of the questionnaire was designed for identifying the intensity of firm information exchange from and to both customers and suppliers and type of information used. In general are Demand (D), Production planning (P), Capacity(C) and Storage (S), as shown in Table 2.

4 Discussion of Results

The Information Extent (IE) for the fifteen enterprises is presented in the Table 1 through as binary form. "1" means information exchange while "0" means no significant information exchange between coupled enterprises. This work considers enterprises sited until two levels upstream to the reference enterprise and two levels downstream to the reference enterprise. Also, weights factors were associated to each level (K = 0,35 to the first level and K = 0,15 for the second level), to express the relative importance of the information. The columns 3 and 4 present the respondent perception related with the cooperation by information exchange with the first level partners up and downstream of the reference enterprise. The second level IE^{ss} index is less relevant than the first level IE^{s} index then its weight is lower.

According to the respondent the information exchange is more intensive with first and second order customers than with the suppliers. It can be confirmed by the dendogram generated from Table 1 and presented in Fig. 1. It also shows the group of enterprises with same behavior regarding to information exchange. The Enterprise 5

(E5), it is totally uncoupled from its upstream neighbor, that is a steel partner, large and strong enough to negotiate with its clients. Table 2 shows the Information Intensity index (II) regarding to the Demand, Storage, Capacity and Production Planning data. Also, the binary representation was assumed (1 information exchange; 0 no information exchange) and the same weight was attributed to the upstream and downstream information exchange, although any other value should be used to consider different way to exchange information. The results demonstrate that actual information exchange practice of the enterprises is inferior to the perception of the respondent expressed in Table 1.

Table 1. Information Extent

Enterprise	Supplier of supplier K^{ss} = 0,15	Immediate supplier K^s = 0,35	Immediate Customer K^c= 0,35	Customer of Customer K^{cc} = 0,15	Index IE
E2	1	1	1	1	1,0
E3	0	1	1	0	0,7
E4	1	1	1	1	1,0
E5	0	0	1	0	0,35
E6	0	1	1	0	0,7
E8	1	1	1	1	1,0
E9	0	1	1	0	0,7
E10	0	1	1	0	0,7
E11	0	1	1	0	0,7
E12	0	1	1	0	0,7
E14	1	1	1	1	1,0
E15	0	1	1	1	0,85
E16	1	1	1	1	1,0
E17	0	0	1	1	0,5
E18	0	0	1	1	0,5
Mean	5/15 =0,33	12/15= 0,8	15/15 = 1	8/15=0,53	11,4/15=0,8

Although the respondent recognizes the importance of information exchange as an element for enterprise competitiveness, the individual measures indicate low level of information exchange than they believe. Second, is observed more information exchange with suppliers than with clients. Most of these enterprises are first level supplier of car manufacturers.

To confirm this unexpected result an unstructured interview with some enterprises was developed. They say to appeal to secondary data to plan its production. Example, new car sale variation can indicate tendencies in future car maker orders. This tendency influences the enterprise production planning and must be considered although not pointed out by the car makers. This finding shows the importance of second level information and the low cooperation among enterprises participants of the research. A resume of Supply Chain Coupling Index is presented in Table 3. The E16 presents the best coupling index and E05 one enterprise with the worst coupling index. These

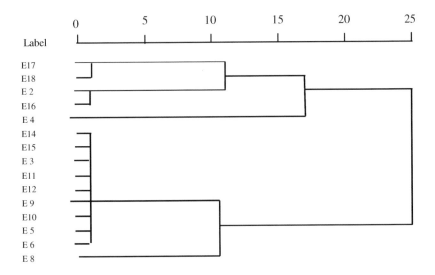

Fig. 1. Customer information exchange dendogram

Table 2. Information Intensity

Enterprise	Neighbor Supplier				Index II^f	Neighbor Client				Index II^c	Index II $(0,5*II^f+0,5*II^c)$
	D	I	C	P		D	I	C	P		
E2	1	0	0	0	0,25	1	1	1	1	1	0,625
E3	1	1	1	1	1	1	0	0	0	0,25	0,625
E4	1	1	1	1	1	1	1	1	0	0,75	0,875
E5	0	0	0	1	0,25	1	0	0	0	0,25	0,25
E6	1	0	0	0	0,25	1	0	0	0	0,25	0,25
E8	1	1	1	1	1	1	0	1	0	0,50	0,75
E9	1	0	0	0	0,25	1	0	0	0	0,25	0,25
E10	1	0	0	1	0,50	1	0	0	0	0,25	0,375
E11	1	1	1	0	0,75	1	0	0	0	0,25	0,50
E12	1	0	0	0	0,25	1	0	0	0	0,25	0,25
E14	1	0	0	0	0,25	1	0	0	0	0,25	0,25
E15	1	0	0	0	0,25	1	0	0	0	0,25	0,25
E16	1	1	1	1	1	1	1	1	1	1	1
E17	1	0			0,75	0			1	0,75	0,75
E18	1	0			0,50	0			1	0,75	0,625
Mean					0,82/15 =0,55					7/15=0,47	7,62/15=0,51

Table 3. Supply Chain Coupling Index - SCCI

Enterprise	Index EI	Index II	SCCI 0,5*EI+0,5*II
E2	1	0,625	0,8125
E3	0,7	0,625	0,6625
E4	1	0,875	0,9375
E5	0,35	0,25	0,3
E6	0,7	0,25	0,475
E8	1	0,75	0,875
E9	0,7	0,25	0,475
E10	0,7	0,375	0,5375
E11	0,7	0,50	0,6
E12	0,7	0,25	0,475
E14	1	0,25	0,625
E15	0,85	0,25	0,55
E16	1	1	1
E17	0,5	0,75	0,625
E18	0,5	0,625	0,5625
MEAN	11,4/15=0,8	7,62/15=0,51	0,6342

indexes represent the point of view of the respondent about cooperation of its enterprise with the supply chain. Also it allows to compare one enterprise against its partners or competitors.

5 Conclusion and Limitation

An analysis of cooperation through information exchange of the Campinas auto parts sector was proposed based in a sample of 15 questionnaires applied to in medium and large size enterprises directly coupled to the car makers or enterprises coupled to the first level suppliers.

The main conclusions are:

1) All the respondent enterprise considers relevant to know the actual status of information integration among its partners.
2) In the automotive Brazilian sector exists cooperation mainly related to the first level supplier.
3) The information exchange with car makers is mainly demand, followed storage and production capacity.

4) The respondent perception about information exchange importance is not confirmed when compared to the indexes that qualify the extent of information exchange between partners enterprises.

5) Analyzing the part 1questionnaire results with customer information exchange dendogram, Figure 2, the enterprise size has no significant influence on the SCCI pattern (see E4 and E8).

The present work is focused on customer and supplier integration. Future work would include the internal dimension of integration. It would be interesting to analyze the cooperation by information exchange considering all the elements of a supply chain from the final customer to the raw material suppliers. This study could identify local actions to be implemented to reach better performance for the entire supply chain. Also, would be interesting to calculate the information exchange assuming value between 0 to 1 to obtain to IE(s) and IE(c) in a continuous space between 0 and 1, to consider different ways of information exchange on production, demand, capacity and storage. Finally this tool would be very useful in the establishment of investments in information technology.

Acknowledgements

The authors would like to thank the reviewers for their comments and suggestions for future work.

References

1. Barut, M., Faisst, W., Kanet, J.: Measuring Supply Chain Coupling: An Information System Perspective. European Journal of Purchasing & Supply Management 8, 161–171 (2002)
2. Bowersox, D., Cross, D., Drayer, R.: The Digital Transformation – Technology and Beyond. Supply Chain Management Review, 22–29 (January/February 2005)
3. Fisher, L.M.: What is the right supply chain for your Product. Harvard Business Review, 105–116 (March/April 1997)
4. Flynn, B., Huo, B., Zhao, X.: The impact of supply chain integration on performance: A contingency and configuration approach. Journal of Operations Management 28, 58–71 (2010)
5. Frohlich, M.T., Westbrook, R.: Arcs of integration: an International Study of Supply Chain Strategies. Journal of Operation Management 19, 185–200 (2001)
6. Gustin, C.M., Daugherty, J.D.: The effects of Information availability on logistics integration. Journal of Business Logistics 16(1), 1–21 (1995)

Impact of Coordination Mechanisms on the Collaborative Planning Process Components

M.M.E. Alemany, F. Alarcón, and A. Ortiz

Research Centre on Production Management and Engineering (CIGIP), Universidad
Politécnica de Valencia, Camino de Vera s/n, Valencia 46022, Spain
mareva@omp.upv.es, faualva@omp.upv.es, aortiz@cigip.upv.es

Abstract. In this paper a conceptual framework for characterizing the Supply
Chain (SC) Collaborative Planning (CP) under a process perspective is presented. When analyzing the CP process view, the definition of coordination
mechanisms among SC members results essential. With the aim of identifying
the possible coordination mechanisms that SC members can implement, the
structural elements necessary to define them are proposed. Finally, the impact
that the coordination mechanisms structural elements have on the definition of
the CP process is presented. The knowledge of the CP process, the coordination
mechanisms and their relationship constitutes the basis for the latter identification of potential activities that can be supported by decision tools and for the
partially or totally automation of the process.

Keywords: Collaborative Planning Process, Supply Chain, Coordination
Mechanisms.

1 Introduction

Collaborative Planning (CP) can be defined as a joint decision making process for
aligning plans of individual Supply Chains (SC) members with the aim of achieving a
certain degree of coordination [1]. Because CP belongs to the SC coordination problems category, CP decisions related to the mid and short-term temporal levels must be
integrated (temporal integration). Furthermore, for each temporal level, the CP decision-making can be centralized if only one decision-maker exists or distributed, in
case several decision makers exist. The plans of these different decision-makers must
be also integrated (spatial integration). Indeed, [2] identifies as a major CP challenge
to simultaneously achieve both types of integration. In a collaborative distributed
context different decision-makers should share some information and should make
several decision cycles involving repetitive sequence of decisions until a stopping
criteria is achieved, in case negotiation exists. In this situation, the knowledge about
the process results essential. Indeed, different authors strength the importance of analyzing the collaboration under a process perspective.

[3] define collaboration as a process in which entities share information, resources
and responsibilities to jointly plan, implement and evaluate a program of activities to
achieve a common goal and therefore jointly generating value. From the process perspective, there are different works that report flowcharts representing the CP process

Á. Ortiz Bas, R.D. Franco, P. Gómez Gasquet (Eds.): BASYS 2010, IFIP AICT 322, pp. 185–192, 2010.

for a specific distributed decision environment (e.g. [4], [5], [6]). However, these CP processes are specifically designed for particular situations being necessary a generic approach that help in the definition, characterization and analysis of CP processes in general. In this sense, [7] conclude that a process will be defined when the answers to the following questions are known: (a) What activities are to be carried out?, (b) Who is responsible to carry them out and with what?, (c) When and how are they to be carried out?, (d) The process inputs, (e) The process outputs, (f) The process objectives, and (g) The performance indicators.

Through the CP process approach it is possible to implement the coordination mechanisms that link the SC members' plans. In this sense, [8] consider that the coordination mechanisms states how the SC members' relationship is operationalized (e.g. rules and protocols to exchange information, which decisions must be taken, by whom and when). [9] affirms that the coordination mechanisms for Distributed Decision-Making systems for a two-level hierarchical environment are: anticipation, instruction and reaction. [10] categorize the supply network (SN) coordination mechanisms into four classes: SN contracts, Information Technology, Information Sharing and Joint Decision Making. [11] establish that a coordination mechanism for a decentralized SN system should include at least three components: (i) an operational plan to coordinate the decisions and activities of SN members, (ii) a structure to share information among the members, (iii) an incentive scheme to allocate the benefits of coordination so as to entice the cooperation of all members. [1] states that the interaction between the parties involved in a CP scheme can be documented by a protocol defined by the following structural elements: the incorporation or not of a mediator, the initial solution, the number of rounds and the number of offers to be exchanged (stopping criteria) and the final results SN members can expect. In the context of agent technology applied to CP, [12] present the main characteristic of automated negotiations (collaboration level, number of participants, number of issues, decision sequence and learning ability), decision mechanisms that can be followed by agents (game theoretic negotiation, argumentation-based negotiation, auctions and heuristic based negotiation). [13] proposes an approach that breaks from the hypothesis that planning must always be conducted in the same way. By using multi-behaviour agents they propose to provide planning agents with the ability to adapt their planning behaviours according to changes in the environment.

From the literature reviewed, it can be concluded that there is a strong relationship between the CP process view and the coordination mechanisms that, in our opinion, requires a deeper analysis. This paper attempts to contribute to clarify this relationship being, therefore, the objective of this paper manifold: 1) to propose a conceptual framework for the CP process that support the characterization, definition and analysis of the CP under a process perspective, 2) to identify the structural elements of the CP coordination mechanisms and 3) to define the impact of the coordination mechanisms structural elements on the components of the CP process. The knowledge of the CP process, the coordination mechanisms and their relationship is essential for the latter development of any supporting decision-making tool and the partially or totally automation of the process.

The rest of the paper is organized as follows. In section 2 the conceptual framework for characterizing the CP process is described. The coordination mechanisms structural elements for the CP are defined in section 3 and their impact on the CP process components is shown in section 4. Finally, section 5 reports some conclusions.

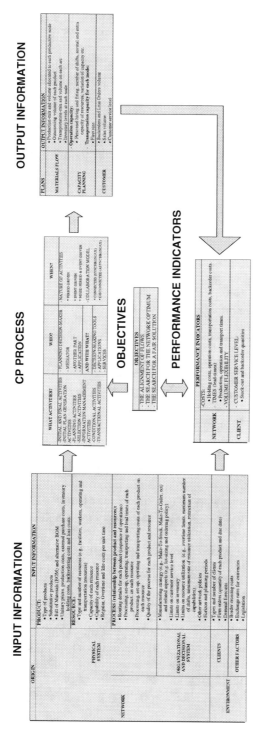

Fig. 1. Conceptual framework components for the CP process and their relationships

2   Conceptual Framework for the CP Process Characterization

As [7], we consider that a process is characterized when the answers to the questions (a)-(g) are known (Table 1). The answer to each question corresponds with the characterization of a specific component of the CP process conceptual framework. For a deeper explanation of the CP process conceptual framework, the reader is referred to [14].

The order to answer each question is not sequential, i.e., during the CP process characterization the answer to some questions are interrelated. Furthermore, though global process inputs, outputs, objectives and indicators exist and should be determined for the entire CP process, each activity of the process presents its own inputs, outputs, objectives and performance indicators.

Therefore, to properly define the coordination mechanisms in SCs, the exchanged information among activities should be reflected. This internal information flow is missing if the only analysis of inputs and outputs under a general process perspective as a whole is performed.

As a consequence, the questions (a)-(g) will be answered not only from a whole process perspective but also, when it will be necessary, from an activity perspective. In Fig. 1, a more detailed view of each conceptual framework component and the relationship between them are provided.

Table 1. Components of the CP process conceptual framework

THE PROCESS ITSELF	THE INFORMATION	EVALUATION ASPECTS
(a) What activities are to be carried out? (b) Who is responsible, who has the authority to carry them out and with what? (c) When and how are they to be carried out?	(d) The process inputs, (e) The process outputs,	(f) The process objectives, (g) The performance indicators

3   Structural Elements of CP Coordination Mechanisms

In this section, the structural elements that should be specified in order to characterize coordination mechanisms in a CP context are proposed. Through this characterization, an analysis of possible alternatives for implementing the interdependence relationships between SC members will be made. The proposed structural elements are derived from the analysis of the conceptual literature cited in the introduction section combined with the abstraction and generalization of particular CP models and the own experience of the authors.

Number of decision-makers: it makes reference to the number of SC members that are either under the responsibility of a SC planning domain at a certain planning temporal level or should coordinate and integrate the different plans of other decision-makers (a mediator). It is of relevance the distribution of the decision-makers along the SC tiers and the number of decision-makers in each one. The most common situations discussed in the literature [12] are centered on a two tier SC and are the following: one-to-one, one-to-many and many-to-many negotiations.

Collaboration level: it represents the degree of interest in decision makers' performance. Agreed collaboration level is intensely related with the final results decision-makers should expect, the decision-makers' goal congruence, the information the SC members are in position to share and the trust between them. It is possible distinguish between three main levels of collaboration:

- *Strong collaboration* (altruistic partners that puts the SC goals before its local goals)
- *Low collaboration* (self-interested partner that makes decisions mainly following its local goals)
- *Balanced collaboration* (any degree of balance between the two previous levels)

Interdependence relationships nature: the sharing of power between SC decision-makers could be not homogeneous. The relative position of each decision-maker in the SC depends on different factors that impact the influence of each decision-maker in the definition of the interdependence relationships. Two differentiate cases could be distinguished:

- *Hierarchical*: the sharing of power between SC members is not homogeneous and, then, CP interdependence relationships are dominated by decision makers with more power in the SC. Their leadership could be reflected in the interdependence relationships in several ways (e.g., defining the negotiation stopping criteria)
- *Non-hierarchical*: all the SC members are recognized with the same power and, therefore, all the interdependence relationships are equally agreed.

Interdependence relationships type: because SC planning decisions are made at different temporal levels and at each temporal level different decision-makers could exist, two different types of plans integration should be distinguished:

- *Temporal integration*: it involves coordinating planning decisions across different timescales or across various levels of decision-making (tactical and operational). This collaboration type is always hierarchical.
- *Spatial integration*: it involves coordinating the plans of different decision-makers at the same temporal level. Depending on the sharing of the power between SC members it could be hierarchical or non-hierarchical.

Number of coordination mechanisms: it refers to the number of different protocols under which the different decision-makers interact.

- *Unique*: there is an only one protocol that is independent on the environment and other situation characteristics.
- *Various*: when the environment is characterized by high levels of variability, it can be advantageous to define different coordination mechanisms to work under different scenarios. In this case, different options exists:
  - Pre-defined (non-learning ability): the number of coordination mechanisms are defined in advanced. The situations under which a specific mechanism should be employed and their characteristics should be specified.
  - Not pre-defined (learning ability): the decision-makers have the ability to acquire experience from previous negotiations (i.e. they are able to adapt their

strategies with changing opponents, topics, concerns and user preferences) and to adapt to the context. They can modify their local planning behaviors and/or in concordance with the rest of the decision-makers.

Criteria to select the operation under specific coordination mechanism (available time to make decisions, source of the perturbation in the environment, etc.) in case several coordination mechanism exists.

Information exchanged: for each coordination mechanism the information exchanged between the decision-makers can make reference to SC attributes and decision-makers' outputs:

- *SC attributes*: they consist of known characteristics of the planning SN elements and their environment (demand forecasts, capacity of facilities, operating costs, incentives, penalizations, etc.). It is known in the literature as information sharing.
- *Decision-makers' outputs*: they are those decision variables/ criteria values which, in some way, are passed to other decision-makers. This output data becomes input data for others activities, more specifically they become interdependent parameters of other planning activities. It is known in the literature as joint decision-making and it is the essence of collaborative planning. Depending on the possibility of changing the final value of the outputs by the interdependent decision-makers, two outputs categories could be distinguished:
  - o   Final Decision Variables/Criteria: their values cannot be changed under any condition during the negotiation process or, simply, because there is no negotiation.
  - o   Non-Final Decision Variables/Criteria: their values can be modified during the negotiation process due to:
    - ▪   Temporal integration: disaggregation of decisions should be made for being implemented (e.g. production volume of families should be disaggregated referred to articles)
    - ▪   Spatial integration: their values are adjusted before reaching the stopping criteria of the negotiation process (e.g. ordered/supplied quantities)

Information processing: the exchanged information for each coordination mechanism could be incorporated in different ways by each decision-maker. Part of the share information can be simply evaluated by other decision-makers (i.e. an ordered pattern can be evaluated by a supplier to know the value of his performance criteria when he does not deviate from the buyer pattern). Other exchanged information can be incorporated in the planning problem of a decision-maker by affecting his decisional space (introduction of constraints) and/or his criteria (penalizations or incentives for deviating from a constraint)

Decision sequence characteristics: it allows define how the coordination mechanisms will be managed.

- *Beginning of the coordination mechanism*: for each coordination mechanism it is necessary to specify when beginning (period, event-driven or a mixed), and how beginning (initial solution by upstream planning, downstream planning, random, by a coordinator, etc.)

- *Sequence of decisions*: the order in which the different decision-makers act and the decisions simultaneously made by different SC members should be specified.

Stopping criteria of the coordination mechanism: in case negotiation exists, the conditions for ending a coordination mechanism could be defined in terms of number of rounds, limited time and the achievement of a determined aspiration level related with the final results the SN members can expect.

4 Impact of Coordination Mechanisms Structural Elements on the CP Process Components

In this section, the relationship between the components characterizing the CP under a process perspective and the structural elements of the coordination mechanisms is presented (Table 2). A grey cell in the matrix means that the definition of the specific CP process component is either influenced or it is dependent on the characteristics of the coordination mechanism structural element. For instance, because the number of planning activities should be at least as the number of decision-makers, a grey cell appears in the intersection of the both items.

Table 2. Relationship between CP process components and the coordination mechanisms structural elements

COORDINATION MECHANISMS	CONCEPTUAL FRAMEWORK FOR THE CP PROCESS					
	PROCESS ITSELF			INFORMATION	EVALUATION ASPECTS	
					(Ex ante)	(Ex post)
Structural elements	What activities?	Who and with what?	When and How?	Process Inputs & Outputs (shared information)	Objectives	Performance Indicators
Number of SC decision-makers	▓	▓				
Colllaboration level						
Interdependence relationship nature			▓	▓	▓	▓
Interdependence relationship type			▓	▓		
Number of coordination mechanisms	▓	▓				
Criteria to select a coordination mechanism	▓		▓			
Information exchanged				▓		
Information processing				▓		
Decision sequence characteristic	▓	▓	▓			
Stopping criteria	▓		▓			▓

Therefore, table 2 shows the impact of the coordination mechanisms on the CP process facilitating its properly understanding and representation. To understand the process and the relationship between its elements is, indeed, the first step and constitutes the basis to either totally or partially automated the process (e.g., by means of agent technology) or to develop decision support tools for each SC member, (e.g., mathematical programming models).

5 Conclusions

In a distributed decision-making environment, the way the collaborative SC members make its decisions and coordinate them results essential to plan the SC operations in a coherent manner. For this reason, there is a wide body of research that develops decision support tools for SC partners and proposes coordination mechanisms between them. The process view is necessary to implement the coordination mechanisms which are the essence of CP because it allows clearly define the information flows, the sequence and timing of decisions, the number of decision cycles, the stopping criteria, etc. Proper process knowledge and characterization is the first step to identify the potential activities for which developing decision support tools and to automate the process. The automation of the process can allow simulate and evaluate different coordination mechanisms under different scenarios before implementing them.

References

1. Stadtler, H.: A framework for collaborative planning and state-of-the-art. OR Spectrum, 1 31(1), 5–30 (2009)
2. Grossmann, I.: Enterprise-wide optimization: A new frontier in process systems engineering. Aiche Journal 51(7), 1846–1857 (2005)
3. Camarinha-Matos, L.M., Afsarmanesh, H., Galeano, N., Molina, A.: Collaborative networked organizations - Concepts and practice in manufacturing enterprises. Computers & Industrial Engineering 57(1), 46–60 (2009)
4. Jung, H.S., Chen, F.F., Jeong, B.J.: Decentralized supply chain planning framework for third party logistics partnership. Computers & Industrial Engineering 55(2), 348–364 (2008)
5. Sapena, O., Onaindia, E., Garrido, A., Arangu, M.: A distributed CSP approach for collaborative planning systems. Engineering Applications of Artificial Intelligence 21(5), 698–709 (2008)
6. Jain, V., Deshmukh, S.G.: Dynamic supply chain modeling using a new fuzzy hybrid negotiation mechanism. International Journal of Production Economics 122(1), 319–328 (2009)
7. Alarcón, F., Alemany, M.M.E., Ortiz, A.: Conceptual framework for the characterization of the order promising process in a collaborative selling network context. International Journal of Production Economics 120(1), 100–114 (2009)
8. Gaudreault, J., Frayret, J.M., Pesant, G.: Distributed search for supply chain coordination. Computers in Industry 60(6), 441–451 (2009)
9. Schneeweiss, C.: Distributed decision making in supply chain management. International Journal of Production Economics 11 84(1), 71–83 (2003)
10. Arshinder, K.A., Deshmukh, S.G.: Supply chain coordination: Perspectives, empirical studies and research directions. Int. J. Prod. Econ. 115(2), 316–335 (2008)
11. Li, X.H., Wang, Q.N.: Coordination mechanisms of supply chain systems. European Journal of Operational Research 16 179(1), 1–16 (2007)
12. Forget, P., Monteiro, T., D'Amours, S., Frayret, J.-M.: Collaborative agent-based negotiation in supply chain using multi-behaviour agents, CIRRELT-2008-54, 1-21 (2008)
13. Forget, P., D'Amours, S., Frayret, J.-M., Gaudreault, J.: Study of the performance of multi-behaviour agents for supply chain planning. Computers in Industry 60, 698–708 (2009)
14. Alemany, M.M.E., Alarcón, F., Lario, F.C., Poler, R.: Conceptual Framework for the Interoperability Requirements of Collaborative Planning Process (2010) (accepted for I-ESA)

Revision to Theory of Constraints

Sofía Estellés Miguel, Teresa Barbera Ribera, José Miguel Albarracín Guillem,
and Carlos Manuel Dema Pérez

Departamento de Organización de Empresas, Universidad Politécnica de Valencia,
Camino de Vera s/n 46022 Valencia
soesmi@omp.upv.es, mabarri@upvnet.upv.es,
jmalbarr@omp.upv.es, cmdema@omp.upv.es

Abstract. It's intended to give an approximation to the Theory of Constraints
(TOC), to achieve that goal we explain the conceptual bases, the thinking process, the flow management and later on we will focus on its application into
production, also known as DBR (Drum-Buffer-Rope). A usual critic in the academic environment is that TOC techniques produce results that are feasible but
not always optimal. Although defenders of TOC reply that optimal results are
very elegant but need to reduce or eliminate variability of systems, while TOC
is an appropriate method to work with variable worlds, such as the real one.
Anyway, this creates a gap relative to production programming and sequencing,
establishment of batch sizes, measures of initial buffer size and determination
of the optimal product mix.

Keywords: DBR, Drum-Buffer-Rope, Theory of Constraints, TOC, Goal,
Thinking-Process.

1 Introduction

TOC is a systemic methodology of company management and improvement. The
concepts in which is based are compiled from most of the literature published over
the topic, we will highlight the concepts goal and constraint. Contribution of TOC can
be divided into 2 groups [1]:

- Thinking Process: Set of tools that ease the analysis and search of systemic solutions for problematic situations.
- Robust applications based on Systemic thinking and Operations research methods: Production, Operations, Supply Chain, Project Management, Decision-
  making, etc….

There also exist some studies showing evidence that from the start of introducing
TOC, companies achieve to increase its production quantity at the same time as they
reduce both inventory and cycle time [2]; [3]; [4]; [5]. Some academicals tests validate that using TOC techniques produce a better performance than using MRP, Lean
Manufacturing and JIT [6], [7]; [8]; [9]; [10]; [11]. The result of these studies show
that TOC systems produce higher production levels as they reduce inventory, production time or "lead time", and the cycle time standard deviation.

Á. Ortiz Bas, R.D. Franco, P. Gómez Gasquet (Eds.): BASYS 2010, IFIP AICT 322, pp. 193–201, 2010.
© IFIP International Federation for Information Processing 2010

2 Theory of Constraints

It is a systemic business management and improvement methodology. It's based on the following concepts [12]:

1. The goal of any profit company is to earn money in a regular way. If it does not it is because its constraints do not let it.
2. In any company just exist a few constraints.
3. A constraint can be physical or political.
4. Systemic thought defends that the maximum performance of a system is achieved by the maximum performance of its constraints.

2.1 Continuous Improvement Cycle

We cannot talk about TOC without mentioning the continuous improvement process in which is based, [13]:

1. IDENTIFY the limitation of the system.
2. Decide how to EXPLOIT the limitation of the system.
3. SUBORDINATE everything else to the previous decision.
4. ELEVATE the limitation of the system.
5. If, in a previous step, the limitation has been broken, return to step 1. Do not let that INERTIA turns out into a limitation of the system.

3 Evolution of TOC

When trying to perform a study or a chronology of the TOC philosophy evolution, its evolution can be segmented into 5 eras [14]:

1. The OPT era (Optimized Production Technology). The secret algorithm.
2. "The Goal" era, using DBR programming (Drum-Buffer-Rope).
3. "The barn syndrome" era, using the TOC measuring systems.
4. The "It's not matter of luck" era, applying reasoning processes to various topics.
5. The "Critical Chain" era or TOC applied to Project Management.

We can see the evolution in the figure 1.

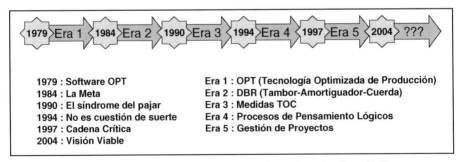

Fig. 1. Eras of TOC evolution. Source: Own adaptation from [14]

The mechanisms used by TOC for each of its Management processes, instead of following the eras chronologically, although they could be easily addressed to the eras mentioned before.

The application of TOC techniques has been discussed in literature in a variety of Management sub-disciplines:

- In production: [15]; [4]; [16]; [17], [5].
- Project management: [18], [19]; [20]; [21]; [22]; [23]; [24].
- Distribution: [25]; [26].
- Supply Chain management: [27]; [28]; [29].
- Improvement processes: [30]; [31]; [32].

4   Reviews to TOC

Besides the reviews already mentioned in the introduction, it is usually reproached to TOC that most of the knowledge that is used is based on already existent theories:

- TOC is based on systemic thought [33].
- The Solutions that propose TOC for operations and Project Management are based on the queues theory and the statistical theory of aggregation. [34].
- The Concepts proposed by TOC for Decision making are the method "Direct Costing" that appears in management books from the fifties [1].
- The solution that TOC proposes for Distribution is basically the application of the aggregation theory [34].
- The thinking processes of TOC are simply the verbalization of common sense, and have also been extracted from Edward De Bono's books. [35].

The true achievement of Dr. Goldratt and his team (Donn Novotny, Dale Houle, Dee Jacobs, Oded Cohen, etc) has been to develop a method to be able to use these Tools together in the resolution of problems. The worth has been to find a way for these tools to be used in companies with a high chance of producing excellent results.

5   Contributions of TOC

5.1   Thinking Process

The reasoning processes are an analytical tool developed by the Abraham Y. Goldratt Institute (AGI) [1], but based on the reasoning processes from the author Edward de Bono [35].

The Tools used in the reasoning processes are based on the systemic use of the logical relationships of cause-effect, necessity and generalization, so once acquired they result easy to handle and to understand.

They are used for [36]:

- To achieve an exact understanding of any aspect of reality and to find way of improving it (understanding of reality).

- To improve the communications capacity, because intuition is not enough to express common sense and to achieve understanding with the others.

Tools uses are:

- Current reality tree.
- Conflicts elimination.
- Future reality tree.
- Pre-requirements tree.
- Transition tree.

These tools are used to answer the following questions.

- What should be changed?
- What should we change to?
- How to produce the change?

Not every tool has to be used at the same time, depending on the kind of problem are used some tools or others.

The cost/benefit balance results more favourable for the use of reasoning processes as they become more complex and therefore more difficult to maintain in a strictly intuitive level [37].

5.2 TOC in the Commercial Area

It is a generic application of the reasoning processes used in TOC. The application of TOC in Marketing and sales has as goal the adequate orientation of the company in dynamic, uncertain, open and highly competitive today markets.

The high level of uncertainty in the markets demands to provide the company with flexibility of offer. TOC looks for increasing that flexibility both in the short and the long term to reduce the vulnerability of the company towards the uncertainties of the demand and the attacks of the competition [36].

The keys of flexibility are the market dynamic segmentation starting from offers that include competitive differentials and in the long term, the concept of strategical limitations, and essential competences over which to spread the offers in function of the alternations in the markets. Segment the market, not the resources [38].

We could talk widely about the differences that exist between the TOC commercial approach and the traditional offers, but this is not the goal of the present article. But it could also be resumed saying that we are looking for solutions "win to win" [39] (process in which both sides win equally).

Examples of this application can be found in various publications: [26], [40]; [38]; [41]; [42].

5.3 Flow Management in TOC

The existence of flows is a common characteristic of the production environments (industrial or services), projects and distribution.

The TOC systemic management model is applied to the management of these flows in the environments defined in function of the following premises [36]:

- The uncertainty existent in any environment and the dependence between the flows processes entail that its output is not determined by all the processes it goes through.
- The final output must be planned in function of the clients and the resource that is pretended to regulate the flow, in other words, the desirable tactical limitation (DTL). If the limitation is inside the system.
- Processes performed by DTL must be planned. This should always be done whenever it is not the demand what determines the volume of output for excess of system capacity. This happens if the limitation is located in the market.
- Buffers (pools of shared resources among non-planned resources), are the mechanism that make possible the subordination of the rest of the system to what was planned letting a higher flexibility.
- Buffers can be time-related (production and projects) and resource-related in ace of distribution.
  TOC Flow Management applications are known as:
- DBR (Drum-Buffer-Rope) in Production.
- Projects Critical Chain. Reposition in Distribution.

In this section are going to be explained the areas previously mentioned except DBR, that will be explained in more retail in the next section.

5.3.1 Application to Project Management

Its goal is to conclude the projects within time, budget and scope. In Project Management 2 limitations interact: time and resources. TOC handles them subordinating project to the "critical chain" through a concentrated buffers in selective points strategy. [18]; [24].

According to Goldratt two problems can be found when working in projects, the student's syndrome and the Parkinson's Law (the work expands to fill all available time), therefore a Project has great chances of not being finished on time. [38].

The buffer concept and its application on activities planning are considered an innovation respect the traditional schema of time Management and a big contribution to Project Management [43].

To evaluate the state of a project it is used: [38]:

1. Critical chain accomplishment percentage.
2. Rate between product buffer consume and the already finished critical chain.
3. Penetration rate in the Project buffer.

The difference in the TOC Project Management is based on one side by the treatment of resources for which different activities of the Project compete, and on the other hand TOC takes into account the almost general fact that the intensity of the effort dedicated to one activity is concentrated on the time immediately previous to the milestone of the ending of itself. Protect the critical chain and not each one of the activities [18]; [24].

5.3.2 Application to Distribution

The application of TOC to Distribution is known by the name of Reposition, it is a system for scheduling and control of the distribution system.

The goal of a distribution system is to assure sells with the minimum amount of stocks in the system. The limitation is the investment in stocks.

The application of TOC to distribution is based on the reposition of used material in each point of distribution/sell from the previous distribution point. Each distribution/sell point must keep a dimensioned stock in function of the predictable consumption along the supply time from the previous distribution point [36]. Buffers management is adapted for stock control in the different distribution/sell points.

The difference in the application of TOC to Distribution is based on the containment strategy "upstream" of the materials demanded in various distribution/sell points against the "push" strategy to protect each consumption point with its own stocks in function of the local predictions, each TOC stock protects every consumption point "Downstream" in function of the global previsions, that use to be more reliable than local ones.

Inventories must not be kept as near as they can to the market. They must be located in function of their impact on the system on its global. Change from "push" to "pull" [38].

6 TOC Applied to Production: DBR

Manufacturers have historically tried to balance capacity through a sequence of processes in a try to level capacity with market demand [44]. TOC instead of this, tries to balance the product flow through the system. When the flow is balanced, capacities are not. This is the reason why instead of balancing capacities it must be balanced the flow of product through the system. To change from a CONWIP system to a CONLOAD system.

TOC solution begins from the premise that different resources have different capacities [1].

TOC states that some variability cannot be eliminated and the process cannot be totally balanced, especially in JOB-SHOP environments [45].

Appears DBR as a solution to the application of TOC to production. The problem is to supply an excellent accomplishment of delivery term as the same time as inventories are minimized.

6.1 TOC Control Measures in DBR

Two kinds of measures are proposed:

- From a financial point of view (management) [46]:
    o Net benefit.
    o Profitability (ROI).
    o Liquidity.
- From an operative point of view (exploitation) [1]
    o Net income.
    o Inventory.
    o Operation expenses.

The relationship between Management measures and the 2 main exploitation measures is:

$$BN = T\text{-}OE$$
$$ROI = (T\text{-}OE)/I \tag{1}$$

There are other secondary measures like the throughoutput-dollar-day that is a measure of delivery terms accomplishment and inventory-dollar-day that measures the excess of inventory.

7 Conclusions

One of the main benefits of introducing TOC uses to be the generation of clear and realistic productivity indicators, related with the goal of the company.

Many companies present great hidden production capacity, caused by the waste of their bottle necks that, in a majority of cases without investments and through the implantation of TOC can flourish.

Theory of constraints is a coherent and logical frame for complex process Management knowing that is not possible to eliminate all variability.

The difference between DBR and other planning and production control techniques is the concentration of planning and control in a very few points.

While JIT can be similar to a CONWIP system, TOC would be similar to a CONLOAD system. This is a new concept.

At last we should say that some problems are usually found when introducing TOC into production and not to the rest of the company, because generally production is able to improve its own processes to the point that the limitation jumps into the market.

References

1. Noreen, E., Smith, D., Mackey, J.T.: La teoría de las limitaciones y sus consecuencias para la contabilidad de gestión. Ediciones Díaz de Santos S.A. Año de la traducción (1997)
2. Aggarwal, S.C.: MRP, JIT, OPT, FMS? Harvard Business Review 63(5), 8–16 (1985)
3. Johnson, A.: MRP? MRP II? OPT? CIM? FMS? JIT? Is any system letter-perfect? Management Review 75(9), 22–27 (1986)
4. Koziol, D.S.: How the constraint theory improved a job-shop operation. Management Accounting 69(11), 44–49 (1988)
5. Tseng, M.F., Wuz, H.H.: The study of an Easy-to-Use DBR and BM system. International Journal of Production Research 44(8), 1449–1478 (2006)
6. Ramsay, M.L., Brown, S., Tabibzadeh, K.: Push, pull and squeeze shop floor control with computer simulation. Industrial Engineering 22(2), 39–45 (1990)
7. Fogarty, D.W., Blackstone, J.H., Hoffman, T.R.: Production and Inventory Management. South-Western Publishing Co., Cincinnati (1991)
8. Cook, D.P.: A simulation comparison of traditional, JIT, and TOC manufacturing systems in a flow shop with bottlenecks. Production and Inventory Management Journal 35(1), 73–78 (1994)

9. Duclos, K., Spencer, M.S.: The impact of a constraint buffer in a flow shop. International Journal of Production Economics 42(2), 175–185 (1995)
10. Holt, J.R.: Candid Comparison of Operational Management Approaches, pp. 1–11. Washington State University, Vancouver (1999)
11. Mabin, V., Balderstone, S.: The World of the Theory of Constraints: A review of the International Literature. Saint Lucie Press (November 1999)
12. AGII, 1998: Asociación Goldratt Institute Ibérica, La Meta: Cómo ponerla en práctica. Apuntes de un seminario, Valencia, 19 de Mayo de (1998)
13. AGII, 1998b: Asociación Goldratt Institute Ibérica, Producción: Cómo mejorar con TOC. Apuntes de un seminario, Valencia 26 y 27 de Noviembre de (1998)
14. Watson, J.K., Balcktone, J.H., Gardiner, S.C.: University of New Orleans, College of Business Administration, United Stated, The evolution of a management philosophy: The theory of constraints. Journal of Operations Management 25, 387–402 (2007), http://www.sciencedirect.com (Disponible 12 de junio de 2006)
15. Jacobs, R.F.: The OPT Scheduling System: A Review of a Production Scheduling System. Production and Inventory Management 24(4), 47 (1983)
16. Lambrecht, M.R., Segaert, A.: Buffer stock allocation in serial and assembly type of production lines. International Journal of Operations and Production Management 10(2), 47–61 (1990)
17. Raban, S., Nagel, R.N.: Constraint-based control of flexible flow lines. International Journal of Production Research 29(10), 1941–1951 (1991)
18. Goldratt, E.: Cadena Crítica (critical chain): Una novela empresarial sobre la gestión de proyectos, Ed. Díaz de Santos, Madrid (2001)
19. Leach, L.P.: Critical chain Project Management improves Project performance. Project Management Journal 30(2), 39 (1999)
20. Umble, M., Umble, E.: Manage your projects for success: an application of the theory of constraints. Production and Inventory Management Journal 41(2), 27 (2000)
21. Steyn, H.: An investigation into the fundamentals of critical chain project scheduling. International Journal of Project Management 19(6), 363 (2001)
22. Cohen, I., Mandelbaum, A., Shutb, A.: Multi-project scheduling and control: a process-based comparative study of the critical chain methodology and some alternatives. Project Management Journal 35(2), 39–50 (2004)
23. Leach, L.P.: Lean Project Management. In: Eight Principles for Success: Combining Critical Chain Project Management and Lean Tools to Accelerate Project Results Advanced Projects Inc., Boise, ID. Also available as e-book (2005)
24. Woeppel, M.J.: Projects in Less Time: A Synopsis of Critical Chain, Pinnacle Strategies, Plano, TX (2006)
25. Gardiner, S.C.: Measures of product attractiveness and the theory of constraints. International Journal of Retail and Distribution Management 21(7), 37–40 (1993)
26. Goldratt, E.: No es cuestión de suerte (It's not luck) Ed. Díaz de Santos, Madrid (1995)
27. Rahman, S.: The theory of constraints thinking process approach to developing strategies in supply chains. International Journal of Physical Distribution and Logistics Management 32(10), 809 (2002)
28. Watson, K.J., Polito, T.: Comparison of DRP and TOC financial performance within a multi-product, multi-echelon physical distribution environment. International Journal of Production Research 41(4), 84–93, 741–765 (2003)
29. Simatupang, T.M., Wright, A.C., Sridharan, R.: Applying the theory of Constraints to supply chain collaboration. Supply Chain Management: An International Journal 9(1), 57–70 (2004)

30. Schragenheim, E., Ronen, B.: B. Buffer Management: a diagnostic tool for production control. Production and Inventory Management Journal 32(2), 74–79 (1991)
31. Atwater, J.B., Chakraravorty, S.S.: Using the theory of constraints to guide the implementation of quality improvement projects in manufacturing operations. International Journal of Production Research 33(6), 1737–1761 (1995)
32. Gattiker, T.F., Boyd, L.H.: A cause-and-effect approach to analyzing continuous improvement at an electronics manufacturing facility. Production and Inventory Management Journal 40(2), 26–31 (1999)
33. Monzó, J.: (2007), http://jmonzo.net/blogeps/eps1.pdf (consultado Octubre de 2.009)
34. Debernardo, H.: Boletín sobre la Teoría de las Restricciones, http://www.cimatic.com.ar (Noviembre de 2000)
35. Dogget, M.: A statistical comparison of three root curse analysis Tools. Journal of Industrial Technology 20(2), 2–9 (2004)
36. AGII, 1999: Asociación Goldratt Institute Ibérica, Información General (Noviembre de 1999)
37. Rizzo, T.: The Theory of Constraints, http://www.rogo.com/cac/rizzo11.html (Año 1997)
38. AGII, 1999b: Asociación Goldratt Institute Ibérica, Cuaderno del Asistente del Programa Satélite de Eli Goldratt (1999b)
39. Mabin, V.J., Davies, J., Kim, S.M.: Applying the TOC thinking process in supply chain management to achieve a strategic level win-win solution. Paper Presented at 4th ANZAN Operations Management Symposium, Wellington, June 6-7, pp. 2601–2613 (2006)
40. Servera, P., Quetglas, P., Horrach, M.: Vols Nous, una experiencia de TOC en el cambio estratégico de una pequeña empresa. Artículos accesibles solo para asociados, http://www.goldratt.es (Año 1999)
41. Woehr, W.A., Legart, D.: Unblock the Power of Your Sales Force! Delta T-Selling. Neuer Wissenschaftlicher Verlag, Vienna (2002)
42. Roff-Mars, J.: Reengineering the Sales Process. Ballistix Pty Ltd., Brisbane (2005)
43. Briceño, J.A., Montilla, A.A.: Dimensionamiento Efectivo de los amortiguadores. In: Ponencia en el 3er Congreso Iberoamericano de Gerencia de Proyecto Cadena Crítica. Caracas (Año 2000)
44. Chase, R.B., Aquilano, N.J., Jacobs, F.R.: Administración de Producción y Operaciones. In: Manufactura y Servicios, 8ª Edición. Editorial: Mc.Graw-Hill (Año 2000)
45. Cespón, R., Ibarra, S., Marrero, F.: La selección del sistema de gestión de la producción en empresas manufactureras. In: Ponencias del IX Congreso de Ingeniería de Organización, Gijón (Septiembre 2005)
46. Goldratt, E.: El Síndrome del pajar (Haystack syndrome), Ed. Díaz de Santos, Madrid (1994)

Part IV
New Trends in Digital Factories

Distributed Intelligent Automation Solutions for Self-adaptive Manufacturing Plants

Alessandro Brusaferri, Andrea Ballarino, and Emanuele Carpanzano

Institute of Industrial Technologies and Automation,
National Research Council, via Bassini 15,
20133 Milan, Italy
{alessandro.brusaferri,andrea.ballarino}@itia.cnr.it,
{emanuele.carpanzano}@itia.cnr.it

Abstract. Nowadays, a new generation of responsive factories is needed to face continuous changes in product demand and variety, and to manage complex and variant production processes. To such an aim, self-adaptive automation solutions are required, capable to adapt their control strategy in real-time to cope with planned as well as unforeseen product and process variations. In such a context, the present paper describes an automation solution based on a modular distributed approach for agile factory integration and reconfiguration, integrating a knowledge based cooperation policy providing self-adaptation to endogenous as well as exogenous events. The proposed approach is discussed through its application to a plant for customized shoe manufacturing.

Keywords: Distributed Control Systems, Multi-Agent, IEC 61499, Reconfigurable Manufacturing Systems.

1 Introduction

To face new consumer centered manufacturing paradigms, like mass customization and personalization, factories must be capable to adapt themselves in real time to continuously changing market demand. Thus, the whole production cycle for small or even single batches has to be executed in very short times, i.e. a few days or even hours. In order to properly approach such complex and strict requirements adaptive knowledge based production systems have to be developed. In particular, the conception and development of a new generation of automation solutions, that integrate all factory levels from machines controls up to shop-floor supervision and production planning in a unique real time framework, is mandatory.

Future factory automation systems have to be modular, open, agile and knowledge based in order to promptly self-adapt themselves to changing exogenous conditions, like consumers expectations, market dynamics, design innovation, new materials and components integration. For such an aim, a new generation of intelligent, highly-interoperable and self-reconfigurable control systems is a fundamental enabling technology.

Á. Ortiz Bas, R.D. Franco, P. Gómez Gasquet (Eds.): BASYS 2010, IFIP AICT 322, pp. 205–213, 2010.

To tackle such a challenge, agile manufacturing paradigms - particularly flexible manufacturing systems (FMS) - have been adopted, often proving to be expensive and difficult to manage due to overall complexity. Furthermore, the integration of flexibility capability is not feasible for any kind of application. Therefore, to overcome such barriers and to provide cost effective flexible solutions, Reconfigurable Manufacturing Systems (RMS) have been introduced, characterized by strongly modular architectures and easy reconfiguration capabilities. In such a direction [1] identify modularity, integrability, diagnosability, customization and convertibility as key features of a RMS.

Among these, system modularity can surely be considered the most important, as outlined in [2] where implications and relationships between the architecture of a logic control system, its modularity and overall level of system reconfigurability, are discussed.

The problem of agile system reconfiguration has been faced mainly from the mechanical point of view with the development of easily pluggable mechatronic solutions. Nevertheless, proper solutions addressing a fully modular and reconfigurable control system have still to be identified.

As a matter of fact, present automation approaches and architectures - adopted in industry - are still based on rigid, loosely-coupled solutions, difficult to manage and to adapt, while current methods and tools for control system programming do not effectively support control system reconfigurability [3].

The integration of a new device within the overall production system or the replacement of a faulty device very often requires a critical stop of the system, to perform physical connections and allocations of the new device, as well as partial/total reprogramming of some parts of the control system, and modifications in production plans, which need time consuming commissioning operations to be executed afterwards [4].

The present paper proposes a self-adaptive control solution in order to support the RMS agility. Particularly, section II briefly analyzes the current state of the art related to the development of self-adaptive control solutions for Reconfigurable Manufacturing Systems and summarizes the main features to be guaranteed; section III presents the proposed overall system architecture; section IV reports conclusions and next developments are acceptable.

2   Requirements and Available Technologies

2.1   RMS Architecture

Typically, Reconfigurable Manufacturing Systems architectures may be structured into three major hierarchical layers as shown in Figure 1: unit level, cell level and system level. In particular, the overall system is composed by the aggregation of different cell modules, according to the system layout, while, in its turn, a cell module is constituted by the aggregation of more units. Specifically, units can be either operating machines or modules dedicated to parts handling and transportation, e.g. conveyors, rotating tables and manipulators.

Starting from last sampled status of underlying controlled objects, each module of the RMS control system - being unit control module, cell control module or system control module – decides and performs its control actions according to the fixed decision policy defined and hard-coded during the control system development phase. The interactions between modules are established ex ante and implemented according to fixed bindings between different modules interfaces.

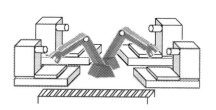 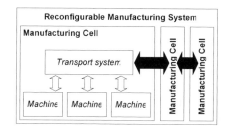

Fig. 1. Reconfigurable Manufacturing System Overall Architecture

Such a strictly coupled architecture is very difficult to modify during RMS reconfiguration phases, as time and costs required for such operations grow rapidly with the increase in system complexity. To such an aim, a new generation of loosely –coupled control architectures, based on a distributed easy-reconfigurable architecture, integrating a flexible knowledge based decision policy, has to be introduced.

2.2 Currently Available Enabling Technologies

Today, the required levels of modularity and distribution of control solutions are not properly adopted in industrial practice due to the lack of well defined and accepted reference models. Major consequences of this lack are twofold. First of all, implemented control and supervision strategies are today typically based on rigid centralized approaches organized into strictly coupled sequences of operations. Difficulties in reconfiguration and in real-time adaptation to production needs are most relevant resulting problems. As a second major consequence, suitable readability, portability and integrability of overall control and automation solutions are not supported. Therefore, the capitalization and reuse of company specific know-how on process and control is very difficult. Flexibility, optimization and failure management features are not properly tackled as well, thus critically impacting the overall production process efficiency and fault tolerance.

Great research efforts have been spent in recent years to conceive a common and well accepted reference model. In such a direction, the multi-agent system (MAS) paradigm shall be mentioned as one the major efforts for development of robust distributed control systems. Such a paradigm is based on autonomous modules, which integrate knowledge-base for decision making inference, high-level communication protocols and languages to support loosely coupled architectural organizations [5]. Despite its potential capabilities, major limits of such an approach for complex industrial test-cases reside in difficulties of guaranteeing strict execution time requirements.

Recently different research projects as SIRENA[1], RIMACS[2], SOCRADES[3], have considered an alternative architectural solution for developing systems composed of autonomous and interoperable units: the Service Oriented Architecture - SOA. Such paradigm is characterized by coarse-grained service interfaces, loose coupling between service providers and service consumers, and message-based, asynchronous communication [6]. Leveraging the SOA paradigm allows for services to be re-used across processes and systems, and systems to be "built for change". Reliability is improved as applications and systems can be made up of tested and proven components. SOA offers the potential to provide the necessary system-wide visibility and interoperability in complex systems subject to frequent changes and operating in a multi-vendor environment. Nonetheless, Service Oriented solutions are still unable to reach the hard-real time constraints in particular for controlling complex manufacturing processes with huge amounts of data and high numbers of units. Furthermore, the decisional logic is not supported by SOA, thus, intelligence has to be integrated onto the SOA level.

In particular, self-adaptivity needs self-interoperability of information: the knowledge has to be structured in order to be understood by autonomous intelligent agents able to interpret the domain conditions and taking the proper decisions. For such reason, a major research effort is ongoing widespread to exploit the adoption of Semantic Web approaches into the factory automation domain. Such paradigm is oriented to the implementation of machine interpretable information supporting the implementation of intelligent control solutions based on formal knowledge models. The formal definition of classes properties and instances allows inferring new knowledge from knowledge already structured into a model.

To cope with real time distributed control, a formal model has been proposed within the IEC 61499 standard of the International Electrotechnical Commission, promoted by the international O3NEIDA network[4]. The normative states the common interfaces and structure of the embedded solutions from simple basic function blocks, to composite functional integrations, up to overall control systems applications. It also provides guidelines for the application distribution within multi-vendor control execution devices. Nonetheless, it does not provide structured indications related to self-adaptive control systems design.

Several research actions have been also oriented to the integration of the low level, hard real-time, control layer and the high level, low real-time, control/supervision layer. In particular, [7] propose an interface for the integration of an heterogeneous low level control based on IEC 61499 standard and a Multi-Agent System for the manufacturing domain. [8] propose the integration of Service Oriented Architecture and a Multi-Agent System (MAS) in order to build a control architecture suitable for automated reconfigurability. [9] introduce a holonic manufacturing control architecture integrated with the logic control layer, designed to improve the agility and reconfigurability of production systems.

---

[1] SIRENA Project www.sirena-itea.org.
[2] RIMACS Project www.rimacs.org.
[3] SOCRADES Project www.socrades.eu.
[4] O3NEIDA Network www.oooneida.org.

Despite the performed research effort and the emerged benefits, such paradigms are currently not implemented within industrial solutions. In fact, the real world applicability needs to be demonstrated through complex industrial test cases highlighting the concrete advantages and providing guidelines for industrial applications.

3 Deployed Control Architecture

Present section describes main architectural and functional aspects regarding the proposed self-adaptive control solution. In particular, a real industrial plant is considered as a test-case in order to properly support the description and provide application details. Nonetheless, proposed solutions can be integrated within any manufacturing automation system. Obviously, a proper configuration of specific control rules and knowledge base classes is required.

3.1 The Focused Industrial Plant

Before starting the description of the deployed control architecture, the considered real industrial application, an innovative shoe manufacturing plant managed by ITIA-CNR, is presented, see Figure 2. For the sake of brevity, a simplified version of a part of the manufacturing system is here considered.

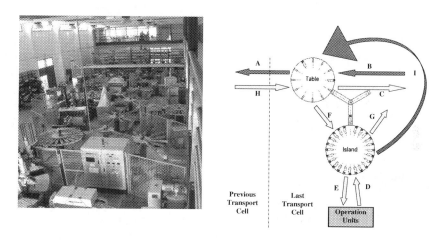

Fig. 2. Shoe manufacturing plant and work pieces flows

The considered manufacturing system integrates an innovative transport line for moving the semi-finished shoes from a machining station to another one according to operations requests. The innovative molecular structure enhances the modularity, scalability, integrability and reconfigurability properties of the production system, increasing the overall flexibility of the plant.

The basic element of the molecular structure is the "Tern", which is constituted by two rotating tables, called "Table" and "Island", and by a rotating three arms manipulator. The Table moves the semi-finished shoes either to the next Tern or to the Island of the same Tern. Moreover, it moves backward the lasts flowing back towards the warehouse (the last is the object around which the semi-finished shoe is built upon). The Island directs the semi-finished shoes towards the different machining stations, laid around the Island itself. The manipulator carries out the transport of the semi-finished shoes and lasts between Tables and Islands. The arrows in Figure 2 depict the possible movements that involve a generic semi-finished shoe or last in a generic single Tern.

3.2   The Deployed Control Solution

Starting from the process specification, a modular and distributed control architecture has been defined, integrating a real-time IEC 61499 distributed control layer and a multi-agent semantic enriched control and supervision layer. First of all, to achieve the desired agility objectives, object-oriented concepts have been exploited within control system development. For such an aim, the IEC 61499 standard has been adopted as design paradigm due to its orientation to the deployment of modular and distributed control solutions [10]. In particular, the molecular line has been considered as a set of interacting Terns, each one with its own independent control system. Each Tern control module communicates with the related Table, Island and Manipulator control modules, as shown in Figure 3. Moreover, each Tern control module is connected to the adjacent Terns control system modules, to coordinate the exchanges of semi-finished shoes and lasts.

Furthermore, each basic function block encapsulates the control logic by means of a state machine responsible for the activation of dedicated IEC 61131[5] based control algorithms depending on run-time events and conditions. For more details regarding function blocks internal structure see [3].

Tern Control modules represent the low level control layer, responsible for real time control tasks. In particular, tasks dedicated to manage nominal and failure operating condition have been integrated.

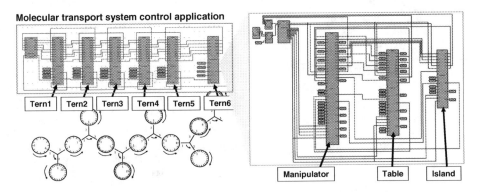

Fig. 3. Control architecture of the Molecular transport line

---

[5] International Standard IEC 61131 - www.iec.ch.

Such control modules have been implemented within the ISaGRAF 5 Workbench[6]. By supporting IEC 61499, such environment acts as backbone for the overall application development, from design to implementation and validation. Furthermore, the distributed hardware architecture can be defined by properly assigning the Resources (Virtual PLCs) executed within each device. Moreover, each device integrates I/O interfaces connected to the factory field.

The application can then be designed as a unique control program. Furthermore, the developed control application can be generated into target-independent C code, executable by a firmware, which emulates a virtual machine on hardware, being it an Industrial PC, an embedded board or a tiny controller. Therefore, portability and scalability of the developed application is guaranteed.

In order to provide self-adaptive capabilities to the deployed automation solution while reconfiguring manufacturing resources (i.e. adding, removing operational units or integrating manufacturing functions) a multi-agent control and supervision layer has been integrated onto the object-oriented real-time control layer. In particular, each Tern control module has been connected to a Tern agent, responsible for the interaction within the high level control layer. The interface between the IEC 61499 modules and the multi-agent layer, deployed in Java language, has been developed by means of the Java Native Interface provided by Sun Microsystems Inc[7].

Besides, the higher level control layer is responsible for the coordination of the low level real-time control layer in response of predicted as well as unforeseen events. In fact, the decisional logic has to be dynamically adapted to follow changing products features/requirements contextually to machine operational capabilities reconfiguration, tools integrations, and new machines implementation into production cells. The higher level control layer is also aimed at interacting within MES and ERP systems so to receive incoming production orders as well as provide a run-time updated factory image to the management layers. To such an aim, dedicated interaction mechanisms have been implemented.

Furthermore, the self-adaptation mechanism has also to react when operational capabilities become unavailable due for example to failures or maintenance operations. To such an aim, a dedicated management agent has been integrated, implementing a knowledge based reasoner connected to complementary knowledge model based on a common formal domain description:

- *Product knowledge base model*: aimed at the structuring of information related to products to be processed by the manufacturing system, as required operations and priorities with reference to the overall production plan.
- *Resource knowledge base model*: aimed at the formal description of the intelligent units run-time integrated within the production facility, i.e. the operations provided and execution state.

Such models are dynamically updated by means of a dedicated Interface agent, in order to be aligned to the process evolution, supporting the optimal real-time decision strategy. Two dedicated model update mechanisms have been implemented: the first has in charge the management of the products entering/leaving the system

---

[6] Isagraf Workbench - www.isagraf.com
[7] Java Native Interface - http://java.sun.com/j2se/1.4.2/docs/guide/jni/

and their operational state change due to processed manufacturing tasks performed within the RMS; the second supervises the resources integrated within the system, updating their available operations depending on their evolving execution state and/or reconfigurations.

Thanks to the adoption of such an asynchronous policy, the model adaptation task is called only when required, reducing the overall execution time. Furthermore, semantically-rich based descriptions have been adopted to implement the knowledge based solution. In particular RDF and OWL-DL W3C[8] standards coming from the Semantic Web area have been considered. Therefore, machine reasoning has been used to perform automatic matchmaking of required and offered services using logical inference, rather than performing hard-coded one-to-one mappings.

Such type of matchmaking enables the use of services that did not exist or were not known when the requestor side was programmed, enabling automation system reconfiguration without control logic reprogramming. The overall control architecture is outlined in Figure 4.

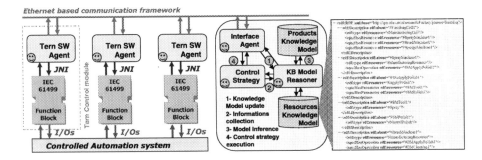

Fig. 4. Overall multi-agent control architecture

Once a new operational unit is plugged into the production system its agent asks for the registration service to the manager passing is description as argument, formally reporting the operations to be provided and the required resources (i.e. tools) to be used during operation execution. The operations to be provided and the resources to be used are described with reference to a common ontology.

The manager interprets the ontological description of the intelligent unit and integrates it into a dedicated knowledge base within the manager architecture. A searching algorithm is then executed in order to find the run-time available manufacturing resources capable of providing the requested operations.

4   Conclusions

The present paper describes a self-adaptive control architecture deployed for a real industrial plant. To such an aim, a modular and distributed approach has been adopted, integrating an IEC 61499 based control solution for real-time control

---

[8] OWL Web Ontology Language - http://www.w3.org/TR/owl-guide/

purposes and a semantically enriched multi-agent control layer for dynamic supervision strategy. Main focus of the paper is kept on the description of the overall solution structure, highlighting the capabilities of run-time updating of the knowledge model used for control decisions, while factory products and resources changes occur.

Next efforts will mainly regard the integration of dedicated supervision and on-line dispatching/scheduling facilities onto the deployed control architecture.

References

1. Koren, Y., Heisel, U., Jovane, F., Moriwaki, T., Pritschow, G., Ulsoy, G., Bruseel, H.V.: Reconfigurable manufacturing systems. Ann. CIRP 1999 48(2), 527–540 (1999)
2. Almeida, E., Luntz, J., Tilbury, D.: Event-Condition-Action Systems for Reconfigurable Logic Control. IEE Transaction on Automation Science and Engineering 4(2), 167–181 (2007)
3. Brusaferri, A., Ballarino, A., Carpanzano, E.: Enabling Agile Manufacturing through Reconfigurable Control Solutions. In: Proc. at 14th IEEE International Conference on Enabling Technologies and Factory Automation (ETFA 2009), Mallorca, Spain (September 2009)
4. Carpanzano, E., Jovane, F.: Advanced Automation Solutions for Future Adaptive Factories. Annals of the CIRP 56(1), 435–438 (2007)
5. Pechoucek, M., Marík, V.: Industrial deployment of multi-agent technologies: review and selected case studies. Autonomous Agents and Multi-Agent Systems Journal, 397–431 (May 14, 2008)
6. Lastra, J., Delamer, I.: Web Services in Factory Automation: Fundamental Insights and Research Roadmap. IEEE Transactions on Industrial Informatics 2(1), 1–11 (2006)
7. Lepuschitz, W., Vallée, M., Merdan, M., Vrba, P., Resch, J.: Integration of a Heterogeneous Low Level Control in a Multi-Agent System for the Manufacturing Domain. In: Proc. at 14th IEEE International Conference on Enabling Technologies and Factory Automation (ETFA 2009), Mallorca, Spain (September 2009)
8. Herrera, V., Bepperling, A., Lobov, A., Smit, H., Colombo, A.W., Lastra, J.L.: Integration of Multi-Agent Systems and Service-Oriented Architecture for Industrial Automation. In: Proc. at IEEE International Conference on Industrial Informatics (INDIN 2008), Daejeon, Korea, July 13-16 (2008)
9. Leitao, P., Restivo, F.: Implementation of a Holonic Control System in a Flexible Manufacturing System. IEEE Transactions on Systems on, Man, and Cybernetics - Part C: Applications and Reviews 38(5), 699–709 (2008)
10. International Electro-technical Commission (IEC), International Standard IEC61499, Function Blocks, part 1-4, IEC, Edition 1.0. (January 2005), http://www.iec.ch/

Exploiting Knowledge Based Systems to Support Manufacturing of Functional Food Products

Stefania Bandini[2], David Martínez-Simarro[1], J.M. Pinazo Sánchez[1],
Fabio Sartori[2], and Giuseppe Vizzari[2]

[1] Ainia centro tecnológico Valencia-Spain
[2] CSAI (Complex Systems and Artificial Intelligence research centre-University of
Milano-Bicocca)

Abstract. In recent years consumers' concern about food safety and health is
becoming crucial. The development of healthier products seems to be a promise
challenge, since functional foods are identified as one of the central pillars for
the future progress of the food industry internationally. Artificial Intelligence
techniques such as Knowledge Engineering, Rule Based reasoning and Expert
systems are presented here as a way of technological innovation towards a
knowledge-based and sustainable manufacturing in food sector. We show how
these techniques are applied in a case study to support companies in the formulation of new chocolate products that reduce the impact on health status, reducing selected risk factors associated with obesity and coronary disease
(fat, sugar).

1 Introduction

In last years the interest of technology platforms[1], public health organizations and
consumers in knowing the relation between diet and health has increased considerably. The experts in nutrition recommend to follow a healthy, diverse and balanced diet
as the best way of preventing or at least reducing the risk of suffering certain altera-
tions or diseases in short and long term: hypertension, obesity, diabetes, cardiovascu-
lar diseases, disorders on food habits and even certain types of cancer related to the
nourishment.

Consumers are increasingly interested in the health benefits of foods and have
started to look beyond the basic nutritional benefits of food to the disease prevention
and health enhancing compounds contained in many foods. This combined with a
more widespread understanding of how diet affects disease, health-care costs and ag-
ing populations have created a potentially sustainable market for functional foods.

The aim of this paper is to propose an approach based on the exploitation of
knowledge artifacts [1] in a collaborative environment to support the development of
functional products. In this paper we present a conceptual and computational framework for the development of knowledge-based systems (KBS) to support experts of
small and medium enterprises involved in the formulation of functional healthier food
products. The paper investigates how functional knowledge can be profitably acquired

---

[1] European Technology Platform Food For Life, http://etp.ciaa.be

Á. Ortiz Bas, R.D. Franco, P. Gómez Gasquet (Eds.): BASYS 2010, IFIP AICT 322, pp. 214–223, 2010.
© IFIP International Federation for Information Processing 2010

and represented through the usage of a specific knowledge artifact, namely ontologies and T-Matrix [2]. Ontologies [3] are one of the most suitable approaches to represent functional knowledge about a domain. In our framework, ontologies are used to specify the structure of the food product (formula) with respect to the functional nature of the relationships existing among its raw material or additives (ingredients). The T-Matrix tool allows representing how different structural ingredients of a food product can be aggregated from the functional point of view (nutritional properties), as well as the relationships existing between functions and the final performances (performance properties) the product must have to be successful. T-Matrix is thus a specific model for the representation of such ontological aspects. The participation of a KBS in this case guarantees both the sharing of the knowledge model among users (user defined ontology) and suggesting solutions to the compounding problem [1] (rule based decision support). The proof of concept we have realised enables an intuitive and highly integrated formula and recipe development, collaboration tools and global regulatory compliance support.

The related case study shows an experiment of our intended application to the reformulation of chocolate products. The work was related to modify the ingredient profile of the standard recipe of traditional products, increasing some ingredients while reducing others in conjunction with maintaining commercial viability.

This paper is organized as follows: The next Section 2 deals with the context and motivation of the related work. In Section 3, a flexible and extensible approach to the support of formulating new food products based on knowledge systems is presented. The design strategy, the domain vocabulary and discussion on the proposed approach are offered as well. Later on, a case study is presented there by means of the application of the approach to a specific problem: the reformulation of chocolate products. Finally, Section 4 points out some remarks and future works.

2 Context and Motivation

A functional food[2] is one that has demonstrated a significant effect on the body beyond adequate nutrition, in a way that improves health and well-being and reduces disease. Functional foods provide an opportunity to improve the health of European inhabitants and reduce health care costs while support economic development in several areas. Researchers, scientific community and food industry work all together with the aim to promote the concept of healthy food. Recent advances in molecular biology and nutrition technologies give food industry a starting point for the design and development of new ingredients and additives for healthy life styles [4-5].

In order to achieve healthier food products and derivatives (even with functional properties), it is necessary to avoid undesired substances (natural or otherwise) or reduce them to appropriate limits, and to increase the levels (naturally or by programmed additions) of other substances with beneficial properties (functional ingredients). Essentially, three kinds of strategies are used to that end in food sector: these are associated with animal or plant production, the handling and processing of raw materials, and the reformulation of intermediate or final products.

---

[2] European Food Information Council (EUFIC). http://www.eufic.org

At this stage reformulation is used as far as possible to develop a range of derivatives with custom-designed composition and properties. To that purpose, there are two possible types of complementary intervention. The first involves reducing some compounds normally present in these foods to appropriate amounts, for example, fat, Saturated Fatty Acids (SFA), salt, sugar, nitrites and so on. The second is to incorporate ingredients that are potentially health-enhancing (functional), for example, fibre, certain types of vegetable proteins, Mono Unsaturated Fatty Acids (MUFA) and Poly Unsaturated Fatty Acids (PUFA), antioxidants, etc.

There are numerous aspects to consider in the development of this kind of products [6]. The new derivative product must have the appropriate technological, sensory and nutritional properties, and be safe and convenient for consumption. Ignoring such requirements, which are demanded by the reference products if they are to be improved, not only compromises the success of the derivatives concerned but also projects a bad product image and creates a lack of confidence which is difficult to surmount.

In the reformulation process, compounding problem stands for the research of the most suitable way of combining ingredients in order to design a product described by a recipe [1]. This indicates which ingredients are involved in the construction of the product by the indication of their amount. The problem has been tackled involving the use of KBS in several domains. For instance the compounding problem has been faced in tablets [7] and colors [8] design and, in particular, in rubber compounding [9].

In the food domain, several new products are launched to the market every year[3]. When companies try to reformulate, the typical situation is that a technically skilled expert has specific knowledge about the domain (ingredients, processes and products). Therefore, the master has the adequate expertise to combine relevant entities in an appropriate way to achieve the desired goal: the formulation of a new product with functional benefits. Not surprisingly, this approach is totally valid, but modern information technologies could be thoroughly integrated into everyday activity of food product formulation and improve the efficiency and effectiveness of related tasks:

First of all, thanks to the use of knowledge elicitation techniques and representation, the development of new products could be extended beyond the basic formulation of a recipe to include marketing considerations. By this way, product innovation is not only aligned to the basic specifications and regulatory compliance but also to the product nutritional properties, performance needs and consumer preferences and acceptances, such as price, format (objective), as well as taste, noise, color, flavour, texture and so on (subjective). See Figure 1 below with the aimed approach.

Secondly, to revise a recipe and assess the development of healthier products, a KBS can be used to support decision making processes [10] in the formulation of safety derivatives both of skilled and expert users and of beginners. The participation of a KBS in this process is threefold:

- sharing the knowledge model (i.e. the contents of the knowledge base) among involved users,
- training beginner/non-expert users (i.e. allowing a rapid technology transfer and prototyping: virtual lab)
- and suggesting solutions to particular problems (i.e. the results of computations made by the inferential engine on the contents of the knowledge base).

---

[3] Global National Product Database, http://www.gnpd.com

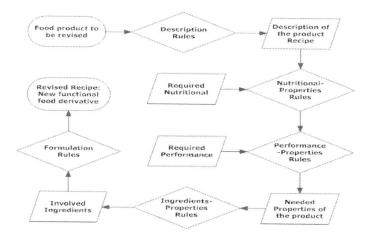

Fig. 1. Challenging approach for functional food formulation

The effectiveness of the KBS and the quality of its contribution in supporting decision making processes will depend mainly on two classes of aspects: internal (e.g. correctness and integrity) and external (e.g. adherence with the application domain and maintainability level).

In our aforementioned approach we apply the KBS to:

- The resolution of a real problem by means of the use of knowledge from the application domain.
- The resolution of a problem that requires a great amount of expert knowledge when it is solved by not experts or beginners.

Not in a substitution approach, but rather with the aim of smoothing the decision making process.

3   Application Scenario

The chocolate and other derivatives of the cocoa have been consumed in diverse forms throughout centuries. Nowadays, chocolates can be found in several ways and formats: tablets, pills, liquid chocolate, sweet, nougats, creams, etc. Basic ingredients of its composition are the cocoa solids and cocoa butter, fats and oils (whose composition obey rheological characteristics and about melting point adapted to every need), sugar, milk powder and / or lacteal and dried fruits (almond, hazelnut, nut ...). All that does chocolate a particularly energetic product for the presence of glucides and lipids: from 500 to 550 Kcal for 100g. The half of this contribution comes from the present lipids in several raw materials. The oily total contribution in chocolates registers from 25 to 40 % of the weight of the product. This proportion difficultly can diminish, since it is requested by production needs or by the organoleptic perception for the final consumer.

3.1 Chocolate Recipe Characterization

Within this context, the tackled problem is the formulation of components in new food product development. The results of compounding activity are fundamental for the definition of the raw materials and additives (i.e. the ingredients) to be used in the formulation of the product. The amount of each ingredient is measured in % values. In food domain, nutritional properties are of paramount importance since they represent our needs for vitamins, minerals, fatty acids and proteins. For instance, the consumption of too many saturated fats is the leading cause of high cholesterol. Unsaturated fats are healthier in moderation than saturated fats. Proteins are essential nutrients for growth and digestion.

The first objective of the project has been a complete characterization of food product from the structural (nutritional properties) and functional (performance) point of view. To this aim, an ontology of the product (chocolate) has been defined and implemented in Protégé. The hierarchical organization of the different concepts and individuals of the ontology is partially represented in Figure 2.

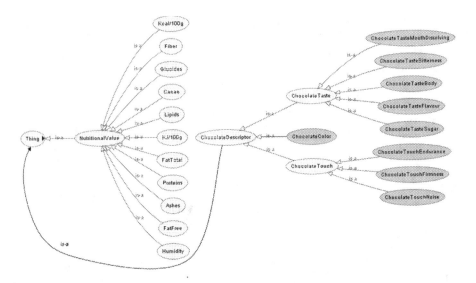

Fig. 2. Partial representation of chocolate ontology

Domain entities resulting from the performed ontological analysis are distributed in recipe names, ingredients, nutritional and performance properties. These constitute the Terms of the grammar.

```
<nutritional property> ::= "np1" | "np2" | ...
<performance property> ::= "pp1" | "pp2" | ...
<recipe> ::= "RECIPE_1" | "RECIPE_2" | ...
<ingredient> ::= "ingredient_1" | "ingredient_2" | ...
```

A previously reported, recipes are made up of ingredients, each one belonging to a family (e.g. sugars, lacteals, flours).

<family> ::= "F1" | "F2" | "F3" | ...

For instance, the recipe name Black Chocolate involves ingredients Cacao Butter, Cacao Powder, sugar, vanilla and lecithin. Each ingredient has a nutritional property table that implies a side effect in the final recipe.

Within a recipe it is possible to identify sets of ingredients made up of elements of the same family and with a role in the final formula. Each role is a functional group of ingredients (system), inserted in the recipe in order to provide particular feature to the final recipe (e.g. basis, sweeteners, flavourings).

<system> ::= "S1" | "S2" | "S3" | ...

By this way, it is possible to represent if there is an association between each ingredient (i.e. cacao powder) and its influence in the final recipe as in Figure 3.

Some constraints that define boundaries for the construction of recipes suitable for derivative development can be described. Generally, these constraints depend on the purpose of the product. It is the case of constraints on combinations cardinality, combination amount, ingredient amounts and continuous attribute value limits.

These constraints (description, nutritional, performance, ingredients and formulation rules) will be defined with the help of a rule engine. But, initially, we make use of a T-Matrix (see Table 1) to represent the correlations among ingredients, nutritional properties and performance.

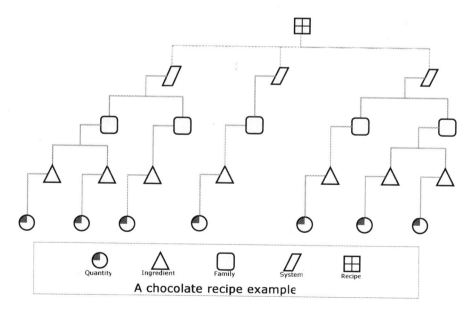

A chocolate recipe example

Fig. 3. A chocolate recipe example

Table 1. T-Matrix for nutritional and high level properties

	Fat	Proteins	Fiber	Carbo-hydrates	Humidity	Calories	Minerals	Vitamins
RI1	↑■	×	×	×	×	↑▪	↑□	↑□
RI2	↑□	↑□	↑▪	↑▪	↑▪	↑□	↑▪	↑▪
RI3	×	×	×	↑■	×	↑■	↓▪	↓▪
RI4	×	↑■	×	↑■	↑□	↑■	↑□	↑□

	Solubility	Bitternesss	Cacao	Cost	Flavour	Color	Texture	Noise
RI1	↑■	↓■	↑□	↑□	↑▪	↑▪	↑■	↑■
RI2	↓■	↑■	↑■	↑□	↑■	↑■		
RI3		↓■						

Correlation	■	Strong	Proportionality	↑	Direct
	□	Good		↓	Reverse
	▪	Weak			
	×	No correlation			

It is possible to create a T–Matrix for each possible formula recipe. For a particular usage of the ingredients the relationships reported in the T–Matrix show the effects of recipe interventions in terms of variations of nutritional properties (i.e. calories) and the effects on product performance (i.e. taste). Two sets of additional terms are respectively dedicated to represent the grade of correlation and the proportionality.

3.2 Software Prototype

The proof of concept of the system consists of a knowledge base, a database, and a user interface. The basic architecture of the system is described and two important issues, knowledge representation and natural language processing, are discussed. The aim of the system is to provide the process expert a tool to simplify the recipe transformation process and to help them to control the recipe management activity during the formulation of functional products with health benefits. Knowledge elicitation and representation techniques, and rule based programming combined with object programming (Java + Drools[4]) are employed in the system.

The user interacts with the system through a user interface which may use menus, natural language or any other style of interaction. Then an inference engine is used to reason with both the expert knowledge (extracted from our friendly expert) and data specific to the particular problem being solved. The expert knowledge will typically be in the form of a set of IF-THEN rules. The case specific data includes both data provided by the user and partial conclusions (along with certainty measures) based on

---

[4] Drools Project, http://www.jboss.org/drools/

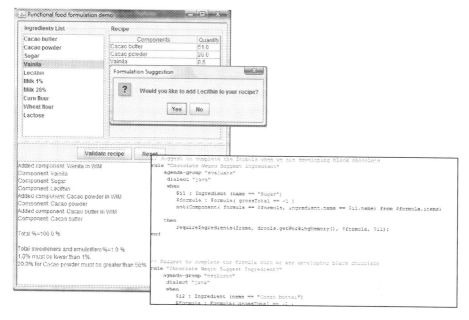

Fig. 4. KBS proof of concept for formulation of functional chocolate

this data. In a simple forward chaining rule-based system the case specific data will be the elements in working memory.

The Figure 4 below illustrates the aspect of the prototype system and shows an intended trial for the modification of the ingredient profile of the standard black chocolate recipe. This included increasing fibre while reducing both fat and sugar.

4   Concluding Remarks and Future Development

This work shows an innovative sustainable and knowledge-based product and manufacturing model to support the development of functional food. The present approach looks promising since it allows redefining the way in which food companies' value-creation process must be conceived and realized, in this case applied to a concrete food scenario for:

- Designing new formulations that include the new potentially interesting ingredients for healthy effects in the targeted product.
- Receiving an assessment and decision support for the generation of new formulations with low content in harmful ingredients (sugar, fat).
- Studying and representing the influence of the different ingredients and additives in the final formula and their relation to performance properties such as color, flavour, taste, smell, image, etc.

Of course our work is a first experiment and the primary future direction is the realisation of a concrete application in collaboration with an end-user. Likewise, due to the relevance of the field in the food sector, a challenging line of work is open and future developments could exploit further potentialities of the system:

- Study and represent the influence of the different stages of the process (mixed, warming, etc.) in the selected ingredients and the formula.
- Exploit the ability to reformulate products while keeping the same taste, texture and consumer satisfaction, enabling the interaction between the consumer and the product-life cycle development through a co-innovation network.
- Enrich the access to a wide variety of functional ingredients by means of the integration of several data sources through information retrieval techniques.
- Take the advantage of registered data (physical measures of process, product and environment, actions and other incidents) to automatically generate and retune recipes. On line comparison of product evolution with previous (finished, classified and registered) ones and also after consumers' perception trials could be used to improve productions in terms of quality, productivity or homogeneity. Case Based Reasoning (CBR), could be proposed in order to reach this goal: compounding is performed designing a recipe by adapting a previous one.
- A mixed approach combining RBR and CBR could be also potentially exploited to support product formulation for food safety.

Acknowledgments

This paper describes some of the results achieved during the collaboration between CSAI in Milano and ainia technological center in Valencia thanks to the *"Programa de Alta Especialización de Tecnólogos"* financed by the Valencian Institute for SMEs IMPIVA.

References

1. Bandini, S., Colombo, E., Vizzari, G.: The The Role of Knowledge Artifacts in Knowledge Maintenance, Department of Informatics, Systems and Communication, University of Milano-Bicocca. Via Bicocca degli Arcimboldi, 8, 20126 Milan, Italy (2005)
2. Bandini, S., Sartori, F.: From From handicraft prototypes to limited serial productions: Exploiting knowledge artifacts to support the industrial design of high quality products. In: AIE, Artificial Intelligence for Engineering Design, Analysis and Manufacturing, CSAI—Complex Systems and Artificial Intelligence Research Center. University of Milano, Milan (2009)
3. Gruber, T.R.: Toward Principles for the Design of Ontologies Used for Knowledge Sharing. Stanford Knowledge Systems Laboratory 701 Welch Road, Building C Palo Alto, CA 94304, http://gruberksl.stanford.edu
4. Pszczola, D.E.: Addressing functional problems in fortified foods. Food Technology 52(7), 38–46 (2001)
5. Pszczola, D.E.: Ingredients that get to meat to matter. Food Technology 53(4), 62–74 (1999)
6. Jiménez-Colmenero: Fat replacers in meat products (2000)

7. Craw, S., Wiratunga, N., Rowe, R.: Case Based Design for Tablet Formulation. In: Proceedings of the 4th European Workshop on Case Based Reasoning, pp. 358–369. Springer, Berlin (1998)
8. Cheetham, W., Graf, J.: Case-Based Reasoning in Color Matching. In: Leake, D.B., Plaza, E. (eds.) ICCBR 1997. LNCS, vol. 1266, pp. 1–12. Springer, Heidelberg (1997)
9. Bandini, S., Manzoni, S.: Modeling Core Knowledge and Practices in a Computational Approach to Innovation Process. In: Magnani, L., Nersessian, N. (eds.) Model-Based Reasoning: Scientific Discovery, Technologicy, Values, pp. 369–390. Kluwer Academic/Plenum Publishers (2002)
10. Holsapple, C., Joshi, K.: Organizational Knowledge Resources. Decision Support Systems, pp. 39–54 (2001)

Using the Life-Cycle Paradigm to Support Factory Planning Approaches

Roberto da Piedade Francisco, João Bastos, and Américo Azevedo

INESC Porto & Faculdade de Engenharia da Universidade do Porto,
Rua Dr. Roberto Frias S/N
4200-465 Porto, Portugal
{roberto.piedade,joao.bastos,ala}@fe.up.pt

Abstract. In order to fulfill all challenges related to design, management, evaluation and reconfiguration of new or existing facilities, the development of a new, integrated and holistic factory framework is required. In this context, a new requirements model is proposed in the context of the innovative framework called Virtual Factory Framework. Using this approach in factory planning it is expected to improve the ability to generate better and more sustainable solutions over the entire factory life-cycle. This paper underlines the use of the life-cycle paradigm in order to enable the future factory planning approaches.

Keywords: Factory Planning, Virtual Factory Framework, Life-Cycle Paradigm.

1 Introduction

The Virtual Factory Framework is a new foresight to the Next Generation Factory, viewing the factory as a new and complex type of product. It is appropriate to consider factories as long life and complex products, since they have to follow the same steps in its origin as products. They also have to be permanently adapted to the needs and requirements of markets and economic efficiency, applying the life-cycle paradigm to the factory as a product [1].

The new line of thought in manufacturing management is directed to the optimization and value creation of products, processes and technologies throughout the factory life-cycle. The main objectives are to improve the effective use of the decreasing time available to reach the market and the increasing need to reduce design, implementation and production costs.

The present work addresses state of the art concepts and research issues in the context of an RTD European project entitled "Holistic, extensible, scalable and standard Virtual Factory Framework", namely in the topic of factory planning and the concept of "factory as a product".

This document is organized as follows: the second section presents the next generation factory concepts; the third section presents two contemporary factory planning approaches; the fourth section addresses the virtual factory framework and the supporting requirements model; and finally, the conclusions and further works are presented in the last section.

Á. Ortiz Bas, R.D. Franco, P. Gómez Gasquet (Eds.): BASYS 2010, IFIP AICT 322, pp. 224–232, 2010.
© IFIP International Federation for Information Processing 2010

2 Next Generation Factory Concepts

In a factory development project, the factory can be seen as a product that requires a complex life-cycle and the use of techniques already used for product development. This new paradigm can be introduced to support manufacturers in the creation of value through new solutions (products, processes and technology) that improve quality, reduce ramp-up and product delivery time, and also reduce production costs in order to achieve greater competitiveness. Some initiatives have been developed in order to reach these objectives. One of the most recent and robust is ManuFuture [2]. This initiative aims to promote investments in innovation that will ensure the future of European industry in a knowledge-based economy. At the same time, its aim is to speed up the rate of industrial transformation in Europe, providing High-Adding-Value employment and reaching a major share of the world's manufacturing output in the future knowledge-driven economy, seeking to achieve Competitive Sustainable Manufacturing [2].

Every factory and production facility is a distinctive entity. Each factory is different in terms of its products, processes, layout, structure, human resources and corporate philosophy. However, the common denominator for them to guarantee their survival is to make production facilities adaptable. The adaptability is becoming a top priority for modern enterprises and is a continuous task for management.

Modern factories have to be modular, scalable, flexible, open, agile and knowledge-based in order to be able to adapt, in real time, to the continuously changing market demands, technology options and government regulations.

In a manufacturing company, the job of a production facility is to perform competitively on the market, with high levels of adaptability, by producing (material) goods as products in line, as much as possible, with the market demand. In order to achieve this adaptability, its companies need to have an integrated perspective. The interrelationship between the products, processes and factory thus requires that the different actors are highly involved and interdependent (Figure 1). The product required by the market determines the process characteristics and configuration, such as equipment, organization and product volume and mix. The process determines the plant with the equipment, support facilities and services that individuals operate, control and supervise. And finally the factory determines the product volume, mix and cadence. Changing one component causes other components to change as well. This cannot only be applied to production facilities, but also to an entire factory [3].

Fig. 1. Interdependence between product, production process and factory plan

One of the factors that have a profound impact on adaptability is flexibility. Hence the constant need to strengthen and improve flexibility in the design of production processes and factory planning. Thus, the need for new methodologies that support the design of the factory as a product is increasingly obvious. But, since this is a highly complex task, it is necessary to study and analyze the approaches followed by experts and experienced implementers in the field.

A first notion that must be present at this stage is the fact that the design of the factory cannot be separated from the planning process and product design, particularly due functional interdependencies and due to the similarity and parallelism observed in their life-cycle, as represented in Figure 2.

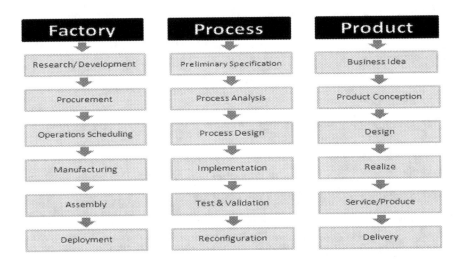

Fig. 2. Factory, process and product life-cycle

Indeed, the benefits of applying this concept are feasible and desirable if a factory planning can be carried out using knowledge on life-cycle paradigm, process planning, factory planning and new product development (NPD).

The product life-cycle is the time period between the moment that the product is conceived (concept, plan, design, idea, notion, or thought) and when its production is no longer profitable [4]. This is a paradigm that can properly conduct the phases of product management through the concepts and tools applied in product development. Then, when taking the concept of the factory as a product, it can also extend the paradigm to this new perspective.

The product life-cycle phases can be studied in different organizational areas such as: marketing, product management, manufacturing and computer systems. For instance, the concept of PLM (Product Lifecycle Management) has to do with the management of activities and product requirements from the viewpoint of processes development, manufacturing and product utilization in the context of data management, while the traditional concept of product life-cycle applies to product marketing and service life [5]. Although the PLM is currently presented as software, in fact, it is a methodology supported in an integrated set of software tools oriented to life-cycle management that is used to manage specific tasks and to plan the entire process of product management.

In fact, the life-cycle paradigm can be applied in order to harmonize and integrate the life-cycle of the product and factory (manufacturing view) simultaneously, providing the idealization of its phases, as shown in Figure 3.

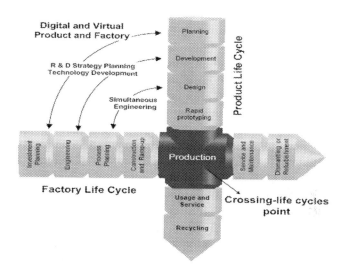

Fig. 3. Factory life-cycle crossing product life-cycle [6]

This approach intends to set up a foundation for factory planning in order to establish the phases that can be standardized in the context of factory design. This harmonization approach of the converging life-cycles makes it possible to use simulations in the design of an object-oriented collaborative product, starting at the vision of the virtual factory to the real factory at the intersection so-called "Crossing-life-cycles point" [6].

According to this idea, we will now present some methodologies followed in Factory Planning and Product Life-Cycle mentioned in the literature.

3 Factory Planning Approaches

In the context of the project research, it was possible to identify several factory planning approaches. The next paragraphs present a brief overview of two of them which have presented relevant contributions for the Virtual Factory Framework requirements definition on the factory design phase.

Systematic and Situation-driven Planning Methods [3] - Planning production facilities means envisioning several aspects that includes the products that are going to be produced, the processes required to produce them and the physical infrastructure required to the production. This approach requires the use of methodologies that efficiently design the planning process. According to Schenk [3], a planning project can be developed systematically and/or situation-driven on the basis of various planning process and procedural model views.

A systematic, methodical approach is influenced by situation-driven decisions. It serves the development of a planning project through internal and external planning activities on the basis of various planning process and procedural model views. These production facility and factory lifecycle design planning phases and stages are represented in figure 4.

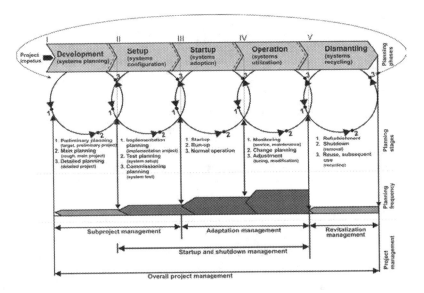

Fig. 4. Production facility and factory lifecycle design planning phases [3]

The planning activities span a production facility's entire life-cycle from development/planning through setup, execution and operation to phase-out [3].

Therefore, the Systematic Planning Processes have the following steps:

1. Rough sequence of processes and manufacturing plants planning
2. The project design takes place with the following sequence:
   a) Main process (parts manufacturing or assembly)
   b) Main process storage; main process transports system; production process control; quality assurance; fixtures tools and testing equipment;
   c) Manufacturing equipment engineering; maintenance; auxiliary materials storage; power conversion equipment; waste treatment facilities,
   d) Management; power generation; social, medical and sanitary facilities.
3. Complex planning model - this consists of the following planning complexes:
   a) Project definition
   b) Project development
   c) Project implementation

An enhancement of the systematic approach is the situation-driven method for factory planning also presented by Schenk *et al.* [3]. The situation-driven planning differs from the systematic planning in that, as a result of operational decisions (e.g. changes in target, data, product, technology, requirement, time, profitability or quality specifications), all or part of the planning process and sequences have to be changed.

According to this situation-driven approach the planning model acquires reactivity and is adaptable to operational changes. Its redevelopment is based on the current situation and uses selected systematic planning components and activities to ensure the accomplishment of the goals.

Factory planning supported in simulation tools – Simulation tools are popular in various industrial fields as decision support systems. Since factory planning is one of the most complex tasks, the need of decision support tools was especially comprehensible. Several commercial solutions have been appearing in the last decade to the market as appropriate to deal with the problem of factory planning.

Mertins *et al.* [7] presents a scalable, flexible and adaptive simulation model used in factory planning based on existing ERP (Enterprise Resource Planning) and MES (Manufacturing Execution System) data. The objective of this work is to enable an industrial engineer without simulation expertise to perform the simulations that are necessary to support several tasks including process planning and factory planning. Moreover, the simulation model facilitates an analysis of the results for different scenarios, using the actual data from the ERP and MES systems.

In their research, Wenbin *et al.* [8] report a development in a production engineering-oriented virtual factory - a planning cell-based manufacturing systems design approach. This manufacturing systems design process is based on a planning cell reengineered according to the concept of concurrent engineering. The process modeling of a production engineering-oriented virtual factory is proposed at both generic and detailed levels. With logic level simulation (discrete event simulation, etc.) and physical level simulation (ergonomics simulation, immersed virtual reality, etc.), a distributed, layered and integrated simulation model can be used to build a virtual factory environment for concurrent manufacturing systems design during the whole lifecycle of production engineering, including production system configuration, factory layout, and so on. Therefore, the designed manufacturing systems can be evaluated and optimized before their implementation.

Once the planning methodologies and the life-cycle paradigm are presented, the next step is based on the development of a conceptual model to support the design of the new generation factories - the Virtual Factory Framework.

4 Virtual Factory Framework

4.1 Framework Overview

In the virtual factory context, the manufacturing attributes are migrating to other forms which include concerns on how to solve highly complex tasks under increasing demand for adaptability, cost, efficiency, durability, reliability, scalability and security

[6]. Thus, the aim of designing the future factories is accomplished if the process planning in a virtual factory can be synchronized with the real factory through basic components that can be simulated by aligning the factory design and decision-making process during the factory life-cycle.

A virtual factory can build designs of manufactured components (geometric models) and their respective process plans to make it possible for any manufacturing process to be defined, modeled and implemented.

So, this work is being developed within the authors' contribution for the Project VFF - "Holistic, extensible, scalable and standard Virtual Factory Framework", a European collaborative project supported by the European Commission that includes about thirty partners from several European companies, universities and research centers. The project's goal is to define the next generation of Virtual Factory Framework, encouraging the European industry to improve its knowledge in terms of design, management, evaluation and reconfiguration of new or existing facilities. At the same time, it seeks to promote major time and costs savings, supporting the capability to simulate the dynamic complex behavior over the entire life-cycle factory interpreted as a complex long living product that synchronize the Virtual Factory with the Real Factory.

4.2 VFF Requirement Analysis for Factory Design

The first task to building up a framework that supports virtual factory relies on extensive requirements analysis of the real factory environment model. The present work have identified four main requirements blocks for the entire factory life-cycle characterization: Strategic Planning, Facility Planning, Process Planning and Factory Operation (Figure 5).

On each requirement's blocks there are subsets of requirements which deal with the main functionalities required in the design, management, evaluation and reconfiguration of new or existing facilities. As an example: the building requirements in the Facility Planning block comprises: *Economic requirements* (operation and maintenance costs; low energy costs, flexibility, operating supply materials, etc.); *Sustainability requirements* (emissions, reusability, reutilization, etc.); *Location requirements* (building plot, logistic connections, accessibilities, etc.); *Layout requirements* (optimal room geometry, utilities integration, modifiable structure configuration, etc.); *Technological requirements* (technological, changeability, capacity feasibility, ergonomics, etc.); *Protection requirements* (health and safety norms, supply protection, materials handling, etc.); *General requirements* (structural integration, optimal infrastructure, architecture, etc).

With this approach, it can be considered that the requirements blocks are iteratively adapted during the factory life-cycle in order to cope with the real changing environment. On each block construction, for each factory instantiation, there are constraints which are propagated to the next block of requirements. In fact, it intends to achieve a "continuous performance improvement" through a reference model fine-tuning for each cycle of iteration.

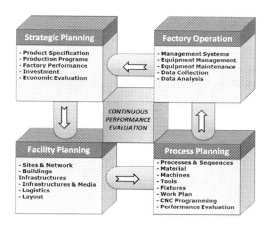

Fig. 5. VFF main requirements blocks

5 Conclusions and Further Work

This paper addresses the problem of factory planning during the entire factory life-cycle through a holistic, extensible, scalable and standardized virtual factory framework. It presents also some of the available methodologies for factory planning and how it can be integrated with the paradigm of product life-cycle.

The challenge of factory design derives from the interdependence between the factory planning, process planning and product development. Since this is a complex task with implications in a large number of functions and stakeholders, as well as time constraints, there is a need for a support framework. This need impelled a new area of research, with the involvement of academic and industry partners, aiming to develop a new generation virtual factory framework that will meet the challenges of integration, flexibility and sustainability of designing the next generation factories.

Finally, this paper addressed the requirements conceptual model within the Virtual Factory Framework project by presenting a set of requirements obtained in a short example.

The ongoing VFF project aims to provide the industrial managers with a more powerful toolset to support the decision making during the entire factory life-cycle. Any future work foreseen in this project involves development and implementation of the VFF framework with factories templates on several industrial scenarios.

References

1. VFF Consortium. Holistic, extensible, scalable and standard Virtual Factory Framework, FP7-NMP-2008-3.4-1 (2009)
2. Jovane, F., Westkamper, E., Williams, D.: The ManuFuture Road: Towards Competitive and Sustainable High-Adding-Value. Springer, Berlin (2009)
3. Schenk, M., Wirth, S., Muller, E.: Factory Planning Manual, 1 ed. Springer, Berlin (2010)

4. Mital, A., Desai, A., Subramanian, A., Mital, A.: Product Development: A Structured Approach to Consumer Product Development, Design and Manufacture. Elsevier, Amsterdam (2008)
5. Saaksvuori, A., Immonen, A.: Product Lifecycle Management. Springer, Berlin (2005)
6. Pedrazzoli, P., Bathelt, J., Chryssolouris, G., Rovere, D., Pappas, M., Boër, C.R., Constantinescu, C., Dépincé, P., Westkämper, E.: High Value Adding VR Tools for Networked Customer-Driven Factory. In: Proceedings of the Digital Enterprise Technology (2007)
7. Mertins, K., Rabe, M., Gocev, P.: Integration of Factory Planning and ERP/MES Systems: Adaptive Simulation Models. In: Lean Business Systems and Beyond. Springer, Boston (2008)
8. Wenbin, Z., Juanqi, Y., Dengzhe, M., Ye, J., Xiumin, F.: Production Engineering-Oriented Virtual Factory: A Planning Cell-Approach to Manufacturing Systems Design. International Journal of Advanced Manufacturing Technology (2006)

Part V
Agent-Based Simulation and Management of Complex Systems

An Agent Based Information System for Project Portfolio Management

José Alberto Arauzo, Adolfo Lopez Paredes, and Javier Pajares

INSISOC, University of Valladolid
{arauzo,adolfo,pajares}@insisoc.org

Abstract. With the increase in globalization, integration of world markets, and rise in the concept of transnational corporations, the importance of project management has increased many folds. An efficient project management helps new enterprises to achieve competitiveness, speed of response, and closeness to customer demands by improving their flexibility and agility, while maintaining their productivity and quality. But for project management to be successful in the new competitive and dynamic environment management, systems should incorporate new characteristics. In these circumstances, the current challenge is to develop information and control systems for project management that exhibit intelligence, robustness and adaptation to the environment changes and disturbances. The introduction of multi-agent systems paradigms addresses these requirements, bringing the advantages of distribution, autonomy, scalability and re-usability. This paper proposes a distributed information and control system for project portfolio management that integrates strategic issues, planning and control into a community of software agents.

Keywords: information systems, multi-agent systems, project portfolio, scheduling.

1 Introduction

Projects affect success rate of the organization and thus are vital for them. A project results in bringing something new. It can be a new product or service, increasing sales or capturing of new markets, reducing cost, or an innovative feature in the existing product. Project management helps organizations working in various places integrating their operations and achieving goals.

Project portfolio managers are involved in developing methodologies for valuing projects, selecting the best ones, balancing the portfolio in terms of risk, cost, etc, and coordinating the joint execution of individual projects, so that synergies can be achieved. The output of this process is a set of projects to be done, ranked in terms of strategic and financial importance to the firm.

Once the firm knows the "right projects to do", it is necessary to plan how "to do things right". Therefore, project schedules need to be developed, taking into account the availability of resources during each period.

Moreover, uncertainty overruns and dynamic changes make portfolio management more complex. Priority changes over time because of the addition of new interesting

Á. Ortiz Bas, R.D. Franco, P. Gómez Gasquet (Eds.): BASYS 2010, IFIP AICT 322, pp. 235–242, 2010.

projects, changes in corporate strategy or simply, because of feedback information about individual project overruns affecting their expected returns.

In this paper, we propose an auction approach for online dynamic scheduling in multi-project environments, where projects can be rejected as a result of the scheduling tatônnement process. We use a multi-agent system where both the resources and the projects are artificial agents which play in real time an auction to maximize the portfolio efficiency.

This agent-based approach has two distinctive aspects with respect to other works: the integration of strategic decisions (accepting or rejecting new projects) and operative aspects (resource allocation), and the ability to manage resource flexibility.

2 Multi-agent Systems for Project Planning and Control

Projects are characterized by complexity (they include many components and dependencies), uncertainty (about the availability of resources, task durations), dynamic behavior (changes in the scope of the project, adding or removing unexpected tasks, re-scheduling processes) and are inherently distributed (each task may be completed by different resources or in different geographical locations). In the case of a multi-project environment, each one of these features is severely intensified.

In the last decade, many ideas of Artificial Intelligence (AI) have been proposed to solve operation management problems [7]. Multi-agent systems are a distributed IA paradigm precisely designed to deal with problems of these characteristics. As Jennings and Wooldridge point out, multi-agent systems are suitable for problems having the following properties: *complexity, openness* (components of the system are not known in advance, can change over time, and are highly heterogeneous, dynamic in project management terms), with *dynamical and unknown environments changing over time* (uncertainty) and *ubiquity* (the activity is distributed over the complete structure) [5][11].

Depending on the physical or organizational structures, many problems can be abstracted and managed as distributed systems using the multi-agent paradigm as metaphor. This decentralized approach in project management has been used since the last decade [13], but it is in the last years when market based approaches [2] are receiving a growing interest. Recently, Lee, Kumara and Chatterjee [8][9] have proposed a multi-agent based dynamic resource scheduling for distributed multiple projects using market mechanisms. Following the same research line, Confessore et al [3] propose an iterative combinatorial auction mechanism as coordination mechanism to resolve the same problem.

Other examples of agent based approaches in project management field can be found in the work of Kim and colleagues [6], Wu and Kotak [12] or Cabac [1]. As underlined in the introduction, our work makes use of a market metaphor and an auction mechanism to help project managers to take portfolio decisions about resources and about portfolio composition.

3 Multi-project Environment Definition

We define a multi-project scheduling environment in which the information system must operate.

At any instant t there are I projects in the system, each one denoted by i. Each project is characterized by a value V_i, that can be interpreted as the revenue obtained for the project, a weight w_i representing the strategic importance given to the specific project, a desirable delivery date D_i, a limit delivery date D_i^* that cannot be exceeded, an arrival date of the project to the system, B_i, and a limit answer date R_i that represents the latest date to decide to reject the project.

The system is considered dynamic: while some projects are being developed other projects can be included or rejected in real time.

Each project i consists of J_i activities, each one denoted by ij where $i \in \{1, 2,..., I\}$ and $j \in \{1, 2,..., J_i\}$. Let d_{ij} the standard duration associated to activity ij and M the set of available resources. Each resource $m \in \{1, 2, 3...M\}$ can just be assigned simultaneously to one activity (figure 1).

A set H of K competences $H=\{h_1, h_2, ... h_K\}$ are necessary to complete the projects. Each resource is endowed with a given cost rate per unit of time, c_m, and a subset H_m of H of competences that can be performed. Each resource has a certain grade or ability to perform a competence. Therefore, the work capacity of resources can be symbolized by means of a vector of abilities per resource $e_m=(e_{m1}, e_{m2},...,e_{mk})$, where $e_{mf} \geq 0$ shows the ability degree of resource m to perform the competence h_f. If $e_{mf} = 0$ then the resource m has not got the competence h_f, if $0 < e_{mf} < 1$ the resource is able to perform inefficiently the competence h_f, if $e_{mf} = 1$ it has standard efficiency to perform the competence, and if $e_{mf} > 1$ it will do it efficiently.

Every activity j of project i is associated with a competence $h(i,j)$. Any activity ij with a given $h(i,j)$ can be performed by a resource m just if $e_{m,h(i,j)} \geq 1$. The duration of the activity ij depends on the resource assigned to perform it. We denote this duration as d_{ijm} (duration of activity j of project i in resource m). It is calculated according to $d_{ijm}=d_{ij}/e_{m,h(ij)}$, where d_{ij} is the standard duration of activity j of project I (activity duration when is performed by a resource that has standard efficiency).

We include explicitly the option of reassigning resources in real time when a new project arrives to the system or when a disruption happens. The activities can be assigned to any resource that has the specific competences to perform it.

The overall efficiency (E) of the system will be evaluated by the average benefit obtained in a certain time interval T according to [1]:

$$E = \frac{B_T}{T} = \frac{\sum_i (V_i - TC_i)}{T} \qquad (1)$$

where i are each one of the projects finished in T and TC_i is the total cost to complete the i project. This cost has two components, the resource direct cost and the delay cost (expression 2).

$$Cost_i = \sum_{j=1}^{J_i} c_{m(i,j)} \cdot d_{ijm} + w_i \cdot \phi \qquad (2)$$

$$where \quad \phi = \begin{cases} 0 & si \ F_i \leq D_i \\ w_i \cdot (F_i - D_i)^2 & si \ D_i < F_i \leq D_i^* \\ \infty & si \ F_i > D_i^* \end{cases}$$

The first addend corresponds to the resource direct cost to finish each activity j of project i. m(i,j) denotes the resource selected to comply with activity ij, and $c_{m(i,j)}$ the cost rate per unit of time of selected resource. The second addend is the delay cost associated to the project, where F_i is the real conclusion date of the project. This cost is zero if the project is concluded before the desirable delivery date D_i. If the project conclude between D_i and the limit delivery date D_i^{*}, the cost will be proportional to the square of the delay over D_i (F_i-D_i). If the project is concluded after D_i^{*} the cost will be consider infinite. The problem considers the decision to reject projects if the benefit of perform the project don't compensate the increment of total cost.

4   Multi-project Environment Definition

The system is mainly composed of two groups of agents: project and resource managers. A third type of agent is required in the system: The Monitoring-Auctioneer-Creator Agent (MAC). There is only one agent instance of this type which receives bids and asks from projects and resources and computes the exchange price to allocate resources to projects.

4.1   Project Manager Agents

Each project is represented by a Project Manager Agent (PMA) which is created and deleted in real time (new projects are evaluated to be accepted in the existing project portfolio, while the projects which finish are removed from the portfolio). Each one is characterized by its tasks, precedence relationships, due date, value, local programs and their execution state. The individual objective of each project agent is to look for 'contracts' with resources that can perform the required activities and hence completing successfully the project. In order to achieve their goal, project agents make a plan that takes into account only their own activities (local schedule).

4.2   Resource Manager Agents

The system includes as many Resource Manager Agents as resources are considered. They are defined by their competences or skills and efficiencies. Each resource agent is aiming at performing tasks from project agents. The use of a resource is controlled by means of a *Resource Manager Agent*. Its goal is to increase it's the level of occupation of the resources and the incomes. Project manager agents and resource manager agents make contracts to perform pending tasks of projects. The contracts will be based in the prices that emerge from an auction which is handled by the MAC Agent (Monitoring-Auctioneer-Creating Agent).

4.3   Monitoring-Auctioneer-Creating Agent (MAC)

The MAC agent plays three roles of centralized nature: (i) it creates manager Project Manager Agents when new projects are added to the system, (ii) it monitors the resource activities, and (iii) it plays as an auctioneer in a market procedure. This agent compiles real time data of resource states (i.e. availability, allocated activities, and current operations in resources) and shows a summary of this information. Moreover, as an auctioneer, it bids available time intervals of resources to projects, initiating an auction procedure that allocates activities to time intervals of resources.

4.4 Auction Interactions

In our distributed multi-project system, the decision-making system is decentralized; it is distributed among every agent. Thus, each project creates its own schedule (local schedule) based on its own goal and information. In principle, this procedure entails some weaknesses, e.g. it can bring incompatible local schedules (several projects use simultaneously the same resource) and the local schedules can be globally inefficient, profitable projects may be rejected; most important projects may be delayed, etc. Accordingly, if we aim to design a functional decentralized scheduling process we need to resolve these difficulties. To do that, we propose a market mechanism (it was initially proposed by Davis R and Smith RG [4]) that ensures that local schedules are nearly compatible and globally efficient according to the expression (1). This market based multi-project scheduling approach is founded on Lagrangian Relaxation [10], [14], a decomposition technique for mathematical programming problems.

In order to apply the market metaphor, the periods of time when resources are available are subdivided in a set small time intervals or time slots. Each time slot of every resource is modelled as a 'good' that can be sold in an auction where the auctioneer acts as a seller. Thus, a local schedule is a bundle of time slots that has been allocated to a project.

The auctioneer (MAC Agent) proposes a price for each time slot from the current time to the end of the scheduling horizon. The scheduling horizon changes dynamically by coinciding with the latest time slot that some project has asked at any moment.

Project agents play the role of 'bidders' in the auction mechanism. They bid for the required set of time slots needed to complete their pending tasks at the current time. Project agents try to find a set of time slots (Z_i) through the resource pool while incurring the minimum possible local cost (LC_i). This cost has two components (expression 3), the sum of the price of the selected time slots and the delay cost.

$$LC_i = \sum_{mt \in Z_i} p_{mt} + w_i \cdot (D_i - F_i)^2 \tag{3}$$

where p_{mt} is the price of the time slot (t) of the resource (m).

If a project agent do not find a set of time slots that allows to schedule all the pending tasks before D_i^* with a cost smaller than the project value (V_i), it will not ask for any set of time slots. This indicates that the project is unprofitable at the correspondent round of bidding and must be rejected.

Depending on the demand of bids, each resource agent modifies the price of its time slots to maximize its revenue, reducing at the same resource conflicts. In order to get this goal a subgradient optimization algorithm is used to adjust prices at each round of bidding. By means of this algorithm resource agents increase the price of the time slots where there is conflict (i.e. more than a project have asked for this time slot) and reduce the price of those time slots that have not been demanded. The process of price adjustment and bid calculation continues indefinitely decreasing the number of resource conflicts at each round.

4.5 Contract Interactions

The auction mechanism described above allows project agents to build compatible and globally efficient local schedules for their pending activities. Agents also interact through a complementary process to make firm agreements based on their local schedules. These agreements determine fixed programs for earliest scheduled tasks. When an agreement is closed, project agents remove the task involved in the agreement from the pending task queue.

5 Working Example

To show the system performance we present a little example. We consider three different resources (R1, R2 and R3), endowed with the competences C1, C2 and C3 respectively. In table 1, we show a portfolio of five projects, and the tasks needed to complete the project.

Table 1. Example

Projects	Task 1	Task 2	Task 3	Arrival date	Starting Date	DD1	DD2	Value
A	C1 35	C3 40	C1 25	0	0	120	180	30000
B	C3 50	C1 25	C2 30	0	0	120	180	10000
C	C2 30	C3 50	C1 10	50	90	150	270	15000
D	C2 40	C3 45	C2 10	0	0	180	240	12000
E	C3 45	C2 20	C3 50	50	90	150	270	30000

Each task is defined by means of the pertaining competence and expected standard time to be completed. The arrival date is the date when the project is included in the system. Projects can start in the starting date; otherwise, they should have been rejected before this date. Due Date 1 (DD1) is the most desirable duration whereas Due Date 2 (DD2) is the maximum allowed. All the projects have a weight of 1.

Figures 1 shows the system state at a given time (current time). In the upper area of the figures the relative duality gap evolution is presented. The prices of time slots are the solution of the dual problem and the duality gap is a measure of the difference between the primal and dual objective function, and hence it quantifies the quality of the solution [10]. The relative duality gap is calculated as the duality gap divided by the dual solution. A small relative duality gap means that the prices are representative of the system state, thus, a good solution is achieved. In the lower part of the picture, charts of resources are presented.

In figure 1, we show the evolution of the tasks performed by each resource and the prices of the time slots after finishing the simulation. This picture is from the monitoring provide by the MAC Agent. We can see how the duality gap increases when the projects C and E arrive to the system. At this moment previous prices did not reflect the new system state (there are new projects in the system). After some time, the prices change to adapt themselves to the new system conditions, and the gap decreases again. The system not only gives us the dynamic schedule and the rejected projects, but the value of each resource as well.

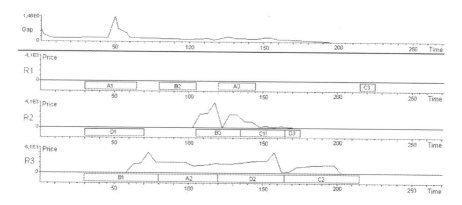

Fig. 1. Tasks performed by resources. Tij denotes Task j of project Pi

6 Conclusions

Project portfolio management is a management process designed to help an organization to acquire and view information about all of its projects, then sort and prioritize each project according to certain criteria. Currently, in the global market, these activities have high influence in the enterprise competitiveness and.

We propose a multi-agent system and an auction mechanism for online dynamic project selection, scheduling and control in multi-project environments. Projects have tasks to be completed, so they compete for the resources endowed with the capabilities required to do some pieces of work. The prices of resources emerge endogenously by means of an auction process.

We show some of the possibilities of our multi-agent approach to deal with some of the decisions that a manager needs to take within multi-project environments. The system allocates in real time resources to projects, and decides about project acceptance or rejection taking into account project value, profitability and (feedback) operational information. We also show how it is possible to discover which resources are the most valuable, so they should be preserved or added to the firm.

References

1. Cabac, L.: Multi-agent system: A guiding metaphor for the organization of software development projects. In: Petta, P., Müller, J.P., Klusch, M., Georgeff, M. (eds.) MATES 2007. LNCS (LNAI), vol. 4687, pp. 1–12. Springer, Heidelberg (2007)
2. Clearwater, S.: Market-Based Control: A Paradigm for Distributed Resource Allocation. World Scientific Publishing Company, Singapore (1996)
3. Confessore, G., Giordani, S., Rismondo, S.: A market-based multi-agent system model for decentralized multi-project scheduling. Annals of Operations Research 150, 115–135 (2007)
4. Davis, R., Smith, R.G.: Negotiation as a Metaphor for Distributed Problem Solving. Artificial Intelligence 20, 63–109 (1983)

5. Jennings, N.R., Wooldridge, M.J.: Applying agent technology. Applied Artificial Intelligence 9, 357–369 (1995)
6. Kim, K., Paulson, J., Levitt, R.E., Fischer, M.A., Petrie, J.: Distributed coordination of project schedule changes using agent-based compensatory negotiation methodology. In: Artificial Intelligence for Engineering Design, Analysis and Manufacturing: AIEDAM, vol. 17, pp. 115–131 (2003)
7. Kobbacy, K.A.H., Vadera, S., Rasmy, M.H.: AI and OR in management of operations: history and trends. Journal of the Operational Research Society 58, 10–28 (2006)
8. Kumara, S.R.T., Lee, Y.H., Chatterjee, K.: Distributed multiproject resource control: A market-based approach. CIRP Annals - Manufacturing Technology 51, 367–370 (2002)
9. Lee, Y.H., Kumara, S.R.T., Chatterjee, K.: Multiagent based dynamic resource scheduling for distributed multiple projects using a market mechanism. Journal of Intelligent Manufacturing 14, 471–484 (2003)
10. Luh, P.B., Hoitomt, D.J.: Scheduling of Manufacturing Systems Using the Lagrangian Relaxation Technique. IEEE Transactions on Automatic Control 38(7), 1066–1079 (1991)
11. Wooldridge, M.J.: An Introduction to Multiagent Systems. John Wiley & Sons Ltd., New York (2002)
12. Wu, S., Kotak, D.: Agent-based collaborative project management system for distributed manufacturing. In: Proceedings of the IEEE International Conference on Systems, Man and Cybernetics, pp. 1223–1228 (2003)
13. Yan, Y., Kuphal, T., Bode, J.: Application of Multi-Agent Systems in Project Management. In: Working Notes of the Agent-Based Manufacturing Workshop 1998, pp. 160–170 (1998)
14. Zhao, X., Luh, P.B., Wang, J.: Surrogate Gradient Algorithm for Lagrangian Relaxation. Journal of Optimization Theory and Applications 100(3), 699–712 (1999)

An Agent Based Model of the Nash Demand Game in Regular Lattices

David Poza[1], José Manuel Galán[2], José Ignacio Santos[2], and Adolfo López-Paredes[1]

[1] Grupo INSISOC, Dpto. de Organización de Empresasy CIM, Escuela de Ingenierías Industriales, Universidad de Valladolid, Pso del Cauce S/N, 47011 Valladolid
[2] Grupo INSISOC, Área de Organización de Empresas, Dpto. de Ingeniería Civil, Escuela Politécnica Superior, Universidad de Burgos, Edificio La Milanera, C/ Villadiego S/N, 09001 Burgos
djpoza@gmail.com, {jmgalan,jisantos}@ubu.es, adolfo@insisoc.org

Abstract. In this work we propose an agent based model where a fixed finite population of tagged agents play iteratively the Nash demand game in a regular lattice. This work extends the multiagent bargaining model by [1] including the spatial dimension in the game. Each agent is endowed with memory and plays the best reply against the opponent's most frequent demand. The results show that all the possible persistent regimes of the global interaction game can also be obtained with this spatial version. Our preliminary analysis also suggests that the topological distribution of the agents can generate new persistent regimes within groups of agents with the same tag.

Keywords: Agent-based modeling, Nash demand game, game theory, negotiation, segregation, tags, social norms.

1 Introduction

The gist of agent-based modeling consists in the individual abstraction of the entities that participate in a given target system as computational entities – agents – in a model [2], [3]. It also facilitates to establish a direct correspondence between the interactions observed as agent's interactions, and hence to analyze the emerging behavior.

In the last twenty years, this technique has become popular in almost every scientific domain, such as natural resources management [4], biology [5], project management [6], etc. Nonetheless, it has been particularly useful in economic and social systems as a formalization tool.

The role that norms play as regulator mechanisms of certain aspects of social, economic and organizational behaviors has been thoroughly studied in social sciences [7], and even by means of agent-based modeling [8]. Once a norm has been established, it acts as a self-reinforcement mechanism of behavior. However, the emergence of norms is, in general, exempt from explicit mechanisms of control. This is a key factor to understand the informal behavior of the organizations.

In this work, we analyze the emergence of norms using the agent-based model proposed by [1], AEY's model from now on, which is an extension of the well known

Á. Ortiz Bas, R.D. Franco, P. Gómez Gasquet (Eds.): BASYS 2010, IFIP AICT 322, pp. 243–250, 2010.

Nash demand game. By studying the transient and the asymptotic dynamics of this model, Axtell et al proved that self-reinforced norms can emerge spontaneously. These emergent norms may be completely different from one another even though all the agents of the population have the same behavior rule. Moreover, when agents are endowed with a tag (which initially has no meaning) and remember the past behaviors of their opponents and their tags, it is possible to demonstrate that segregation, in terms of different behavior within and outside a group, can emerge endogenously.

We have generalized the original model by adding a new behavior rule that requires less cognitive abilities than those required in the original paper. Furthermore, when agents used this new behavior rule, the segregation emerged even more frequently. In our analysis, we have also incorporated the influence of the topology on the results of the game. To this aim, we have considered the spatial dimension of the game by introducing a regular spatial structure.

This work is organized as follows: first, we will briefly explain the extensions and modifications that we have performed to generalize the AEY original model. Next, we will describe the results that we have obtained when agents are randomly distributed. Afterwards, we will discuss some cases where several persistent regimes can simultaneously emerge and the possible relation with mesoscopic topological effects. We will finish with conclusions and extensions of this work.

2 AEY's Model in Regular Spatial Structures

In AEY's model there is a population of n agents that repetitively play a bargaining game. The interaction process in the model consists in the following: two agents – randomly selected from the population of agents – demand some portion of a pie (which is a metaphor of something that is going to be shared between two persons). The portion of the pie that each agent gets depends on the corresponding portion demanded by her opponent: they get what they demand as long as the sum of both demands is not higher than the whole of the pie; otherwise both get nothing.

In order to simplify the analysis we will assume that agents have only three possible demands: low (30%), medium (50%) and high (70%). Table 1 shows one agent's reward depending on her opponent's demand –[9] study the influence of payoffs in the game–.

Table 1. Payoff matrix

	H	M	L
H	0,0	0,0	70,30
M	0,0	50,50	50,30
L	30,70	30,50	30,30

Agents have a memory in which they keep the latest m decisions taken by their opponents in previous games (where m is the memory length). Agents check their memory and take their decision depending on the strategies followed by their opponents in the previous matches. When the game starts, the agents' memories are initialized with m random values between the three options they can demand (low, medium or high).

There is a small probability of a player not following the rational decision rule and playing a random strategy instead, called the mutation probability ε. In the most sophisticated version of the model, each agent can be identified as a member of one of the two possible groups by means of a tag: agents store in their memory their opponents' demands conditioned by the corresponding group.

In our simulation model, agents take decisions by using two different decision rules: either maximizing the expected utility in function of the memory vector, or demanding the best reply against the opponent's most frequent demand.

In the original model by AEY, players randomly paired at each tick could play with any other in the population. However, in our spatial version of the model where agents are placed on a 10x10 toroidal reticule, each one interacts with one of her eight spatial neighbours located in a radius-1 Moore neighbourhood.

A simulation run stops when the system reaches a persistent regimen. As there are no absorbent states for ε>0, we consider that a persistent regimen has been reached either when all the agents have at least (1- ε)·m instances of 'medium' behaviour in their memories (an equitable norm) or when there are, at most, ε·m instances of 'medium' behaviour in their memories (a non-equitable norm). When tags are considered in the game, the stop criterion is applied to both agents' memories corresponding to same and different tagged opponents.

3   Equilibrium in a Random Scenario

We have studied the model in different scenarios. In the first one, tagged agents are randomly distributed in the grid (see Figure 1).

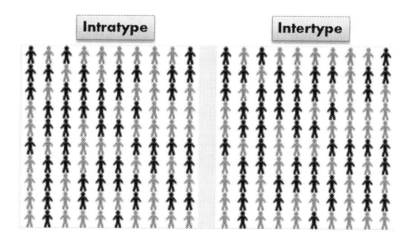

Fig. 1. A sample of random distribution of agents in the grid. In order to show clearly the players' strategies for both kind s of contacts, two symmetric grids are used to represent interactions between agents with the same tag (the left one) and with different tag (the right one), called "intratype" and "intertype" interactions respectively.

The system is an ergodic time-homogeneous Markov chain [10]. Although there is a strictly positive probability of finding the system in each of its states in the long run, some states are more persistent than others -the probability of staying in them is higher-. The best way of representing the state space is a simplex of the agents' memory states. Because the memory of an agent is made by two partitions, corresponding to the past demands of the two classes of opponents, we use two simplexes to represent both ones.

The pure strategy equilibrium MM of the Nash demand game, or equity norm, is a stochastically stable equilibrium for mutation rates small enough -once it is reached, it is very unlikely the system leaves it-. However, other regions of inequality strategies can be considered as pseudo-stable because the transition time to go from them to the equity norm is enormously long, and it grows exponentially with the number of agents and the memory length m, so the system can permanence in them over a long time.

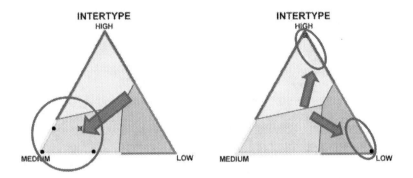

Fig. 2. Most probable states (persistent regimens) in the intertype game

Figure 2 depicts two important states of the memory of agents playing against opponents of different tag -intertype game- On the left simplex, everyone plays the strategy one-half, whereas on the right one every agent of one group (circles in the example) demands high against agents of the other group (squares), who consequently demand low.

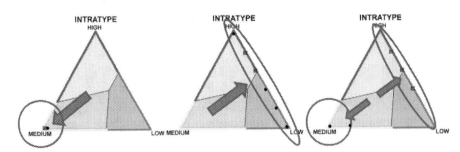

Fig. 3. Most probable states in the intratype game

Figure 3 shows the three possible final states of the intratype interactions. In the first one (left), equity emerges within two groups (circles and squares). The second one (middle) represents a fractious state where both groups have members demanding simultaneously low and high. And finally, the third state (right) depicts a segregated situation in which equity emerges within one group (circles) whereas the other group (squares) plays inequality strategies.

4 Other Persistent Regimes

The results commented in the previous section confirm that the same six combinations of intertype and intratype persistent regimes pertaining to the global interaction game can also be obtained in the regular lattice game. Notwithstanding, when we run random intensive simulations in the spatial game we find that there is someone that needs a much higher time to converge to one of the mentioned regimens than the average time. This fact could suggest the appearance of some other basins of attraction beyond the mentioned combinations of states. This might imply that there are more situations where the transient dynamics of the system differs from the long run behavior of the system. A deeper insight into the tag spatial distribution puts forward two different types of situations (see Figure 4).

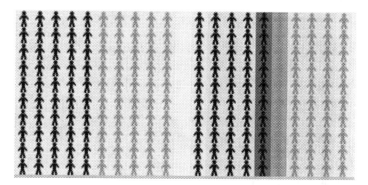

Fig. 4. The intertype plot (right) shows two different persistent regimens: one LH at the center and another MM at the right and left borders. Notice that the lattice is a torus.

A first case occurs when the particular distribution of tagged agents in the grid results in isolated areas of players with the same tag, without any contact between them. The behavior of disconnected frontiers of agents of the same type can produce different persistent regimens in each frontier. An extreme case of this effect is represented in Figure 4.

However, the other kind of situations is much more interesting. Now, the system state is characterized by non-disconnected clusters of agents -with the same tag- playing simultaneously different types of intertype coordination. The key difference with the previous case is the existence of an interconnection between the clusters.

The analyzed cases suggest that this last regime only appears when there is a strong community structure in the underlying network topology of the players, and that each regime corresponds to a different community. Our hypothesis is that the regimes obtained in the regular lattice version of the game are influenced by a mesoscale dimension between the individual and the complete population. In order to verify this intuition we have studied the community structure of an idealized case when this phenomenon frequently appears (see Figure 5).

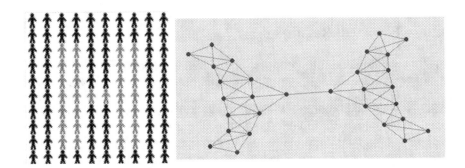

Fig. 5. We have analyzed the effects that appear in the stylized configuration showed on the left of the figure. On the right we represent the underlying interaction structure for the intratype game of grey-tagged players.

In order to find out the community structure of the network, we have used the Girvan-Newman algorithm [11] based on the iterative removal of the nodes with more betweenness. Our results depicted in Figure 6 show that, as predicted, the different regimes correspond to the partition of the network in communities detected by the algorithm.

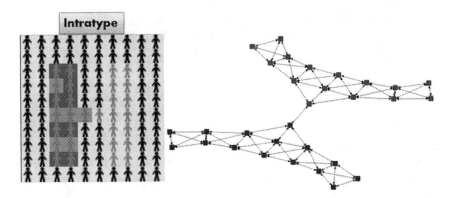

Fig. 6. On the left of the picture we can observe two different simultaneous persistent regimes in a connected population of agents with the same tag (h-shaped area). The different regimes correspond exactly to the different communities obtained in the underlying network of neighbors.

5 Conclusions

In this work we have analyzed the Nash demand game played by a finite population of tagged agents situated in a regular lattice and playing as decision rule the best reply against the opponent's most frequent demand. Our results confirm that all the different regimes obtained in the global interaction model, including discriminatory norms, can emerge. Furthermore, computational simulations show that different persistent regimes can appear simultaneously within a group of agents with the same tag depending on the topology –especially the mesoscopic characteristics of the network-. Some results correspond to the trivial case, when there are disconnected clusters of players with the same tag, but also to other non-evident distributions of tagged agents in the grid. A preliminary study suggests that the community structure of the network of players with the same tag could be a strong predictor of these special regimes of the spatial version of the Nash demand game.

Acknowledgments

The authors have benefited from the financial support of the Spanish Ministry of Science and Technology (project TIN2008-06464-C03-02), of the Junta de Castilla y León (project BU034A08) and Caja Burgos (project 2009/00148/001 and project 2009/00199/001).

References

1. Axtell, R.L., Epstein, J.M., Young, H.P.: The Emergence of Classes in a Multi-Agent Bargaining Model. In: Durlauf, S.N., Young, H.P. (eds.) Social Dynamics. MIT Press, Washington (2004)
2. Galán, J.M., Izquierdo, L.R., Izquierdo, S.S., et al.: Errors and artefacts in agent-based modelling. Journal of Artificial Societies and Social Simulation 12, 1 (2009)
3. Izquierdo, L.R., Galán, J.M., Santos, J.I., del Olmo, R.: Modelado de sistemas complejos mediante simulación basada en agentes y mediante dinámica de sistemas. EMPIRIA Revista de Metodología de Ciencias Sociales 16, 85–112 (2008)
4. López-Paredes, A., Hernández, C.: Agent-based modelling in Natural Resource Management. Insisoc, Madrid (2008)
5. Walker, D.C., Hill, G., Smallwood, R.H., Southgate, J.: Agent-based computational modelling of wounded epithelial cell monolayers. IEEE Transactions on Nanobioscience 3, 153–163 (2004)
6. Araúzo-Araúzo, J.A., Galán-Ordax, J.M., Pajares-Gutiérrez, J., López-Paredes, A.: Gestión eficiente de carteras de proyectos. Propuesta de un sistema inteligente de soporte a la decisión para oficinas técnicas y empresas consultoras. DYNA Ingeniería e Industria 84, 761–772 (2009)
7. Coleman, J.S.: Foundations of social theory. Belknap Press of Harvard University Press, Cambridge (1994)
8. Galan, J.M., Izquierdo, L.R.: Appearances Can Be Deceiving: Lessons Learned Re-Implementing Axelrod's 'Evolutionary Approach to Norms'. Journal of Artificial Societies and Social Simulation 8, 2 (2005)

9. Poza, D., Villafáñez, F.A., Pajares, J.: Impact of Tag Recognition in Economic Decisions. In: Hernandez, C., Posada, M., López-Paredes, A. (eds.) Artificial Economics. The Generative Method in Economics. Springer, Heidelberg (2009)

10. Izquierdo, L.R., Izquierdo, S.S., Galán, J.M., Santos, J.I.: Techniques to understand computer simulations: Markov chain analysis. Journal of Artificial Societies and Social Simulation 12, 6 (2009)

11. Girvan, M., Newman, M.E.J.: Community structure in social and biological networks. Proceedings of the National Academy of Sciences of the United States of America 99, 7821–7826 (2002)

Cloud Computing Integrated into Service-Oriented Multi-Agent Architecture

Sara Rodríguez, Dante I. Tapia, Eladio Sanz, Carolina Zato, Fernando de la Prieta, and Oscar Gil

Departamento de Informática y Automática, Universidad de Salamanca
Plaza de la Merced, s/n, 37008, Salamanca, Spain
{srg,dantetapia,esanz,carol_zato,fer,oscar.gil}@usal.es

Abstract. The main objective of Cloud Computing is to provide software, services and computing infrastructures carried out independently by the network. This concept is based on the development of dynamic, distributed and scalable software. In this way there are Service-Oriented Architectures (SOA) and agent frameworks which provide tools for developing distributed systems and multi-agent systems that can be used for the establishment of cloud computing environments. This paper presents CISM@ (Cloud computing Integrated into Service-Oriented Multi-Agent) architecture set on top of the platforms and frameworks by adding new layers for integrating a SOA and Cloud Computing approach and facilitating the distribution and management of functionalities.

Keywords: Cloud Computing, Multi-Agent Architecture, SOA.

1 Introduction

The main objective of Cloud Computing is for the network to independently provide software, services and computing infrastructure. This concept is based on the development of dynamic, distributed and scalable software. These types of software usually require the creation of increasingly complex and flexible applications, so there is a trend toward reusing resources and sharing compatible platforms or architectures. In some cases, applications require similar functionalities already implemented into other systems, which are not always compatible.

For this reason, it is necessary to develop new functional architectures capable of providing adaptable and compatible frameworks and allowing access to services and applications regardless of time and location restrictions. There are Service-Oriented Architectures (SOA) and agent frameworks [16], [17], [18], which provide tools for developing distributed systems and multi-agent systems [8], [11], [2] that can be used for the establishment of cloud computing environments. However, these tools do not solve the development requirements of these systems by themselves. Therefore, it is necessary to develop innovative solutions that integrate different approaches in order to create flexible and adaptable systems, especially for achieving higher levels of interaction with people in a ubiquitous and intelligent way.

One of the most prevalent alternatives in distributed architectures is agent and multi-agent systems which can help to distribute resources and reduce the central unit

Á. Ortiz Bas, R.D. Franco, P. Gómez Gasquet (Eds.): BASYS 2010, IFIP AICT 322, pp. 251–259, 2010.

tasks [1]. CISM@ (Cloud Computing Integrated on Service-oriented Multi-Agent) architecture is set on top of the platforms and frameworks by adding new layers for integrating a SOA and Cloud Computing approach and facilitating the distribution and management of functionalities. A distributed agent-based architecture provides more flexible ways to move functions to where actions are needed. Additionally, the programming effort is reduced because it is only necessary to specify global objectives so that agents cooperate in solving problems and reaching specific goals, thus giving the systems the ability to generate knowledge and experience. Unfortunately, the difficulty in developing a multi-agent architecture lies in the need of having more complex analysis and design stages, which implies more time to reach the implementation. Moreover, the system control is reduced because the agents need more autonomy to solve complex problems.

The main purpose of this research is to design and implement an architecture that is applicable to the development of intelligent highly dynamic environments. The architecture proposes several features capable of being executed in dynamic and distributed environments to provide interoperability in a standard framework. These features can be implemented in devices with limited storage and processing capabilities. CISM@ integrates intelligent agents with a service-oriented philosophy.

In the next section, the problem that has motivated the development of the CISM@ architecture, combining concepts of Cloud Computing, SOA and Multi-Agent, systems will be explained. The specific characteristics and the agent-based architecture will be described in section 3. Finally, section 4 will present the results and the conclusions obtained.

2 Problem Description

Distributed architectures are aimed at achieving interoperability between different systems, distribution of resources, and the lack of dependency of programming languages [4]. Functionalities are linked by means of standard communication protocols that must be used by applications in order to share resources in the network [1]. The compatibility and management of messages between functionalities is an important and complex element in any of these approaches.

Agent and multi-agent systems (MAS) combine classical and modern functional architecture aspects. We have that an agent is anything with the ability to perceive its environment through sensors and respond in the same environment through actuators, assuming that each agent may perceive its own actions and learn from the experience [10]. MAS is defined as any system composed of multiple autonomous agents with incomplete capabilities to solve a global problem, where there is no global control system, the data is decentralized and the computing is asynchronous) [15].

Multi-agent architectures and frameworks such as Open Agent Architecture (OAA) [8], RETSINA [11] and JADE [2] define agent-based structures to resolve distributed computational problems and facilitate user interactions. Nevertheless, integration is not always achieved because of two reasons. The first is the incompatibility between the agent platforms. To resolve this, two alternatives are possible. One of them is centered on the communication between the different models of the platform [3] and the other is focused on the integration of distributed services in the agent infrastructure [9]. The second reason is that Cloud-based architectures usually do not provide intelligent computational and interactive mechanisms. CISM@ combines both paradigms, trying to take advantage of their strengths and avoid their weaknesses.

Although these developments provide an adequate background for developing distributed MAS with a cloud computing approach based on Web Services, most of them are in early stages of development, so it is not actually possible to know their potential in real scenarios. In addition, CISM@ not only provides communication and integration between distributed agents, services and applications; it also proposes a new method for facilitating the development of distributed MAS by means of modeling the functionalities of the agents and the systems as services and applications based on cloud computing.

Cloud Computing is an innovative concept, which is based on the compendium of a group of technologies. These proportionate a computational paradigm to offer services in three different levels: IaaS, PaaS y SaaS [5], [13], [7].

The IaaS (Infrastructure as a Service) level is oriented to provide hardware and/or software equipment (operating system, process capacity, storage, etc.) as a technology environment in different developments. The capacity to vary under demand is also included in the characteristics of the services [12], [14]. The PaaS (Platform as a Service) level offers integration but with higher abstraction, allowing the construction of customized services by different services [6]. The SaaS (Software as a Service) level offers software with a specific purpose that is totally functional and available through the Internet.

Although the concept of providing services at three different levels is clearly accepted, the needed standards and interfaces are currently still not defined and therefore, the interoperability between different Cloud Computing platforms is an open problem today [10]. CISM@ aims to solve these problems, by specifying a well-defined architecture that integrates the main frameworks of intelligent agents in order to provide Cloud Computing services, both at software (SaaS) and platform (PaaS) level.

CISMA@ allows the development of MAS with increased scalability and reutilization of resources. In addition, CISMA@ allows the extraction and modeling of the agents functionalities as independent services and applications, giving as a result, lighter agents in terms of computational processing. A distributed approach provides the architecture with a greater capacity for recovery from errors, and thus, a greater flexibility to adjust its behavior in execution time.

3   CISM@ Architecture

CISM@ is a novel architecture which integrates a cloud computing approach with SOA and intelligent agents for building systems that need be dynamic, flexible, robust, adaptable to changes in context, scalable and easy to use and maintain. The architecture proposes a new and easier method to develop distributed intelligent systems, where cloud services can communicate in a distributed way with intelligent agents, even from mobile devices, independent of time and location restrictions. The architecture focuses on distributing the majority of the systems' functionalities into remote and local services and applications. The functionalities of the systems are not integrated into the structure of the agents; rather they are modeled as distributed services and applications that are invoked by the agents acting as controllers and coordinators. Because the architecture acts as an interpreter, the users can run applications and services programmed in virtually any language, but have to follow a communication protocol that every cloud service must incorporate. Another important functionality is that, thanks to the agents' capabilities, the systems developed can make use of reasoning mechanisms or learning techniques to handle cloud services according to context characteristics, which can change dynamically over time. Agents and cloud services can communicate in a distributed way, even from mobile devices. This makes it possible to use resources no matter its location. It also allows the starting or stopping of agents, services or devices separately, without affecting the rest of resources, so the system has an elevated adaptability and capacity for error recovery.

CISM@ is based on agents because of their characteristics, such as autonomy, reasoning, reactivity, social abilities, pro-activity, mobility, organization, etc., which allow them to cover several needs for highly dynamic environments, especially ubiquitous communication and computing and adaptable interfaces. CISM@ combines a cloud computing approach built on top of Web Services and intelligent agents to obtain an innovative architecture, facilitating ubiquitous computation and communication and high levels of human-system-environment interaction. It also provides an advanced flexibility and customization to easily add, modify or remove services on demand, independently of the programming language. The goal in CISM@ is not only to distribute services, but also to promote a new way of developing highly dynamic systems focusing on ubiquity and simplicity. CISM@ provides a flexible distribution of resources and facilitates the inclusion of new functionalities in highly dynamic environments based on Cloud Computing concept. It also provides the systems with a higher ability to recover from errors and a better flexibility to change their behavior at execution time.

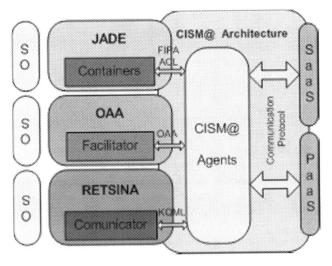

Fig. 1. CISM@ Architecture over Different Agent Platforms

CISM@ sets on top of existing agent frameworks by adding new layers to integrate a cloud computing approach and facilitate the provision and management of services at two different levels, Software as a Service (SaaS) and Platform as a Service (PaaS) [5]. Therefore, the CISM@ framework has been modeled following the Cloud Computing model based on SOA, but adding the applications block which represents the interaction with users. These blocks provide all the functionalities of the architecture. CISM@ adds new features to common agent frameworks, such as OAA, RETSINA and JADE and improves the services provided by these previous architectures. These previous architectures have limited communication abilities.

As can be seen in Figure 1, CISM@ defines four basic blocks:

1. *PaaS (Platform as a Service).* This involves all the custom applications that can be used to exploit the system functionalities. Applications are dynamic and adaptable to context, reacting differently according to the particular situation. They can be executed locally or remotely, even on mobile devices with limited processing capabilities, because computing tasks are largely delegated to the agents and services.
2. *Agent Platform.* This is the core of CISM@, integrating a set of agents, each one with special characteristics and behavior. The agents act as controllers and administrators for all cloud services, managing the adequate functioning of the system. In CISM@, services are managed and coordinated by deliberative BDI agents with distributed computation and coordination abilities.
3. *SaaS (Software as a Service).* These represent the activities that the architecture offers. Services are designed to be invoked locally or remotely and they can be organized as local services, Web Services, Cloud services, or even as individual stand-alone services. Services can make use of other services to provide the functionalities that users require. CISM@ has a flexible and scalable directory of services, so they can be invoked, modified, added, or eliminated dynamically and on demand.
4. *Communication Protocol.* This allows applications and services to communicate directly with the agent platform. The protocol is completely open and independent of any programming language, facilitating ubiquitous communication capabilities. This protocol is based on SOAP specification to capture all messages between the platform and the services and applications [4]. All external communications follow the same protocol, while the communication amongst agents in the platform follows the FIPA Agent Communication Language (ACL) specification.

One of the advantages of CISMA@ is that the users can access the system through distributed applications, which run on different types of devices and interfaces (e.g. computers, cell phones, PDAs). All requests and responses are handled by the agents in the platform. The agents analyze all requests and invoke the specified services either locally or remotely. Services process the requests and execute the specified tasks. Then, the services send back a response with the result of the specific task.

A simple case can better demonstrate the basic functioning of CISM@ when it is requesting a service. A user needs to calculate the sum of two numbers and wants to do it through a mobile device (e.g. PDA) remotely connected to the system. The user executes a mathematical toolkit, which provides him with a large set of formulas from which he selects the sum function, introduces a set of values, and clicks a button to get the result. When the user clicks the button, the application sends a request to the platform to find a service that can process that request. The agents invoke the appropriate service and send the request. The service processes the request and sends the result back to the agents, which in turn, send it to the application. It is obvious that invoking a remote service to execute a sum is not the best choice. But imagine a large-scale process that uses complex AI (Artificial Intelligence) techniques, such as genetic algorithms, data mining, neural networks, etc. where the limited processing capacity of the mobile device makes it impossible to calculate. In this case, the service may be in a powerful computer and could be remotely invoked by the mobile device.

The Web Services Architecture model uses an external directory, known as UDDI (Universal Description, Discovery and Integration), to list all available services. Each service must send a WSDL (Web Services Description Language) file to the UDDI to be added to the directory. Applications consult the UDDI to find a specific service. Once the service is located, the application can start communication directly with the selected service. However, CISM@ does not include a service discovery mechanism, so applications must use only the services listed in the platform. In addition, all communication is handled by the platform, so there is no way to interact directly between applications and services. Moreover, the platform makes use of deliberative agents to select the optimal option to perform a task, so users do not need to find and specify the service to be invoked by the application. These features have been introduced in CISM@ to create a secure communication between applications and services. They also facilitate the inclusion of new services regarding their location and application that users can make use of.

CISM@ is a modular multi-agent architecture, where services and applications are managed and controlled by deliberative BDI agents. There are different kinds of agents in the architecture, each one with specific roles, capabilities and characteristics. This fact facilitates the flexibility of the architecture when incorporating new agents. However, there are pre-defined agents, which provide the basic functionalities of the architecture.

The CISM@ pre-defined agents are described next:

1. *PaaS Agent.* This agent is responsible for all communications between applications and the agent platform. It manages the incoming requests from the applications to be processed by services. It also manages responses from services (via the platform) to applications. All messages are sent to Security Agent for their structure and syntax to be analyzed.

2. *SaaS Agent.* This agent is responsible for all communications between services and the agent platform. The functionalities are similar to PaaS Agent but backwards. All messages are sent to Security Agent for their structure and syntax to be analyzed. This agent also periodically checks the status of all services to know if they are idle, busy, or crashed.

3. *ServiceDir Agent.* This agent manages the list of services that can be used by the system. For security reasons, the list of services is static and can only be modified manually; however, services can be added, erased or modified dynamically. There is dynamic information that is constantly being modified: the service performance (average time to respond to requests), the number of executions, and the quality of the service (QoS). This last data assigns a value between 0 and 1 to all services. All new services have a quality of service value set to 1. This value decreases when the service fails (e.g. service crashes, no service found, etc.) or has a subpar performance compared to similar past executions. Security must be a major concern when developing this kind of systems. For this reason CISM@ does not implement a service discovery mechanism. However, agents can select the most appropriate service (or group of services) to accomplish a specific a task.

4. *Control Agent.* This agent supervises the correct functioning of the other agents in the system.

5. *Security Agent.* This agent analyzes the structure and syntax of all incoming and outgoing XML messages.

6. *Manager Agent.* The Manager Agent decides which service must be called by taking into account the QoS and users' preferences. Users can explicitly invoke a service, or can let the Manager Agent decide which service is the best to accomplish the requested task

7. *Interface Agent.* This kind of agent was designed to be embedded in users' applications. Interface agents communicate directly with the agents in CISM@. These agents must be simple enough to allow them to be executed on mobile devices, such as cell phones or PDAs. All high demand processes must be delegated to services.

CISM@ is an open architecture that allows developers to modify the structure of the agents described before. Developers can add new agent types or extend the existing ones to conform to their projects needs. However, most of the agents' functionalities should be modeled as services, releasing them from tasks that could be performed by services.

4 Conclusions and Future Work

CISM@ facilitates the development of dynamic and intelligent multi-agent systems. Its model is based on a cloud computing approach where the functionalities are implemented using Web Services. The architecture proposes an alternative where agents act as controllers and coordinators. CISM@ exploits the agents' characteristics to provide a robust, flexible, modular and adaptable solution that can cover most requirements of a wide diversity of distributed systems. All functionalities, including those of the agents, are modeled as distributed services and applications.

One of the objectives of the research activity is testing the application of Cloud Computing and Cloud services to systems and platforms oriented to Ambient Intelligent environments. Therefore, the next step in this research will be the testing of the proposed architecture in a real case study; in particular, its implementation in an e-health system to enhance assistance and health care for patients with dependencies. This system is suitable for validating the architecture because includes a large number of distributed services with different natures which can be integrated to test the architecture.

As a conclusion we can say that although CISM@ is still under development, preliminary results demonstrate that it is adequate for building complex systems and exploiting composite services. However, services can be any functionality (mechanisms, algorithms, routines, etc.) designed and deployed by developers. CISM@ has laid the groundwork to boost and optimize the development of future projects and systems that combine the flexibility of a cloud computing approach with the intelligence provided by agents. CISM@ makes it easier for developers to integrate independent services and applications because they are not restricted to programming languages supported by the agent frameworks used (e.g. JADE, OAA, RETSINA). The distributed approach of CISM@ optimizes usability and performance because it can obtain lighter agents by modelling the systems' functionalities as independent services and applications outside of the agents' structure, thus these may be used in other developments.

Acknowledgments

The heading should be treated as a 3rd level heading and should not be assigned a number.

References

1. Ardissono, L., Petrone, G., Segnan, M.: A Conversational Approach to the Interaction with Web Services. Computational Intelligence 20, 693–709 (2004)
2. Bellifemine, F., Poggi, A., Rimassa, G.: JADE–A FIPA-compliant Agent Framework. In: Proceedings of PAAM, pp. 97–108 (1999)
3. Bonino da Silva, L.O., Ramparany, F., Dockhorn, P., Vink, P., Etter, R., Broens, T.: A Service Architecture for Context Awareness and Reaction Provisioning. In: IEEE Congress on Services, pp. 25–32 (2007)
4. Cerami, E.: Web Services Essentials: Distributed Applications with XML-RPC, SOAP, UDDI & WSDL. O'Reilly Media, Inc., Sebastopol (2002)
5. Foste, I., Zhao, Y., Raicu, I.,, Lu, S.: Cloud Computing and Grid Computing 360-Degree Compared. In: Grid Computing Environments Workshop (GCE 2008), pp. 1–10 (2008), doi:10.1109/GCE.2008.4738445
6. Google App Engine, http://code.google.com/intl/es-ES/appengine/
7. Gruman, G., Knorr, E.: What Cloud Computing really means. Info World. Electronic Magazine (April 2008), http://infoworld.com/article/08/04/07/15FE-cloud-computing-reality_1.html
8. Martin, D.L., Chever, A.J., Moran, D.B.: The Open Agent Architecture: A framework for Building Distributed Software Systems. Applied Artificial Intelligence 13, 91–128 (1999)
9. Ricci, A., Buda, C., Zaghini, N.: An agent-oriented programming model for SOA & web services. In: 5th IEEE Conference on Industrial Informatics (INDIN 2007), Vienna, Austria, pp. 1059–1064 (2007)

10. Russell, S.J., Norvig, P., Canny, J.F., Malik, J., Edwards, D.D.: Artificial Intelligence: a Modern Approach. Prentice Hall, Englewood Cliffs (1995)
11. Sycara, K., Paolucci, M., Van Velsen, M., Giampapa, J.: The RETSINA MAS Infrastructure. Autonomous Agents and Multi-Agent Systems 7, 29–48 (2003)
12. S3 Amazon, http://aws.amazon.com/s3/
13. Vaquero, L.M., Rodero-Merino, L., Caceres, J., Lindner, M.: A break in the Clouds: Towards a Cloud Definition. In: SIGCOMM Comput. Commun. Rev., vol. 39(1), pp. 50–55. ACM, New York (2009)
14. Varia, J.: Amazon white paper on cloud architectures (September 2008), http://aws.typepad.com/aws/2008/07/white-paper-on.html
15. Wooldridge, M.: An Introduction to MultiAgent Systems. Wiley, Chichester (2002)
16. Maamar, Z., Kouadri, S., Yahyaoui, H.: Toward an Agent-Based and Context-Oriented Approach for Web Services Composition. IEEE Transactions on Knowledge and Data Engineering 17(5), 686–697 (2005)
17. Buhler, P., Vidal, J.M.: Integrating Agent Services into BPEL4WS Defined Workflows. In: Proceedings of the 4th International Workshop on Web-Oriented Software Technologies, pp. 244–251 (2004)
18. Fuentes-Fernández, R., García-Magariño, I., Gómez-Sanz, J.J., Pavón, J.: Integration of Web Services in an Agent-Oriented Methodology. International Transactions on Systems Science and Applications 3, 145–161 (2007)

Collaborative Tactical Planning in Multi-level Supply Chains Supported by Multiagent Systems

Jorge E. Hernández[1], Raúl Poler[1], Josefa Mula[1], and David de La Fuente[2]

[1] CIGIP (Centro de Investigación Gestión e Ingeniería de Producción), Dpto. Organización de Empresas, Escuela Politécnica Superior de Alcoy, Universidad Politécnica de Valencia, Edificio Ferrándiz y Carbonell, 2, 03801 Alcoy (Alicante), Spain
{jeh,rpoler,fmula}@cigip.upv.es
[2] Dpto. de Administración de Empresas, Escuela Politécnica Superior de Ingenieros Industriales, Universidad de Oviedo, Campus de Viesques s/n. 33204 Gijón (Asturias), Spain
david@uniovi.es

Abstract. In the supply chain modeling context, the agent-based model aims to represent not only each node, but also the information sharing process among these nodes. Despite the complexity of the configuration, the agent-based model can be applied straightforwardly to support the collaborative planning process. This allows the parties to achieve common goals effectively. Thus by sharing accurate, action-based information, collaboration among the nodes will emerge to improve the decision-making process in supply chain planning processes. Therefore, this paper presents a novel collaborative planning model in multi-level supply chains that considers a multiagent system modeling approach to carry out the iterative negotiation processes which will support the decision-making process from a decentralized perspective.

Keywords: Collaborative planning, supply chain management, negotiation, multiagent systems.

1 Introduction

The decisions linked to the supply chain management process can affect three decisional levels: strategic, tactical and operational. The first relates with long-term decisions, which include design processes. The second implies decisions at the mid-term level, which will influence planning activities at the operational level. Finally, the third mainly involves the execution of planned activities, where a decision has to be made from a short-term perspective. Thus, high uncertainty in the planning horizon will have a significant effect at this level because, in most cases, there is not enough reaction time to meet the new requirement. Thus, the system will need to consider high inventory levels to cover this uncertainty, which will imply and increase cost rates. This impact may be stronger if the system is composed of a multi-level supply chain where suppliers, warehouses, 3PL, retailers, etc., are directly affected by strategic and tactical decisions. Hence, a system should be studied from three viewpoints in relation to its products, information and decision flows [6]. Therefore, the on-time

Á. Ortiz Bas, R.D. Franco, P. Gómez Gasquet (Eds.): BASYS 2010, IFIP AICT 322, pp. 260–267, 2010.

and right decisions in the tactical planning process might avoid, and also optimize, these unnecessary levels and rates. Furthermore, [12] established that tactical planning covers those planning decisions in which short-term decisions are defined, such as synchronized planning policies for procurement, production, distribution and sales. In a supply chain context, it is possible to state that the planning process takes into account the coordination and integration of the key business activities which are normally undertaken by enterprises, ranging from the procurement of raw materials to the distribution of final products to end customers [5]. In addition, lead times are one of the important factors to be considered in the supply chain planning process, as suggested by [1]. Thus, it is important to consider lead times at the tactical level because lead times vary in terms of environmental uncertainties, which is precisely one of the serious factors that challenge suppliers and buyers in a supply chain when it comes to defining the mean and variance. In this context, supply chain management offers new opportunities for conducting operations strategy research [17]. Nevertheless, supply chain management at the information system level is becoming a high core competency, and enterprise resource planning systems are expected to become an integral component of supply chain management. Moreover, installing such systems is expensive and risky, and managers must decide how to use their limited resources and how to invest in the right products [15].

Therefore, this paper is set out as follows: Section 2 briefly reviews the relevant literature on collaborative planning and multi-agent systems in a supply chain management context. Section 3 establishes the formal formulation for the novel collaborative planning proposal in multi-level supply chains. Section 4 provides a brief example of the proposal application. Finally, Section 5 offers the main conclusions drawn and also briefly describes our future work.

2 Background

Despite the complexity of these systems, there are significant benefits at the collaborative level from a supply chain perspective, where the information exchanging process occupies a relevant place in supporting the planning processes among the nodes. Hence, as defined by [6], collaborative activities also imply a distributed decision-making process which involves several supply chain nodes. So in relation to the collaboration that may exist among these supply chain nodes, planning will consider the answers that customers send to the manufacturer which, in turn, will be sent to suppliers; thus, messages will flow effectively. The planning process is then supported by considering more effective answers in relation to demand/orders, and the agreement processes may also be supported by considering the corresponding negotiation processes [7].

In addition, this collaborative process can be seen from two perspectives: centralized and decentralized. From the centralized perspective, a virtual node controls the supply chain information process to support the planning processes. An example of this is highlighted in [11]. Then, from the centralized viewpoint, however, collaborative planning (among supply chain partners) can be achieved by simple coordinated upstream planning by providing the collaboration partners an opportunity to modify the suggested order/supply patterns iteratively [2]. Meanwhile from a decentralized collaboration viewpoint, each node will consider its collaborative and non collaborative partners (customers and suppliers) to carry out its planning processes [13]. This last perspective leads to a more realistic current supply chain process. In addition, examples of this decentralized perspective relating to logistic supply chain planning, supply chain coordination, a collaborative supply chain decision-making model and a supply chain coordination under demand uncertainty, can be found in [9], [3], [8] and [16], respectively.

Consequently, and as mentioned earlier, information technology systems must be set up irrespectively of the collaborative approach that the supply chain possibly considers to support such aspects as the information flow among the nodes in order to support supply chain planning and the communication processes. In the same context, and by considering the robustness presented by the multi-agent system, [10] proposed a novel architecture to support the inter-enterprise functions/resources integration and collaboration in a networked context. Moreover, [4] present auctions experiments, supported by multiagent systems, to view the impact at the operative level. To support this, modeling methodologies like MASCOT [14] or SCAMM-CPA [7] can be considered where a full literature review has been contemplated. Thus, the aim of multiagent proposals is to support the development of a system with a collaborative purpose by exchanging information without sharing a common system, but one that also considers the related ontology's with a view to supporting the communication process, hence leading to collaborative behavior. Therefore, this technology has been considered to support the following proposal.

3   The Collaborative Tactical Planning Formulation in Multi-level Supply Chains

The proposed planning process is about to consider the right and on-time information to support the decision-making process. Thus, the decision-making process is supported by a manufacturing requirement planning (MRP) system which, like the main information for all the n periods, considers inputs such as demand (D), inventory level (IL), the sell price (SP) and capacity (CAP). On the other hand, the main MRP outputs are the following: planned orders (PO), Delay on Demand (DoD), Profit and SP. Then, each node considers its own MRP mechanism (M).

The collaborative perspective of this proposal, as seen in Fig. 1, establishes communication at the multi-level area of the supply chain by considering the customer node's PO, which will be contemplated as D in the directly relating tier suppliers, as will the PO relating with the CAP information that the customer owns.

So the main idea is support a negotiation process by incrementing the SP with an increased P factor. In fact, if no agreement is reached among the nodes, the proposal will be improved by raising the SP.

Hence from the decentralized and collaborative perspectives, each node in the multi-level decision-making process considers its own database (or information repository) to link the communication process. This kind of communication is considered decentralized and collaborative because.

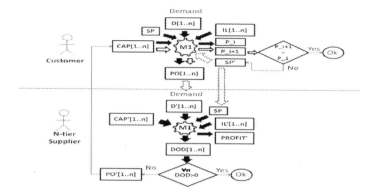

Fig. 1. Collaborative planning mechanism

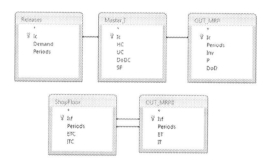

Fig. 2. Structure of the database supporting decentralized collaborative planning

In addition, Fig. 2 shows how the information system structure is composed of five main tables. These tables aim to collect the inputs and outputs generated by the MRP mechanism. In this case, the Releases table is about demand information. The Master_I table includes the information related to holding costs (HC), unitary costs UC, delay on demand costs (DoDC) and the sell price (SP). The OUT_MRP table collects information relating to the final level of the IL, P and DoD. This table holds information that will support the decision-making process of the planning process.

MRP systems also consider that information relating to ShopFloor activities, which mainly relate to CAP, ETC and ITC. Then, each answer the system generates will be restricted by the information in this table. Thus given the collaborative planning proposal, this information will consider the answer from the tier supplier to evaluate the planning proposal's level of profit. Then along with the OUT_MRPII table, the supply chain will be able to evaluate its decision by considering the right and on-time information in an iterative decentralized negotiation process.

$$ic = \sum_{N=1}^{M} \sum_{i=1}^{n} (OUT\_MRP.Inv_{Ni} * Master\_I.HC_{Ni}) \tag{1}$$

$$pc = \sum_{N=1}^{M} \sum_{i=1}^{n} (OUT\_MRP.P_{Ni} * Master\_I.UC_{Ni}) \tag{2}$$

$$dc = \sum_{i=1}^{n} (OUT\_MRP.DoD_{1i} * Master\_I.DoDC_{Ni}) \tag{3}$$

$$extratc = \sum_{i=1}^{n} (OUT\_MRPII.ET_{Ni} * ShoopFloor.ETC_{1i}) \tag{4}$$

$$idletc = \sum_{N=1}^{M} \sum_{i=1}^{n} (OUT\_MRP.IT_{Ni} * ShoopFloor.ITC_{Ni}) \tag{5}$$

$$sr1 = \sum_{i=1}^{n} (Releases.Demand_{1i} * Master\_I.SP_{1i}) \tag{6}$$

$$sr2 = \sum_{i=1}^{n} (MRP.DoD_{1i} * Master\_I.SP_{1i}) \tag{7}$$

$$PROFIT = sr1 - sr2 - ic - pc - dc - extratc - idlec \tag{8}$$

Finally, the profit level (8) will lead not only to the negotiation process, but also to the decisions relating to the planning process in each n period of the planning horizon. The calculus of this profit consider the following information for each period: inventory costs at each period (1), production costs (2), delay on demands costs (3), extra time costs (4), costs of the idle time of resources (5) and sell revenues (6 and 7). Thus by considering the answers from suppliers, the customer node will evaluate renegotiation by taking the new profit value which is directly affected by the raised product's sell price. The negotiation process will finish when new price changes no longer have an impact on the profit level or when no DoDc for the suppliers exist. Hence, an example of the application of this novel proposal to a multi-level supply chain is briefly provided in the following section.

4   A Multiagent-Based System to Support Collaborative Tactical Planning in Multi-level Supply Chains

The collaborative planning model (Fig. 3) for supply chain networks which considers a multiagent system modeling approach is supported by MPL/CPLEX, JADE 3.6 and ECLIPSE. The communication process among agents is supported by behaviors that aim to generate demands and firm orders, and to also send and receive the corresponding messages, by considering the FIPA standard communication protocols, which are mainly supported by the Contract-Net protocol. The system has been tested in a real concurrent environment, thus each agent considers its own thread.

As Fig. 3 illustrates, each node considers its own planning mechanism, as well as its own database (DB) repository. In addition, each agent is independently governed by its own behaviors, including its wishes and beliefs. Next, the multi-level supply chain is composed of the customer agent (CA), the first-tier supplier agent (FTSA1) and two second-tier supplier's agents (STSA1 and STSA2). Then, each node will validate its proposals by obtaining the related values at the profit level.

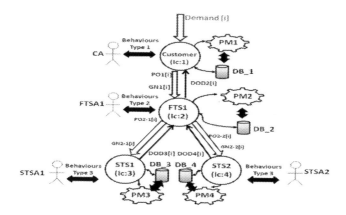

Fig. 3. A Multi-Tier Supply Chain example

```
private int GetProfit(int ShoopFloor){
int profit=0, sr1=0, sr2=0, pc=0, ic=0, dc=0, idletc=0, extratc=0;
BeginConection(ShoopFlor);

try {
Statement jeh = con.createStatement();

...
ResultSet sr1 = jeh.executeQuery("SELECT Sum([Releases]![D]*[Master_I]![SP]) AS sr1 FROM Releases
INNER JOIN Master_I ON Releases.Ic = Master_I.Ic WHERE ((([Releases]![IBDc])=1) AND
(([Master_I]![IBDc])=1))");

...
ResultSet sr2 = jeh.executeQuery("SELECT Sum([OUT_MRP]![DoD]*[Master_I]![SP]) AS sr2 FROM OUT_MRP
INNER JOIN Master_I ON (Master_I.IBDc = OUT_MRP.IBDc) AND (OUT_MRP.Ic = Master_I.Ic) WHERE
((([OUT_MRP]![IBDc])=1) AND (([OUT_MRP]![Periods])=30) AND (([Master_I]![IBDc])=1))");

...
ResultSet pc = jeh.executeQuery("SELECT Sum([OUT_MRP]![P]*[Master_I]![UC]) AS pc FROM OUT_MRP INNER
JOIN Master_I ON (OUT_MRP.IBDc = Master_I.IBDc) AND (OUT_MRP.Ic = Master_I.Ic)");

...
ResultSet ic = jeh.executeQuery("SELECT Sum([OUT_MRP]![Inv]*[Master_I]![HC]) AS ic FROM OUT_MRP INNER
JOIN Master_I ON (Master_I.IBDc = OUT_MRP.IBDc) AND (OUT_MRP.Ic = Master_I.Ic)");

...
ResultSet dc = jeh.executeQuery("SELECT Sum([OUT_MRP]![DoD]*[Master_I]![DoDC]) AS dc FROM Master_I
INNER JOIN OUT_MRP ON (OUT_MRP.IBDc = Master_I.IBDc) AND (Master_I.Ic = OUT_MRP.Ic) WHERE
(((([Master_I]![IBDc])=1) AND (([OUT_MRP]![IBDc])=1))");

...
ResultSet idletc = jeh.executeQuery("SELECT Sum([OUT_OUT_MRPII]![IT]*[ShoopFloor]![ITC]) AS idletc
FROM OUT_OUT_MRPII, ShoopFloor");

...
ResultSet extratc = jeh.executeQuery("SELECT Sum([OUT_OUT_MRPII]![ET]*[ShoopFloor]![ETC]) AS extratc
FROM OUT_OUT_MRPII INNER JOIN ShoopFloor ON (OUT_OUT_MRPII.Periods = ShoopFloor.Periods) AND
(OUT_OUT_MRPII.Ir = ShoopFloor.Ir)");

profit = sr1 - sr2 - pc - ic - dc - idletc - extratc;

Return profit;
}
```

Fig. 4. JAVA – Extract of the SQL profit calculus code

Then, the negotiation process supported by the profit algorithm calculus (8) is presented in its technical JAVA-SQL approach (see Fig. 4). Fig. 5 presents the communication process which considers the main planning decision relating to the negotiation process (supported by the profit level).

Therefore from a decentralized perspective, the system implementation, as Fig. 5 highlights, considers that each agent in the collaborative planning supported by the multi-agent system is in its own machine; that is, in its own container. Thus, each thread is composed of sub-threads that are supported by the relating FIPA contract-net protocols. Every agent belonging to the highest level will wait for the negotiated answers from the lower levels, and each node will evaluate its profit evolution.

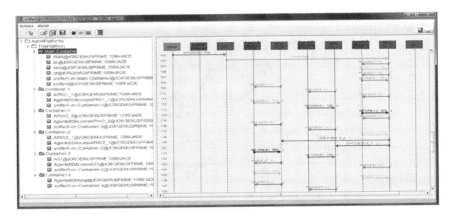

Fig. 5. Sniffer agent. Validation of the collaborative planning process

5   Conclusions

A novel multiagent-based collaborative planning model for multi-level supply chains has been proposed. The modeling basis is supported by the fact that each node considers its own information repository from a decentralized viewpoint, hence its own databases. In addition, the MRP mechanism supports the decision-making processes. The main idea is that these mechanisms will consider some inputs from the lower levels of the supply chain (suppliers) to, in turn, consider their answers about their profit calculus. Hence, the negotiation process will be composed of both the inputs and outputs relating to the decision, and the answers from all the supply chain levels; and all this from a decentralized perspective. In addition, a prototype has been developed that offers a good possibility of establishing the multi-agent system.

In future research, the proposed model will be applied to a real supply chain network in the automobile supply chain sector with a view to implementing the mobility agent by scaling the platform prototype and by considering real demand data. Furthermore, this novel proposal will also be compared with other negotiation mechanisms to test its suitability.

Acknowledgments. This research has been supported by the EVOLUTION project (Ref. DPI2007-65501) which is funded by the Spanish Ministry of Science and Education, www.cigip.upv.es/evolution.

References

1. Chaharsooghi, S.K., Heydari, J.: LT variance or LT mean reduction in supply chain management: Which one has a higher impact on SC performance. International Journal of Production Economics 124, 475–481 (2010)
2. Dudek, G., Stadtler, H.W.: Negotiation-based collaborative planning between supply chains partners. European Journal of Operational Research 163(3), 668–687 (2005)
3. Gaudreault, J., Frayret, J., Pesant, G.: Distributed search for supply chain coordination. Computers in Industry 60, 441–451 (2009)
4. Gomez-Gasquet, P., Franco, R.D., Rodríguez, R., Ortiz, A.: A Scheduler for extended supply chains based on combinatorial auctions. Journal of Operations and Logistics 12, V1–V12 (2009)
5. Gupta, A., Maranas, C.D.: Managing demand uncertainty in supply chain planning. Computers and Chemical Engineering 27, 1219–1227 (2003)
6. Hernández, J.E., Mula, J., Ferriols, F.J.: A reference model for conceptual modeling of production planning processes. Production Planning & Control 19(8), 725–734 (2008)
7. Hernández, J.E., Alemany, M.M.E., Lario, F.C., Poler, R.: SCAMM-CPA: A Supply Chain Agent-Based Modelling Methodology That Supports a Collaborative Planning Process. Innovar. 19(34), 99–120 (2009)
8. Hernández, J.E., Poler, R., Mula, J., Lario, F.C.: The reverse logistic process of an automobile supply chain network supported by a collaborative decision-making model. Group Decision and Negotiation Journal (2010) (in Press)
9. Jung, H., Chen, F.F., Jeong, B.: Decentralized supply chain planning framework for third party logistics partnership. Computers & Industrial Engineering 55, 348–364 (2008)
10. Nahm, Y.E., Ishikawa, H.: A hybrid multi-agent system architecture for enterprise integration using computer networks. Robotics and Computer-Integrated Manufacturing 21, 217–234 (2005)
11. Ortiz, A., Franco, R.D., Alba, M.: V-Chain: Migrating From Extended To Virtual Enterprise Within An Automotive Supply Chain. In: PRO-VE 2003, Proceedings. Processes and Foundations for Virtual Organizations, pp. 145–152 (2003)
12. Ouhimmou, M., D'Amours, S., Beauregard, R., Ait-Kadi, D., Chauhan, S.S.: Furniture supply chain tactical planning optimization using a time decomposition approach. European Journal of Operational Research 189, 952–970 (2008)
13. Poler, R., Hernández, J.E., Mula, J., Lario, F.C.: Collaborative forecasting in networked manufacturing enterprises. Journal of Manufacturing Technology Management 19(4), 514–528 (2008)
14. Sadeh, N.M., Hildum, D.W., Kjenstad, D., Tseng, A.: MASCOT: An Agent-Based Architecture for Coordinated Mixed-Initiative Supply Chain Planning and Scheduling. In: Third International Conference on Autonomous Agents. Workshop on Agent-Based Decision Support for Managing the Internet-Enabled Supply Chain, Seattle WA (1999)
15. Su, Y., Yang, C.: Why are enterprise resource planning systems indispensable to supply chain management? European Journal of Operational Research 203, 81–94 (2010)
16. Xiao, T., Shi, K., Yang, D.: Coordination of a supply chain with consumer return under demand uncertainty. International Journal of Production Economics 124, 171–180 (2010)
17. Zhao, X., Lee, T.: Developments and emerging research opportunities in operations strategy and supply chain management. International Journal of Production Economics 120, 1–4 (2009)

Evolutionary Model of an Innovative and Differentiated Industry

José I. Santos[1], Ricardo del Olmo[1], and Javier Pajares[2]

[1] INSISOC, University of Burgos, Spain
{jisantos,rdelolmo}@ubu.es
[2] INSISOC, University of Valladolid, Spain
pajares@insisoc.org

Abstract. In this paper, we propose an agent based model that describes the spatial and temporal evolution of an industry composed of a set of heterogeneous firms distributed in different regions. The model formalizes a particular hypothesis about spatial agglomeration and industrial concentration phenomena in which innovation occupies the central place of economic and geographical growth explanation. Each company owns one or more manufacturing divisions that produce an exclusive variety of product. Economic selection is modeled as a monopolistic competition market where competitive pressure depends on consumers' preference for variety. Moreover, firms may enjoy more competitive advantages innovating in processes, product characteristics and new commodities. The purpose of the model is integrating theories which come from research areas traditionally separated into a single formal proposal.

Keywords: evolutionary economics, industrial dynamics, economic geography.

1 Introduction

Traditionally, Economics theory has left aside the spatial dimension of economic phenomena, and in particular agglomeration and industrial concentration phenomena[1], with the aim of developing a tractable and analytic framework [1]. However, industrial dynamics are usually characterized by economic forces that tend to agglomerate firms in particular locations and concentrate market power in a few group of companies. Because of this, different scientific disciplines, not exclusively economic, have given increased attention to these phenomena in the last two decades.

Due to the complexity of these phenomena, there are few and quite heterogeneous formal models that address the problem. A significant contribution comes from some economists of the new Economic Geography, who propose a new family of microeconomic models [1]. The main assumption of these models of spatial economic agglomeration is based primarily on the effect of local market size and the relationship between scale economies and transportation costs.

---

[1] Economic Geography often uses the term agglomeration to describe the spatial distribution of an industry over regions and countries. In this paper, we keep this assumption and use the term concentration to refer to the distribution of the market shares within an industry.

Á. Ortiz Bas, R.D. Franco, P. Gómez Gasquet (Eds.): BASYS 2010, IFIP AICT 322, pp. 268–275, 2010.
© IFIP International Federation for Information Processing 2010

However, new Economic Geography models intentionally forget the dynamic dimension of industries to make the problem analytically tractable. In contrast, selection and innovation processes are of fundamental importance to other scholars [2]. For example, Audretsch and Feldman [3] demonstrate how R&D activities of many knowledge-based industries tend to be agglomerated in a few locations. Similarly, Baptista and Swann [4] show empirically the greater intensity of innovation activity in UK industrial clusters.

Evolutionary dynamics of industries are characterized by complex spatial-economic interdependence, insofar as firms' economic performance is conditioned by geographical factors, which at the same time are influenced by firms' performance. Industrial dynamics evolve simultaneously in both economic and geographic dimensions, making quite difficult, or even impossible, any intent to separate one from another.

Frenken and Boschma [5] integrate evolutionary theories of industrial dynamics with other geographical theories of regional growth and innovation to propose a new theoretical framework for developing geographic and evolutionary formal models, and this theoretical approach is the starting point of our work. We try to develop an evolutionary formal model of industrial dynamics in which innovation plays a key role as the engine of economic and geographical growth.

2 Cumulative Causality of Industrial Agglomeration and Concentration Phenomena

The model is built on the following assumptions:

- The industry is formed by heterogeneous firms which are different in their capacities, knowledge and routines [6].
- Selection processes operate through a monopolistic competition market in which firms enjoy an imperfect monopolistic position producing differentiated products [7].
- Innovation is the source of diversity and competitive advantages. Firms do not only seek to improve processes and products, but also develop new products, and hence they can grow and strengthen their position in the industry [5].
- The synergy of knowledge within the firm as well as the knowledge diffusion (knowledge spillovers) outside the firm through labor mobility and personal contacts influence innovation results, reducing uncertainty and increasing the chances of success [3].

All these assumptions can be summarize in a hypothesis about spatial agglomeration and industrial concentration phenomena that we call it cumulative causality: a positive reinforcing chain of causes and effects. Figure 1 depicts graphically this cumulative causality: (1) innovation generates improvements in manufacturing processes (process innovation) and in the characteristics of products (product innovation), and therefore provides firms with competitive advantages; (2) innovation also makes possible the creation of new products (product differentiation) that promote the expansion of firms; (3) the growth of firms may have a positive effect on their R&D activities through scale economies; (4) the growth of firms entails consequently the growth of the region where they are located; (5) the geographical proximity between firms facilitates knowledge externalities (knowledge spillovers) that influence all types of innovative activities.

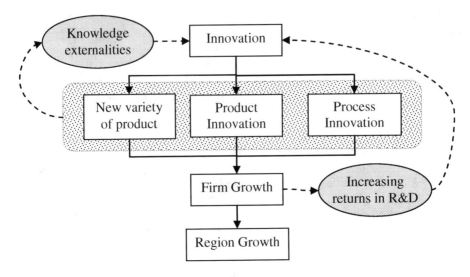

Fig. 1. Main hypothesis of the model: cumulative causality of spatial agglomeration and industrial concentration phenomena [5]

3 Agent Based Model of a Differentiated Industry

We use the Agent-Based Modeling (ABM) paradigm to formalize the theoretical hypothesis outlined before. The model[2] describes the spatial and temporal evolution of an industry initially composed of a group of firms distributed in different locations (regions). Each company owns one or more manufacturing divisions that produce an exclusive variety of product. Economic selection is modeled as a monopolistic competition market, where consumers' preferences are determined by an aggregate utility function with constant elasticity of substitution (CES) between varieties. The income that consumers spend on products evolves exogenously according to a logistic curve, characteristic of the life cycle of the industry. Firms may enjoy competitive advantage innovating in processes and product characteristics or creating new products.

3.1 Monopolistic Competition Market

Selection processes in the industry is modeled as a competition between imperfect substitute varieties of products, each one is a monopoly of a single division of a firm. We incorporate a particular abstraction of imperfect monopolistic competition borrow from Dixit and Stiglitz [9] where consumers' behavior is fully described by an aggregate utility function U (Eq.1) with CES between varieties $j \in \{1, 2, ..., m\}$

$$U = \left(\sum_{k=1}^{m} \left(f_k(t) q_k(t) \right)^{\theta} \right)^{1/\theta} = \left(\sum_{k=1}^{m} \left(f_k(t) q_k(t) \right)^{\frac{\sigma-1}{\sigma}} \right)^{\frac{\sigma}{\sigma-1}} \qquad 0 < \theta < 1 \qquad (1)$$

---

[2] The model has been implemented in Repast [8].

where q_k denotes the quantity of commodity k and $f_k(t)$ the consumers' predilection for it. The parameter $\theta \in (0,1)$ governs consumers' preference for variety, and therefore the degree of monopolistic competition in the market. Higher values of θ denote weaker preferences for diversity. In particular, $\theta = 1$ represents the situation where consumers do not distinguish between products, and the competition is similar to a homogeneous product market.

The family of CES utility functions in Eq.1 facilitates the derivation of the demand curve for each product j in Eq.2, where $Y(t)$ represents consumers' income. We assume that consumer's income evolves exogenously according to a logistic equation that characterizes the life cycle of the industry [10].

$$p_j(t) = \frac{f_j(t)^\theta}{q_j(t)^{1-\theta} \sum_{k=1}^{m} \left(f_k(t) q_k(t) \right)^\theta} Y(t) \qquad (2)$$

It is interesting to observe how the demand for each commodity is affected by the total number of products in the industry (see Fig. 2), due to the particular abstraction of monopolistic competition used in the model. Note that new commodities in the market push down demand curves of all products, and this competitive pressure is higher as consumers' preference for variety declines, i.e., as $\theta \to 1$.

3.2 Firm Behavior

The firm i is formed by one or more divisions $\{j\} \in i$ responsible for a variety of product, all them located in a region r. At time period t, the division j belonging to the firm i produces $Q_{ij}(t)$ units of the corresponding commodity according to the production function of Eq.3, which relates the output with the productivity of the division $A_{ij}(t)$ and its stock of physical capital $K_{ij}(t)$.

$$Q_{ij}(t) = A_{ij}(t) K_{ij}(t) \qquad (3)$$

The division j invests part of its capital $r_j^{pc}(t)$ in process innovations, which may improve the productivity $A_{ij}(t)$, and other part $r_j^{pd}(t)$ in product innovations, which may improve consumers' predilection $f_k(t)$. Similarly, the firm i invests part of its capital (the sum of capital over its divisions) $r_i^{nv}(t)$ in innovation of new varieties of products.

We assume that the total production of the division j, $Q_{ij}(t)$, is sold at price $p_j(t)$, which is determined by Eq.2. Division j's profits $\Pi_{ij}(t) = p_j(t)Q_{ij}(t) - c_{ij}(t)K_{ij}(t)$ are the difference between revenues and costs, where $c_{ij}(t)$ represents the cost per unit of capital of the division (Eq.4); the parameter c quantifies the cost of capital, which is identical for all divisions.

$$c_{ij}(t) = c + r_{ij}^{pc}(t) + r_{ij}^{pd}(t) + r_i^{nv}(t) \qquad (4)$$

At time period t, the division j estimates the capital investment rate $I_{ij}(t)$ according to a simple adaptive rule [6], expressed in Eq.5.

$$I_{ij}(t) = \max\left(0, \min\left(I_{ij}^{\max}(t), I_{ij}^{des}(t)\right)\right) \qquad (5)$$

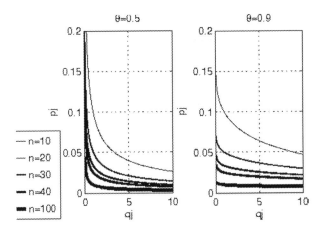

Fig. 2. Family of demand curves of products (Eq.2) for two scenarios of a monopolistic competition market, $\theta = 0.5$ on the left and $\theta = 0.9$ on the right, where $Y = 1$, $f_i(t) = 1 \forall i$, $q_i(t) = 1 \forall i \neq j$. In each graph, the demand curve of a product j has been drawn for different values of the number of products n in the market. Looking at both graphs simultaneously we observe that the sensitivity of the demand curve to changes in the number n is modulated by consumers' preference for variety θ.

The maximum capital investment rate $I_{ij}^{max}(t)$ is limited by division j's profits in the period, and the desired investment rate $I_{ij}^{des}(t)$ depends on how far division j is from the optimal situation in which its marginal revenue is equal to marginal costs. This deviation from the optimum can be expressed easily, Eq.6, by means of a desired margin $mg^{des}(t)$, which depends on the elasticity of the demand curve, and an expected margin $mg^{exp}(t)$, which depends on expected price and marginal costs.

$$I_{ij}^{des}(t) = 1 + \delta - \frac{mg^{des}}{mg^{esp}(t)} \tag{6}$$

Then, division j's stock of capital is updated according to Eq.7, where δ modulates the depreciation of capital. Whenever the division j gets an expected margin higher than the desired margin, it decides to increase its stock of capital and consequently the quantity to be produced and sold in the next period.

$$K_{ij}(t+1) = K_{ij}(t)\left(1 - \delta + I_{ij}(t)\right) \tag{7}$$

3.3   Innovation and Knowledge Spillovers

We model innovation as a stochastic process of two steps. First, a division/firm has a chance of innovating according to a probability of innovation. Second, if it achieves success, it assesses the scope of the innovation. The probability of innovation (for the three types of innovations considered in the model) is defined by Eq.8.

$$P^{in} = P_{max}^{in} - (P_{max}^{in} - P_{min}^{in})\exp(-\alpha^{in} X^{in}) \tag{8}$$

The parameters P_{max}^{in} and P_{min}^{in}, which represent the maximum and minimum probability of innovating, determine the technological opportunity regime in the model – innovating can be more difficult in some industries than in others [11]–. The parameter α^{in}, which governs the growth rate of the probability function, represents the productivity of innovative efforts X^{in}. Not every division/firm invests the same resources in innovative activities, and they are not equally efficient due to returns to scale and knowledge externalities [12].

The innovative effort X^{in} is modeled as a Cobb-Douglas function of increasing returns (Eq.9), where $X_{division}^{I+D}$ represents the division's capital expenditure in R&D, X_{firm}^{I+D} the corresponding one in the firm, and X_{region}^{I+D} the total expenditure in the region in which the firm is located.

$$X^{in} = X_{division}^{I+D} \left(X_{firm}^{I+D} \right)^{\beta_{firm}} \left(X_{region}^{I+D} \right)^{\beta_{region}} x_{scala}^{1+\beta_{firm}+\beta_{region}}$$
$$0 < \beta_{region} < \beta_{firm} \ll 1 \tag{9}$$

The parameters β_{firm} and β_{region} govern the importance of knowledge externalities within the firm and the region respectively. We assume that the former are more important than the latter, insofar as firms have more tools to manage them, and that both do not condition excessively the probability of innovation ($\beta_{region} < \beta_{firm} \ll 1$), which depends mainly on each division's innovative effort.

In short, the probability of innovating is positively reinforced by: (1) returns to scale in the division's expenditure in R&D; (2) knowledge externalities within the firm [5]; and (3) knowledge spillovers in the region [3].

The scope of innovations in processes and products are modeled as a random leap forward from the current state of the division's productivity $A_{ij}(t)$ and consumers' predilections $f_j(t)$ according to a uniform distribution defined in Eq.10.

$$A_{ij}^{in}(t) = U\left(A_{ij}(t),(1+\gamma^{pc})A_{ij}(t) \right)$$
$$f_j^{in}(t) = U\left(f_j(t),(1+\gamma^{pd})f_j(t) \right) \tag{10}$$

The parameters γ^{pc} and γ^{pd} are considered to be constant and equal to all firms in the industry. Moreover, we suppose that any innovation in processes or products gives the same order of competitive advantage, so it is not difficult to demonstrate a relation between them (Eq.11).

$$(1+\gamma^{pc}) = (1+\gamma^{pd})^{\theta} \tag{11}$$

A firm can also create a new product, starting a new division responsible for its manufacturing. The new division j^* replicates the capacities of its parent according to a stochastic process (Eq.12) that is function of all divisions' features of the firm. Furthermore, there is a probability $p^{spinoff}$ that the new division becomes a new independent spin-off [13].

$$A_{ij*}(t) = U\left(\min(A_{ik}(t)), \max(A_{ik}(t))\right) \quad k \in i$$
$$f_{j*}(t) = U\left(\min(f_k(t)), \max(f_k(t))\right) \quad k \in i \tag{12}$$

We incorporate a noise in the model with the entry of new firms at each time period according to a Poisson distribution of parameter λ_{entry}, which it is assumed to be constant throughout the simulation. Finally, if a division reduces its stock of capital below a minimum threshold, it exits the industry; consequently, if all divisions of a firm exit, the company leaves de industry too.

5 Conclusions

We have proposed a formal model of an innovative and differentiated industry where a set of heterogeneous firms localized in different regions compete in an imperfect monopolistic market. The model is built on a particular hypothesis about spatial agglomeration and industrial concentration phenomena –that we call it cumulative causality– in which innovation occupies the central place of economic and geographical growth explanation. Innovation is modeled as a stochastic process where firm's probability of innovating depends not only on its innovative effort, but also on knowledge externalities within the firm and knowledge spillovers in the region.

The main contribution of the model is that we integrate theories which come from research areas traditionally separated into a single formal proposal. Thus, we incorporate the concepts of diversity, development and selection from Evolutionary Economics, and some theories about innovation and knowledge spillovers from Economic Geography and Geography of Innovation.

Acknowledgments

The authors have benefited from the financial support of the Junta de Castilla y León (project BU034A08 and VA006A09) and Caja Burgos (project 2009/00148/001 and project 2009/00199/001).

References

1. Fujita, M., Krugman, P., Venables, A.J.: The spatial economy: cities, regions and international trade. MIT Press, Cambridge (1999)
2. Boschma, R.A., Lambooy, J.G.: Evolutionary economics and economic geography. Journal of Evolutionary Economics 9(4), 411–429 (1999)
3. Audretsch, D.B., Feldman, M.P.: R&D Spillovers and the Geography of Innovation and Production. American Economic Review 86(3), 630–640 (1996)
4. Baptista, R., Swann, P.: Do firms in clusters innovate more? Research Policy 27(5), 525–540 (1998)
5. Frenken, K., Boschma, R.A.: A theoretical framework for evolutionary economic geography: industrial dynamics and urban growth as a branching process. Journal of Economic Geography 7(5), 635–649 (2007)

6. Nelson, R.R., Winter, S.G.: An evolutionary theory of economic change. Harvard University Press, Cambridge (1982)
7. Santos, J.I., Olmo, R., Pajares, J.: Selection processes in a monopolistic competition market. In: Hernandez, C. (ed.) Artificial Economics: the generative method in Economics. Lecture Notes in Economics and Mathematical Systems, vol. 631, pp. 67–77. Springer, Heidelberg (2009)
8. North, M.L., Collier, N.T., Vos, J.R.: Experiences Creating Three Implementations of the Repast Agent Modeling Toolkit. ACM Transactions on Modeling and Computer Simulation 16, 1–25 (2006)
9. Dixit, A.K., Stiglitz, J.E.: Monopolistic Competition and Optimum Product Diversity. American Economic Review 67(3), 297–308 (1977)
10. Klepper, S.: Industry life cycles. Industrial and Corporate Change 6(1), 145–181 (1997)
11. Klevorick, A.K., Lewin, R.C., Nelson, R.R., Winter, S.G.: On the sources and significance of interindustry differences in technological opportunities. Research Policy 24(2), 185–205 (1995)
12. Santos, J.I., Olmo, R., Pajares, J.: Innovation and knowledge spillovers in a networked industry. In: Consiglio, A. (ed.) Artificial Markets Modeling: Methods and Applications. Lecture Notes in Economics and Mathematical Systems, vol. 599, pp. 171–180. Springer, Heidelberg (2007)
13. Klepper, S.: Employee startips in high-tech industries. Industrial and Corporate Change 10(3), 639–674 (2001)

Human Attributes in the
Modelling of Work Teams

Juan Martínez-Miranda and Juan Pavón

Facultad de Informática, Universidad Complutense Madrid
Ciudad Universitaria s/n
28040 Madrid, Spain
jmartinez@microart.cat, jpavon@fdi.ucm.es

Abstract. This paper presents a summary of relevant research findings that have been used as the theoretical background in the design of an agent-based model to simulate the human behaviour within work teams (the TEAKS model). It underlines some of the main trends in the modelling of human behaviour in teams, and the rationale for selecting the attributes to represent real team candidates as software agents in the TEAKS model.

1 Introduction

Computer simulations to analyse and understand complex phenomena have been applied in several research disciplines including Automation [1], Economics [2], Social Sciences [3] and Environmental Sciences [4]. The success in the use of simulations within these research areas relies on the feasibility to *play* with the behaviour of the modelled phenomenon under study by changing the conditions of its environment and its internal parameters to observe the consequences in a controlled experiment.

The study of human behaviour under specific contexts and circumstances has been one of these complex phenomena under study since early 70's [5]. Over the past few decades, tools and techniques for modelling and predicting human performance in complex systems have evolved and matured, for instance, considering task network models [6] and situational awareness models [7], among others.

In the last years, agent-based modelling has emerged as a relative new technique to model social behaviour, particularly helpful for the modelling of individuals immerse in a social environment such as groups, organisations or societies. The key characteristic of agent-based models is the concept of *Agent,* which is an autonomous software entity with the ability to interact with other agents and with the environment. Autonomy means that agents are active entities that can take their own decisions. This is not the same with objects, as they are predetermined to perform the operations that someone else requests them. An agent, however, will decide whether to perform or not a requested operation, taking into account its goals and priorities, as well as the context it knows. In this sense, the agent paradigm assimilates quite well the individual in a social system.

This paper presents a summary of relevant research findings that have been used as the theoretical background in the design of an agent-based model to simulate the

Á. Ortiz Bas, R.D. Franco, P. Gómez Gasquet (Eds.): BASYS 2010, IFIP AICT 322, pp. 276–284, 2010.

human behaviour within work teams, which has been implemented as the TEAKS model [8]. It first underlines some of the main current trends in the modelling of human behaviour in teams. Then, it focus on explaining the rationale behind the selection of the human attributes that have been included in the TEAKS model to represent real team candidates as software agents.

2 Modelling Human Behaviour in Work Teams

The modelling of human behaviour is a great challenge due to the instability, unpredictability and the ability to perform independent actions of human nature. Nevertheless, in the recent years several models and techniques have emerged that clearly indicate that some contextual-limited modelling of human-like behaviours are possible such as in training and learning [8], and for the representation of crisis and emergency situations [9], among others.

An interesting scenario where models of human behaviour are applied is for the analysis and understanding of the different dynamics that take place within groups and teams under specific context. Some examples of works where group behaviours are analysed using agent-based models include the presented in [10], which analyses the behaviour of a group of agents facing the management of common pool resources. Also, [11] report the analysis of the performance in military combatants, studying the effect on their behaviour of individual and social factors. The analysis of a group's behaviour and dynamics when facing the adoption of a new software application is other application described in [12].

One type of teams particularly interesting is the one formed by people in front of their daily activities at work to perform a set of tasks. The analysis of the behaviour and performance of these work teams can support the decision making process of managers to select the right persons to form better work teams taking into account the fact that a group of people with optimal individual abilities may perform suboptimally acting as a work team [13]. From a research point of view, this scenario offers several dimensions to be studied given that the work team's performance is influenced not only by the personal expertise and responsibilities of each team member, but also by some personal characteristics that influence individual, and in consequence, team performance [14].

In this context we have developed TEAKS (TEAm Knowledge-based Structuring), an agent-based model where a virtual team can be configured using the characteristics of the real candidates to form a team of software agents, and given a set of tasks, the model generates statistical information about the possible performance of the agents obtained from the interaction between all the team members and with their assigned tasks [8].

The representation of the real candidates through software agents required a careful study about the individual (internal) attributes to model in the software agents. It is difficult to include all the internal human attributes that affect, influence and direct the behaviour of a person. The most common strategy to follow is to select only those attributes that are important in the context of the phenomenon that will be studied. In this sense, the next section presents a brief review of existent research that indicates the importance of some specific internal attributes in human behaviour, in the context of human behaviour at work and within work teams. Additionally, a brief review of some existent artificial systems and architectures that implement the identified attributes are mentioned.

3   Individual Attributes in the Modelling of Human Behaviour

A key set of human attributes that influence and direct behaviour within work teams were identified and included in the TEAKS model. Four human attributes were selected and implemented in the model: *creativity, emotions, personality traits* and *trust*.

3.1   Creativity

The research discipline that traditionally has focused on the study of human behaviour is the Psychology. The psychological cognitive approach focuses on how humans think with the belief that such thought processes affect the way in which humans behave. The interest and development of this psychological approach has been increased from the 1960s originating the Cognitive Science.

According to [15], the central hypothesis of cognitive science is that thinking can best be understood in terms of representational structures in the mind and computational procedures that operate on those structures, i.e. the Computational-Representational Understanding of Mind. The mental processes that are studied in cognitive science include *comprehension, inference, decision-making, planning* and *learning*. All these mental processes produce at the end an intelligent human behaviour with the capabilities to develop highly routine tasks to extremely difficult, open-ended problems.

In the context of human behaviour at work, several studies along the years have proved the high influence of the cognitive abilities on work performance across different types of jobs [16]. One particular outcome originated from the different mental processes that has been deeply studied in the analysis of work performance is the *creative behaviour* [17]. Research has linked five specific cognitive abilities that influence creativity: *problem framing, divergent thinking, mental transformations, practice with alternative solutions*, and *evaluative ability*. The concept of creativity has received much attention (mainly in the Organisational Psychology and Human Resources disciplines) due that it is considered the basic ingredient to be innovative [18], which in turn is a key factor to increase the success in the work performance of an individual, group or organisation.

Moreover, the cognitive and creativity research topics have not remained to exclusively understand work behaviour and/or performance at individual level, but both have been extended to cover the understanding and improvement of behaviour in work teams. In concrete, the term *team cognition* has been linked to effective team performance and it includes knowledge about team members, task-specific information, and team processes [19]. Team cognition has been also attracted the attention of researchers on creativity to analyse and better understand the creative processes and outcomes that take place at group/team level [20].

3.2 Emotional Behaviour

In the past, for many years the main belief was that emotions are an undesirable product of the human rational mind, and thus the less emotional a person was, the more intelligent and reasonable the person was. Nevertheless, in recent years some researchers have proved that emotions are a relevant part of the human reasoning and necessary for an intelligent behaviour [21].

In the context of human behaviour at work, the influence of emotions is also recognised of great importance. The clearest example of this importance is the development of the relatively new concept of Emotional Intelligence. According to [22], Emotional Intelligence is composed of four abilities: *(1)* the ability to identify one's own and others' emotions to accurately express own emotions to others; *(2)* understanding how emotions orient people toward important information and how different emotional states can induce varying approaches to problem solving; *(3)* understanding the meaning, progressions, and complexity among emotions; and *(4)* the ability to stay open to feelings, to detach, and to manage one's own and others' emotions promoting emotional and intellectual growth.

With regard to the influence of emotions within work teams performance, despite the fact that group researchers have long acknowledged the importance of group's emotional life in its performance, there is relatively little research to date. Most of the studies have focused on individual level issues to show a positive relationship between emotional expression and organisational commitment [23]; a positive relationship between emotions and work motivation [24] and the different types of emotions that can be experienced at work [25]. Some others have concentrated efforts on evaluate the effects of mood (different than emotions) into work team performance [26]; and only few studies have reported how emotions influence directly (e.g. *envy* in work teams [27]) or indirectly (e.g. analysing the role of emotions in conflict management within work teams [28]) the work team performance.

From the existent psychological theories of emotions, the cognitive appraisal theories focus on the elicitation of emotional experiences as result from constant evaluations of the subjective significance of construed situations and events, according to specific dimensions or criteria [29]. The key characteristic of these theories is that the emotional process is seen as the permanent assessment of the environment according to the person's goals, intentions and standards, i.e. *appraisal*. Due that cognitive appraisal theories are focused on emotion as a process rather than in the descriptive characterisations of emotions in dimensional or categorical models, several works in modelling human behaviour are based on these theories. One of the most influential theories for implementation in artificial systems has been the often referred as the OCC model [30]. In summary, the OCC model relates types of emotional reactions to types of emotional responses. An individual can have positive or negative reactions to a specific situation depending on how the object of the appraisal (an event, and action of somebody or an actual object) is relevant to the individual's goals, to the standards it tries to uphold, or to its tastes. The OCC model is used as the theoretical basis in several applications, and more deeply referred to model an intelligent and believable behaviour in synthetic characters [31].

The above mentioned theories, studies, and implementation works are only small evidence about the increasing interest in the study and modelling of emotions, a deeper analysis can be found in [32]. It is clear the high importance that the emotional behaviour has on the global human behaviour and the modelling of it in artificial systems has originated great efforts such as the development of new research branches (e.g. Affective Computing [33]) and large research associations (e.g. HUMAINE: http://emotion-research.net/).

3.3 Personality Traits

Another branch of the Psychology that has dedicated efforts, since long time ago, to the study of human behaviour based on the identification and classification of individual differences is Personality Psychology [34]. Due to the development of different theories of personality, there is not an achieved consensus about the definition of the concept, but the different definitions of personality have some common features. In [34], three main features are proposed: *i) uniqueness of the individual*: each person is different; *ii) uniformity of behaviour*: behaviour of the individual is consistent over time and across situations; *iv) Content and processes*: personality consists of something that influences behaviour, e.g. how our expectations in one situation influence our behaviour in others?

The different theories of personality have originated also different models containing various dimensions to assess the distinct (but consistent) styles of behaviour. In 1923 Carl Jung [35] proposed two types of attitudes in people: *extraversion* and *introversion* which modify four Jung's proposed functions of consciousness: perceiving (Sensation and Intuition) and judging (Thinking and Feeling). Other model of personality was proposed by Hans Eysenck [36] based on the biological perspective of personality. The Eysenck's model, known as the P-E-N model, initially includes two dimensions of personality: *extraversion* and *neuroticism*, adding afterwards the third *psychoticism* dimension.

Probably the most accepted (but not exempt of criticism) personality model is the known as the Big Five model [37]. The five big factors of personality, also known as the OCEAN model, include *Openness, Conscientiousness, Extroversion, Agreeableness* and *Neuroticism*.

In the context of human behaviour at work, one of the studies that have focused on the identification of the personal styles that affect the job performance and relationships is the presented in [38], where four styles of behaviour were found represented in any occupation. The four proposed patterns of behaviour at work are *Amiable*: the Relationship specialist; *Analytical*: the Technical specialist; *Driver*: the Command specialist; and *Expressive*: the Social specialist.

Regarding the influence of the personality traits within work teams, several studies have been developed to relate the different traits of personality with the team performance. A study developed with an engineering team found that team members who possess high level of conscientiousness manifested increased task performance, while those with minimum composite level of extraversion are highly successful in managing product design processes [39]. More recently, a different study was developed using 78 college students working in 10 long-standing teams competing in a business simulation, finding that emotional stability (the opposite trait of *neuroticism*) predicted task performance and agreeableness predicted cohesion within the work team [40].

It can be argued that the results obtained from the different studies largely depend on the types of activities of each work team, but it is unquestionable that the personality traits are another important factor that directs the behaviour of a person. Due to this fact, the interest to include models of personality into artificial systems has been increased in the last years (just as same as the emotions) to reproduce more realistic human behaviours. In the development of synthetic characters (more commonly known as virtual characters) different theories of personality psychology are applied to direct the behaviour of these artificial entities. Virtual characters with personality have been used for pedagogical purposes [41], the simulation of bargaining in e-commerce [42] and entertainment [43] among some others.

3.4 Trust

Additional relevant factors that directly affect human behaviour are the actions and behaviours of the other people whom the individual is interacting in its same environment. This is especially important when talking about work teams due to the importance that human relations have to achieve team-working behaviours (such as good communication and co-ordination among the team members) and are the foundation of *healthy and productive work environments* [44].

An important factor that contributes to create and maintain the productive work environments is the concept of *trust*. The increasing interest in trust within organisations could be explained as there are more and more large companies and consortiums where several people need to work together from different geographically locations. New theories and hypotheses about the thinking and functioning of organisations have been replacing traditional aspects of management by collaborative approaches emphasising ideas of coordination, sharing of responsibilities and risk taking [45]. More recently, and with the great development of applications in Internet, the interest in the study of trust has grown up and some research works put efforts towards the modelling of trust and reputation concepts addressed mainly to e-Commerce applications. Most of these models of trust and reputation use software agents as the entities where the relationship of trust takes place and is represented using specific characteristics of each model [46]. Some other models and studies have been developed in the Human Resources and Management disciplines to analyse the importance of trust within work teams and how it is related with performance effectiveness [47].

4   Conclusions

All the studies presented in this paper show the relevance of different individual attributes in the generation of human behaviour. Even that the selected set of attributes is not, of course, the complete spectrum that produces, influences and directs the human behaviour, it is at least, an important part of the complete picture and allows the study and understanding of work team dynamics.

Acknowledgments

This work has been done in the context of the project Agent-based Modelling and Simulation of Complex Social Systems (SiCoSSys), supported by Spanish Council for Science and Innovation, with grant TIN2008-06464-C03-01.

References

1. Gupta, R.P., Srivastava, S.C.: A distribution automation system Simulator for training and research. International Journal of Electrical Engineering Education 45(4), 336–355 (2008)
2. Marks, R.E.: Validating Simulation Models: A General Framework and Four Applied Examples. Computational Economics 30(3), 265–290 (2007)
3. Gilbert, N., Troitzsch, K.G.: Simulation for the Social Scientist. Open University Press, Stony Stratford (2005)
4. Gernaey, K.V., van Loosdrecht, M.C.M., Henze, M., Lind, M., Jørgensen, S.B.: Activated sludge wastewater treatment plant modeling and simulation: state of the art. Environmental Modelling and Software 9(9), 763–783 (2004)
5. Dutton, J.M., Starbuck, W.H.: Computer Simulation of Human Behaviour. John Willey, New York (1971)
6. Wetteland, C.R., Miller, J.L., French, J., O'Brian, K., Spooner, D.J.: The Human Simulation: Resolving Manning Issues Onboard DD21. In: Proc. of the 2000 Winter Simulation Conference (2000)
7. Sawaragi, T., Murasawa, K.: Simulating behaviours of human situation awareness under high workloads. Artificial Intelligence in Engineering 15(4), 365–381 (2001)
8. Martínez-Miranda, J., Pavón, J.: An Agent-Based Simulation Tool to Support Work Teams Formation. Advances in Soft Computing 50(2009), 80–89 (2008)
9. Kozine, I.: Simulation of human performance in time-pressured scenarios. Proc. of the Institution of Mechanical Engineers, Part O: Journal of Risk and Reliability 221(2), 141–151 (2007)
10. Pahl-Wost, C., Ebenhöh, E.: Heuristics to characterise human behaviour in agent based models. In: Proc. of iEMSs 2004 Int. Congress: Complexity and Integrated Resources Management (June 2004)
11. Luscombe, R., Mitchard, H.: Exploring Simple Human Behaviour Representation Using Agent Based Distillations. In: Proceedings of SimTecT 2003, Adelaide, Australia, May 26-29 (2003)
12. Wu, J., Hu, B.: Modeling and simulation of group behavior in E-Government implementation. In: Henderson, et al. (eds.) Proc. of the 2007 Winter Simulation Conference, Washington (2007)
13. Steiner, I.D.: Group process and productivity. Academic Press, New York (1972)
14. Morgeson, F.P., Reider, M.H., Campion, M.A.: Selecting Individuals in Team Settings: The Importance of Social Skills, Personality Characteristics and Teamwork Knowledge. Personnel Psychology 58(3), 583–611 (2005)
15. Thagard, P.: Mind: Introduction to Cognitive Science, 2nd edn. MIT Press, Cambridge
16. Zyphur, M.J., Bradley, J.C., Landis, R.S., Thoresen, C.J.: The Effects of Cognitive Ability and Conscientiousness on Performance Over Time: A Censored Latent Growth Model. Human Performance 21(1), 1–27 (2008)
17. Gilson, L.: Why be Creative. A Review of the Practical Outcomes Associated With Creativity at the Individual, Group, and Organizational Levels. In: Shalley, C., Zou, J. (eds.) Handbook of Organizational Creativity, pp. 303–322. Lawrence Erlbaum Associates, Mahwah (2008)
18. Shalley, C.E., Zhou, J.: Organizational Creativity Research. A Historical Overview. In: Shalley, C., Zou, J. (eds.) Handbook of Organizational Creativity, pp. 3–31. Lawrence Erlbaum Associates, Mahwah (2008)

19. Fiore, S.M., Salas, E.: Why we need team cognition. In: Salas, E., Fiore, S.M. (eds.) Team Cognition: Understanding the Factors that Drive Process and Performance, pp. 235–248. American Psychological Association, Washington (2004)

20. Paulus, P.B., Nijstad, B.A.: Group Creativity: Innovation through collaboration. Oxford University Press, New York (2003)

21. Gray, J., Braver, T., Raichele, M.: Integration of Emotion and Cognition in the Lateral Prefrontal Cortex. In: Proceedings of the National Academy of Sciences USA, pp. 4115–4120 (2002)

22. Mayer, J.D., Caruso, D., Salovey, P.: Emotional intelligence meets traditional standards for an intelligence. Intelligence 27, 267–298 (1999)

23. Allen, N.J., Meyer, J.P.: The measurement and antecedents of affective, continuance and normative commitment to the organization. Journal of Occupational Psychology 63, 1–18 (1990)

24. George, J.M., Brief, A.P.: Motivational agendas in the workplace: The effects of feelings on focus of attention and work motivation. Research in Organizational Behavior 18, 75–109 (1996)

25. Rafaeli, A., Sutton, R.I.: The expression of emotion in organizational life. Research in Organizational Behavior 11, 1–42 (1989)

26. Jordan, P.J., Lawrence, S.A.: The impact of negative mood on team performance. Journal of Management & Organization 12(2), 131–145 (2006)

27. Duffy, M.K., Shaw, J.D.: The Salieri syndrome: Consequences of envy in groups. Small Group Research 31, 3–23 (2000)

28. Desivilya, H.S., Yagil, D.: The Role of Emotions in Conflict Management: The Case of Work Teams. In: IACM 17th Annual Conference Paper, SSRN: http://ssrn.com/abstract=602041

29. Scherer, K.R.: Psychological models of emotion. In: Borod, J.C. (ed.) The Neuropsychology of Emotion, pp. 137–162. Oxford University Press, New York (2000)

30. Ortony, A., Clore, G.L., Collins, A.: The Cognitive Structure of Emotions. Cambridge University Press, Cambridge (1988)

31. Taihua, L., Yuhui, Q., Peng, Y., Guoxiang, Z.: Exploiting Model of Personality and Emotion of Learning Companion Agent. In: Int. Conf. on Computer Systems and Applications, pp. 860–865 (2007)

32. Martínez-Miranda, J., Aldea, A.: Emotions in Human and Artificial Intelligence. Computers in Human Behaviour Journal 21(2) (March 2005)

33. Picard, R.W.: Affective Computing. MIT Press, Cambridge (1997)

34. Carducci, B.J.: The Psychology of Personality, 2nd edn. Wiley-Blackwell (2009)

35. Jung, C.G.: Psychological Types. In: Collected Works of C.G. Jung, vol. 6. Princeton University Press, Princeton (August 1, 1971)

36. Eysenck, H.: Dimensions of Personality. Trubner & Co., Ltd., Kegan Paul (1947)

37. Goldberg, L.R.: The Structure of Phenotypic Personality Traits. American Psychologist 48(1), 26–34 (1993)

38. Merrill, D.W., Reid, R.H.: Personal Styles & Effective Performance. CRC Press LLC, Boca Raton (1999)

39. Kichuk, S.L., Wiesner, W.H.: The Big Five personality factors and team performance: implications for selecting successful product design teams. Journal of Engineering and Technology Management 14(3), 195–221 (1997)

40. O'Neill, T.A., Kline, T.J.B.: Personality as predictor of teamwork: a business simulator study. North American Journal of Psychology (March 1, 2008)

41. Martínez-Miranda, J., Jung, B., Payr, S., Petta, P.: The Intermediary Agent's Brain: Supporting Learning to Collaborate at the Inter-Personal Level. In: Proceedings of the 7th Conference on Autonomous Agents and Multiagent Systems AAMAS 2008, vol. 3, pp. 1277–1280 (2008)
42. Nassiri-Mofakham, F., Ghasem-Aghaee, N., Ali Nematbakhsh, M., Baraani-Dastjerdi, A.: A personality-based simulation of bargaining in e-commerce. Simulation Gaming 39(1), 83–100 (2008)
43. Campano, S., Sabouret, N.: A socio-emotional model of impoliteness for non-player characters. In: Proceedings of AAMAS 2009, vol. 2 (2009)
44. Pyoria, P.: Information technology, human relations and knowledge work teams. Team Performance Management 11(3-4), 104–112 (2005)
45. Vangen, S., Huxham, C.: Nurturing Collaborative Relations: Building Trust in Interorganizational Collaboration. J. of App. Behavioral Science 39(1), 5–31 (2003)
46. Sabater, J., Sierra, C.: Review on Computational Trust and Reputation Models. Artificial Intelligence Review 24(1), 33–60 (2005)
47. Costa, A.C.: Work team trust and effectiveness. Personnel Review 32(5), 605–622 (2003)

Metamodelling for Agent Based Modelling: An Application for Continuous Double Auctions

Rubén Fuentes-Fernández[1], José M. Galán[2], Samer Hassan[1], Juan Pavón[1], and Felix A. Villafañez[3]

[1] GRASIA, Universidad Complutense de Madrid, Spain
{ruben,samer,jpavon}@fdi.ucm.es
[2] INSISOC, Universidad de Burgos, Spain
jmgalan@ubu.es
[3] INSISOC, Universidad de Valladolid, Spain
villafafelix@eis.uva.es

Abstract. Agent-Based Modelling is gaining wider acceptance as a paradigm for social research. However, it still present limitations in the management of the process to generate the simulations from the initial conceptual models. Thus, it is difficult to reuse the knowledge from available models and adapt it to different hypotheses. This paper proposes the use of metamodels in order to define explicitly the core concepts of a problem and to differentiate the aspects involved in the process. A case study for continuous double auctions shows how to define the related metamodel and use it to address alternative situations in these auctions. The case study drives the discussion on the advantages and limitations that metamodelling can bring to social simulation.

1 Introduction

Agent-Based Modelling (ABM) has become over the past years a widely used technique for research in Social Sciences [4]. One of its key advantages lies on its core abstractions for modelling, i.e. agents and their societies. Agents are intentional and social entities, which are capable of rational and complex individual behaviour. As they share these features with humans, they are expected to facilitate the specification of the human target systems. Besides, these abstractions can be refined with concepts closer to the target simulation platforms, bridging the gap between the conceptual models and the simulation ones.

The actual use of agent-based models still has a lot of room for improvement [1]. The situation in which agents constitute general and reusable modelling primitives for ABM, with standardise processes to translate them to simulation models has not been reached. In fact, researchers in ABM have different perspectives on what agents are. Moreover, they do not tend to follow a clear translation of those perspectives in their formal agent models, frequently adopting ad-hoc translations of them in the simulation code.

In order to address these limitations, some researchers [7, 12] have proposed the use of metamodelling techniques. Metamodels define modelling languages, which

Á. Ortiz Bas, R.D. Franco, P. Gómez Gasquet (Eds.): BASYS 2010, IFIP AICT 322, pp. 285–292, 2010.

describe the modelling primitives available to describe a problem. Researchers create their models instantiating these primitives. If required, they can use extension mechanisms to modify the language in a controlled way, introducing new elements.

This approach has several advantages. Firstly, metamodels can be processed by software tools. This allows, for instance, the building of graphical editors for these models, and to provide automated transformations that partly carry out the propagation of information from abstract formal models to actual simulations. This tool support reduces the probability of making unintended mistakes when modelling and provides the basis for comparison (and thus replication) among works.

The main obstacle to apply this approach is to define suitable metamodels. There is an inherent difficulty in capturing the knowledge to describe complete domains of problems with a formal definition. A metamodel must be rich enough to capture all the variability of a domain, but also to constrain modellers to produce correct models that can be translated to simulation code in a semi-automated way.

Our work attempts to provide guidelines, intermediate languages for metamodelling in ABM and software tools that facilitate the definition of these metamodels. In order to illustrate this approach, this paper discusses the formalisation of the well-known problem of continuous double auctions.

The rest of the paper is organised as follows. Section 2 provides a brief introduction on ABM. Section 3 considers how our approach use metamodels in ABM and Section 4 applies such approach to model auctions. Finally, Section 5 discusses the implications of the process together with some concluding remarks.

2 Related Work

ABM describes models for social analysis using agents as the key abstraction. The complete process entails different stages of designing, implementing and using agent-based models. Initial steps usually begin with non-formal conceptualizations of the target system that successively are refined to shape a formal model that can be computationally implemented. This process is often got around in literature and only few works explore the migration from conceptualisations to formal models.

[12] considers the problems emerging from the usual lack of background in software programming of social researchers and the difficulties to compare similar models implemented over different platforms. They propose adapting the model-driven engineering methodology INGENIAS [10], which focuses on the development of Multi-Agent Systems (MAS). Their approach extends the INGENIAS modelling language with additional primitives for specific problems. It also uses the INGENIAS process to generate the simulation source code. The main limitation of this work is its use of predefined extension mechanisms of the INGENIAS language, with concepts with an inherent software bias, which are not very appropriate for social researchers.

[7] defines a MDE approach for ABM. Its language has as core concept the *Mentat*, an agent skeleton with mental properties that researchers can extend for their models. The main issue of this work is that it is constrained to data-driven simulation, which complicates its application for other kind of problems.

Looking to overcome these limitations, our approach tries to achieve a MDE approach for ABM with two main features: it must be adaptable to different agent-oriented approaches and support alternative uses of models and their reuse.

3 INGENIAS Metamodels for ABM

INGENIAS [10] is a software development methodology for MAS. It adopts a MDE approach with two basic components: a modelling language and software tools.

A metamodel specifies the INGENIAS modelling language. It defines the available concepts and relationships, together with their properties and constraints. As it is aimed for modelling MAS, it includes the concepts of agent and group. An agent is characterised in terms of its goals and the capabilities it has to accomplish them. Groups include agents and external resources, coined environment applications, that agents can use. Agents participate in interactions with other agents to achieve global goals. Models can also include code components to specify low-level details that depend on the platform, such as formulas about preference policies or location algorithms.

The INGENIAS Development Kit (IDK) software tool allows processing models with their modules. Standard modules available with the distribution support model auto-completion for certain tasks, documentation and code generation. Both of them require the availability of templates. A template gives a general description of a primitive available for modelling with slots that are instantiated with information of specific elements in models. For instance, researchers building a simulation for the MASON platform [9] specify a general template for a MASON agent; when generating code, the IDK instantiates that template with the information of every agent in the specification, generating the source code for those specific agents. The IDK allows the development of new modules that access and change its models, so automated transformations can be adapted to the researcher needs.

The approach of this work uses these elements to provide domain-specific modelling languages and tools, with guidelines for their use [8]. It modifies the INGENIAS metamodel in order to include more flexible extension mechanisms. In particular, inheritance relationships are allowed for any concept, so it can be tailored with additional properties and constraints in common models, without changes in the metamodel. Inheritance implies that a concept acquires all the features of its super-concept. Moreover, it adopts a more declarative approach concerning the tool. It specifies transformations with transformation languages instead of code, which provides a definition closer to the artefacts (i.e. metamodels, models, grammars, code...) that these transformations manipulate. Besides, it proposes developing model transformations (i.e. those that only involve models) with a Model Transformation by Example (MTBE) approach. MTBE [3] defines transformations through prototype pairs of source and target models compliant with certain metamodels. A MTBE tool processes these pairs and automatically generates the resulting transformation. The final component of the approach is a process to guide researchers in the application of this framework [8]. The case study chosen here illustrates this to show the advantages and current limitations of the work.

These decisions are expected to increase the autonomy of social researchers. The final goal is that they mostly develop their models autonomously, requiring only the support of engineers to address new and not-considered features of the domain.

4 Case Study: Continuous Double Auction

4.1 Case Study: Continuous Double Auction

In order to illustrate the exposed approach, this paper considers an auction as paradigmatic case in Economics, in particular the Continuous Double Auction (CDA). As CDA is one of the institutions used more often for real trading, it has been thoroughly analyzed from the experimental and computational point of view [11]; it is also complex enough to exemplify the capabilities of metamodelling. CDA fixes the *Institution* in the triplet IEA (Institution x Environment x Agent's behaviour) that defines any market [13]. This study takes into account the other two dimensions from the classical work of Gode and Sunder [5, 6] where zero-intelligence agents interact in using a single unit per trader. The main features of this CDA are described below.

The CDA considers buyers and sellers. All the sellers are endowed with a unit of a good that is indistinguishable from any other; the buyers want to obtain a unit of this good. The decisions of sellers and buyers depend on certain private values. Each buyer agent is informed of a redemption value v according to a demand function unknown for the other players. The profit obtained by a buyer that buys the good at a price p is v-p. Similarly, each seller agent is endowed with a cost c for the unit of the good. The profit obtain by a seller that sells the good at price p is p-c.

From the point of view of the institution, the auction runs as follows. Any buyer can send a "bid" for a single unit by stating its identity and price. Any buyer can raise this bid. Correspondingly, any seller can "ask" (offer) by stating its identity and price. If asks and bids match or cross, a transaction takes place and both, buyer and seller, leave the market cancelling any unaccepted bids and asks. In the case that a bid and ask do not match but cross, the transaction price is equal to the earlier of the two. After this, the process begins again with the remaining agents. The whole procedure is run several periods of specified duration.

The agents considered in this version [6] are zero-intelligence traders subject to a budget constraint (ZI-C agents). This implies that after a certain amount of time, either a buyer or seller randomly forms a bid or an ask. A seller forms an ask price between its cost and a maximum value (usually the maximum redemption value). A buyer forms a bid price between its redemption value and 0. These constraints suppress the possibility for agents to have losses.

In the game dynamics, each buyer compares its bid with the current state of the market. If its bid is above the best ask, it accepts the best ask and the transaction occurs, while the state of the market is updated. If the buyer's bid is below the best ask and above the best bid or there is not any ask yet, that bid becomes the current best bid; otherwise, in the case that the buyer's bid is below the best bid and according to the auction rules, the agent does not send the bid. The asking process is analogous in the case of sellers.

4.2 Metamodelling

The process proposed in [8] comprehends two main stages: the identification of the core concepts of the domain and the description of their standard interactions. The metamodel for the problem describes these elements as extensions of the primitives available in INGENIAS [10].

INGENIAS has two main components that can perform tasks: *agents* are proactive entities able to initiate tasks following their own and explicit agenda; *applications* are usually reactive (i.e. used by agents), though they can raise events in case of changes in the environment. Agents that share an application belong to the same *group*, and when they also share knowledge, procedures and rules, to the same *organisation*.

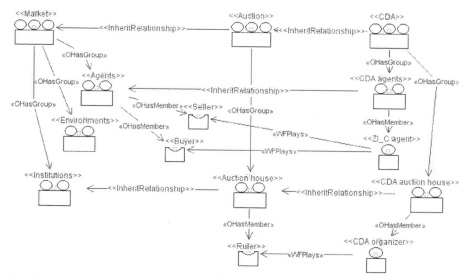

Fig. 1. Partial metamodel for the structural components of the CDA. Stereotypes (i.e. names between guillemets) denote types of entities and relationships.

Fig. 1 illustrates part of the hierarchies of elements proposed for the modelling language of CDA. Following [13], the basis of the hierarchies is the *market* that determines the *institutions*, the *environments* and the *agents*. Agents in market can play two roles, *buyer* and *seller*, which are not exclusive. The *auction* is a particular type of market. The diagram shows this through the *InheritRelationship* between these concepts. The auction is characterised for its institution, the *auction house*. A *ruler* governs this house and implements the common rules for auctions (e.g. turns between buyers and sellers, transactions, availability of goods, or relationships between bids and asks). The most specific market in this hierarchy is the CDA. Following [6], this auction uses a particular type of agents (i.e. *ZI_C agents*) to play the two roles in the group agents of the market. The CDA also adds a specific *CDA organiser* agent to play the ruler role and tailor the institutional behaviour to the norms of CDA.

In this case, there is no need to identify external entities. In order to keep the model simple for this discussion, this metamodel does not explicitly represents the units of goods. These are represented as attributes of the traders. The internal values of these agents (i.e. the redemption and cost value) are also represented as a unique limit value attribute. These attributes appear in Fig. 3 as the components *good units* and *value limit* of the internal state of the ZI_C agent.

The next step is refining the agents and roles in Fig. 1. This refinement implies defining their goals and the capabilities they have available in order to achieve them. Roles define the general features of these elements, which agents implement with specific policies. Fig. 2 shows them for the buyer role. It pursues the goal *acquire good*, which requires stating bids and accepting some of the asks when they are suitable according to its internal demand function. These goals are achieved through two tasks, *generate bid* and *accept ask* respectively.

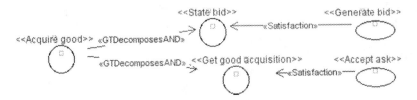

Fig. 2. Goals and tasks for the buyer role and their relationships

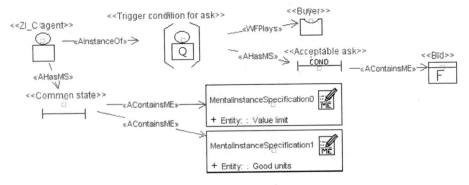

Fig. 3. Mental states for the buyer

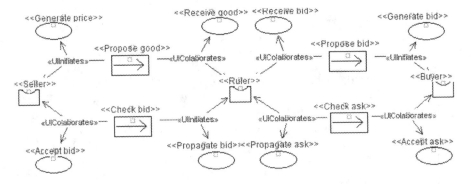

Fig. 4. Metamodel for interactions. Roles execute the activities that trigger the communications represented by the arrows.

Besides specifying the involved goals and tasks, roles need to describe when they initiate the tasks and when the goals are satisfied according to the current system state. Fig. 3 shows an example of these specifications. The *trigger condition for ask* is an instance of the internal state of the ZI_C agent that indicates when the task *accept ask* can be initiated. The condition states that the agent must be playing the role buyer and there must be a bid. The specific condition involving the bid and the limit value of the agent would be recorded in the *acceptable ask*. It can be specified, for instance, as formulae or code. The metamodel could include additional primitives to describe this condition, although it is not advisable: there must be a trade-off between the expressiveness of the language and its value to present a synthesised vision of the problem. Adding primitives to the low-level details would make specifications too verbose, losing their abstraction value.

The final element of the specifications is the interactions describing how agents and roles participate in the global activity of the system. Fig. 4 shows an excerpt involving the previous element and also showing the participation of the ruler.

5   Conclusion and Discussion

This paper has presented the definition of a metamodel that defines a modelling language for CDA. This metamodel illustrates our vision that ABM can benefit from an explicit definition of its modelling languages in several ways: facilitating the specification of problems, their translation to code and the analysis of their results.

Several classical works on CDA have been the basis to identify the key concepts present in this kind of auctions, the attributes that determine their behaviour and their interaction. These elements have been structurally formalised as roles and agents, their goals and capabilities, and groups and organisations. The dynamic behaviour of these elements in auctions has been established through satisfaction relationships between tasks and goals, together with particular conditions, as those used for triggering a task. This metamodel shows the common participants in auctions with the components that researchers need to specify and test different hypotheses. For instance, CDA does not require their agents being zero-intelligence traders; if other traders are going to be tested, researchers may need to add new attributes. Those would participate in conditions or change specific tasks, but the defined roles, interactions and groups would remain unchanged. Besides, the metamodel can define the well-formedness rules for models, allowing the checking of modelling mistakes. For instance, if the model does not include the participation of the buyer proposing bids, it should be revised and corrected.

As stated in sections 1 and 2, the formal models of auctions facilitate applying standardised transformations. Transformations are used to check complex errors, generate documentation, translate them to another modelling language, generate source code, or output result data from models. For instance, a transformation could check that all the traders are going to participate in at least two different auctions if researchers decide so. These transformations are developed and refined over different projects, fixing the potential errors and simplifying the processing.

These advantages are expected to make researchers more autonomous and productive in ABM. These are two necessary conditions to mitigate the main drawbacks of the approach: the high costs of development models and the difficulties to guarantee that the final simulation models are a close translation of the original conceptual models.

References

1. Edmonds, B.: The Use of Models - Making MABS More Informative. In: Moss, S., Davidsson, P. (eds.) MABS 2000. LNCS (LNAI), vol. 1979, pp. 15–32. Springer, Heidelberg (2001)
2. France, R., Rumpe, B.: Model-driven Development of Complex Software: A Research Roadmap. In: 2007 Future of Software Engineering (FOSE 2007), pp. 37–54. IEEE Computer Society, Los Alamitos (2007)
3. García-Magariño, I., Rougemaille, S., Fuentes-Fernández, R., Migeon, F., Gleizes, M.P.: A Tool for Generating Model Transformations By-Example in Multi-Agent Systems. In: Demazeau, Y., Pavón, J., Corchado, J.M., Bajo, J. (eds.) Proceedings of the 7th International Conference on Practical Applications of Agents and Multi-Agent Systems (PAAMS 2009), Advances in Soft Computing, vol. 55, pp. 70–79. Springer, Heidelberg (2009)
4. Gilbert, N., Troitzsch, K.G.: Simulation for the social scientist. Open University Press, Buckingham (1999)
5. Gode, D.K., Sunder, S.: Allocative Efficiency of Markets with Zero-Intelligence Traders - Market as a Partial Substitute for Individual Rationality. Journal of Political Economy 101(1), 119–137 (1993)
6. Gode, D.K., Sunder, S.: Lower Bounds for Efficiency of Surplus Extraction in Double Auctions. In: Friedman, D., Rust, J. (eds.) Proceedings of The Double Auction Market: Institutions, Theories, and Evidence. Santa Fe Institute Series in the Sciences of the Complexity, vol. XV, pp. 199–219 (1993)
7. Hassan, S., Antunes, L., Pavón, J.: Mentat: A Data-Driven Agent-Based Simulation of Social Values Evolution. In: Multi-Agent-Based Simulation X. LNCS. Springer, Heidelberg (2010) (in Press)
8. Hassan, S., Fuentes-Fernández, R., Galán, J.M., López-Paredes, A., Pavón, J.: Reducing the Modeling Gap: On the use of metamodels in agent-based simulation. In: 6th Conference of the European Social Simulation Association (ESSA 2009), pp. 1–13 (2009)
9. Luke, S., Cioffi-Revilla, C., Panait, L., Sullivan, K., Balan, G.: MASON: A Multiagent Simulation Environment. Simulation 81(7), 517–527 (2005)
10. Pavón, J., Gómez-Sanz, J.J., Fuentes, R.: The INGENIAS Methodology and Tools. In: Henderson-Sellers, B., Giorgini, P. (eds.) Agent-Oriented Methodologies, ch. IX, pp. 236–276. Idea Group Publishing (2005)
11. Posada, M., López-Paredes, A.: How to choose the bidding strategy in continuous double auctions: Imitation versus take-the-best heuristics. Journal of Artificial Societies and Social Simulation 11(1), 6 (2008)
12. Sansores, C., Pavón, J.: Agent-Based Simulation Replication: A Model Driven Architecture Approach. In: Gelbukh, A., de Albornoz, Á., Terashima-Marín, H. (eds.) MICAI 2005. LNCS (LNAI), vol. 3789, pp. 244–253. Springer, Heidelberg (2005)
13. Smith, V.L.: Microeconomic Systems as an Experimental Science. American Economic Review 72(5), 923–955 (1982)
14. Wilensky, U., Rand, W.: Making Models Match: Replicating an Agent-Based Model. Journal of Artificial Societies and Social Simulation 10(4), 2 (2007)

Price-Setting Combinatorial Auctions for Coordination and Control of Manufacturing Multiagent Systems: Updating Prices Methods

Juan José Lavios Villahoz[1], Ricardo del Olmo Martínez[1],
and Alberto Arauzo Arauzo[2]

[1] INSISOC, Escuela Politécnica Superior, Universidad de Burgos
Avda, Cantabria s/n, 09006, Burgos, Spain
{jjlavios,rdelolmo}@ubu.es
[2] INSISOC, ETSII Universidad de Valladolid
Pº del Cauce s/n, 47011 Valladolid, Spain
arauzo@insisoc.org

Abstract. Combinatorial auctions are used as a distributed coordination mechanism in Multiagent Systems. The use of combinatorial auctions as negotiation and coordination mechanism is especially appropriate in systems with interdependencies and complementarities such as manufacturing scheduling systems. In this work we review some updating price mechanisms for combinatorial auctions based on the Lagrangian Relaxation Method. We focus our research to solve the optimization scheduling problem in the shop floor, taking into account the objectives of resource allocation in dynamic environments, i.e. -robustness, stability, adaptability, and efficiency-.

Keywords: Multiagent Systems, Combinatorial Auction, Lagrangian Relaxation.

1 Introduction

Scheduling is a decision-making problem devoted to allocate resources on tasks to optimize one or several objectives. Manufacturing and production systems are some of the most known fields of application of this problem. In this context, operations of a given production process are considered as tasks and the different machines in a workshop are considered the resources [1]. This problem is characterized by its highly combinatorial and dynamic nature and its practical interest for industrial applications [2].

Multiagent Systems (MAS) have been proved to be an appropriate paradigm to model complex systems and they constitute a useful framework to define distributed decision-making processes. In this specific domain, agents are used to encapsulate physical and logical entities or even autonomous functionalities of the production systems. The ability of MAS to perceive and react to changes in their environment justifies their use as adaptive systems in manufacturing (some recent reviews in the field can be found in [3], [4] or [5].

Á. Ortiz Bas, R.D. Franco, P. Gómez Gasquet (Eds.): BASYS 2010, IFIP AICT 322, pp. 293–300, 2010.
© IFIP International Federation for Information Processing 2010

2   Market Based Coordination Mechanisms and Combinatorial Auctions

Distributed decision making through MAS are considered an alternative to centralized scheduling systems. They facilitate to take into account local objectives, preferences and constraints of each resource in the decision making process [6]. Combination of individual problem-solving and coordination/negotiation schemes is one of the research challenges in this area [3].

Market based allocation mechanisms are one of the most active branches of decentralized scheduling research. The underlying idea is to allocate resources among tasks by designing an ad-hoc market and setting prices iteratively to find the equilibrium. The process involves the creation of a production schedule based on the prices emerging from the bids sent by tasks. The goal is to design a bid structure and a selling mechanism that leads to an optimal scheduling of resources on a shop floor.

According to [7], the main features of a decentralized scheduling problem are: First, each individual decision-maker follow its own objectives, but coordination will be enabled by prices. Second, decision-makers may have their own private information, such as their valuations of objects, and have no access to the private information of others (objectives, preferences and constraints). Third, complex calculations are distributed among the participating agents, so that the problem is divided into several easier problems which can be solved in parallel, and hence calculations can be sped up. Fourth, the communication overhead is low since it is limited to the exchange of bids and prices between agents and the market mechanism.

Combinatorial auctions have been used as a market mechanism to create schedules. One of the earliest works in this area has been developed by [8]. Combinatorial auction is a type of auction in which participants can place bids on combinations of items rather than just individual items or continuous quantities. Economic efficiency is enhanced if bidders are allowed to bid on bundles of different items when there are complementarities between the different items, [9]. The use of combinatorial auctions as negotiation and coordination mechanism is appropriate in problems in which the value of interdependent items needs to be considered.

Manufacturing scheduling problem presents complementarities. For instance, jobs are required to bid for continuous time slots on a resource (non-preemption constraints) and each job is required to participate in multiple auctions for its different operations, however all these operations have precedence constraints. We use a combinatorial auction-based mechanism to coordinate agents.

Combinatorial auctions can be divided into single round and iterative combinatorial auctions. In single round auctions participants send their valuations over the combinations of products just one time and the auctioneer allocate the items in such a way that the global objective is maximized. On the contrary, in iterative combinatorial auctions prices are fixed after multiple rounds. There are some advantages of using iterative combinatorial auctions instead of single round ones. First, participants do not have to make bids over the set of all possible combinations of bids. Second, participants reveal in each iteration their private information and preferences. Third, iterative auctions are well-suited for dynamic environments (e.g. manufacturing environments) where participants and items get in and out in different moments.

There are two kinds of iterative combinatorial auctions: quantity-setting and price-setting. In the fist one, bidders send their valuation over every possible combination of the items sold. The auctioneer makes a provisional allocation that depends on the submitted prices. Bidders adjust the prices at every iteration. In the second one, price-setting, (or demand query) auctioneer sets the prices for each of the items of the auction. Bidders submit the bundle of items they want to get at the given price. Auctioneer adapts the prices to balance the supply and demand [9].

3   Combinatorial Auctions and Lagrange Relaxation Techniques

The updating methods used in the Lagrangian Relaxation Method to solve the dual problem can be used to update prices in iterative combinatorial auctions, since they share the same structure in their protocols [10]. Auction protocols can be implemented in a non-adaptive standard Walrasian fashion, or as an adaptive tâtonement (price adjustment process). The subgradient optimization can be viewed as a particular version of the tâtonement proccess. While the subgradient optimization tries to penalize infeasibility of dualized constraints and the auctioneer updates the resource prices as to discourage conflicts on the demanded objects, the subgradient algorithm adjusts the prices proportional to the amount of infeasibility and the auction algorithm updates the prices proportional to the excess of demand [6]. Lagrangian relaxation technique relaxes the complex constraints of an optimization problem (i.e. those constraints which make the problem hard to solve), making the problem easier to optimize. The group of relaxed constraints is incorporated to the objective function in such a way that the restrictions that are not fulfilled are penalized. The new objective function is called Lagrangian function. The Lagrangian problem solution is always lower or equal to the solution of the original problem [11]. The iterative process will approach the solution of the Lagrangian problem to the solution of the original problem.

4   Price Setting Iterative Combinatorial Auction

The task scheduling problem can be modeled as an auction where time horizon is divided into slots that are sold through the auction. Tasks participate in the auction as bidders, trying to get the time slots of the resources that they need to perform the operation [10](See Fig. 1). We will relax the constraints that relies on variables belonging to different jobs. Our aim is to divide a complex problem into several easier ones. If we eliminate the restriction of capacity of the resources, we will be able to split the problem into N job subproblems. The mechanism will follow the main principles of distributed systems since the relevant information of the bidders (i.e. due date of the jobs, penalty for the delays, resources needed) will be hidden to the rest of agents [12]. None of the agents knows which other agents belong to the system nor what are the goals of those agents. Prices show the preferences of other agents, providing information to the agent to act consequently. This mechanism have been used to solve different kind of task scheduling problem, e.g. job shop problem [13], [14], flow shop problem [15], or project management [16], [17].

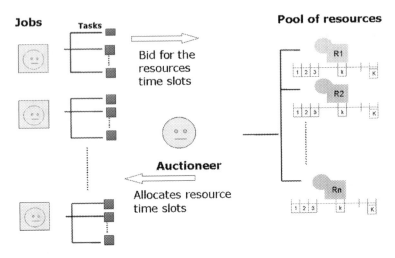

Fig. 1. Auction-based scheduling mechanism

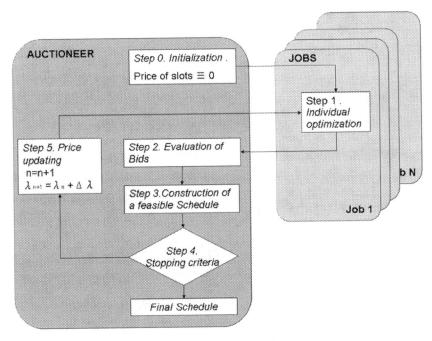

Fig. 2. Price-setting iterative combinatorial auction

It can be described as follows: There exists a central pool of resources (Resource-agent). Each resource has different abilities. The planning horizon of the resource is divided into time slots. These time slots are sold in an auction. Several jobs have to be completed (Job-agents). The jobs need to get the necessary resources to be finished before their due date. Job-agents bid for the time slot of the resources. They try to minimize their cost function. An agent acts as a central node (Auctioneer-agent). The bids sent by Job-agents are received by the Auctioneer-agent, who will update the prices of the slots. Once known the new prices, the Job-agents will remake their bids. This iterative process continues until prices are stabilized or a stop condition is fulfilled. (See fig. 2)

Job-agents are price-takers in the model (See fig. 3). Price is fixed by an iterative process. The prices of the slots are raised or lowered by a walrasian mechanism. The auctioneer compares the demand over a time slot of a resource with the capacity of the resource in this time slot. if there is an excess demand, the auctioneer raises prices. On the other hand, if there is an excess of capacity he lowers them.

$$\lambda^{n+1} = \lambda^n + \Delta\lambda$$

There are many ways to update prices (e.g. constant increase or decrease of prices, proportional to the demand, proportional to the excess of demand).

5   Updating Prices Methods

Subgradient method [18], [11], [19]: It is the method most commonly used to solve the relaxed (dual) problem. Each bidder sends the bundle of time slots that maximizes its utility. Auctioneer computes the excess demand (subgradient) and updates time slots prices along the subgradient. A lower bound of the optimal scheduling cost can be obtained from the dual problem resolution process. Although it is used by many practitioners for its simplicity and low computational overhead, it has many drawbacks: Multipliers zigzag along ridges (intersection of several facets) of the dual function. It suffers from slow convergence, and it can be difficult to solve all the suproblems in big size problems.

Aiming to improve the performance of the subgradient method, [20] developed the conjugate gradient method, also used in [21], [22] or [23] by following a modified gradient step direction that is calculated as a linear combination of the actual vector of excess demand and the precedent modified gradient step direction. It reduces zigzagging with respect to subgradient method.

The surrogate gradient method [24], [25] is based on the idea that it is not necessary to get the best directions to reach the optimum of the dual function. Good directions can be obtained with much less effort. The bundles of time slots sent by the bidders do not have to maximize its utility; they just have to improve the utility of the bidder with respect to the previous bids at the given prices. This method is useful for large problems having many complicated subproblems. The main disadvantage of this method is that the surrogate dual cost is not always a lower bound to the optimal scheduling cost.

The interleaved subgradient is a special case of the surrogate method [26], [13], [24]. Only one subproblem per iteration is solved to obtain a direction and to update the multipliers. The method is called random interleaved subgradient if this process is done in a non predefined order. This idea is attractive for real dynamic environments, where real time dynamics have to be considered. The directions obtained are also smooth for large problems, leading to better performance.

The fuzzy subgradient [27] aims to make use of all the information generated in the job sub-problem resolution. It takes not only optimal solutions of the job sub-problems, but also near optimal solutions combining them to generate "fuzzy gradients". This method reduces the solution zigzagging without much additional computational requirements.

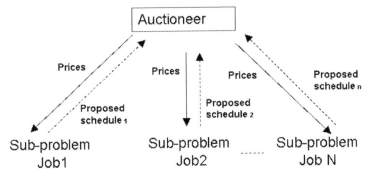

Fig. 3. Problem-solution schema

6 Research Line and Future Work

We search an updating price method for combinatorial auction that meets the requirements of scheduling manufacturing systems in dynamic environments, i.e. they are intended to offer robustness, stability, adaptability, and efficient use of available resources through a modular and distributed design [5]. To the best of our knowledge, currently there is no work which compares the updating prices methods of combinatorial auctions for Job Shop problem.. In our work we will use a specific problem as Job Shop scheduling problem, but we want to extend the conclusions that we will obtain to other problems of the same nature. Our objective is to compare the different methods of updating prices based on those that update the Lagrangian problem.

We will define and implement a distributed task scheduling system based on the Job Shop Problem [1]. We want to compare the different methods of updating prices using as criteria convergence, stability and other points to study in a real case implementation as asynchronous computation. We will use different benchmark as we can find in [28] and the modifications suggested in [29].

Acknowledgements

This work has been partially supported Caja de Burgos through Projects 2009/00199/001 and 2009/00148/001.

References

1. Pinedo, E.P.M.L.: Scheduling, 2nd edn. Springer, New York (2008)
2. Shen, W.: Distributed manufacturing scheduling using intelligent agents. Intelligent Systems 17(1), 88–94 (2002)

3. Shen, W., et al.: Applications of agent-based systems in intelligent manufacturing: An updated review. Advanced Engineering Informatics 20(4), 415–431 (2006)
4. Lee, J.-H., Kim, C.-O.: Multi-agent systems applications in manufacturing systems and supply chain management: a review paper. International Journal of Production Research 46(1), 233–265 (2008)
5. Ouelhadj, D., Petrovic, S.: A survey of dynamic scheduling in manufacturing systems. Journal of Scheduling 12(4), 417–431 (2009)
6. Kutanoglu, E., Wu, S.D.: On combinatorial auction and Lagrangean relaxation for distributed resource scheduling. IIE Transactions 31(9), 813–826 (1999)
7. Wellman, M.P.: A Market-Oriented Programming Environment and its Application to Distributed Multicommodity Flow Problems. Journal of Artificial Intelligence Research 1, 1–23 (1993)
8. Rassenti, S., Smith, V., Bulfin, R.: A Combinatorial Auction Mechanism for Airport Time Slot Allocation. The Bell Journal of Economics 13(2), 402–417 (1982)
9. de Vries, S., Vohra, R.V.: Combinatorial Auctions: A Survey. Informs Journal on Computing 15(3), 284–309 (2003)
10. Dewan, P., Joshi, S.: Auction-based distributed scheduling in a dynamic job shop environment. International Journal of Production Research 40(5), 1173–1191 (2002)
11. Fisher, M.L.: The Lagrangian Relaxation Method for Solving Integer Programming Problems. Management Science 50(12 Suppl.), 1861–1871 (2004)
12. Duffie, N.A.: Synthesis of heterarchical manufacturing systems. Comput. Ind. 14(1-3), 167–174 (1990)
13. Kaskavelis, C.A., Caramanis, M.C.: Efficient Lagrangian relaxation algorithms for industry size job-shop scheduling problems. IIE Transactions 30(11), 1085–1097 (1998)
14. Sun, T., Luh, P., Liu, M.: Lagrangian relaxation for complex job shop scheduling. In: Proceedings 2006 IEEE International Conference on En Robotics and Automation, ICRA 2006, pp. 1432–1437 (2006)
15. Tang, L., Xuan, H., Liu, J.: A new Lagrangian relaxation algorithm for hybrid flowshop scheduling to minimize total weighted completion time. Computers & Operations Research 33(11), 3344–3359 (2006)
16. Ni, M., Luh, P., Moser, B.: An Optimization-Based Approach for Design Project Scheduling. IEEE Transactions on Automation Science and Engineering 5(3), 394–406 (2008)
17. Arauzo, J., et al.: Gestión eficiente de carteras de proyectos. Propuesta de un sistema inteligente de soporte a la decisión para oficinas técnicas y empresas consultoras= efficient projet porfolio management. And intelligent decision system for engineering and consultancy firms. Dyna 84(9), 761–772 (2009)
18. Geoffrion, A.M.: Lagrangean relaxation for integer programming. In: En Approaches to Integer Programming, pp. 82–114 (1974)
19. Guignard, M.: Lagrangean relaxation. TOP 11(2), 151–200 (2003)
20. Camerini, P.M., Fratta, L., Maffioli, F.: On improving relaxation methods by modified gradient techniques. En Nondifferentiable Optimization, 26–34 (1975)
21. Crowder, H.: Computational Improvements for Subgradient Optimization. In: Symposia Mathematica, pp. 357–372. Academic Press, New York (1976)
22. Brännlund, U.: A generalized subgradient method with relaxation step. Mathematical Programming 71(2), 207–219 (1995)
23. Wang, J., et al.: An optimization-based algorithm for job shop scheduling. SADHANA 22, 241–256 (1997)

24. Zhao, X., Luh, P., Wang, J.: The surrogate gradient algorithm for Lagrangian relaxation method. In: Proceedings of the 36th IEEE Conference on Decision and Control, vol. 1, pp. 305–310 (1997)
25. Chen, H., Luh, P.: An alternative framework to Lagrangian relaxation approach for job shop scheduling. European Journal of Operational Research 149(3), 499–512 (2003)
26. Zhao, X., Luh, P.B., Wang, J.: Surrogate Gradient Algorithm for Lagrangian Relaxation. Journal of Optimization Theory and Applications 100(3), 699–712 (1999)
27. Zhao, X., Luh, P.: Fuzzy gradient method in Lagrangian relaxation for integer programming problems. In: Proceedings of the 37th IEEE Conference on En Decision and Control, vol. 3, pp. 3372–3377 (1998)
28. Demirkol, E., Mehta, S., Uzsoy, R.: Benchmarks for shop scheduling problems. European Journal of Operational Research 109(1), 137–141 (1998)
29. Kreipl, S.: A large step random walk for minimizing total weighted tardiness in a job shop. Journal of Scheduling 3(3), 125–138 (2000)

The Design of an Agent-Based Production Scheduling Software Framework for Improving Planning-Scheduling Collaboration

Pedro Gomez-Gasquet, Francisco Cruz Lario Esteban, Ruben Dario Franco Pereyra, and Victor Anaya Fons

Universidad Politécnica de Valencia, Centro de Investigación de Gestión e Ingeniería de la Producción, Cno. de Vera s/n, 46022, Valencia, Spain
{pgomez,fclario,dfranco,vanaya}@cigip.upv.es

Abstract. In the operation management environment, the process of production scheduling is responsible for detailing operating activities by indicating a set of methods and tools that are conditioned, among other restrictions, by the tactical decisions that are made in the production planning environment. Although, theoretically, a bi-directional flow of information should exist among both environments of decisions that permit those who are involved to coordinate both levels in practice, such does not occur because of a structured decision-making tool gap. This document proposes an architecture that is based on agents software designed with INGENIAS methodology and proposed from an analysis of requirements that is based on CIMOSA. Once it is implemented, a prototype that employs JADE has been carried out to test and verify its suitable operation.

Keywords: Production Scheduling, Agent, Collaboration Planning-Scheduling.

1 Introduction

The design of the system that is proposed is initiated once the analysis of the requirements has been completed. In this case, the requirements have been obtained by applying CIMOSA [1][2][3]. It provides optimal, desired images.

The reader should consider the proposed system to be the structural element on which the algorithms, methods, and other resources that are oriented to the scheduling in changing environments will subsequently be placed or where it is necessary to apply rescheduling of the previously established schedules. The functional coordination between the environment of the planner and the scheduler, in this type of environment, is based on cooperation. Communication is the fundamental objective of this software element.

From a technical point of view, the system's design is based on the agent-based paradigm that offers some interesting advantages [4]. Therefore, its design itself includes the employee methodological proposal INGENIA [5], which facilitates the development of systems that are based on agents and multi-agents. Although the design is closely linked to the Technology of Information and Communication (TIC), a vision of the employed methodology is provided in order to connect it with the most conceptual levels of the process of production scheduling.

Á. Ortiz Bas, R.D. Franco, P. Gómez Gasquet (Eds.): BASYS 2010, IFIP AICT 322, pp. 301–308, 2010.
© IFIP International Federation for Information Processing 2010

The remainder work is divided according to the following form: the second paragraph analyzes the conditions in which the process of collaboration between planner and scheduler should occur. In the third paragraph, INGENIAS methodology is deployed in order to obtain the framework of the proposed software. The fourth paragraph is dedicated to commentary about the practical use of the proposed software. The report concludes with a summation of the aforementioned information.

2 Process Analysis of Collaborative Planning-Scheduling Operations

To proceed in the phase of requirement analysis, CIMOSA methodology has been selected. It provides the advantage of offering a vision of the problem to analyze that is structured according to various views (i.e., functional, organizational, resource-based, and informational) that enrich the final analysis. Figure 1 presents the functional point of view that production scheduling is defined like a domain; that is, directly related to the domains of the planning (i.e., tactical), the design of processes and products (i.e., strategic) and the operations control (i.e., operating).

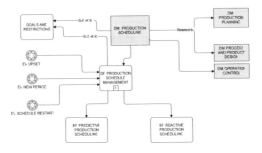

Fig. 1. Main Elements of Functional View of Production Scheduling Domain

The objective that is defined inside the production scheduling domain is to obtain production schedules in which the average of productivity that is reached in the different periods is the highest that is possible. This aspect is fundamental and, from our point of view, implies that the quantitative methods are suitable to give solutions to the corresponding combinatorial problems as well as fundamentally promoting the contribution among the planner. The planner decides the lots that one must carry out in each period. The scheduler manages the capable manufacturing system that offers the service in question. In this sense, one must emphasize that the suitable adjustment of the capacity to the needs of each moment will be the one that facilitates the attainment of the greatest productivity average.

Inside the production scheduling domain, only the domain process has been defined (DP-production schedule management) as being responsible for managing the allocation, sequencing, and timing of the lots that the planner has requested be manufactured in a determined period. Such management implies that the initial schedule is obtained by means of a business process (BP-predictive PS) that employs some algorithm that is adjusted to the characteristics of the problem in function of the known data to priori (e.g., static or predictive schedule). At the beginning of the period, the initial schedule will become the schedule in process. A new business process will run (BP-REVIVE PS) to detect events and, in that case, to try those that can affect the schedule in process (EV-upset, EV-new period, EV-restart) and imply the execution of some method to readjust the schedule in process to the current reality.

The proposed system is focused on a make-to-stock management, although other type of management will be tackled easily. Algorithms and methods should be adapted to each problem. What is provided is an architecture that enables the coordination between the planner and the scheduler to adjust the lot number and its volume of each period by means of an iterative process to carry out the major number of possible units. For example, consider the following in the case of:

- Predictive scheduling (i.e., initial schedule). Normally an upset among the employed times for the calculation in the environment of planning exists and the available time in the environment of scheduling once generated the schedule (e.g., the variable times of process and setups, dependence of the sequences, etc.).
- Reactive scheduling (i.e., schedule in process) consists of detecting the possibility of incorporating some new lot if the schedule in process advances faster than predicted. In other cases, it consists of canceling some lot that is included on the schedule in process if some delay that impedes the ability to carry out the predicted schedule occurs inside the current period.

One must remember that is possible that the initial schedule include some idle time that provides a solution to some small incident that is not predicted without modifying the initial selection of lots. This situation is normal, in order to avoid a high number of cancellations or incorporations of lots in each period.

The views of information and resources indicate that they have established the type of data and capacities that are necessary to manage the productive schedule.

3 The Jade-Based Production Scheduling System

Complex manufacturing systems consist of a number of related subsystems that are organized in a hierarchical fashion. At any given level, subsystems work together to achieve the functionality of their parent system. Each component can be thought as achieving one or more objectives. Thus, entities should have their own thread of control (i.e., they should be active), and they should have control over their own actions (i.e., they should be autonomous). Given this fact, it is apparent that the natural way to modularize a complex system is in terms of multiple autonomous components that act and interact in flexible ways to achieve their objectives. Therefore, the agent-oriented approach is simply the best fit.

In next sections, we present the agent-oriented models and methodology that we have used in the development process of the scheduling problem of production.

3.1 Description of the Modeling Process

INGENIAS methodology employs several meta-models and a meta-model language for constructing models. All meta-models are based on objects, attributes, and relationships.

INGENIAS methodology also integrates its meta-models into the Rational Unified Process (RUP) for developing software systems and offers a graphical development tool called the INGENIAS Development Kit (IDK).

During analysis and the design phases, five different meta-models are used: (i) an organization meta-model, which defines how agents are grouped and identifies the system functionality and the existing constraints in the agents' behavior; (ii) an agent meta-model, which describes the particular agents to be used and their internal mental states; (iii) an interaction meta-model, which details how agents are coordinated and interact; (iv) an environment meta-model, which defines the types of resources and applications that are used by the system; and (v) a tasks and objectives meta-model, which relates the mental state of each agent with its tasks.

This paper focuses on the analysis phase of the production. In the following subsections, we will show analysis diagrams of a distributed, flexible, and autonomous production scheduling system. This system could be easily connected with the other subsystems in order to implement the agile manufacturing enterprise.

3.2 Use Case Diagrams

A use case diagram provides a snapshot model of a set of system behaviors that meets a user goal. Thus, this description represents a functional requirement that shows what happens, but not how it is achieved by the system. As previously mentioned, our study is focused on the scheduling system, in which four main use cases can be identified (Figure 2). In the "calculate predictive scheduling" use case, a feasible initial schedule to be carried out in the following days is created. This schedule is developed according to the manufacture lots that are defined in the master plan which is included in the planner set of use cases (not shown) but that is available with the "get periodic plan" use case. In the "reactive production adjustment" use case, previous schedules in which problems developed during execution are modified. Therefore, those schedules are reconfigured in order to adjust to factory changes. The schedule execution monitoring data is included in the last use case.

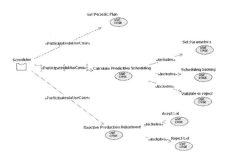

Fig. 2. Use Cases for the Schedule of Production Tasks

3.3 Organization Model

The organization model is defined by the organizational goals and tasks, the workflows that determine associations among tasks and general information about their execution; groups, which may contain agents, roles, resources or applications; and social relationships.

Several roles are distinguished in the organization model for the scheduling process (Figure 3): (i) planner, which is responsible for selecting the lots in a period; (ii) coordinator, which maintains information about all plants' configuration and knows all restrictions and features of each machine and plant element; (iii) scheduler, which has the ability to schedule tasks and resources and supervises actual execution of a schedule in a specific plant; and (iv) worker, which oversees the schedule execution at the plant.

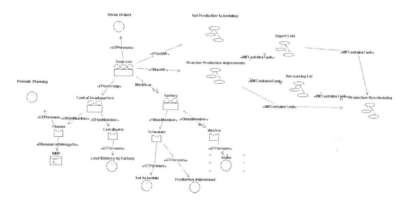

Fig. 3. Scheduling Process Organization Model

3.4 Interaction Model

An interaction model consists of identifying, for each use case, interaction goals, its members (i.e., the initiator and collaborators), nature, and specification (by means of collaboration diagrams). Table 1 shows the defined interactions, the involved agents, and the interaction unit (i.e., message) that is used.

Table 1. Interactions Between Agents and Interactions Units

Interaction	Agent Actors	Interaction Unit
Get Periodic Planning	Planner-Scheduler	Ask for Factory Capacity Notify Factory Capacity Notify Factory Planning
Notify Infeasibilities	Scheduler- Planner	Notify Infeasibilities of Planning
Notify Planning	Planner-Scheduler	Reject Lot Get allocating options Notify Capacity available Modify Planning Ask for a lot Allocating new lot
Notify Scheduling	Scheduler-Worker	Notify new schedule
Notify problems	Worker-Scheduler	Notify the problem

3.5   Agent Model

In an agent model, a specific agent has been assigned to each role that is identified in the organization model. The goals, tasks, and mental states have to be associated for each agent. Figure 4 shows the scheduler agent model. The scheduler agent plays the scheduler role and this example has two main goals (e.g., set a schedule and increase the production rate average) and a set of tasks (e.g., check and load data, parameter adjustment, calculate predictive/reactive scheduling, tuning the schedule, validate/reject the results, notify a new schedule). They are achieved by means of a set of mental states. In the same way, a planner and a worker agent model exists. The first one plays the role of planner and coordinator, and the second plays the role of worker.

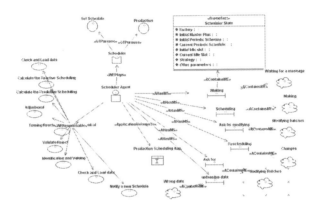

Fig. 4. Scheduler Agent Model

Figure 4 shows how a scheduler agent could be in a different mental state ("AHasMS"). For example, "waiting" for a proposal/message, "scheduling" a batch of jobs, "ask for modifying" a batch of jobs, etc. From a specific mental state, the agent scheduler must reach his goals by using the available functions and tools.

3.6   Task/Goals Model

This model attempts to answer the questions of why, who, and how throughout the analysis process. "Why" refers to the goals that are defined for the system; "who" refers to the agents which are responsible for the goal fulfillment; and "how" refers to the set of tasks which are defined to achieve the goals.

Two major goals have been established: "predictive scheduling" and "scheduling adjustment or rescheduling".

Predictive scheduling comes from the functional view of the production scheduling domain, which is carried out in CIMOSA analysis. Figure 5 shows how this workflow must satisfy three main goals (i.e., satisfy planning, efficient use of resources, and set production scheduling). The "conversation" items that represent interactions between two agents (e.g., scheduler-planner and scheduler-worker) could be highlighted in the figure. These conversations are the core of the negotiation process that occurs in almost all functional processes.

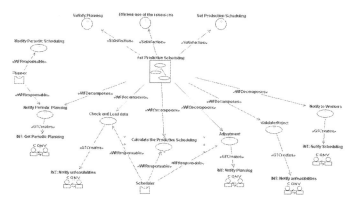

Fig. 5. Predictive Scheduling Tasks/Goals Model

Regarding our analysis, the decomposition of the schedule creation workflow is shown in figure 6 as an example of the tasks/goals model. The associated tasks are the different steps of this workflow which are accomplished according to concrete roles.

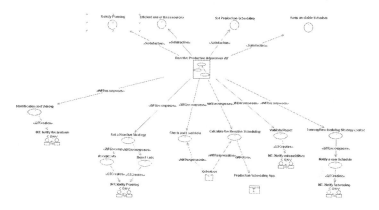

Fig. 6. Scheduling Adjustment Tasks/Goals Model

Scheduling adjustment comes from the functional view of the production scheduling domain, which is carried out in CIMOSA analysis that is named "reactive scheduling." Figure 6 shows how this workflow adds one additional goal, "keep a stable scheduling," and displays what is relevant and characteristic about this function. This task maintains "conversations" as core elements in the process.

3.7 Environment Model

The environment model of the production scheduling organization is shown in order to consider that an internal application is managed by the planner to store and update executed plans that are created by the organization.

4 Using Proposed Software in a Ceramic Tile Factory

The resulting proposed framework software has been transformed in a prototype in order to be used in a typical make-to-stock industry, such as a ceramic tile enterprise. The software programming and deployment has been carried out by using the JADE platform (http://jade.tilab.com/) and JAVA language. The methods and algorithms have been developed in order to solve a hybrid flow-shop problem with sequence-dependent setup times [6][7]. Comparing the current processes at the selected enterprise and the new options that are provided by the prototype, one could observe that, as the top productivity rate is attained (i.e., 10%-25%, depending on the scenario) in the second case, it can be attributed to the overall reduction of idle time. These times have reduced as much for the relocation/sequencing of the lots in process as they have for the incorporation of new lots.

5 Conclusions

This paper presents a methodological development, based on multi-agent technology, of an application with which to overcome the scheduling production problem in a make-to-stock factory. It has been designed according to the actual dynamic production processes needs that allow the selling process to be realized in an online platform. Our approach is based on a medium-time project. This proposal is based on the system capability that offers the most suitable product alternative, even though it could involve scheduling changes if the global quality is improved.

In order to satisfy that goal, it is necessary to integrate the various distributed production steps in a flexible, adaptable, versatile, robust, and natural way. Agent/multi-agent systems technology has been used in the resolution of this problem, since it provides the required characteristics for manufacturing systems. We have currently centred our analysis on the scheduling problem, due to its critical importance in the whole process. The resulting software has been tested in the ceramic tile industry.

References

1. ESPRIT Consortium AMICE. CIMOSA - Open System Architecture for CIM (1993)
2. Kosanke, K.: Cimosa - Overview and Status. Computers in Industry 27(2), 101–109 (1995)
3. Zelm, M., Vernadat, F., Kosanke, K.: The CIMOSA business modelling process. Computers in Industry 21(2) (1995)
4. Wooldrige, M., Jennings, N.R.: Intelligent Agents: Theory and Practice. Knowledge Engineering Review 10(2), 115–152 (1995)
5. Pavon, J., Gomez-Sanz, J.: Agent Oriented Software Engineering with INGENIAS. In: Mařík, V., Müller, J.P., Pěchouček, M. (eds.) CEEMAS 2003. LNCS (LNAI), vol. 2691, pp. 394–403. Springer, Heidelberg (2003)
6. Gomez-Gasquet, P., Andres, C., García-Sabater, J.P.: Dynamic Hybrid Flow-Shop Scheduling with Due Dates and Sequence Dependent Setup Times. In: Proceedings of Production Planning and Scheduling 2004 (PMS 2004), Nancy, France, pp. 254–259 (2004)
7. Gupta, J.N.D.: Flowshop Schedules with Sequence Dependent Setup Times. Journal of the Operations Research Society of Japan 29(3), 206–219 (1986)

Author Index